Craypo

ALSO BY SEYMOUR MELMAN

Dynamic Factors in Industrial Productivity *(1956)*

Decision-making and Productivity *(1958)*

The Peace Race *(1962)*

Our Depleted Society *(1965)*

Pentagon Capitalism *(1970)*

The Permanent War Economy *(1974)*

EDITED BY SEYMOUR MELMAN

Inspection for Disarmament *(1958)*

No Place to Hide *(1962)*

Disarmament: Its Politics and Economics *(1962)*

In the Name of America *(1968)*

Conversion of Industry from a Military to Civilian
Economy, Vols. I–VI *(1970)*

The War Economy of the United States *(1971)*

PROFITS WITHOUT PRODUCTION

PROFITS WITHOUT PRODUCTION

Seymour Melman

ALFRED A. KNOPF   NEW YORK   1983

THIS IS A BORZOI BOOK

PUBLISHED BY ALFRED A. KNOPF, INC.

Copyright © 1983 by Seymour Melman
All rights reserved under International and Pan-American
Copyright Conventions. Published in the United States by
Alfred A. Knopf, Inc., New York, and simultaneously in
Canada by Random House of Canada Limited, Toronto.
Distributed by Random House, Inc., New York.

Library of Congress Cataloging in Publication Data
Melman, Seymour.
Profits without production.
Includes index.
1. Industrial management—United States.
2. United States—Indusries. I. Title.
HD70.U5M425 1983   338.0973   82-48720
ISBN 0-394-51895-0

Manufactured in the United States of America
First Edition

To Lawrence Beryl Cohen,

whose pathfinding research on
production decision-making by
working people portends a future
beyond managerialism

CONTENTS

PREFACE

Preparing this book has been especially exciting. For it has permitted me to draw together and utilize much of what I have learned from the main lines of research I have pursued since becoming a graduate student at Columbia University at the close of World War II.*

As an applicant with interests that yoked together a number of academic fields (as conventionally defined), I was interviewed by Professors Frederick C. Mills and Louis Hacker (economics), Professor Walter Rautenstrauch (industrial engineering) and Dean George B. Pegram (physics). I told them that I hoped to explore the ways in which economic factors, within an individual company and without, determine the design of technology—for example, production machinery. All these scholars were known for their active encouragement of interdisciplinary studies, and all of them were warmly supportive of my own project. For this support I am forever indebted to them.

This line of inquiry was linked to wider concerns with the dynamics of social organization. It shed new light on, and benefited from, a dynamic view of decision-making on production (relations of production) as this relates to machines and their organized use (means of production). These have been the larger defining categories of my work to this day.

For providing me, by his example, with a model of wide-ranging, rigor-

---

*The following are the main research topics that I have dealt with in articles, monographs and books: how cost factors, in cost-minimizing firms, control the design and selection of production equipment; intensity of mechanization and levels of productivity in manufacturing industries; dynamics of administrative cost growth; characteristics of management methods and their cost; the relation of cost of management to productivity; the evolution of forms of management organization; decision-making by workers, and its effect on cost and productivity of labor and capital; technical, managerial and economic determinants of productivity in machinery production; the characteristics of military and other enterprises that operate by maximizing both costs and government subsidies; the organization and consequences of military economy with regard to depletion of production and productivity; requirements for conversion from military to civilian economy.

ously disciplined and highly innovative studies of social processes, I am indebted to Professor Zellig S. Harris (Emeritus, University of Pennsylvania).

Walter Norton, of Walter Norton, Ltd. (London), and Tony Yamazaki of Yamazaki Machinery Works, Ltd. (Nagoya), are senior executives of the machine tool firms that bear their names. I am grateful to them both for sharing generously their ample professional wisdom and broad views of industrial affairs.

In the preparation of this book, I have benefited from the editorial talents and warm support of Robert Hatch, and from the careful and constructive editorial attention that the manuscript received from Ashbel Green and his associates at Alfred A. Knopf.

Professor David Noble of M.I.T. favored me with comments that sharpened the analysis at many points, and generously made available unpublished materials on factors affecting the design of modern machine tools. Alice Amsden, Professor of Economics at Barnard College, applied her considerable knowledge of the machine tool and allied industries to the improvement of the discussion of that vital area in this book.

In what is perforce a less than adequate manner, I wish to acknowledge with appreciation the contributions of the many colleagues whose published works I have cited in this book.

Carol Ann Luten and Philla Osborne patiently and diligently attended to the production of successive drafts of the manuscript, and were especially helpful in the detailed checking of data. For any errors that may remain, I am, of course, alone responsible.

SEYMOUR MELMAN
New York, January 1983

Managerial Success with Production Decay

Until recently, the managers of U.S. industry were the world's best organizers of industrial work—that was the basis of their profits and for their claim to large personal incomes. Since a community must produce in order to live, and since a core task of an economy is to organize people to work, the managers, within the constraints of their profit-making concerns, performed a vital function.

The decision power and personal wealth accorded to managers was one side of a historic exchange, a social contract. In return for these privileges management was expected, by working people and community, to organize work. That social contract was threatened by the Great Depression and was reconstituted as a legitimation for management only when a new contingent of state managers was introduced to share in decision power over the industrial economy. Thereafter, management's economists, informed by the theories of John Maynard Keynes, hoped that a new "public sector" military economy could help to stabilize the functioning of management's decision processes, extending to the "private sector" as well. But the successful pursuit of profits and power by both private and state managers also resulted in a major unanticipated effect. A process of technological and economic depletion of the means of production itself was set in motion, causing major contraction of opportunities for productive livelihood.

Management's social contract with working people and community was broken.

Since the mid-1960s the production competence of many U.S. industries has obviously been deteriorating. By 1980 one-fifth of the steel used in the United States was being supplied from abroad. A fourth of the new machine tools and a third of the automobiles were no longer produced by American workers in American factories. A visit to almost any hi-fi or camera store in an American city will confirm that only a minor part of the sophisticated products offered for sale are made in the United States. The domestic production of these and many other capital and consumer goods has been replaced, increasingly, by products from Western Europe and Japan. Managers in those countries, sometimes using exported U.S. capital, have learned how to compensate for rising wages with rapid improvement of productivity.

While capturing U.S. markets with quality products at competitive prices, they have also bestowed a high, and still rising, level of living on their own populations. In 1980, seven European countries—Belgium, Denmark, West Germany, the Netherlands, Norway, Sweden, Switzerland—paid their industrial workers higher wages, in money and "fringes," than did the United States.[1] If the average rates of the 1970s' wage increases continue, Japanese workers will by 1986 be paid more than their American counterparts. The United States will then be well established as a medium-to-lower-income society, suitable for investments by other countries that want to take advantage of a relatively docile, cheap labor force.

All this is part of a collapsing production competence that occurred as the money-making successes of U.S. managers reached new highs—a possibility that has had no place in mainstream theories about industrial capitalism or U.S. industrial management. It is unprecedented that profit-taking success should be the partner of system-wide production failure.

Even the most confirmed critics of capitalism have accepted the assessment of the productivity of industrial capitalism made by Karl Marx and Friedrich Engels in the *Communist Manifesto* (1848):

> The bourgeoisie, during its rule of scarce one hundred years, has created more massive and more colossal productive forces than have all preceding generations together. Subjection of nature's forces to man, machinery, application of chemistry to industry and agriculture, steam-navigation, railways, electric telegraphs, clearing of whole continents for cultivation, canalisation of rivers, whole populations conjured out of the ground—what earlier century had even a presentiment that such productive forces slumbered in the lap of social labour?

This description also shaped the Marxists' understanding of capitalism's internal operation. They saw production by workers as the necessary basis for management's profit and other gains—cumulatively, the "surplus value" generated by labor but appropriated by management.

Most economists agree that businessmen act as organizers of production, even though many of them differ sharply with the Marxists, seeing profit not as exploitation but as just return for services rendered. And whatever the evaluation of management's role, there is little dissent from the proposition that profit is based finally upon production. Thus, manufacturing firms have been viewed as the productive foundation of a system that could readily support a further superstructure of profit-takers who exact their fees for servicing various forms of exchange or speculation.

The "captains of industry" who assembled the great industrial firms at the turn of the twentieth century attained wealth, power and social eminence as organizers of the largest production organizations in history. Whatever the maneuvers for financial and market control that went on in the boardrooms of industrial capitalism, no one doubted that investing in and efficiently operating the means of production, especially those of basic industry, was the high road to wealth and fame.*

During the latter half of the twentieth century, this pattern of industrial capitalism has shifted. Soon after World War II the marketing executive emerged as the bright star of the American managerial firmament. "Madison Avenue" took center stage. By the 1960s the ideal type, as portrayed in management journals, had become the financier-strategist, the shrewd, nimble operator who combined disparate firms into conglomerates that maximized the short-term profit-taking opportunities afforded by tax laws, securities transfers, the milking of production assets and other financial legerdemain. This is a world of money-making, one that can prosper even as production is neglected or transferred to distant lands. In this world, the optimum condition is profit without any production.

In the same period, the managers of state-subsidized enterprises learned how to marshal the nation's largest single block of capital resources for the military economy. That economy, which produces neither consumer goods nor anything useful for further production, is a money-maker for everyone involved in it.

Military production is often regarded as simply an adjunct to the government's foreign relations and, apart from that, as an undifferentiated part of the economy. Otherwise, military industry is viewed as a concentration point of technical sophistication, "high technology," as against the widening array of decrepit civilian industries.

A major aim of the present work is to show that the special effects of military economy are integral parts of, and major contributors to, the transformations under way in American management, technology and productivity. That is why there is a particular treatment of the military economy in each part of this book.

---

*An exemplary diagnosis of the businessmen of that era is in Thorstein Veblen, *The Theory of Business Enterprise* (Viking Press, 1946).

· · ·

It is not to be thought that any group in American society planned or worked to bring about the erosion of U.S. production capability. It has happened as an unanticipated, derived effect of normal, proper operations by industrial managers, both private and public, all of them acting according to well-accepted rules, exercising decision power and generating profits, while enjoying the income and other rewards of their privileged occupations.

The decline of production competence in the private and state economies of the United States has been caused by two forms of managerial success: profit-taking from expanded private nonproductive or foreign investments; and the ability of government managers to extend their powers of decision over an enlarged military economy.

The historic crises of American capitalism, those revealing the functional incapacities of the system, were typically crises of decision-making, of the interior mechanism of the *business* process, while all the time the production plant was fully competent to serve the market as the buyers of consumer or capital goods appeared. The new and unprecedented development in American capitalism is the collapse of production competence in the manufacturing process itself.

The money-making strategies of private management, combined with the enlarged power of the state managers, result in the looting of the productive capital of the system on behalf of short-term money-making and military-political power. Together, they produce the world's slowest rate of productivity growth and unemployment with inflation.

The "ideal type" of private manager now embraces men who are willing to put the money entrusted to them wherever its rate of return is highest. That includes the large-scale export of finance capital, with an accompanying failure to invest and re-invest in U.S.-based production. These profitable moves often take advantage of opportunities for easy entry into new markets (like the European Common Market) or the chance to make a killing by paying very low wages, as in Taiwan, Singapore and Mexico. The money-making manager is also conditioned to maximize the "bottom line" of a short-term balance sheet. Therefore, the quarterly report becomes primary evidence of good management, and any projection beyond one year is long-range planning. The same money-makers have developed the theory that managing as a profession can be practiced independently of the character and locale of an enterprise—that is, quite apart from the product, production methods, requirements of internal organization, etc. Such managers tend to specialize in financial strategies and operate at a great distance from production, which they view as an operating expense that can reduce profit. They also become increasingly intent on enlarging the scope and intensity of their managerial controls, thus raising the cost of managing at the same time that productivity is often depressed.

These trends in U.S. industrial management have been abetted by a parallel ideology. The American idea of every man for himself, of the individual as responsible for his own success or failure, has fostered the notion of the mobile manager, a new type who acknowledges no loyalty to any particular enterprise, let alone to a community, but only to his own professional advancement. An exaggerated regard for the individual's unique contribution supports a mythology about the supremacy of the single top executive. According to this way of thinking, the wisdom of the chief executive officer, rather than the skills of engineers and workers, the structure and working of an organization, its cohesiveness, its morale, and so forth, is responsible for the success or failure of a productive enterprise. This role inflation is used to justify the large salaries bestowed on men at the top.

The reliance on individualism was given a measure of credence by the long history of the American frontier. Opportunities for acquiring land and for exploiting apparently boundless resources seemed to confirm the possibility that every man for himself could be a really workable idea.

Another, more recent strand of American ideology has also supported the new managerial style. It is the idea that ours is a post-industrial society. From that premise it follows that, aside from high technology, there is little left for U.S. industry to do. The rest of production can be left to the smaller states of Western Europe and the underclasses of the third world. In this view, the United States has achieved a permanent state of technological preeminence, and the idea of money-making without production is entirely justified because the production problems of the private sector have been solved.

Meanwhile, the state managers of American society have been operating a military economy with an annual budget that, every year since 1951, has exceeded the net profits of all U.S. corporations. That military outlay, using up the largest single block of the economy's equivalent capital funds, makes no contribution whatever to the economic product of the society. Although this deployment of funds has depleted the available capital resources of the economy, an elaborate and widely trusted ideology supports its continued operation.

On this point my analysis departs sharply from mainstream economic theories. The latter almost unanimously assume that an economic product is anything that can be assigned a price—a definition that has the marvelous effect of obscuring the influence of the military economy on the rest of the system. By contrast, the idea that nothing can be called an economic product unless it contributes to consumption or to further production exposes the contribution made by the military economy to the deterioration of production competence in the United States.

Also, the true economic role of the state managers has been shielded from view by the idea that preparation for war, like war itself, creates prosperity. Since the American Civil War, no major military operations have taken place within the continental United States. Wars have been perceived by the majority of Americans as distant events, reported in the newspapers or on radio and television, in far-off places to which American soldiers are sent—all with little direct physical impact on American homes, workplaces, or on the material quality of life.

The trends of technology are necessarily shaped by a community's decision criteria. Accordingly, the analyses of decision processes in both private and state management can explain the deterioration of the quality of American technology in the civilian and military economies. None of this means that good workmanship, competent planning and close attention to the details of production are now unknown in U.S. industry. But managements of firms that set the tone for the whole system—U.S. Steel, the Ford Motor Company and a host of other multinational conglomerates—increasingly display the new pattern of profit-making with reduced production. The residual islands of high productivity are surrounded by a sea of concentrated money-making.

Our Depleted Society

The consequences of these developments lead me to frame certain questions: Under what foreseeable conditions could developments in private and state management produce a deterioration of production competence so severe as to be irreversible? And, short of that "worst case" future for the U.S. economy, what is required to generate fresh production competence?

Actually, deterioration in the production competence of U.S. industries has been well in motion since 1960. By 1965 I had diagnosed the processes of that decay in some detail.[2] Predictably, these early warnings of industrial inefficiency were received with skepticism by a population that was still aglow with the euphoria of World War II, still believed that the United States could enjoy both guns and butter, and had just been marshalled for the conquest of space and the first landing of man on the moon. In 1960, the air was full of an election campaign waged against a missile gap. Then came the Bay of Pigs debacle, the Berlin Wall crisis, the Cuban Missile crisis, the trauma of Kennedy's assassination, and the election of Lyndon Johnson—the pro-peace candidate who operated a small war on poverty and a larger war in Vietnam. All this while the universities were awash in money, as the government, with cheers from the populace, demanded more science, more technology, more trained professionals to guarantee U.S. leadership in the space race and the arms race too. In the midst of such excitements, almost no one, apart from those closely affected, paid much attention to the closing of factories in a widening sweep of northeastern and midwestern cities.

The American intelligentsia were seized with dreams of the post-industrial society—so why not hand over low technology and mundane commodities to the Japanese, the Taiwanese, and the lower-paid workers of Western Europe, while the United States concentrated on high technology? Against such a background of ideological reassurance (or was it nationalist arrogance?) few were prepared to consider the full significance of many ongoing events. So the World Trade Center in New York City has a steel framework that was made in Japan—well, after all, the U.S. construction industry has long been backward. So the Alaska pipeline was made in Japan—well, the Japanese steel industry profited from having been destroyed by U.S. bombardments during World War II. So the shoe factories of New England are closing and their machinery and tools are sold abroad—well, in the post-industrial society, Americans should be concerned with high technology and not with demeaning work like shoemaking that can well be done in less developed countries. So the closing of enterprises in the United States during the 1960s and 1970s disrupted the lives of about 15 million people—well, let the labor market handle the problem of reslotting those people into the U.S. economy.

By 1979–1980, American buyers of automobiles, almost one out of three, were passing up the products of General Motors, Ford, Chrysler, and American Motors. That debacle in the U.S. marketplace led to mass unemployment throughout the Midwest, financial losses in the billions for U.S. firms, and near-bankruptcy for Chrysler and others. The U.S. failure in autos was also a culture shock. No one proclaimed that these castoff industrial workers should redeploy themselves into new-look "services" or high-tech occupations. The U.S. automobile industry is more than an industrial colossus: it has long been a central feature of America's self-image. Detroit made of mass production an American and then a worldwide force. If the United States no longer excelled at rolling cars off the assembly line, what was left?

There are some important barriers to seeing, and therefore believing, that the United States has been losing its productive vitality. The decline is well enough understood by working people, technicians, and their immediate communities, who have lost their livelihoods and often been forced into a gypsy-like existence in the quest for jobs. The effect on young people, candidates for entry-level industrial jobs, is particularly devastating. The rest of the town feels at second hand the effects of lost industrial jobs—by the appearance of a *Lumpenproletariat,* that is, a permanently unemployed welfare-dependent population, and by the decline of municipal facilities and services of every sort.

But an important part, about 37 percent, of American society is substantially shielded from these effects. This is the suburban middle class, which is concentrated in occupations that are not related to manufacture. For these people deterioration in the United States' producing capability is hardly visible because the goods and services that they commonly purchase are available in ample supply. They neither know nor care whether the food processor comes from Kentucky, Japan or France, and the firm name on the label is no indication of where the item was produced (you have to look for the small "made in" legend). Durable goods of all sorts are to be had from local dealers, and in middle-class suburbia public amenities are often first-rate. All this has important bearing on the ability of American society to confront a new, culturally astonishing fact: the United States is well on the way to becoming a second-rate industrial country.

Since production backwardness grows out of normal managerial operations in America, it is unlikely that the processes can be reversed by any quick fix, by minor alterations in the managerial pattern, private and public. Thus, it is improbable that asking the schools of business administration to give more attention to production can change the priorities of the present faculties, or the intellectual assumptions and cultural biases that guide those institutions. The low esteem in which blue-collar work is held by the managerial teaching centers of the United States, private and public, cannot be altered by admonitions, however well intentioned, that they mend their ways. Their assumptions have become deeply embedded, linked to the core characteristics of managerialism itself. But are there technically and economically workable alternatives to present managerial-hierarchical ways of making decisions in the area of production?

My plan is first to identify the main aspects of managerialism and how they have been changing. That sets the stage for showing the impact of private and state managers on technology in the United States, for technology is shaped in the image of those who preside over it.

Once in place, the quality of the means of production, together with the ways of organizing work, have a controlling effect on industrial competence, on the productivity of labor and capital. These, in turn, are what finally determine the ability of an industrial system to organize people to work and to sustain industrial production on a high technological level.

When the cumulative effects of the developments in management, technology and productivity are taken into account, a surprising prospect for the United States must be considered: the deterioration in production competence can become irreversible. Short of such a debacle, what conceivable directions of change in economic policies, and decision-making by managers and workers, can deliver industrial and other economic renewal?

In order to help the reader get a handle on such large-scale processes, I thought it would be helpful to show how the main thread of ideas works out in the case of one industrial sphere. That is why the main argument of this book opens with the story of the U.S. machine tool industry.

PROFITS WITHOUT PRODUCTION

How the Yankees
Lost Their Know-how

For a century after the American Civil War, the machine tool industry of the United States was the star performer, worldwide, in the design and production of high-capacity, high-productivity machine tools.

This was no cultural or technological accident, for the drills, lathes, milling machines and other pieces of equipment that are the master tools of every metalworking economy were designed and produced in the United States to meet the requirements of users who, from the start, had to pay wages higher than those prevailing in the industries of Western and Eastern Europe.

In its own shops, the U.S. machine tool industry practiced cost-minimizing, the managers and engineers acting to offset increases in their own costs by improving their own productivity. As a result, the prices of their products, the basic machines for all U.S. industry, rose more slowly than the wages of labor. From 1939 to 1947, average hourly earnings of industrial workers in the United States grew 95 percent, while the prices of machine tools increased only 39 percent.[1] Therefore, all users of machine tools saw the new, higher-performance machinery as an increasingly attractive alternative to the employment of manual workers in industry. As U.S. industry was well served with effective equipment, offered at an attractive price, productivity was improved throughout the entire industrial system. That is how one industry employing 85,000 people had a decisive impact on the competence of the whole U.S. industrial system.*

Rising productivity, then, was a derived effect of the effort by industrial managements, both the producers and the users of machine tools, to retard the growth of their own costs of production. That pattern of general practices was the central mechanism within American industry that yielded the United

---

*In 1978, U.S. industries used 3,365,700 machine tools. National Machine Tool Builders Association, *Economic Handbook of the Machine Tool Industry, 1980/81* (Washington, D.C., 1980).

States the highest rate of output per person in the world, and an average increase in productivity of about 2.5 to 3 percent a year. American economists and historians recognized that growth rate as an integral factor in American prosperity.

Furthermore, the U.S. industrial tradition has included an understanding that it is entirely possible to combine top wages with low costs for quality products. What it takes is systematic attention to product design and all-around plant efficiency, so that increased productivity of labor and capital can offset rising wages. That is how the U.S. auto industry, after World War II, paid the world's highest wages per hour while producing cars in the Ford, Chevrolet and Plymouth lines that were the world's least expensive in terms of price per pound of vehicle.[2]

That is what "Yankee know-how" meant, and the machinery-producing companies were crucial to it. It was their ability to hold down costs that made their products attractive, and yielded the ripple effect of high productivity through the rest of the system. The U.S. machine tool industry also enjoyed a worldwide reputation for the outstanding productivity of its capital, and for machine reliability under taxing conditions.

There is nothing in this record to explain the deterioration in the performance of the U.S. machine tool industry, which began in the 1960s and by 1978 had progressed so far that, for the first time, the United States imported more machine tools than it sold abroad.[3] During 1980, U.S.-based machine tool factories supplied less than three out of four machine tools purchased by American industry. Year by year, in increasing numbers, the factories of Western Europe and Japan have been offering and selling quality equipment at attractive prices in the United States.

What had happened? Beginning in the late 1950s and culminating in the mid-1960s, a new set of rules was installed at the decision-making level of many industrial firms. Government contracts for the military and space agencies were assigned to companies on a cost-plus basis. This gave the contracting firms a strong incentive to run up costs, and the cost overruns were actually encouraged by the Pentagon's managers and the federal government's economists, on the grounds of "bolstering the economy" and "getting America moving again."[4] For the firms involved, high bids and subsequent overruns became normal operating procedure. These rules—exactly contrary to the traditional cost-minimizing—set a pattern of cost-maximizing within limits of available federal subsidy. Cost-maximizing became the dominant theme among the 37,000 industrial firms, or parts of firms, organized by the Department of Defense to meet its requirements. By 1980, prices of the military-serving goods produced by this network of firms were rising 20 percent annually.[5]

The Pentagon had also become a major client-manager of the machine tool firms, and cost-maximizing became the pattern in important parts of that industry, with effects that were far-reaching. In 1981 the Department of Defense owned 103,000 machines in use by major and subcontracting firms. Their value exceeded $1.7 billion. Also, the Pentagon has maintained "two industrial reserves of machine tools," the "General Reserve" and "Plant Equipment Packages" that range from a few machines to complete production lines held as reserve industrial capacity.[6]

In the 1950s, the Air Force became a principal sponsor of technological development in the machine tool field. The Air Force decided to push for computer-controlled machine tools (numerical control)* capable of shaping intricate parts of large size to accurate dimensions, the better to assure a high strength-to-weight ratio for large structural components of major aircraft.

With this new technology, parts of the operation previously assigned to skilled machinists—reading the blueprint, translating that information into movements of the machine tools—was now supplanted by prerecorded control information for the machine, in much the way that the holes in the paper roll control the player piano. This made possible an accuracy in repeatability of operations, especially for intricate metalworking, that was previously unattainable.

Even while the development of ingenious new mechanisms proceeded, the firms engaged in this effort found themselves catering to a state management for whom capability and performance were the dominant requirements, while cost was a matter of less significance. The Pentagon, when assigning "weights" to the criteria used for selecting industrial contractors, gives cost a value of 15 percent.[7] These criteria dominated the selection process among alternative design options in the development of numerical control technology.

So for leading firms of the machine tool industry, those best able to do research and new product development, the relationship with the Department of Defense became an invitation to discard the old tradition of cost-minimizing. It was an invitation to avoid all the hard work—the difficulties of changing internal production methods, modifying design of product, etc.—that is needed to offset cost increases. For now it was possible to cater to a new client, for whom cost and price increase was acceptable—even desirable.[8]

Accordingly, a new management style was encouraged within the machine tool industry of the United States, so that from 1971 to 1978 prices of machine tools rose, on the average, 85 percent, while the average hourly earnings of U.S. industrial workers increased 72 percent.[9] That inversion of

---

*The desired movements of workpieces and cutting tools, corresponding to blueprint specifications, are recorded as numerical information on punched cards, tapes, or in magnetic signal form. Hence the name given to this technology: numerical control.

the classic cost-minimizing pattern now meant that users of machine tools who still sought to hold down their costs had no incentive to purchase the new machines.

This pattern in the United States, from 1971 to 1978, was in dramatic contrast to the relationship between labor costs and machine tool prices in Japan. There, during the same years, machine tool prices rose 51 percent, while average hourly earnings of workers grew 177 percent.[10] Whereupon Japanese industry adopted the strategy of cost-minimizing that had long been recognized as the hallmark of U.S. industrial performance.

The consequences have been far-reaching for U.S. productivity and industrial competence. By 1978 in the United States, where there was a cost deterrent to the purchase of new metalworking machinery, only 31 percent of U.S. machine tools in use were less than ten years old. In West Germany the figure was 37 percent, but in Japan it was 61 percent.[11]

When the prices of American-built machine tools became unattractive to American users, there was no automatic shift to foreign sources at possibly more favorable prices: Machinery buyers are necessarily cautious about changing their suppliers. Managers are leery of buying industrial equipment from unfamiliar sources whose quality and reliability are not well known to them. Machinery buyers value a vendor who is near enough to service the equipment and can supply spare parts speedily. Machine downtime can be very costly. All these are biases in favor of known and accessible machinery suppliers. Therefore a move to purchase new machinery abroad requires more than a major price advantage.

As the age of the U.S. machine tool stock increased, industry began to lose the buoyancy of productivity that had long been the effect derived from the installation of new production equipment. For the important decade 1965–1975 this showed up in the differential productivity growth rates of U.S., West German and Japanese manufacturing. The average annual rates of improvement were 10 percent in Japan, 5 percent in West Germany, 2 percent in the United States. In 1980 U.S. productivity was *minus* 0.5 percent,[12] a stagnation unprecedented in American experience and the lowest rate of productivity growth of any industrialized country in the world.

The editors of *American Machinist*,[13] reflecting on the 1978 age of the U.S. machine tool stock, noted that it was virtually identical with the situation in 1940—at the end of ten years of the Great Depression, a long period of depressed investment in new production equipment. The failure some forty years later to replace old equipment in the United States was the direct consequence, not of depression, but of the collapse of cost-minimizing in the machine tool industry. And the falling rate of U.S. manufacturing productivity growth after 1965 was, in turn, strongly affected by the aging stock of production equipment.

By 1980 U.S. machine tool firms, employing 85,000 people, could no longer supply more than 24.6 percent of the machine tools purchased by American firms. Indeed, by mid-1981 Japan was providing 40 percent of the very important new class of computer-controlled vertical "machining centers" purchased by U.S. firms.[14] A machining center is an exceedingly versatile piece of major equipment, capable of applying many types of tools to the workpiece. Japanese models of this advanced machine tool, of quality comparable to the U.S. product, are offered at about 40 percent below U.S. prices. In 1979 the machine tool industry of Japan produced 14,317 of the new class of machines compared with 7,174 built in the United States.[15]

Again, there is no evidence to suggest that this set of effects was planned or intended by the managers of the U.S. machine tool industry or federal officials in the military, space, and nuclear agencies, who have become increasingly influential as state managers in a widening sector of U.S. industry. The managers of the machine tool firms simply acted to maximize their profits by applying a series of well-accepted methods. These included investment abroad; diversification of U.S. investments into other than machine tool firms; managerial decision-making with an eye to short-term results; a collateral emphasis on money-making by means remote from production—as from investments in the money markets; intensified managerial control in an attempt to make money and extend decision power; alliance with federal government managers in the effort to secure assured sales to federally subsidized, military-serving firms.

Foreign investment, along with licensing and other arrangements by U.S. machine tool firms, supported expansion of machine tool production, especially in Western Europe, to serve growing world markets. The editors of *American Machinist* have compiled reports (unpublished) on "foreign arrangements" by U.S. firms.* The earliest of these listings, in 1966, filled ten typescript pages. By 1974 the tabulation had expanded to thirty pages, and the 1981 roster (incomplete at this writing) will exceed forty pages. By 1972, overseas production facilities accounted for sales of $450 million in Western Europe alone.[16] As the financial fortunes of the U.S. machine tool industry became less tied to the competence of its domestic production, the firms were under less pressure to try for higher productivity in their U.S. plants; instead, they were offering equipment from their foreign production sources at prices

joint — overseas ventures + transfers

---

*American machine tool managers have emphasized licensing agreements with foreign firms, more so than the German industry, which has been an important foreign investor. See Alice Amsden, *Internationalization of the Machine Tool Industry,* United Nations, Centre on Transnational Corporations, 1982. Licensing the use of available designs and technique is an important form of capital export which is not counted in the statistics of "direct foreign investment." Blueprints, details of materials specifications, and production technique all have real value as "capital" but do not have the money form which is the conventional unit of measure of capital import (or export).

attractive to buyers outside the United States. The hard work and innovation needed to enhance efficiency at home could be avoided by managers who were making money from the new foreign production facilities.

Especially during the 1960s, the argument was heard that selling from a U.S. production base was necessarily difficult because of high U.S. wages. At one time machine tool firms, and companies in many other U.S. industries, had applied managerial and engineering competence to offset the U.S. wages. But this demanding managerial enterprise could be avoided once the explicit goal became making money, not making machines. The money-making could be accomplished while the foreign managers, engineers and workers did more of the planning and producing. The top managers and stockholders of U.S. machine tool firms have increasingly preferred that sort of development, even while opportunities for productive livelihood in the United States have deteriorated. By 1980, the almost 25 percent of U.S. machine tool purchases that were imported meant that at least 25,000 jobs in this single, crucial industry were exported. And the sales in Western Europe alone from the foreign-based production of U.S. firms account for at least another 15,000 jobs. These two forms of job loss for Americans add up to almost half the total 1977 employment in the U.S. machine tool industry.

Much like other U.S. industries, the machine tool firms have swung toward short-term profitability. The consequences for the character of their own investments and productivity are far-reaching. The very industry that developed the new computer-controlled (numerical control) machine tool technology has installed few of these machines in its own production system. By 1978 the metalworking equipment used by the machine tool industry itself included only 3.7 percent of numerically controlled machine tools.[17] The managers evidently feared the high fixed costs of the advanced equipment. When operated at a small percent of their capacity, the result is high cost per unit of work done. The larger machines in particular weigh heavily on overhead when sales are depressed.

Therefore the machine tool industry managers designed a production system that would be highly responsive to short-term market fluctuations. This included producing in small lot sizes; massive reluctance to standardize components and develop modular patterns for machine tool design; emphasis on product variety within single factories and firms. As one might expect, this management style boasted of providing "custom-built" machine tools to suit "unique" customer requirements. But the system that served this objective also operated at a relatively low level of productivity and at high cost. And it limited research and development to a few of the industry's larger firms.

By 1980 it had become clear that substantial efforts to design and apply mass production methods to the manufacture of these new instruments of mass production were being conducted primarily outside the United States. In December 1979 and February 1980 I observed the construction of the first computer-controlled production systems in machine tool factories in Budapest, Hungary, and Nagoya, Japan. As I surveyed U.S. and foreign exhibits of numerically controlled machining centers at the International Machine Tool Show (Chicago) in September 1980, I asked a principal U.S. maker, "What is the lot size in which these machines are produced?" The sales manager answered: "Well, you don't produce a $350,000 machine for inventory. When you order one, we make it for you." By contrast, the Japanese firms, both large and small, are manufacturing numerically controlled machining centers on regular monthly schedules. They count on attractive price and high quality to sell their product to a worldwide market. One of the smaller Japanese firms (100 employees) participating in the show announced that its production rate was at a steady thirty units a month. That way, the representative explained, it is possible to schedule delivery of components from various suppliers with long lead times, and also to benefit from good prices under conditions of assured purchase. That is the kind of production system that delivers machining centers at prices averaging 40 percent below comparable U.S.-produced equipment.

At this writing, it is clear that the Japanese strategy succeeds and that the one-at-a-time, even ten-at-a-time, output of the principal U.S. machine tool firms assures them technological backwardness and a loss of market position within the United States and around the world.

To protect themselves against the hazards of an uncertain domestic market for machine tools, U.S. manufacturers sought out various kinds of product diversification in this country and looked for promising investments abroad. At the same time they learned to combine production of machine tool components abroad with assembly and sale in the United States. Several of the important U.S. firms at the 1980 International Machine Tool Show had made advantageous arrangements with companies in Western Europe and Japan to produce for them. The machines would carry the nameplates of the U.S. firms, which would do the merchandising in the United States. A large exhibit displayed by a principal American machine tool firm indicated that half the machines offered were built abroad to the firm's specifications. That company is well on the way to terminating its role as a producer and limiting itself to money-making by means of market management.

This major shift of emphasis makes for a fine showing on the profit and loss statement, but carries as a liability less design, less production, and therefore less opportunity for productive livelihoods in the U.S. factories of the machine tool industry. The new strategy of the industry's managers has also been developed at high administrative cost. In 1977, for every 100 production workers in U.S. manufacturing industry as a whole, there were on average 43 administrative, technical and clerical employees. In the machine tool industry the ratio was 56 per hundred, 30 percent higher than the general average.[18] That lavish employment of administrative controls adds heavily to production expense, and puts U.S. machine tool firms at a still more severe cost-price disadvantage, even in the U.S. market.

The machine tool industry has long been a key factor in war production, its equipment being vital to the great factories that produced the tanks, artillery and endless tons of munitions for the armed forces of the United States in their various wars. But it was the Air Force in the late 1950s that combined efforts with the machine tool industry and a team of technologists at MIT to produce the new numerical-control (NC) machine tool technology. The service's requirements governed the choice of designs, and these led to the production of a line of machine tools so expensive as to be out of reach of most metalworking firms in the United States. Thus, the principal firms of the U.S. machine tool industry that collaborated with the Air Force in the development of the new technology effectively restricted themselves to the aerospace industry and similar markets.

By 1979, after this technology had been available for more than twenty years and had been endlessly promoted in the trade press, only 2 percent of all the machine tools in use in the United States were of the numerically controlled class. High prices and technical complexity put the American-produced NC machines out of reach for the majority of metalworking firms. It was left to the machine tool industries of Western Europe, and also notably of Japan, to set up high-capacity production systems for the mass production of quality numerical-controlled machine tools of the sizes and classes that are of interest to medium- and small-sized firms.

The Pentagon's central administrative office, which controls the operations of 37,000 industrial prime contractors, is probably the largest single direct owner of machine tools in the United States. This state management has not only sponsored crucial research and development within the machine tool industry, but also has generated the large purchase of machine tools for aerospace, ordnance and related industries. And it has been active in defining problems for research and development. A two-and-a-half-year study, sponsored by the Air Force's Wright Field research establishment and the Lawrence Livermore National Laboratory, and completed in 1980, marshalled the technical brains of American, European, and Japanese universities and technical institutes to define the new problems and goals to be confronted in the design and employment of machine tools. Five volumes of technical papers were published.[19] But entirely missing from this vast study was any reference to productivity, to production organization, to the design of production operations in the industry. It was apparently assumed that the organization and conduct of production were in such good order as to require no discussion. For the needs of the Air Force, they probably are.

From the standpoint of the national economy's stake in improved productivity, the enterprise was obviously flawed. And it also contributed to an already strong alliance between major machine tool firms and the state managers. When the U.S. Army convened a mobilization exercise conference in 1980, the chief executive officers of two of the major U.S. machine tool companies were among the handful of top industrial managers invited to attend.

Historically, the productivity of labor has been addressed by managers as a principal way to take maximum advantage of resources in production. Following the teachings of Frederick Winslow Taylor, managers have sought to subdivide and simplify production tasks, removing discretion in the conduct of work from the individual performer. So, reliance on the simplification of work and the transfer of discretion to engineers and technicians has been characteristic of the managerial tradition in U.S. industrial life. Skill on the plant floor has meant mainly manual-manipulative dexterity. The country's machine tool firms seem to have been unaware of or unconcerned by a major transformation in the conditions of industrial work brought about in part by their own industry, notably by the development of numerically controlled machine tools.

With numerically controlled machine tools, manual dexterity is the bare beginning of the skills required of the operator. If there is to be a stable and high utilization of equipment, the operator must understand how the machine performs, must be prepared to intervene when there is malfunction, must anticipate such malfunction, and adjust programs that, being man-made, can include error.

With the new technologies, productivity of capital becomes more important in terms of cost than productivity of labor. Optimum results are obtained, not by maximizing manual dexterity or physical exertion, but rather through sustained optimum use of the capital equipment. But managements have yet to recognize this change and to make the appropriate alteration in wage, employee training and similar policies.

For the most economic operation under these conditions, machinists and allied workers, to the limit of each person's ability, must be upgraded into computer technology, and responsibility and discretion must be delegated to the machine operator. But that view of the matter is hardly discussed in American industry. However, in 1979 I found that at a major

Japanese machine tool firm the importance of capital productivity was fully understood and that management had been able to achieve rates of equipment utilization, reductions of downtime and the like, reductions of working capital requirements, to a degree probably unprecedented in the machine tool industry.

By treating numerical-control technology as another device for deskilling workers, lowering job ratings (and job pay rates), U.S. managers have discovered a new device for their contest with workers. At the same time, they have introduced a grave contradiction. For whenever the organization of work contradicts the requirements of technology, a sure result is an economically flawed use of the latter. In the present case the harmonious mode of work organization must include systematic cooperation (rather than "every man for himself"), elaboration of worker skills rather than simplification, and motivation for stable, reliable work as a built-in style of producing.

The managers of the U.S. machine tool industry have held to their methods of operation with great tenacity. These are the ways and the skills they grew up with and have always known, the ones that for a long time were good enough to build a worldwide reputation for U.S. machine tools, and even now can sustain a profit position for their enterprises. However, these methods have meant less employment for all the relevant occupations, as factories outside the United States have displaced at least one out of four U.S. technicians, engineers and blue-collar workers.

The range of consequences for the machine tool managers' financially successful style of operation can be confidently forecast, for the basic pattern has already been seen. The example is the machine tool industry of Great Britain, whose managers, operating in the cradle of the industrial revolution, had created a long, enterprising, and financially successful tradition. However, after World War II major forces in the industry gave priority to new strategies for making money rather than to innovations for making machines. By 1980 more than 65 percent of England's new machine tools were imported. The managers of the industry aimed at near-term profits and ignored requirements for production competence. Alfred Herbert Ltd., the flagship firm of British industry, sustained by government subsidies for about a decade, had 7,000 employees as recently as 1979; only 350 remained in 1981. That startling decline contributed to the loss of production competence in the rest of British metalworking.

In 1959,[20] I reported on the low productivity style of operation in the machine tool industry of Great Britain and other Western European countries. The report said two things: first, that the industry that produced the implements of mass production was not using that mode of organization in its own operations; second, that in order to recognize the feasibility of doing so, the industry needed to gain certain new knowledge. Accordingly, I designed a set of about fifteen inquiries that could be carried out in a short time.*

The British industry's management, seconded by a formal government report,[21] was notably vigorous in rejecting all the principal recommendations of that study with respect to improving productivity of operations in their industry. The "old boy" network of senior managers succeeded in fending off that momentary disturbance to their well-established managerial status quo. By the mid-1970s, however, major firms of the British machine tool industry had reached a terminal condition of business deterioration. The pattern of production deficiency coupled with short-term money-making had finally run its course.

The managements of the U.S. machine tool industry have followed a parallel path. When *The New York Times* reported on my 1959 report, the National Machine Tool Builders Association were asked their opinion. A spokesman reserved comment until the findings could be studied and discussed; that study and discussion are apparently still going on.[22]

In papers to the American Society of Mechanical Engineers, I attempted to press these points, recommending that as a public service ASME should sponsor an inquiry into ways of raising the productivity of the U.S. industry and urging "that stable production systems must be introduced into machine tool and allied industries in order to make possible the production of quality products at low prices . . . to encourage modernization of U.S. manufacturing equipment and a firm position in the international market."[23] Establishment consensus has continued in a pattern exactly opposed to the recommendations first made in 1959.[24]

One of the interesting features of these patterns of managerial decline is the unwavering allegiance of the principal managements in the industry to an ideology that justifies their ways of operating and thus the relevance of their own job skills. They argue that as long as their market is as unstable as it has been for decades, then the technologies of mass production are fundamentally inappropriate to their industry. However, they have also declined to investigate possible strategies for effectively stabilizing market demand. And yet they could ponder the example of the Japanese and Western European ma-

---

*These inquiries were designed to answer a series of rather straightforward questions. For example: What proportion of machine tool components could be composed of standardized sets of gears, shafts, slides, hand wheels, bearings, etc.? To what degree is it feasible to compose diverse machine tools from sets of modules, so that modules could be produced in quantity but used in diverse arrangements to construct the desired stock of machine tools? What cost reductions and productivity gains would be obtained by such methods?

chine tool firms, which have learned to operate in diverse markets so as to stabilize their net market situation, while offering quality equipment at prices attractive enough to generate markets.

By 1981 the managers of the U.S. machine tool industry were clearly locked into a pattern that combined money-making and low productivity with investment abroad and short-term financial strategies. They also modified important parts of the older tradition of cost-minimizing in their own operations to take advantage of cost pass-along, even cost-maximizing, in the service of the federal government's state managers.

As an inevitable result of these changes in mode of operation, prices of U.S. machine tools have become progressively less attractive as tradeoffs for industrial labor. Accordingly, the U.S. machine tool industry has been diminished as a production entity, being progressively less able to supply even the domestic market in the face of competition from abroad.

At the same time the state managers of the United States can regard themselves as well served by the same U.S. machine tool industry. The firms that design and construct equipment for them within a cost-maximizing framework are well suited to the state management's needs. Thus, the normal functioning of the state managers contributes to the deteriorating competence of the U.S. machine tool industry with respect to its wider civilian market.

The private and state managers within and around the U.S. machine tool industry have pursued their normal objectives of profit-making and power expansion with acceptable success. But the production consequences of these strategies have included backwardness in the design of products and in the production operations of the industry, finally resulting in a growing inability to supply their vital products to the rest of U.S. industry.

What has been described here as a pattern of the U.S. machine tool industry is important not only in its own right but as a model that has been repeated many times over in other basic industries of the United States. The almost 25 percent dependence on imports for machine tools in U.S. industry is slated to rise to 30 percent and more. As this process continues, the discussion of a point of no return will cease to be an academic exercise.

MANAGING FOR PROFITS/POWER

Managerialism, the main method of decision-making in industry, has a number of sustaining features: the work of decision-making tends to be separated from producing; the decision occupations are organized in hierarchies; the command for every manager is to strive to become a more important manager; finally, income is directly related to position in the hierarchy. But these characteristics of managerialism can operate in various organizational frameworks: as managers are oriented primarily to profit or primarily to production, to short- or long-term profits, together with profit-making (as in a business firm) or with direct power accumulation (as in government).

What has been happening to managing for profit and managing for power in the United States?

1

Exporting Capital,
Exporting Jobs

By their resolve to maximize money profits and managerial decision power, American corporate managers have set in motion the deindustrialization of entire regions of the United States. The closing of thousands of factories is the central feature of this process, the associated effects being the transfer of production to other parts of the United States or to foreign lands. Massive shocks are thus dealt to the employees and to their communities.

There are virtually no reliable national figures on the number of factories shut down, people displaced, and plant closings accompanied by new investments in other states or outside the country. However, there is enough information about particular firms and localities to confirm that an industrial nightmare has been taking place in the United States. It has been diagnosed, thus far, by only a handful of venturesome scholars.

Frank Georges is a steelworker, long employed at the Youngstown, Ohio, works of the U.S. Steel Corporation. On November 27, 1979, he arranged a bank loan for the purchase of a $56,000 house. On the way home from the bank he heard on his car radio that U.S. Steel was planning to close the Ohio works, along with several other plants. Altogether, the corporation discharged 13,000 steelworkers.[1]

Inquiring reporters have learned that, while financial analysts and industry specialists regarded the aging Youngstown works as facing poor economic prospects, the corporation's local general manager had told the workers that the Youngstown plants would be kept open as long as they were profitable. Accordingly, the union made a number of cost-reducing concessions to the management.

In a three-year period, from 1977 to 1980, almost every steel corporation of any size in the United States closed some of its factories, many of them permanently. U.S. Steel laid off people in Chicago, Gary, Youngstown and Pittsburgh. Armco dropped workers in Houston and Middletown, Ohio. Bethlehem Steel cut employment at Lackawanna, New York, and Johnstown,

Pennsylvania. And the Youngstown Sheet and Tube Company shut down its Youngstown plant, putting 5,000 employees out of work.[2]

Pleading losses of $293 million in 1979 to justify factory closings, U.S. Steel management reported earnings of $504 million in 1980, even though most of its plants operated at 50 percent capacity.[3] How could the corporation be making more money while producing less? The answer lies in the long-range strategy of U.S. Steel's management, which has elected to neglect research and development, technological improvement and new capital investment in its steel manufacturing, while making large investments in chemicals, oil and gas, coal and real estate. Indeed, "by 1978, 44 percent of U.S. Steel's total worldwide assets were in non-steel operations."[4] The non-steel proportion has been growing steadily.

By mid-1980, there was speculation that management might be considering getting out of the steel business entirely, but that issue was apparently resolved when David M. Roderick, chairman of U.S. Steel, told a stockholders' meeting that "we are both a steel company and a capital management company," and further that "we expect to be a steel producer for the balance of this century."[5]

Roderick reported that his firm had, from 1975 to 1980, invested about $6.8 billion, the largest part of it outside the steel industry. One result is that the number of its blast furnaces has dropped from forty-six to twenty-seven and its capacity to produce raw steel "is expected to shrink to about 34 million tons from the 38 million produced in 1978."[6]

In April 1981, U.S. Steel announced a plan to invest "several hundred million dollars" to modernize and redesign its 100-year-old steel mill on Chicago's industrial South Side.[7] That is the corporation's first major capital investment in this factory in ten years. To a layman, this may seem a large sum. But its significance must be gauged in terms of the corporation's other, non-steel investments. The purchase of Marathon Oil by U.S. Steel required an outlay at least twenty times the size of the belated modernization of U.S. Steel's Chicago plant.

While these details are specific to the U.S. Steel Corporation, they are part of an overall pattern—that of U.S. corporate managers following the practice of transferring money to whatever places offer the most favorable rate of return. Ordinary maintenance and new investment are dispensed with, the better to accumulate capital funds for investment in new industries, new products, new locations. Then, when the factories so deprived are finally shut down on grounds of high operating costs, inability to compete with the Japanese, or stringent union work rules, management is in a position to score a financial gain in the presence of apparent losses. For the marvelously contrived tax laws of the United States permit a corporation to declare a loss from the closing of a production plant, the size of the loss being determined by appropriately creative accounting. This figure can then be used to reduce tax liability for the remainder of the firm's operations. Thus loss is transformed into profit.

Meanwhile, the financial pages hail "The Turn-around at U.S. Steel— Diversified Concern Is Now Profitable after Plant Closings."[8] But these celebrations of financial well-being and managerial success evoke no cheers from the working people in the steel towns, where by the tens of thousands they have been declared unneeded and unwanted. And indeed they are expendable, since about a fifth of the U.S. economy's steel requirement is now being met by imports.

Having attained their goals of maintaining decision power and enlarging profits, the managers of U.S. Steel evidently congratulate themselves on meeting their responsibilities. That view of their work is endorsed by the consensus that sees workers as commodities and managerial gain as the ultimate social value. Thus, what is described in economic theory as mobility of capital translates into shattered lives, decaying communities and a net loss of production competence in the nation as a whole.*

While factory closings are crucial to the deindustrialization of the United States, no count is made by the U.S. Bureau of the Census or any other federal agency of plants actually shut down. However, employment data are regularly maintained by government and industry, and they show that from 1967 to 1976 1.5 million manufacturing jobs were lost in the northeastern and midwestern states, while 936,000 were gained in the rest of the country.[13]

From 1969 to 1976, New York City alone lost 620,000 industrial jobs.[9] Akron, Ohio, long the center of the U.S. rubber industry, lost 16,000 of its 100,000 manufacturing jobs between 1969 and 1979. The central offices for principal rubber companies remained in Akron, some of them even adding to their white-collar work forces.[10] Further losses of employment from factory closings continued in the Northeast and the Midwest through the end of the

---

*The American pattern is quite different from law and custom in Western Europe. In 1979 a team of U.S. trade union officials reported on *Economic Dislocation, Plant Closings, Plant Relocations and Plant Conversion* policies and programs in three countries (Sweden, England, West Germany), May 1979 (jointly published by United Automobile, Aerospace and Agricultural Implement Workers of America, United Steelworkers of America, International Association of Machinists and Aerospace Workers). They found that countries of the Common Market were bound by "minimum standards for national legislation in order to regulate corporate behavior with respect to plant shutdowns and mass layoffs: actual standards equaled or exceeded the minima with respect to advance notification, joint consultation, provision for income maintenance and alternative employment, etc."

1970s. "In the heavily populated counties of northern Ohio, unemployment has been running considerably above the national average, as high as 16 percent, and much higher among inner city minority groups."[11]

Once corporate managements begin to treat the parts of their enterprises as money machines, the nature of the product becomes secondary. What counts primarily is the magnitude and especially the rate of return on the investment. A prime attention to profit is nothing new in industrial capitalism, but a managerial style that includes disregard for the product, work force and community, and a readiness to move resources to wherever they will earn the greatest money return, has been extended and intensified by the growth in number and importance of conglomerates in the industrial world.

Industrial firms were originally enterprises that made a particular product or set of products. Sometimes, as in some chemical and metallurgical operations (like foundries), the emphasis was on a process rather than a product. Such firms grew either by enlarging their baseline operations or by "horizontal" or "vertical" growth. Horizontal growth means acquiring other enterprises in the same product line; vertical growth means acquiring enterprises that supply raw materials or components to a particular industry, or enterprises that use the product of a particular firm.

Departing from this homogeneity of interest, the conglomerate industrial firm is a complex of enterprises (sometimes "divisions") that provide a diversity of products. The chart on pages 22–23 shows the remarkable array of products represented by the firms that Textron acquired from 1943 to 1968. Relatively few of the concerns in this vast "package" are related, either horizontally or vertically, to Textron's original function, the manufacture of textiles.

The top management of a conglomerate firm is not oriented to a particular product or process, nor can it hope to develop any real knowledge of the diverse technologies represented by the firms it controls. Accordingly, controls of a financial sort, which can be applied uniformly to a multitude of enterprises, are preferred and elaborated. Profitability then becomes a key criterion of control, and the managers of conglomerates are ever ready to dispose of manufacturing facilities when that serves the profit interest of the firm.

It is therefore significant that from 1926 to 1968 the record of corporate mergers shows a dramatic rise in the relative importance of conglomerate acquisitions. From 1926 to 1930 and again from 1940 to 1947 the conglomerate form accounted for an average of 20 percent of corporate mergers in the United States. After 1950 there came an explosion of conglomerate mergers; from 1951 to 1955 they represented 48 percent of corporate mergers and by 1966–1968 82 percent of mergers were of the conglomerate type.[12] Detailed studies of business closings in New England, and particularly in Massachusetts, from 1969 to 1976, show that during the time when the conglomerate form of merger was dominant, conglomerate firms showed a high rate of business closings.[13] At this writing there is no evidence of any change in these patterns, and the following illustrations are still relevant:

Early in 1981 the management of Penn Central, the former railroad company, described itself as a conglomerate of real estate, oil and gas properties and amusement parks. The ability of this firm to engage in active search for profitable acquisitions is strongly supported by the formal financial loss recorded when the Pennsylvania Railroad went into bankruptcy. Under the tax laws that loss, amounting to $600 million in 1981, is a "carry forward" which can be charged against earnings into the future and serves as a shield against payment of income taxes until 1985. The search for acquisitions is taking this firm mainly into two areas—the oil service industry and electronics.[14]

Sante Fe Industries, Inc., the parent company of the Atchison, Topeka and Sante Fe Railway Company, must now allot capital between the maintenance and new investment needs of a modern railroad, and the highly profitable natural-resources enterprises in which the firm has recently invested. It is a sign of the times that the management has been attracted to a possible merger with the Southern Pacific Railroad because the latter's non-railroad holdings include oil, gas, minerals, real estate and pipelines.[15]

The president of the U.S. Steel Corporation announced that about half of the firm's $975 million of capital spending in 1980 was allotted to the steel operations of the firm and the remainder to the firm's various operations in other industries. One thing that U.S. Steel won't be spending any money on any time soon is a new steel plant.[16]

The imaginative managers of conglomerates have developed myriad methods for maximizing their profits, with or without production. Milking a subsidiary, one of the more common devices, involves severe restrictions on maintenance of plant and equipment, reduced outlays for research and development, and no spending on new plant and equipment. Thus, operational overhead is restricted to wages, salaries, power and materials. As long as the subsidiary can survive on this starvation diet, it functions as a "cash cow," an accumulator of money to be spent by the conglomerate central management for further acquisitions. To be sure, this parasitic strategy is limited by the continuing ability of the subsidiary to produce anything that is salable, at a price that covers the out-of-pocket minimal expenses of operation. Any manufacturing facility that is given the "cash cow" treatment will finally be exhausted not only financially but also as a physical production entity.

It appears that this practice was followed by the Lykes Company after it took over the Campbell Works of the Youngstown Sheet and Tube Company

ACQUISITIONS OF

Horizontal and Vertical

TEXTILES
(All resold by 1964)

SUNCOOK MILLS, Suncook, N. H., 1943
Cotton, rayon and other synthetic griege goods, cotton fabrics

LONSDALE CO., Providence, R. I., 1945
Cotton fabric, chambrays, lawns and broadcloth, shirtings, bleaching

MANVILLE JENCKES CORP., Woonsocket, R. I., 1945
Cotton and rayon fabric, taffeta, drapery fabrics, rayon

GOSSETT MILLS, 1946
Cotton and rayon fabric, cotton broadwoven fabric

NASHUA MANUFACTURING CO., Nashua, N. Y. 1946
Cotton and rayon fabric, blankets, pajamas, sheets, pillow cases, bedspreads

THE ESMOND MILLS, INC., Esmond, R. I. 1948
Subs Clarence Whitman & Sons, Inc.
The Esmond Mills, Limited
Esmond Mills, Ontario, Limited
Esmond Virginia, Inc.
The Wilkes-Barre Mfg. Co.
Infant blankets

R. W. BATES PIECE DYE WORKS, INC. Groverville, N. Y., 1951
Cotton broad woven fabrics

VASS COTTON MILL CO., Vass, N. C. 1951
Cotton Fabrics

AMERICAN WOOLEN CO. New York, N. Y. 1955
Woolen and worsted fabrics, blankets and upholstery fabrics, industrial brushes, wool yarn

ROBBINS MILLS, INC., New York, N. Y. (Incorporated New Jersey) 1955
Rayon and acetate fabrics, gray goods, nylon

INDUSTRIAL BATTING

F. BURKHART MANUFACTURING CO. St. Louis, Mo., 1953
Industrial batting

CAROLINA BAGGING CO. Henderson, N. C. 1956
Industrial batting, padding, upholstery filling, polyurathane foam

Oakland Plant of
NATIONAL AUTOMOTIVE FIBRES, INC. Oakland, Calif., 1959
Cotton pad and batts for automobile seating

AIRCRAFT AND PARTS

M. B. MANUFACTURING CO. New Haven, Conn., 1954
Engine mounts and vibration elimination equipment

ACCESSORY PRODUCTS CORP. Whittier, Calif., 1957
Servo actuators, flight control systems, inertial guidance and navigation equipment

BELL AIRCRAFT CORP. Wheatfield, N. Y. 1960
Defense business, including Bell Aerospace Corp. and 3 divisions Helicopters, rocket engines, research and development on propulsion systems, space vehicle equipment, etc.

ELECTRONIC EQUIPMENT

DALMO VICTOR CO. San Carlos, Calif., 1954
Airborne radar antennas and refatec equipment

RYAN INDUSTRIES, INC. Detroit, Mich., 1955
Electromechanical products, photographic equipment, jigs, dies, and fixtures

CALIFORNIA TECHNICAL INDUSTRIES Belmont, Calif., 1957
Electronics

GLOBE ELECTRONICS Council Bluffs, Iowa, 1959
Radio equipment

SCHAFER CUSTOM ENGINEERING Burbank, Calif., 1959
Automation equipment for radio and TV broadcast equipment

ALLEGHANY INSTRUMENTS CO., INC. Cumberland, Md. 1960
Gas regulators, thrust and pressure measuring devices, electronic and electromechanical vibration systems

ELECTRONIC RESEARCH CO Kansas City, Mo. 1960
Electronic components, radio frequency crystals, related power supplies, airborne radar antennas

Nuclear energy operations of
ALCO PRODUCTS New York, N.Y. 1962

COLLEGE HILL INDUSTRIES Warwick, R. I., 1964
Inertia compensated tape recorders for space vehicles, specialized pressure and inertia switches and pressure-sensing capsules; research in other commercial and defense electronic products

ELECTROCRAFT, INC. Chicago, Ill., 1959
Plugs and jacks

ROBOTOMICS ENTERPRISES, INC. Phoenix, Arizona, 1963
Decades and displays for electronic counters

OPTICAL INSTRUMENTS

SAURON OPTICAL CO. Geneva, N.Y., 1958
Optical lab equipment, including interference filters, spectacle frames, cases and lenses

SPECTROLAB, INC. Hollywood, Calif., 1960
Optical lab equipment including interference filters

MODERN OPTICS, INC. Houston, Tex., 1961
Lenses, optical

CONTINENTAL OPTICAL CO. Indianapolis, Ind., 1963
Spectacle frames, cases and lenses

INDUSTRIAL FASTENERS

CAMCAR SCREW & MANUFACTURING CORP., Rockford, Ill., 1955
Industrial fasteners, rivets, bolts

TOWNSEND CO. New Brighton, Pa. 1959
Industrial fasteners, rivets, bolts, cold-heading machinery, wire-drawing equipment, rivet setting machines and electrical contacts

BOUTS AIRCRAFT NUT CORP Norfolk, Conn., 1960
Lock nuts, engine nuts

AMERICAN SCREW CO Willimantic, Conn. 1962
Industrial fasteners, rivets, bolts

TUBULAR RIVET & STUD CO. Wollaston, Mass., 1961
Rivets

FABRICATED PRODUCTS CO West Newton, Pa., 1960
Specialty building seals, washers, closures and fasteners

BOSTITCH, INC. East Greenwich, R. I., 1966
Industrial staplers and stitchers

HARMIL MANUFACTURING, INC Downey, Calif., 1966
Sealing washers

IRON AND STEEL CASTINGS

CAMPBELL WYANT & CANNON FOUNDRY CO. Muskegon, Mich., 1956
Gray iron and steel castings for automotive, railroad, agricultural, implement refrigeration, marine and other industries

PITTSBURGH STEEL FOUNDRY CORP Glassport, Pa., 1959
Steel and alloy castings

CHAIN SAWS

HOMELITE CORP. Port Chester, N.Y. 1955
Chain saws and pumps, electric power plants, centrifugal pumps gas engines

MEASURING INSTRUMENTS

SPRAGUE METER CO., INC Bridgeport, Conn., 1961
Gas meters, gas regulators, thrust and pressure measuring devices; electronic and electromechanical vibration systems

RESEARCH

NUCLEAR METALS, INC. Cambridge, Mass., 1959
Nuclear and metallurgical research

FITTINGS AND PRESSURE VALVES

M. B. SKINNER CO. South Bend, Ind., 1961
Service fittings for utilities, pressure valves

LEDEEN, INC Los Angeles, Calif., 1964
Hydraulic and pneumatic control equipment.

Source: *Economic Report on Corporate Mergers,* Federal Trade Commission, Bureau of Economics, Commerce Clearing House Edition, Fig. 8–8.

TEXTRON, INC. 1943-1968

CONGLOMERATE

DIE CASTINGS

PEAT MANUFACTURING CORP
Norfolk, Calif., 1956
Nonferrous die castings

METAL STAMPINGS

THE RANDALL CO. Cincinnati, Ohio, 1959
Wagner Mfg. Co., Sydney, Ohio, 1959
(Subsidiary)
Appliance stampings and aluminum kitchen utensils

ZENITE METALS CORP.
Blytheville, Ark., 1963
Trim for auto and appliance industry

METAL PIPE AND TUBING

CROWELL TUBE CO., INC.
Lexington, Mass., 1960
Small-diameter metal tubing

ERIE TOOLWORKS AND LAKEVIEW
FORGE CO., Erie, Pa., 1965
Pipe wrenches, vices and bomb legs

BATHROOM FIXTURES

HALL-MACK CO., Los Angeles, Calif., 1956
Bathroom fixtures and accessories

METAL WORKING MACHINERY

PRECISION METHODS AND MACHINES
Waterbury, Conn., 1958
Rolling mill machinery and equipment

BRIDGEPORT MACHINES, INC.
Bridgeport, Conn., 1968
Small milling machines

MACHINE TOOLS

WATERBURY FARREL FOUNDRY &
MACHINE CO., Waterbury, Conn., 1958
Cold-heading machinery, wire-drawing
equipment, rivet setting machines

JONES & LAMSON MACHINE CO.
Springfield, Vt., 1963
Machine tools

THOMPSON GRINDER CO.
Springfield, Ohio, 1967
Precision grinders

FOUNDRY SUPPLIES

FANNER MANUFACTURING CO.
Cleveland, Ohio, 1958
Foundry supplies, industrial hardware for
iron and steel foundries, machine tools

AMSLER MORTON CORP.
Pittsburgh, Pa., 1959
Industrial hardware for iron and steel
foundries, metal processing, industrial
furnaces

MOTOR VEHICLE PARTS AND ACCESSORIES

VAN NORMAN INDUSTRIES
Springfield, Mass., 1958
Automotive replacement antennas

MILFORD MACHINE CO.
Leesburg, Ind., 1960
Crank shafts and connecting rods

ELECTRICAL TRANSMISSION EQUIPMENT

Underfloor division of
WALKER BROTHERS, 1964
Underfloor line for electrical distribution
system

AMERICAN CROSSARM & CONDUIT CO.
Niles, Ill., 1967
Crossarms, braces, insulator pins

BROADCASTING EQUIPMENT

American Microphone Division of
ELGIN NATIONAL WATCH CO.
Elgin, Ill., 1958
Broadcasting equipment

PAINTS

VITA VAR CORP., Newark, N.J., 1962
Industrial paints and protective coatings

FLOOD AND CONKLIN MANUFACTURING
CO., Newark, N.J., 1964
Paints and industrial coatings

Patterson-Sargent and Allied Divisions of
H. K. PORTER CO., No. Brunswick, N.J.
1965
Paints

BEARINGS

FAFNIR BEARING CO.
New Britain, Conn., 1968
Precision ball and roller bearings

PARKERSBURG-AETNA CORP.
Parkersburg, W. Va., 1962
Ball and roller bearings, oil field production equipment, pre-engineered metal
buildings

PLYWOOD

COQUILLE PLYWOOD CO.
Coquille, Ore., 1955
Plywood

MYRTLE POINT VENEER CO.
Norway, Ore., 1955
Plywood

BANDON VENEER & PLYWOOD
ASSOCIATION, Bandon, Ore., 1956
Plywood

PLASTIC PRODUCTS

KORDITE CORP., Macedon, N.Y., 1955
Plastic products, specialty food and industrial bags

FEDERAL LEATHER COMPANIES
Belleville, N.J., 1956
Proxylin-coated fabric and vinyl coated
fabric

OLD KING COLE, INC.
Louisville, Ohio, 1965
Vacuum and rotary forming of plastic

ABRASIVE PRODUCTS

CLEVELAND METAL ABRASIVE CO.
Cleveland, Ohio, 1965
Iron and steel shot and grit

A. P. De SANNO & SON, INC.
Phoenixville, Pa., 1967
Grinding wheels and abrasive products

BOAT BUILDING AND MARINE HARDWARE

FAEGEOL MARINE ENGINE CO.
San Diego, Calif., 1958
Rights to manufacture marine engines and
turbines

DORSETT PLASTIC CORP.
(Dorset Marine), Santa Clara, Calif., 1960
Inboard and outboard runabout cruisers

SOUTH COAST MARINE CO.
Newport Beach, Calif., 1965
Marine hardware

PASSENGER LINER

S. S. La GUARDIA renamed
S. S. LEILANI, 1956
Tourist passenger line

FURNITURE

Ames Maid Division of
O. AMES CO., Parkersburg, W. Va., 1963
Kitchen and juvenile furniture

Pennant division of
NOVO INDUSTRIAL CORP.
New York, N.Y., 1964
Kitchen and bar stools, juvenile furniture

DURHAM MANUFACTURING CO.
Muncie, Ind., 1964
Folding metal furniture

UNDERWATER EXPLORATION

GERALDINES, LTD., Annapolis, Md., 1962
Products and services for commercial and
underwater exploration

AGROCHEMICALS

SPENCER KELLOG & SONS, INC.
Buffalo, N.Y., 1961
Soybean oil, soybean oil meal, lecithin,
linseed oil, castor oil, linseed oil meal,
livestock feed

S. R. MILLS FEED CO.
Freehold, N.J., 1965
Poultry and livestock feeds

POULTRY FARMING

BYARD V. CARMEAN, INC.
Laurel, Del., 1963
Poultry farm

CAROLINE POULTRY FARMS, INC.
Federalsburg, Md., 1963
Grower and processor of poultry

PHARMACEUTICALS

ZOTOX PHARMACAL CO.
Stanford, Conn., 1961
Pharmaceutical preparations

OLD KING COLE, INC.

TILDEN CO., New Lebanon, N.Y., 1961
Pharmaceutical preparations

SHOES

ALBERT H. WEINBRENNER CO.
Milwaukee, Wis., 1960
Men's, boys' and children's shoes

STORM DOORS

BENANDA ALUMINUM PRODUCTS CO.
Girard, Ohio, 1956
Storm doors and windows, awnings, siding
material for building

GOLF CARTS

E-Z-GO CAR CORP., Augusta, Ga., 1960
Electric golf carts

WATCH BRACELETS

SPEIDEL CORP., Providence, R.I., 1964
Watch bracelets, chains, identification
bracelets

WRITING INSTRUMENTS

W. A. SHEAFFER PEN CO.
Ft. Madison, Iowa, 1965
Writing instruments, electronic hearing
aids

ZIPPERS

TALON, INC., Meadville, Pa., 1968
Slide fasteners (zippers)

SILVERWARE

GORHAM CORP., Providence, R.I., 1967
Fine silverware, school supplies and
stationery

DISTRIBUTORS

HENRY W. SAARI, INC.
Seattle, Wash., 1967
Distributor, Bostitch products

EDWARD SICKLES & CO.
Philadephia, Pa., 1967
Distributor, Speidel products

OTHER

NEWMARKET MANUFACTURING CO.
Lowell, Mass., 1954

Walsco-Schott division of
TELAUTOGRAPH CORP.
Los Angeles, Calif., 1956

COMPONENT PARTS CO.
Whittier, Calif., 1959

FUEL ENGINEERING CORP.
Torrance, Calif., 1962

in 1969. Analysts of Lykes' responsibility for closing the Youngstown Campbell works have judged that thereafter Lykes did virtually nothing to modernize its steel operations, especially those in Youngstown. According to *Business
Week* (October 3, 1977), "Lykes failed to invest sufficiently to refurbish the
pre–World War I open hearth and blast furnaces in Youngstown. . . . Spending in the crucial years 1970–73 averaged only $27 million, little more than
enough to cover the cost of basic maintenance of the furnaces. Less efficient
than most of its competitors because of its old facilities, Youngstown has had
trouble competing with its more modern rivals. . . ." During this time when
plant maintenance and investment were withheld from the Youngstown steel
works, the Lykes Corporation enjoyed high cash-flow earnings, which enabled the conglomerate to expand other operations and take over additional
companies, including an insurance company, three large highly automated
cargo ships, the W. R. Grace Company's share of a jointly owned steamship
line, the Ramseyer and Miller Company and, in 1975, the Great Western Steel
Company.[17]

Internal accounting practices can produce an appearance for a given firm
of higher earnings, or higher assets, per share of stock than could be supported
by actual conditions of production. Conglomerate managements profit from
this sort of creative bookkeeping because it encourages higher prices for the
firm's securities on the stock exchanges, and these in turn become more
valuable assets for use in buying more enterprises. The manipulation of inventory valuation to show increases or decreases in assets is one such accounting
device.

Since profitability is so widely recognized as a central goal of business
operations, it is important to emphasize that the conglomerate strategies
include the closing of productive subsidiaries that are in fact profitable. The
trouble is that they are not doing well enough to clear the "profit hurdle"
set by conglomerate managements. Their "target rates of return" can
force the shutting down of enterprises where records, by other standards
such as producing desirable products, affording sustained livelihood,
and maintaining technical competence, are entirely satisfactory. Barry Bluestone and Bennett Harrison have assembled important illustrations of these
processes:

At Cornell University, William F. Whyte and his colleagues have been studying cases
of conglomerate destruction of viable businesses. Among their findings are numerous
examples of abandonment of going concerns by conglomerates whose target rates of
return were not met. For example,

The Herkimer [New York] plant, producing library furniture, had been acquired
by Sperry Rand in 1955. The plant had made a profit every year except one
through the next two decades, and yet Sperry Rand decided to close the plant and

sell the equipment [in part because it] was not yielding a 22 percent profit on invested capital. That was the standard used by this conglomerate/management in determining an acceptable rate of return on its investments. . . .

Another example is offered by the Bates Manufacturing Co., a leading Maine textile manufacturer. After several exchanges of ownership following World War II, all of the mills except one at Lewiston were sold to textile conglomerates. Finally the Lewiston facility was also sold to two New York investors who were more interested in the coal and energy business which was thrown in with the Bates transaction. The energy business promised a 15–20% return on investment, in contrast to Bates' steady but small 5–7% return. As a long-standing manager put in, "These guys were not textile men, they were money men." Not surprisingly the new owners decided to close the Lewiston Mill in 1977. The jobs were saved only when the mill's workers and some of the former managers chose to buy it . . . through an ESOP arrangement. . . .*

. . . in the current economic era, viable businesses *can* be closed because, although they are making a profit, it is not *enough* of a profit. Perhaps the most dramatic example of this phenomenon involved Uniroyal's closing of its 87-year-old inner tube factory in Indianapolis in 1978. . . .

The factory has long been the country's leading producer of inner tubes. It operates profitably. Its $7 million to $8 million annual payroll sustains the families of nearly 600 employees.

The company, in a formal statement, cited "high labor costs" and "steadily declining demand." Union and management officials who worked at the plant tell another story. They say that Uniroyal could have kept the plant operating if it wanted to but that under pressure from the securities markets, management decided to concentrate its energy on higher-growth chemical lines. Interviews with securities analysts support this theory. Richard Haydon, an analyst at Goldman, Sachs & Co., says: "You have one very large entity looking at a very small entity, but the small entity being very large to those people that work there. I think it's a truism that many companies have grown too big to look at the small market."

. . . this particular case has a happy ending. Together with the president of the City Council and the aid of the Rubber Workers Union president, Peter Bommarito, the workers were able to get local financiers to put up the capital to purchase the plant from Uniroyal. The jobs were saved, two union representatives now sit on the board of directors, and it is forecast that after one year, about $500,000 in profits will be distributed among the workers and a matching $500,000 will be invested in new machinery.[18]

The record even includes the making and unmaking of profitability for particular subsidiaries of a conglomerate according to management decisions

---

*ESOP—Employee Stock Ownership Plan, enabling employees, with support from the federal Economic Development Administration, to purchase a firm threatened by closure.

on the assignment of the administrative costs and charges of its central operations to each of its subsidiaries. The tax laws encourage such operations inasmuch as various outlays, including political lobbying, can be charged as business costs rather than having to be paid from the profits of the firm. Similarly, when a factory is closed and its equipment is shifted to other subsidiaries in other localities, the expense of those moves can usually be charged to cost. Thus, the federal government, by loss of tax revenue, pays approximately half the expense.

Finally, conglomerates are especially well positioned for such operations because they can charge calculated losses, as from shutting down a particular factory, against past or future profits of the conglomerate enterprise as a whole. A conglomerate can milk a subsidiary, causing the physical deterioration of its assets, but yet maximize the declared value of those assets as "losses" for tax purposes. "Losses" then become effective net profit by reducing tax liability. Such mechanisms realize profits by diminishing production capability and, finally, by terminating production altogether.* Federal laws on investment tax credits and rapid depreciation also encourage investment in altogether new buildings and industrial machinery rather than in maintenance that sustains or improves existing equipment and facilities.

Especially during the 1960s and 1970s conglomerate and other U.S. corporations relentlessly sought out money and managerial gain by moving production operations to more advantageous locations. Among the considerations bearing on such decisions, two have clearly dominated: first, cheap, nonunionized labor, and second, a production base in rapidly expanding, high-income economies, notably the countries of Western Europe.[19]

The pursuit of lower wages for industrial workers has been a frequent spur to factory closings. The American Shoe Machine Company has reportedly arranged to shut down competent shoe manufacturing plants in various Massachusetts towns "in order to acquire their machinery."[20] In testimony to the House of Representatives Committee on Ways and Means, one investor reported that he had "purchased a modern U.S. shoe factory, shut it down, and

---

*Since the declining rate of productivity growth in U.S. industry has become a national issue, it is worth defining the connection between plant closing and relocation, within the United States, and industrial productivity. John E. Ullmann and Jeffrey Wenzel of Hofstra University have examined changes in productivity for major industry groups in relation to location. They find that "there is no systematic relationship between changes in productivity and Sunbelt location, but rather that the changes in productivity appear to be nationwide in scope. They are a function of the industry itself, rather than where it happens to be located. The documented decline in productivity cannot merely be attributed to a decaying industrialized North, and it is *not* compensated for by the Sunbelt developing its own comparable industrial base. . . . Troubles, for industries as for people, frequently have a habit of following their owners." John E. Ullmann and Jeffrey Wenzel, *Regional Changes in Manufacturing Productivity,* Hofstra University, 1981.

shipped the lasts, dies, patterns, management, and much of the leather to Europe," where he was able to continue with shoe manufacturing while paying workers fifty cents an hour as compared to three dollars an hour in Massachusetts.[21]

The closing of American factories, especially in the Midwest and the Northeast, is often the initial step in a process whereby financial resources are moved, first to states of the American South and then, in increasing numbers since 1950, to foreign locations. A 1974 book documented the closing of forty-two separate factories in the U.S. consumer electronics industry and the subsequent relocation of their operations outside the United States.[22] While there is no national count of the number of facilities that have been shut in the United States only to reappear somewhere abroad, observers of multinational corporations and of international capital shifts have identified many cases of individual factory closings and their consequences. Some examples:

In 1966, as an alternative to expanding its older, unionized TV factory in Cincinnati, RCA opened a 4,000-employee facility in Memphis. When the Memphis workers organized a union, RCA closed *both* plants and moved all of its black-and-white TV production to Taiwan.

The General Instrument Corporation is a New York–based firm that produces electronic equipment. . . . In the early 1960s, General Instrument employed 14,000 production and maintenance workers in plants at Chicopee Falls, Mass., Newark, N.J., and eventually in Kentucky as well. By 1978, all of these plants had been closed, and the production operations, including existing machines and designs for new ones, shifted to—once again—Taiwan.

During the 1960s, Litton Industries, a famous conglomerate, acquired Royal Typewriter. Over the next fifteen years, domestic production was shifted from Hartford, Conn., to Springfield, Missouri, and then to Portugal and England, to get inside the Common Market tariff wall. This last move eliminated some 4,000 American jobs. . . .

Bulova has transferred production to a new plant near Pago Pago, American Samoa, where 60 Samoans assemble some 210,000 watch movements flown in from Switzerland for eventual shipment to the U.S. market. . . . Says Bulova's President Harry B. Henshel, "We are able to beat foreign competition because we *are* the foreign competition." . . .

In 1965, the Mexican government offered cheap labor to American business, this time on its side of the border. The new Border Industrialization Program allowed entirely foreign-owned companies to set up operations within a virtually tax and tariff-free 12 1/2 mile strip of the border. The Mexican Minister of Commerce told *The Wall Street Journal* (May 25, 1967): "Our idea is to offer an alternative to Hong Kong, Japan and Puerto Rico for free enterprise." Through U.S. tariff code regulations 806.30 and 807.00, U.S.-owned corporations could assemble products in this zone and import them into the country, paying duty only on the value added in the assembly process—the cost of the cheap Mexican labor.

With the impetus, then, from both the U.S. and Mexican governments, U.S. garment, electronics and toy companies moved quickly into the border area. Among the pioneers were Litton Industries, Transitron, Motorola, Fairchild, Hughes Aircraft, and General Electric. Beginning with 72 authorized U.S. plants in 1967, they had . . . reached 665 in late 1974 . . . sending nearly $450 million in "added-value" to the U.S. in 1974.

Other multinational corporations operating *maquiladoros*—the word used by Mexican workers to describe these border assembly plants—include North American Rockwell, Burroughs, General Instrument, GTE, Sylvania, RCA, Levi-Strauss, Puritan, and Kayser-Roth. In a period of less than ten years, the *maquiladoros* came to employ almost 13 percent of the border region's labor force.[23]

In 1977, the U.S. Commerce Department found that 3,540 U.S. companies had 24,666 foreign affiliates. All told, these companies had a combined direct investment stake of about $200 billion by 1980 in overseas plant and facilities, up from not quite $12 billion in 1950.[24]

The full significance of this vast transfer of financial capital from the United States can best be appreciated by observing the effect on physical resources used in production and on employment opportunity in the United States. The automobile industry is a good place to start.

A Dodge dealer in Mount Kisco, New York, reportedly offered a bumper sticker in November 1980 that proclaimed: "This vehicle built in America by Americans for Americans." Actually, about 15 percent of the Dodge Omni and its related Plymouth Horizon was manufactured outside the United States. A more important omen of things to come is the "world car," an idea heralded by the major auto companies. The Ford Escort draws on the following countries for components:

Japan	manual transaxles	France	hub and bearing
Spain	shock absorber struts		clutch assembly
Brazil	rear brake assembly	Mexico	door lift assembly
Britain	steering gears	Taiwan	wiring
Italy	engine cylinder heads	W. Germany	valve-guide bushing[25]

Ford has also "introduced the Fiesta, designed and developed in Europe, assembled in three countries, and which includes an engine from Britain and Spain, windshield glass from Oklahoma, road wheels from Belgium, a transmission from France, a distributor from Northern Ireland and a fuel tank from West Germany."[26]

Apart from the four major U.S. auto companies, there are large firms, like Borg-Warner, that specialize in the manufacture of parts for automobiles. Borg-Warner has factories in Japan, Australia and Europe. Its director for Asia has stated that "in Japan we have a joint venture with Japanese partners, and we deliver about 95 percent of our output to Japanese auto manufacturers, primarily for export." The Eaton Corporation, long centered in Cleveland, Ohio, now "manufactures hydraulic lifters and intake and exhaust valves at several sites in Europe. It manufactures valves in Spain for autos built in Britain, provides parts for Volkswagen engines built in West Germany that are then shipped to the United States, and it supplies parts from its Saginaw, Mich., facility for the Ford Erika being built in Britain. It is also building a valve plant in Mexico with a Mexican partner."[27]

The parts operation is anything but trivial. In 1979 $6.8 billion worth of parts and components were manufactured abroad for automobiles to be assembled in the United States. Assuming average hourly earnings of fifteen dollars an hour in the auto industry and a 2,000-hour man-year, these imported parts in 1979 accounted for the equivalent of about 226,000 direct and indirect man-years of U.S. labor. The expectation in the automobile industry is that it will import about 10 percent of the parts for U.S.-built motor vehicles by 1985 and 15 percent by 1990.[28]

The guiding principle behind the "world car" is that multiple manufacturing locations for the components of a given vehicle will be set up in major world areas (Europe, South America, North America, East Asia) and coupled with assembly plants for that vehicle in the same general locations. That done, the management of the international auto firm can draw components to assembly plants in the quantities and at the times that they are needed. The availability of alternative supply locations makes management dramatically less vulnerable to union pressures in any particular location. The world car is part of an estimated $80 billion new capital investment plan by the major U.S. auto companies, described by sympathetic journalists as a "rescue plan, an astronomical gamble that will tolerate few mistakes, an investment . . . that the auto men hope will buy back lost prestige and market dominance."[29]

Assuming that the rescue plan works and that it regains for the U.S. auto companies their prestige and market dominance, what will this success mean for working people in the United States?

The auto industry has long occupied a central place in the manufacturing economy of the United States. Therefore, when, by the end of 1980, imported cars accounted for 28 percent of dollar-valued automobile sales in the United States, a crisis was signaled for the American industrial system. As described by the Secretary of Transportation, Neil Goldschmidt, in a report to President Carter on January 11, 1981,

The auto industry sits at the center of this country's manufacturing economy. Together with the steel, rubber, aluminum, iron, glass and electronics industries, it exerts an enormous influence on our economic course and that of the other nations of the world:

- Roughly one of every six jobs in America is related to the auto industry; in total, more than 4 million people directly owe their employment to the automobile.
- It utilizes 21 percent of the nation's steel output; 60 percent of the synthetic rubber; 11 percent of the primary aluminum; 30 percent of the ferrous castings; 25 percent of the glass; 20 percent of the machine tools; and significant percentages of plastics and electronics.
- Production of the auto involves a vast and expensive industrial network: There are more than 100 plants involved in the manufacturing process of each automobile; over 2,000 companies produce goods primarily for the auto industry, which each year purchases $40 billion of equipment and material from suppliers.
- The auto itself is also a major user of energy. Almost 34 percent of the oil we consume goes to fuel America's fleet of autos.[30]

The situation that was disturbing Goldschmidt can be grasped most readily, perhaps, from the two listings in the next pages. The first shows factory closings in the auto industry by the end of 1980. Job losses are given for the Chrysler and Ford factories; similar figures are not available from General Motors, but they are surely larger than those of Chrysler and Ford combined. By September 1980, about 340,000 blue- and white-collar workers in the U.S. auto firms had been laid off or discharged. About three times that many, "an estimated million workers in the automotive supply industries have lost their jobs."[31]

These factory closings are part of a long-term process of production relocation in the auto, steel and tire industries. By far the largest relocation of U.S. auto production will now be outside the United States. That is shown in the second table, which tabulates arrangements by U.S. automobile firms to buy foreign-made parts for automobiles to be assembled in the United States. The bulk of that $80 billion "rescue plan" for the U.S. auto industry is, more exactly, a rescue plan for the top managements of these firms. But the working people involved will be replaced, to a substantial degree, by counterparts in Mexico, Japan, Brazil, France, West Germany and Italy.

Harley Shaiken, a specialist in auto industry technology, finds that "computer technology and telecommunications allow basic decisions to be made at corporate headquarters, while manufacturing is decentralized around the world to exploit low wages and other advantages abroad. The scramble to build engine plants in Mexico is a case in point. Attracted by low wages, GM is building a Mexican facility capable of producing 500,000 6-cylinder engines per year; Chrysler is doubling the annual capacity of its yet-uncompleted Mexican plant to 440,000 units. Ford is constructing a 500,000-unit factory

RECENT PLANT CLOSINGS

Chrysler Plants

Shutdowns	*Job Loss*
Lyons Trim, MI	700
Hamtramck Assembly, MI	5,600
Fostoria Iron Foundry, OH	650
Eight Mile/Outer Drive Stamping, Detroit, MI	2,400
Windsor Engine, ONT	2,400
Missouri Truck Assembly, St. Louis, MO	4,100
Warren R.V. Assembly, MI	2,000
Huber Av. Foundry, Detroit, MI	2,400
Cape Canaveral, FL	500
Mack Av. Stamping, Detroit, MI	4,100
Employment Loss from Peak	24,850

Ford Plants

Shutdowns	*Job Loss*
Los Angeles Assembly, CA	2,300
Mahwah Assembly, NJ	4,800
Dearborn Foundry, MI	1,100
Windsor Foundry, ONT	1,600
Flat Rock Foundry, MI (announced possible future closing)	—
Cleveland Engine, OH (indefinite)	2,300
Employment Loss from Peak	9,800

GM Plants

Shutdowns	*New Locations*
Pontiac Assembly, MI	Orion Township, MI
St. Louis Assembly, MO	St. Charles, MO
St. Louis Corvette, MO	Bowling Green, KY
Detroit Cadillac Engine, MI	Livonia, MI
Flint Foundry, MI	(Consolidation)
Kansas City (possible)	Kansas City Area
Detroit Cadillac Assembly	Detroit (negotiation)
	Dayton, OH (mini-truck and engine)

Source: U.S. Department of Transportation, *The U.S. Automobile Industry* (Washington, D.C., 1981), p. xvi.

FOREIGN SOURCING—RECENTLY ANNOUNCED COMMITMENTS BY U.S. AUTOMOBILE MANUFACTURERS
TO PURCHASE FOREIGN-MADE COMPONENTS FOR USE IN DOMESTIC VEHICLES PRODUCTION

Description of Component	Intended Use	Manufacturing Source	Approx. No. of Components	Period
		G.M.		
2.8 liter V-6	Cars	GM de Mexico	<400,000/year	1982–
2.0 liter L-4 with transmission	Mini-trucks	Isuzu (Japan)	100,000/year	1981–
1.8 liter diesel L-4	Chevette	Isuzu (Japan)	small numbers	1982–
1.8 liter L-4	J-car	GM de Brazil	250,000/year	1979–
THM 180 automatic transmission	Chevette	GM Strasbourg (France)	~250,000/year	1979–
		Ford		
2.2 liter L-4	Cars	Ford-Mexico	<400,000/year	1983–
Diesel L-4	Cars	Toyo Kogyo	150,000/year	1983–
2.0 liter L-4	Mini-trucks	Toyo Kogyo	<100,000/year	1982–
2.3 liter L-4	Cars	Ford de Brazil	~50,000/year	1979–
Diesel 6 cyl.	Cars	BMW/Steger	100,000/year	1983–
Turbo-diesel/4 cyl.	Cars	BMW/Steger	—	1985–
Manual transaxles	Front Disc Cars	Toyo Kogyo	100,000/year	1980–
Aluminum Cylinder Heads	1.6 liter L-4	Europe, Mexico	—	1980–
Electronic Engine control devices	Cars	Toshiba	100,000+/year	1978–
Ball Joints	Cars	Musashi Seimibu	1,000,000/year	1980–1984

Chrysler

L-6 and V-8 engines	Cars	Chrysler de Mexico	<100,000/year	early 1970s
2.2 liter L-4	K-body	Chrysler de Mexico	<270,000/year	1981
2.6 liter L-4	K-body	Mitsubishi	1 Million	1981–85
1.7 liter L-4	L-body (Omni)	Volkswagen	1.2 Million	1978–82
1.6 liter L-4	L-body	Talbot (Peugeot)	400,000 total	1982–84
2.0 liter Diesel V-6	K-body	Peugeot	100,000/year	1982–
1.4 liter L-4	A-body (Omni replacement)	Mitsubishi	300,000/year	1984–
Aluminum Cylinder Heads	2.2 liter L-4	Fiat		

AMC

Car components and power train	AMC-Renault	Renault in France and Mexico	300,000/year	1982–

VW of America

Radiators, Stampings	Rabbit	VW de Mexico	250,000/year	1979–
L-4 diesel and gas	Cars	VW de Mexico	300,000+/year	1982–

Sources: Compiled from *Automotive News*, *Ward's Engine Update*, *Ward's Automotive Report*, *American Metal Market*, Detroit *Free Press*, and *Japan Economic Journal*. U.S. Dept. of Transportation, *The U.S. Automobile Industry* (Washington, D.C., 1980), p.viii.

south of the border, and Volkswagen has canceled plans for a U.S. engine plant in favor of a 300,000-unit expansion of its present Mexican facility."[32]

While GM is "spending $3 billion to build or remodel six assembly plants in the United States," it is, at the same time, committing "$2 billion more to build new car and assembly production facilities in Spain and Austria."[33] The Ford Motor Company at the end of 1980 had "cut back its North American investments, but it plans to reinforce its European and Latin American operations with worldwide spending of almost $36 billion by 1985."[34]

The construction of new factories outside the United States continues a pattern that the major U.S. auto companies have pursued doggedly since 1950. But the behavior of the U.S. auto firms is by no means unique. For some time *Forbes* has been assembling from U.S. multinational firms information on the scale of their foreign operations. A table (see Appendix I) summarizes the magazine's 1979 information on foreign assets as a percent of the total assets of each of seventy-six major manufacturing firms. The point here is plain enough: the Ford Motor Company, as of 1979, had located 54 percent of its assets outside the United States. General Motors will probably move up quickly in this respect as a result of its massive capital investment plan for the 1980s. On average, the firms on the *Forbes* list retain 63 percent of their assets inside the United States—and from that one may plausibly estimate that 37 percent of their employment is now outside the United States. (I have excluded from this listing the oil and other mining companies whose asset location is largely controlled by the natural occurrence of minerals in the earth's crust.)

As might be expected, American trade unions have been particularly alert to the behavior of multinationals in less developed countries. The industrial union department of the AFL-CIO reported in 1975 that

> U.S.-based multinationals are now employing prison labor in Colombia. The minimum wage in Bogotá, the capital city, was recently *raised* to the equivalent of $1.33 per day! U.S. companies like B. F. Goodrich and the Container Corporation of America, among others, found this meager sum too much to pay. Instead they employ 6,000 prisoners at below the minimum wage, with no fringe benefits and no possibility of strikes.
>
> The Dole Corporation used to produce the bulk of its pineapples in Hawaii, paying its organized agricultural workers about $3 per hour. Now it has moved its plantations to the Philippines, where it pays $.30 an hour. The price of pineapple paid by U.S. consumers is unchanged.[35]

U.S. government agencies are extolling the virtues of foreign locations for direct American investment. Thus, a Commerce Department publication describes Taiwan's "liberal tax and other incentives to attract foreign capital," and then gives the following appraisal of labor relations: "Taiwan does not have an active labor movement and the government does not interject itself into wage negotiations. Strikes are virtually unheard of . . . there is little activity in the way of collective bargaining." Similarly, the U.S. Agency for International Development has suggested Rumania as a likely place for foreign investment opportunities: "The dependable, low cost, and controlled labor force of Rumania, with its well-trained workers eager to learn advanced Western technology and techniques, is especially appealing to Western firms, interested in the more labor-intensive industries. Internal, political and economic risks are minimal."[36]

Direct foreign investments by U.S. firms in 1950 totalled $11.8 billion, and by 1980 had reached $200 billion. Furthermore, these original investments appreciated as they were used to construct and operate industrial and other facilities. Thus, by 1973 investments originally totaling $100 billion had a book value of about $160 billion. Applying the same multiplier to the $200 billion of direct foreign investment that was reached by 1980, it is safe to assume that the current value is $320 billion. About 40 percent of these investments have been in manufacturing industries, 30 percent in petroleum and 30 percent in other fields.[37]

By 1970, capital controlled by U.S. firms in manufacturing industries abroad was equal to 26.1 percent of the U.S. corporate capital in the domestic manufacturing industry. For some manufacturing industries the foreign percentage was much higher. Thus, capital placed overseas by auto firms equaled 95 percent of their total domestic capital—almost the same. In the important machinery industries, U.S. foreign capital was equal to 48 percent of the domestic capital.[38]

Since 1950, foreign investment appears to have accelerated. In manufacturing as a whole, U.S. foreign spending for new factories and equipment from 1957 to 1961 amounted to 12 percent of the domestic outlay. From 1967 to 1970, however, foreign investing equaled 21 percent of the domestic expenditure. These dry money statistics translate directly into the presence and, by implication, the absence of jobs.

The United Electrical Workers, a union whose members have been especially hard hit by exportation of employment from the United States, reports: "In 1966 U.S. electrical manufacturers invested six times as much in domestic plant and equipment as they did in their foreign locations—$1.2 billion compared to $200 million. By 1979 the tables had turned. U.S. multinationals invested $5.1 billion at home but $13 billion—more than twice as much— abroad."[39]

By 1970 U.S. multinationals were employing, in all industries outside the United States, 4,780,000 people, or 7.8 percent of such employment in the United States. In manufacturing industry, however, foreign employment by

U.S. firms was 3,293,000, or 17.1 percent as much as was available in all the U.S. manufacturing industries. For motor vehicles, the ratio of employment abroad to that at home was 73 percent and for machinery-producing industries the figure was 25.9 percent. All told, the export of capital has produced a major enlargement of employment opportunity outside the United States.

For every billion dollars of direct foreign investment by U.S. industrial firms, about 26,500 domestic jobs are eliminated in the United States.[40] This means that the direct foreign investment of $200 billion from the United States had by 1980 transferred about 5,300,000 jobs from the United States to the overseas operations of U.S. corporations.[41]

Over the same years the foreign affiliates of U.S. manufacturing firms were of course producing and selling their goods abroad. For manufacturing as a whole, foreign-controlled affiliates of U.S. firms produced 2.3 times as much as the United States exported. In the motor vehicle industry the figure was 4.6, and for machinery industry firms it was 1.5.[42]

The prospects for employment in the United States, and the prospects for the technological competence of U.S. industry, are both strongly affected by the relation between the output of U.S. subsidiaries abroad and U.S. exports. In 1957, in the crucial machinery industry field that ratio was 2.25. From 1963 to 1966 it was 2.4, and by 1974–1976 it had climbed to 3.7.[43]

Plainly, employment opportunity as well as productive capacity in the United States was diminished by the parallel success of U.S. firms producing and distributing from their bases abroad.

But suppose it were said that the relationships summarized here between the foreign and domestic performance of American multinational firms are illusory: that foreign investments by U.S. firms have taken their business from other foreign firms. A crucial assumption is that it is feasible now, as in the past 100 years, to design, produce and sell competitively to both United States and world markets from production facilities in the United States. As in the past, attention to civilian product development, and capital investment to increase productivity, can offset American costs well enough to be competitive at home and abroad. Industries in Western Europe that pay higher than average U.S. wages and salaries are able to design, produce and export quality products to the U.S. market. Alternatives in technology that would enable American-based producers to do just as well are available, but have not been drawn upon by managers who have focused on fast, short-term financial returns, whose model achievement is not the well-planned production system but a financial coup with the least effort.

The outflow from the United States of corporate financial capital and employment opportunity has been strongly spurred by a series of remarkable tax advantages that have been accorded U.S. investments abroad. The Foreign Tax Credit provides a subsidy to the foreign operations of the U.S.

multinationals. When a foreign subsidiary pays taxes to local and national governments abroad, the sum is credited against the U.S. parent firm's corporate tax liability. Should it happen that the foreign tax exceeds the U.S. domestic tax for a given subsidiary, then that "surplus" tax can be transferred as a credit against the U.S. tax payable by another subsidiary in the same country. Furthermore, such tax "surpluses" can be carried forward or backward to be applied to future or past taxable income.

When a foreign subsidiary of a U.S. multinational reinvests its profits abroad, that money, not having been returned to U.S. jurisdiction, is not subject to any U.S. tax. Accordingly, U.S. multinational corporations in the vital machinery-producing industries have been disposed to draw an increasing proportion of their new investment money, year by year, from the "undistributed" earnings of subsidiaries abroad. Thus, on the average during 1966–1969, new investments around the world by U.S. machinery-producing multinationals consisted of 38 percent new outflow from the United States and 62 percent undistributed earnings from the overseas subsidiaries. By 1975–1978, 87 percent of the new investment was drawn from the profits of overseas subsidiaries and only 13 percent came from home.[44] This means that the firms have grown very rich very rapidly, thanks in large part to the federal government, which has collected no income taxes on the bulk of the funds used for fresh investments abroad.

The federal government also operates OPIC, the Overseas Private Investment Corporation, which insures American investors abroad against danger to their investment from "expropriation, war, revolution and insurrection." In situations where private insurance firms might be hesitant to underwrite against political risk, OPIC will write twenty-year policies at attractively low rates. Furthermore, the OPIC insurance is backed by "full faith and credit of the United States Government." This insurance fund also helps to convert foreign profits into U.S. dollars, and offers investors abroad liaison with other federal agencies interested in these matters.[45]

The American financial press has emphasized the contribution to the nation's balance of international payments from the flow of profits to the United States from investments made over a long period by the U.S. multinational firms.[46] Some writers have even invented the idea of a "trade surplus" consisting of the exports of goods by a given firm compared to the imports of goods by the firm.[47] But all these approaches ignore the consideration that is central in this analysis: How does the export of capital affect production capability and job availability within the United States?

In the case of U.S. corporate investments in the third world, a massive wage advantage promises attractively low costs of operation, and this, coupled with the federal tax subsidies of foreign investment and the availability of OPIC-type insurance, has spurred U.S. third world investment. Nevertheless, by far the greater part of U.S. direct foreign investment in manufacturing industries has gone to Western Europe. What are the big attractions there, and in third world countries?

Obviously, one of them is to be found in the hourly wages paid to production workers in manufacturing here and in several less developed countries. The following schedule is for 1977:[48]

United States	$7.60	Singapore	0.85
Brazil	1.40	South Korea	0.64
Mexico	1.82	Taiwan	0.75
Hong Kong	1.05		

By way of contrast, it is instructive to see what has happened to U.S. industrial wages compared to those of other industrialized countries. At mid-year 1980 here is what managers paid in hourly "compensation" to production workers in manufacturing industry in each country. (Compensation includes money as well as fringe, nonmonetary, payments.)

United States	$10.00	W. Germany	12.26
Canada	9.04	Italy	8.26
Japan	5.61	Netherlands	12.17
Belgium	13.18	Sweden	12.51
France	9.23	United Kingdom	7.37

Four countries among those listed here paid higher wages to their production workers than did the United States in mid-1980. So too did Denmark, Norway and Switzerland.[49] The idea that the United States is the highest-wage country in the world is out of date. At mid-1980, the United States ranked ninth among countries in the world with respect to wages of industrial workers. This was certainly not the case during the 1950s and 1960s, when lower wages in Western Europe attracted direct foreign investment by U.S. industrial firms.

At one time it seemed that U.S. investors moved into Western Europe to profit from low wages, but this is now history. In fact, one of the important economic facts of our time is that the rate of wage increase in the countries of Western Europe exceeded that of the United States during the 1960s and 1970s.[50]

Some people have reasoned that U.S. firms nevertheless continued to concentrate on Western Europe in order to get into the Common Market and avoid the obstacle of tariff barriers. But the Japanese have been doing extremely well in Western Europe, selling a great array of products, directly from their manufacturing base in Japan. Similar reasoning applies to the idea that it is probably advantageous to become rooted in a rapid economic growth area like the Common Market by establishing enterprises directly in the field. The fact is that the Japanese have been outstandingly successful at exporting machinery of all classes and other high-technology products into the Common Market area. They have been able to compete there on the basis of product design, quality, and a price competitiveness derived from the high productivity of their manufacturing system. What, then, are the possible gains that apparently continue to lure new U.S. investment abroad?

First, once made, the investments become a continuing source of new capital. That capital, reinvested abroad and thus free of U.S. federal taxes, yields a much higher effective profit rate than can be obtained from comparable investments in the United States. This is confirmed by analyses of comparative profit rates for U.S. firms abroad as against their operations in the United States.[51] Also, by initiating and expanding operations in modern plants overseas, U.S. industrial managements have avoided the hard work and expense of upgrading products and manufacturing facilities at home.

All in all, the closing of U.S. manufacturing facilities and the transfer of capital abroad provide a major opportunity for expanding profits and control. The same actions also diminish U.S. production and U.S. employment. But the profit and control gains, not products and jobs, are central in managerial decision-making.

The American pattern outlined in this chapter is not the world's first example of conflict between private profit and community well-being founded on production competence. Analysts of British economic development have noted: "It [British overseas investment] was a fine system while it lasted, but it contained a fatal weakness. . . .

"The British exported immense amounts of capital and, in the short term, they made a lot of money. But this led to the atrophy of the British industrial base. To the extent that they were developing the world, they neglected to develop their own economy."[52]

2

Managing for Short-Term Profit

"The short term, the current twelve months, is what matters; the next twenty-four don't." That, in 1980, was a senior industrial manager's description of the managerial planning that prevailed in his firm. In the 1950s, he said, many decisions were made in accordance with a long-term view. "Short term" and "long term" refer to the time required to carry out important and continuing production activities. In contrast to the twelve-month planning period for budgeting and financial targeting that is now preferred by the top managers of one of America's largest industrial firms, here are some illustrations of time spans ordinarily encountered in industrial life:

- Time to develop major new products in the chemical and pharmaceutical industry—five years plus.[1]
- Production life of a new car model—five years.
- Production life of an automobile engine and transmission—ten years plus.
- Planning and installing a new manufacturing facility—five years.
- Useful life of railroad rolling stock—ten years plus.
- Machinist's apprenticeship training (after high school)—four years.
- Engineer's formal education (after high school)—four years.

Research managers of U.S. firms report that "their labs are no longer as committed to new ideas as they once were and that the pressures on their resources have driven them into a defensive research shell, where true innovation is sacrificed to the certainty of near-term returns."[2]

Of course, some people in industrial management still think about long-term issues, but the point is that their orientation now tends to be overshadowed by plans that promise very quick results. A good example of long-range calculation is the following estimate that Jacob E. Goldman, then director of the Ford Motor Company's science laboratory, offered to a meeting of the American Physical Society in 1956:

If there is any industrial area in the U.S. where an important new idea is absolutely necessary for survival, it is in the automobile industry. The oil prospects for the world are so very dim that this largest of all American industries must have an important, original, inspired breakthrough sometime within the next 25 years, or by then we shall have to kiss goodbye to any means of locomotion which requires for its use the internal combustion of fossil fuels. What we must have is something so new, so radical, and so unanticipated that it would be folly to compartmentalize our thinking into how to go about pursuing this.[3]

But that is precisely the kind of dedication to long-term research that was not pressed by the automobile industry during the subsequent twenty-five years.

As is evident from the examples of production times cited above, there is a definite contradiction between "short-termism" and the requirements for orderly planning and execution of many industrial operations. Therefore, insofar as priority is given to short-term calculations and results, production operation must suffer various forms of neglect. A management under pressure to deliver short-term results will soon discover that it can avoid risks by letting a subcontractor handle the selection of equipment and the management of production over a long period of time. And for such production as they retain, managers interested in short-term gains without long-term commitments will forgo the major changes in plant and equipment required to upgrade productivity. Instead, they will seek ways to get more from existing equipment and labor force—for example, by deferring preventive maintenance while hoping to continue operations by relying on troubleshooting as breakdowns occur.

What has happened to industrial firms in the United States—externally and internally—to create this emphasis on short-term calculations and short-term gains? What happened to compress the time span of U.S. industrial managers to the point where any planning beyond the current twelve months gets scant attention?

Industrial firms in the United States operate today in an environment that coerces managers to take the short-term view. We can identify the factors that press in that direction, even though it is not possible to specify the relative importance of each element.

Since 1965, price inflation in the United States has given a nightmarish quality to many attempts at long-range industrial planning. There is available no theory or empirical procedure for reliably predicting future prices and industrial costs. This lack makes highly dubious every calculation of costs for materials, energy and labor. Pricing and contracts for future delivery become chancy. As a result, industrial managers are driven toward cost, production and price planning within very short time spans. For them a single year seems the longest meaningful planning time.

The uncertain value of the currency, as indicated by unpredictable inflation, also drives up the cost of borrowing and using money. In 1960, U.S.
industrial firms paid out only 1.7 percent of their total revenues as interest on
borrowed capital; by 1977 they were paying out 3.7 percent.[4] This increase in
interest charges has caused a dramatic rise in the cost of capital, which is
recognized as one of the hurdles that must be overcome by any productive
investment. Thus, if $1,000 is borrowed for ten years when the interest rate
is 8 percent, the compounding effect of interest payment requires that over
the ten-year period $1,158 will be paid in interest for the use of that initial
$1,000. But when $1,000 is borrowed at 15 percent, the interest charge for ten
years amounts to $3,045. Over the ten-year period when the borrowed $1,000
is being used, the average annual cost of interest at the 8 percent charge would
be 11.5 percent, while at the 15 percent rate, also compounded, the effective
average annual interest payment comes to 30.4 percent. Obviously, the higher
interest rate compels industrial managers to restrict new capital outlays to
changes in equipment and processes that can yield extraordinarily high rates
of return. Responding to the pressure for limiting risk, even large firms have
been putting ever more severe requirements on proposals for product and
process innovation. For example: "Gould Inc. [electrical equipment, electron-
ics] now specifies that development to market introduction can take no longer
than three to five years, the total market for the product must run $50 million
and be growing at least 15 percent per year, the product must be capable of
producing a pretax return of 30 percent on sales and 40 percent on investment,
and it must establish Gould as either a technical or market leader in the
product's field."[5]

The high cost and relative shortage of investment capital for productive
investments have weighed most heavily on attempts to form smaller, tech-
nology-innovating companies. In 1969 there were 698 such companies
financed in the United States; in 1977, only 30.[6]

A young engineer who went to work in the emissions control section of
a U.S. automobile firm was given a twofold mission: first, to meet the federal
air pollution standards; second, to conserve the company's capital investment.
Translated, the latter meant that he was to introduce design changes that
would extend the life of the existing engine-producing facilities in such a way
as to draw upon a minimum of new capital investment. In short, he was to
make excellent bricks with almost no straw.

The federal government shapes the policies of industry in two main ways:
directly, as a manager-contractor for the 137,000 firms involved in the military
industry network; and, indirectly, by the effects of the federal tax system on
managerial behavior. The relationship between the federal government and
the contracting firms is formalized, in part, by a number of arrangements that
have a common feature—they are all variants on the assumption that the

government will pay cost-plus for the work that industrial firms do in the military field. Accordingly, the Pentagon provides capital and guarantees of income that cannot be matched in the civilian marketplace. Also, it has become the practice to subdivide a major weapons system into a multitude of subcontracts for parts to be supplied within specified short periods of time. Thus, a Pentagon "buy" can include a stated number of particular airplanes that are to be purchased during a given year at an agreed price. But that price is based upon costs to be incurred during that year and does not necessarily refer to the longer-term costs of research, development, design, test and evaluation that had been incurred in previous years. The effect is one of make-believe: the price of the aircraft in a given year is based upon the supposed expenses incurred during that year, but a stream of activities and costs from many previous years are not necessarily accounted for. The formal price of a particular "buy" therefore may appear to be low insofar as it does not include costs incurred earlier (or later) as part of the "program" for a weapon system. The perspective, then, of a given contract is definitely short term in character.

On the tax side, the shaping effect of the federal government is well illustrated by the Reagan scheme for accelerating the depreciation of business investments: ten years for buildings, five years for machinery, three years for cars, light vehicles and research equipment. Ostensibly, the purpose is to encourage rapid growth of investment in machinery and rapid reinvestment. But whatever the intention, "10–5–3 depreciation would exact a price in inefficiency. American corporations are rightly accused of myopia; plans that would raise productivity a decade down the road are often shelved in favor of those that goose next year's (or next quarter's) profit. Yet by raising the tax credit on short-lived equipment, the Reagan plan would only exacerbate the distortion; it would offer the greatest reward for capital purchases that pay out the fastest."[7]

While these external factors have played a part in restyling the procedures of American industry, the fact is that a shift toward short-term planning was visible before the inflation of 1965 or the high interest rates of the 1970s and 1980s. One must, therefore, identify also the internal factors that have turned U.S. industrial managers away from long-term productive investment and toward minimum-risk, short-term money-making.

Seizing opportunities for profit is an old-fashioned and thoroughly respected idea in business. But special consequences follow when fast maneuvers for larger profits are carried out by very large corporations. General Motors, for example, is not just another company. By the late 1970s its annual sales exceeded $66 billion, a volume of money larger than the gross national product of forty-one sovereign nations.[8] According to a former top executive of General Motors, John Z. DeLorean,

The best interests of the country were certainly not being considered when General Motors announced an average price hike of almost 10 percent per car in the summer of 1974, for inflation was already eating away at the average American family's income. It became a cold and callous decision to my mind after people on the financial staff told me that the size of the increase was raised when it learned that the pricing announcement would come at the time President Nixon resigned from office. The corporate bet was that all of the publicity given to the historic events taking place in Washington would overshadow and diminish the attention given to the GM price hike. And that is precisely what happened.[9]

OPEC now loomed large. The price of gasoline had already soared. A national interest in fuel conservation was clearly high on any thoughtful person's agenda. The major redesign of automotive vehicles would obviously have contributed to the common good. But the management of General Motors was not committed, by custom, tradition or law, to consider what, beyond the immediate effect on profit, is economically useful production. Neither was the management concerned with productivity of operation, except in the narrow sense of yielding a specific cost-and-profit relationship.

Individual managers are, furthermore, committed to their own professional careers, which advance according to the performance of the unit for which the individual manager is formally responsible. Again there is make-believe in this pattern, since it attributes success or failure to the performance of a particular manager and overlooks the performance of an organization that necessarily requires the collaboration of many people. Bonuses given to executives on the basis of monthly and quarterly financial reports become a reason for making moves that will yield quick results and avoiding those whose effects will not be observed for five or ten years.

The application of computer technology to corporate accounting has greatly stimulated the concentration on short-term results, since elaborate accounting reports on various aspects of firm operations can be produced on a monthly, weekly, even daily basis.[10] Managers are supposed to act on reports of changing situations, and more frequent situation bulletins require action over shorter periods of time. The pressure to make a "good" showing in short periods encourages elaboration of techniques for manipulating statistical data. For example, the value of inventories, of work in process and the time period used for allocating classes of "fixed" charges can all be tinkered with to produce the best showing of short-term profit.

Short-term profit targeting is reinforced by individual manager job mobility. As an annual performance record becomes a key to judging the manager's competence, the profit results of the one-year period become a crucial target with major impact on the manager's prospects for his next job. At the top of the world's largest industrial firm

The people running General Motors today tend to be short-term, professional managers. They are in the top spots only a short time, less than ten years. In a sense, they just learn their job, about the time they have to leave. So the concern at the top today is for the short-term health of the company. These professional managers want to produce a good record while they are in office . . .[11]

General Motors awards bonuses to senior executives on the basis of current year's profits. The sums are substantial, reportedly equalling a year's salary. This policy has encouraged the U.S. auto industry's basic thesis that "mini cars mean mini profits."[12] In fact, the commitment to large cars was so strong by 1980 that senior executives of the U.S. auto industry were apparently incapable of "seeing" the prime cause of their collapsed U.S. market. It took a report by the federal government's International Trade Commission to specify that, in the marketplace, "the shift from larger cars appears greater than the shift to imports." So it was not the rise of imports per se that dominated the field but rather the major change in market demand within the United States from large to smaller, more fuel-efficient vehicles.[13] The U.S. auto industry managers were so wedded to the big car–big price strategy for short-term profit that they were moved to "deny" that the American public was losing interest in their gas guzzlers.*

General Motors insiders have reported that economies made to increase profits led to the distribution of defective auto components. The shoddiness of workmanship became evident when the parts and completed units were rejected by other General Motors divisions.

. . . At one time, the assembly plant in Tarrytown, New York, year in and year out, produced the poorest quality cars of all 22 GM U.S. car assembly plants. In some instances, Tarrytown cars were so poorly built, the dealers refused to accept them. At the same time, it had the lowest manufacturing costs in General Motors. So the Tarrytown plant manager was getting one of the biggest bonuses of all the assembly-plant managers while building the worst cars in the company.[14]

The influence of the annual, semiannual and quarterly bonus system on short-term decision-making is reinforced when boards of directors make public announcements of bonus awards.

Another thread in the fabric of American management practice that promotes short-termism is the reliance on the securities market instead of bank loans for capital financing.[15] The general practice today is to sell securities to raise money for both fixed and working capital. But this has led to

---

*Some analysts suggest that management resistance to a major changeover to smaller cars may have also been founded on fears of lost profits during a changeover period. Perhaps that played some part. But careful production planning could permit product conversion with minimum cost and disruption.

elaborate attention being paid to the relation of profit to stock prices (the price-earnings ratio). The connection is obvious. If quarterly reports of profits are sufficiently optimistic, the price of a firm's securities will hold or rise, and investors will be encouraged to buy. Officers of the firm who have been granted bonuses in the form of stock rights score a gain as the price of the stock goes up. The ability of the firm to raise money from the securities market, the personal wealth of many corporate managers and stockholders, as well as the professional standing of the top managers—all become tied to the parade of quarterly profit reports and their effect on the price-earnings ratio of the company's securities.

In Western Europe and in Japan, banks are still the primary source of industrial capital, their loans being made for extended periods at fixed rates of interest. This more traditional form of capital financing outweighs the equity (securities) sources by about two to one in Western European and Japanese practice—approximately the reverse of the U.S. pattern. Consequently, the attention of European and Japanese industrial managers is focused on the longer-term considerations for operating their enterprises, since the interest on debt and for repayment of principal are fixed factors.

That is why observers of the American corporate scene note that

Rare is the American Chief Executive who, in a philosophical moment, away from the daily fray, will not say that corporations should focus more on the future. However, in the next breath, many of these same executives will say that the verdict of Wall Street—and, hence, their survival in office—depends on producing the steady quarter-to-quarter increases in profits that so please the financial community.[16]

But what exactly is the financial community? If it were composed, for the most part, of a stable body of shareholders, committed to long-term investment in particular enterprises, the stock market would be substantially less affected by quarterly profits. But it appears that many shareholders themselves behave as short-term profit maximizers. A large number of securities customers spend portions of every business day in the customer rooms of their brokers' offices, watching the ticker prices move across the screen. These people are there to buy and sell, and they are augmented by a larger group of customers who are ringing the brokers' phones. All of them are looking for profit opportunities, but few have special knowledge in the form of a predictive theory about stock prices to guide their frantic patterns of buying and selling. Quarterly price-earnings ratios do not reliably forecast long-term enterprise health. The risk-taking can assume the quality of casino gambling rather than competent decision-making.

Buying and selling by large institutional investors (mutual funds, pension funds, large foundations) is necessarily oriented to current-period income maintenance or optimization. The influence of their individual trading can be massive, often large enough to "make the market price." Whatever the more specific short-term aims of such large investors may be, they have not corresponded to the long-term finance capital requirements for sustaining a high rate of productivity growth in industry.

Major Japanese industrial firms are giving a resounding demonstration of how it is possible to operate according to measurements other than short-term profits. Thus, IBM Japan now competes, neck and neck, with Fujitsu, Japan's top computer firm. By 1979 the two companies had an equal volume of sales in Japan, the world's number two market for computers. But "Japanese computer companies often forgo profits and slash prices by as much as 80 percent to win market share." In the words of a senior American computer executive, "the discounting and freebies are worse than anywhere in the world right now." Meanwhile, "IBM's pretax profit margin in 1979 was 22.5 percent, while Fujitsu's was 6 percent to 7 percent. . . ."[17] The major Japanese computer firms, Fujitsu, Hitachi and Nippon Electric, have been advancing aggressively in broad technological competence, product design, and building up research, production and marketing capability, while accepting substantially lower profit rates than IBM. The Japanese firms' strategy is clear: accept the lower short-term profit price for the sake of long-term design, production and market position.

Short-termism has had a major depleting effect on both the manpower and the machinery of U.S. industry. The critical state of U.S. manufacturers is indicated by the age of their machine tools. As U.S. managers required very rapid (short-term) recoupment of new machinery costs as a condition of purchase, less new investment could be justified. This contributed to the aging of American industry's metalworking machinery. By 1978, 69 percent of the U.S. machine tool stock was at least ten years old, which saddles the United States with the oldest stock of basic metalworking machinery of any of the major industrial countries (West Germany, United Kingdom, Japan, France, Italy, or Canada).[18]

Skilled workers are crucial to a society's industrial competence. In 1981, trained machinists were in dramatically short supply, because "the status of the nation's 176,000 tool makers has steadily declined in the past 30 years, as young people have sought out better paying, less demanding jobs." This is just what one would expect, since the entry-level pay scale for machinist trainees is often barely higher than the minimum wage. U.S. management has simply not tried seriously and consistently to teach journeymen machinists the trade. At Cincinnati Milacron, the largest machine tool firm in the United States, no more than ten journeymen machinists a year were being turned out during the early 1980s by the firm's apprenticeship program.[19]

For a long time, significant product improvement was given little thought

by the U.S. automobile industry, the fountainhead of mass production technology that once served as a model for the rest of the world. Former auto
industry executives have described in detailed testimony how cost-cutting was
carried out even at the expense of product quality. A former GM executive
reports that during the 1960s he "felt the emphasis at General Motors had
switched from . . . [delivering real value to the customer, to] . . . taking the
last nickel out of every part to improve profits in the short term."[20] Under
the pressure of maintaining short-term profits U.S. auto firms have paid less
and less attention to product improvement. When Lee A. Iacocca, then
president of Ford Motor Company, was asked in 1974 ". . . about the importance of front-wheel drive as a technological innovation . . . ," he answered
that the public "can't see it," adding, "I say, give 'em leather. They can smell
it."[21]

With the greater intricacy of control equipment in modern industrial
operations the task of assuring reliable production has become increasingly
difficult. Breakdowns are best avoided by sophisticated regular preventive
maintenance and careful monitoring of production, but these standards are
set aside when corner-cutting is tolerated in the interest of cost reduction
and short-term gain.[22] The complicated equipment now on the market requires prompt and competent servicing if it is to be reliable, but pressure
to sell, when given priority, causes the manufacturer to cut back his service
department.*

Under the goad of short-term profits, research and development organizations have been urged to concentrate on modifying existing products, that
being a low-cost approach to fast returns on R & D investment. As a percent
of the gross national product, U.S. R & D peaked at 3 percent in 1964. The
annual average was 2.4 percent during the 1970s and by 1980 had dropped to
1.3 percent.[23] American bankers, observing the scene, judge that "U.S. firms
have fallen badly behind in the rate of productive investment and technological improvement, and are now falling behind in absolute levels as well."[24]

From 1950 to 1980, American and European (mainly American) firms sold
Japanese companies 30,000 licenses to use their technical designs and production know-how. The agreements covered design and production details from
a great array of industries. The total price—trivial for such riches—to the
Japanese purchasers has been estimated to equal about 20 percent of a single

---

*Business Week, November 24, 1980, p. 104. By way of contrast, I am informed that it is the practice
of several Japanese machine tool firms to set up high-grade customer servicing organizations in
Western European countries *before* marketing their product. One result is prompt and competent
servicing for the new users of new equipment. Obviously, this strategy requires the establishment of
the service organization as part of the capital investment for market development.

year of U.S. R & D spending.[25] The revenue from the sale of these licenses was obviously advantageous as short-term profit. But that profit bears little relation either to the social cost of producing the knowledge that was sold, or to the economic value of the technical knowledge as a base for sustained production and livelihood in many industries and communities. An important part of the social heritage of American working people was sold off by management for the sake of quick profits.

Research and development activity usually precedes major investment in productive facilities and equipment. Under the impact of short-term financial planning, managements raised the standard for required rates of return on investment. As a result, firms can meet the higher rate of return, or hold investment down. The evidence of investment held down is clear. The average annual growth rate of fixed business capital per hour worked in U.S. private business was 2.3 percent for the period 1948–1965. Thereafter, from 1965 to 1979, this average annual growth rate declined to 1.8 percent.[26]

In an interview Akio Morita, president of Sony, has stated that "most corporate managers in the United States are now oriented to short-term profit, which tends to discourage them from making important investment in new plants, equipment and research and development." He added that in his opinion "American managers are too worried about short-term profits and too little concerned about their workers."[27]

The path taken by many industrial firms has established a general pattern of production decay:

- Invest and produce in areas of cheap labor abroad for high returns on output.
- Invest abroad in a firm already producing there: that is, join them.
- Hire a foreign firm to supply parts for your firm's product line, while continuing to perform the design function.
- Hire a foreign firm to produce all of your firm's product line, while tapering off the design function.
- Become an agent, or dealer, for foreign firms producing a given class of goods.

These successive states of production decay can maintain profits while burdening the firm with progressively less responsibility for production, for employment, and for all ancillary activities. Responsibility for investment and for changes of technology are also reduced, but the employment of top management and of assisting administrative and marketing groups can continue, and the firm's product name may even be kept alive through the successive reductions of initiative and responsibility. The rate of return on a diminishing investment may even be improved. And by such a sequence of cop-outs the opportunity for productive employment in the United States is steadily reduced.

The hunger for short-term success has produced changes in the general management policy of U.S. industrial firms that range from novel uses of capital to a readiness to break the law. Industrial firms can invest accumulated money in new technology, new products, new production facilities, and in basic and applied research in the sciences and technologies that nourish their particular production competence. But all these operations require hard work. The building of new industrial plants takes considerable time and is beset with complications. Revamping an existing facility is one of the most complex tasks in industrial life.

The managers of major American firms have learned to sidestep important aspects of these tasks. Instead of addressing the problems of new or revised production operations, it is easier to buy entire companies that are earning respectable profits. Thus the Mobil Company acquired Montgomery Ward, a mail-order firm. Atlantic Richfield purchased Anaconda Copper. Exxon, parent firm of the Standard Oil empire, bought into high-technology office equipment and has taken over Reliance Electric. All these companies have advertised their need for larger profits to carry on the search for new oil resources. Yet, "with cash pouring in at a rate of $100 million a day, they are looking eagerly for ways to diversify into other businesses."[28]

The commitment of major U.S. firms to short-term goals has even led to counter-profit and a weakening of strategic position. In the auto industry, eagerness to inflate fast profits by pushing the large car, with its large price tag and large profit per unit, led the main U.S. auto makers into a catastrophic failure of market position, along with major losses. At General Motors, as at the other firms, internal proposals during the 1960s for switching to smaller automobiles were ignored. "These rejections became classic examples of decisions which were made for the short-term benefit (record profits of $2.16 billion and $2.4 billion in 1972 and 1973, respectively) but hurt the company longer term."[29]

In the name of short-term concerns a classic pattern of organization at General Motors was abandoned during the 1960s. The corporation had long been a model of the organization style called decentralization. In that scheme of things, a central administrative office formulates general policy. Managers of subdivisions implement that policy with detailed decisions appropriate to their particular products, manufacturing technologies and marketing requirements. Division managers report results of operations to the central office, which also oversees their compliance with general policy. Senior officers of the firm and their supporting staffs in the central administrative office devote themselves primarily to larger issues and long-range planning, while the division focuses on the problems of day-to-day and quarter-to-quarter operations.

John Z. DeLorean reports that during a career that spanned the 1960s and early 1970s he

watched GM operations slowly become centralized. The divisions gradually were stripped of their decision-making power. Operating decisions were more and more being made on The Fourteenth Floor. This is because men rose in power who did not seem to have the capabilities or broad business outlook necessary to manage the business. . . . They also lost sight of the corporate objective of keeping policy making and control separate from the day-to-day operations of the business. As The Fourteenth Floor began to run the operations of GM, it had no time or inclination for planning the growth and direction of General Motors. There was no forward planning to speak of at GM. . . . The committees and sub-committees which were methodically set up during the twenties, thirties and forties to plan and guide General Motors' growth were not doing that. They spent little time looking at the big picture, instead occupying themselves with minuscule matters of the operation which should have been considered and disposed of in the divisions or much further down the corporate management line.[30]

So powerful and extensive are the pressures for short-term gain that many corporate managers have moved outside the law. *Fortune* magazine reported in 1980 that of 1,043 major corporations included in a study of illegal activity, 117, or 11 percent, have been found guilty of criminal charges or have pleaded no contest to such charges.[31] These company crimes share the common feature of being committed to obtain a short-term profit. The *Fortune* report noted that "The common practice of running a company through decentralized profit centers, giving each manager his head but holding him strictly accountable for the results, often provides a setting in which the rules can readily be bent. The temptation comes when heightened competition or a recession squeezes margins."[32]

Violations of criminal law for large and quick profits have even included the reinstitution of peonage—"virtual slavery," *The New York Times* calls it —by employers in southern and southwestern commercial farming operations, taking advantage of Spanish-speaking aliens who have entered the United States illegally.[33] Reckless, but profitable, dumping of toxic industrial wastes has apparently become a national industry.[34]

A recurring theme in much recent literature about the performance of U.S. industrial managers is the span of years that most senior executives may have to enjoy in the top jobs. Thus, "the typical chief executive of a major corporation is about 60 years old. . . . Assuming retirement at 65, he has five years in the top office, that is, if all goes well. How likely is such a person to reduce this year's profits to invest in some costly new project, the pay-off for which is several years down the road, and uncertain even then?"[35] Also, since individual chief executives are held responsible for the success or failure of major projects, they are understandably unwilling to take risks.

Some of the social costs arising from quick-gain commercial operations have been transformed into business costs by local and federal legislation. That happens, for example, when government regulates waste disposal and air pollution. But the social costs of closing industrial enterprises have yet to be declared a proper component of doing business. Indeed, every effort by working people, their unions, and allied community groups to enact such legislation in the United States has been vigorously and, thus far successfully, fought by industrial management.

The relentless quest for short-run profits has prompted management resistance to any legislation that would raise costs by restricting certain industrial practices. When local, state and national governments have attempted to correct workshop environments that cause "brown lung" in the cotton textile industry, or to stop the reckless disposal of industrial waste that has polluted the water supplies in thousands of neighborhoods, the moves have been denounced as unreasonable "regulation." The prohibition of such industrial practices does constrain short-term profit.

Short-termism, as a sustaining pattern of management practices, is justified by an array of social assumptions:

- that making money is a proper ultimate goal for the operation of industrial enterprise;
- that money made by each firm contributes to economic advance for all;
- that production has value insofar as it contributes to profit;
- that business fulfills its responsibility to the community by maximizing profit;
- that institutions and practices which constrain profit-making, or introduce extra-profit criteria for industrial operation, are to be shunned.

Although the main focus of the foregoing analysis has been on the American economy, short-term business strategies are not restricted to the United States. Britain has a long history of plant closings and the export of capital, with a consequent neglect of production and employment opportunity for the British working people.[36] One aspect of West Germany's 1980 economic troubles was traced to increased investment abroad. Skilled workers and engineers came to be in short supply, and the country's machinery-producing industries did not keep pace with technological development, with the result that "in 1980, for the first time, Japanese makers of machine tools exported more units to West Germany than the Germans sent to Japan."[37] And from Japan came word in May 1980 that some of its firms had been moving factories out of South Korea because "the average wage in South Korea is now measurably higher than that of Taiwan, Korea's chief competitor in such labor intensive industries as electronics and textiles."[38]

In the United States, the special intensity of short-term effects is associated with an ongoing decline in the value assigned to production work of every sort. Money-making and the enhancement of decision-making power are seen as cardinal virtues in the managerial occupations and as yardsticks of achievement. They are displacing such other criteria as organizing people to work, or producing excellent goods, or enhancing the quality of life for a wider community. The development of management with primary emphasis on short-term rates of profit has been further facilitated in the United States by strong ideological support from the schools of business.

3

Wisdom from the
Seminaries of Business

Until a few years ago, the general manager of one of the country's largest shipyards was a man with a long and distinguished career as an engineer specializing in shipbuilding. He then retired, and his successor came into office with a team of bright Masters of Business Administration (MBAs) from one of the prestigious graduate schools of business. Almost the first act of this new management was to draft a letter that was signed by the incoming general manager and addressed to the administrative and technical staff of the enterprise. The key sentence stated: "I remind you all that we are not here to make ships. We are here to make money."

Money and power. And more money in order to expand power. These are the imperatives that an up-to-date business manager is trained to act upon, and never mind the ships.

The growing influence of professional managers, trained by America's schools of business administration to make money, not ships, is an important cause of the production debacle in U.S. industry. The professional behavior of the present generation of U.S. industrial managers has been strongly conditioned by the emphasis their formal training places on finance rather than production. Holders of MBA degrees have been graduating at an astonishing rate from the 500 schools of business now operating in American universities. There were only 303 such schools in 1970, and while the master's degrees awarded in all fields by American universities tripled in the 1960s and 1970s, the 1981 production of MBA degree holders was 54,000, or twelve times the number conferred in 1960.[1] The MBA degree has become a professional job ticket for making it—fast. In 1980, starting salaries for graduates of the nine largest business schools in the United States ran from $26,300 to $31,000.[2]

What is the recipient of an MBA supposed to know? The qualifications can be readily deduced from the front sections of the leading business journals, where one finds newsy details about the latest achievements of top managers of leading firms. Thus, the "In the News" section of *Fortune* celebrates the activities of money managers who arrange mergers, fire large staffs, regroup others, arrange major financial consortiums, trade stocks, buy and sell entire enterprises, cause the value of their firm's securities to escalate and in general wheel and deal from dawn to dusk. The schools of business are the training fields for these business strategists.

Robert B. Reich, former chief of policy planning at the Federal Trade Commission, has formulated a telling contrast between "paper entrepreneurs" and "product entrepreneurs":

Veblen's dickohany

> Paper entrepreneurs—trained in law, finance, accountancy—manipulate complex systems of rules and numbers. They innovate by using the systems in novel ways: establishing joint ventures, consortiums, holding companies, mutual funds; finding companies to acquire, "white knights" to be acquired by, commodity futures to invest in, tax shelters to hide in; engaging in proxy fights, tender offers, antitrust suits, stock splits, spinoffs, divestitures; buying and selling notes, bonds, convertible debentures, sinking-fund debentures; obtaining Government subsidies, loan guarantees, tax breaks, contracts, licenses, quotas, price supports, bail-outs; going private, going public, going bankrupt.

By way of contrast:

> Product entrepreneurs—engineers, inventors, production managers, marketers, owners of small businesses—produce goods and services people want. They innovate by creating better products at less cost: establishing more-efficient techniques of manufacture, distribution, sales; finding cheaper sources of materials, new markets, consumer needs; providing better training of employees, attention-getting advertising, speedier consumer service and complaint handling, more-reliable warranty coverage and repair.[3]

This differentiation captures an essential difference between management activities that are primarily a service to fast profits and control, and management functions that are primarily a service to production.

The main subjects of instruction in business schools range from the internal economics of business firms—accounting and auditing, personnel and industrial relations, finance and general management—on to international business, marketing and sales, production and manufacturing and quantitative methods for business problem-solving. The main area of concentration for one-third of MBA graduates is "general management"; it is followed closely by training in finance, which absorbs one MBA graduate out of four. Marketing and sales have recently attracted 13 percent of the students and the rest are scattered among the other subject majors. During the 1970s production and manufacturing (sometimes called operations management) were the preferred specialties for a scant 3 percent of MBA graduates.[4]

The influx of these MBAs into the industrial world has caused a distinct change in the professional background of corporate staffs. In 1948 22 percent of U.S. corporate chief executives came from backgrounds in finance and law. By 1977 this group accounted for a third of company presidents. At the same time, top people with technical backgrounds of all sorts dropped from 38 to 33 percent, and even the marketing specialists dropped off from 25 to 20 percent of company presidents. Since World War II, U.S. corporations have prized most highly the skills of the moneymen.[5] Accordingly, the business schools have been producing what their executive-suite customers have ordered. A faculty member in one such school told me that, while the 1980 graduates with majors in marketing commanded starting salaries of $26,000, specialists in production (operations management) averaged only $17,000.

The course objectives of the schools of business have responded to these professional trends. Theoretical materials and specific techniques for short-term income maximizing at high rates of profit have been emphasized, instead of strategies involving long-term calculation at lower profit rates. Productive efficiency and product quality are accorded less importance as greater emphasis is placed on financial maneuvers that take advantage of tax laws and ways to control the market. The quality of production equipment is seen as relevant insofar as it affects the calculation of short-term cost; it is not analyzed for its bearing on productivity, product quality or overall technological competence. Corporate capital is treated as a strictly portable item to be invested wherever opportunity beckons and with little concern for the social costs of major industrial displacements. Attempts to translate social costs into business costs are deplored as evidence of excessive government regulation. Production competence and the actual performance of physical work enjoy little prestige; the highest status is accorded to the harvesting of money and the wielding of decision power.

To get a current view of what these institutions are up to, I interviewed the deans of several schools of business administration. Here is what they say:

- Even if the business schools turned out long-term thinkers, they would be pressed into short-term thinking and performance once they got into their first jobs. The firms' quarterly and monthly report practices impose short-term calculations. Pressures in the same direction come from the policy of offering stock options, bonuses and other forms of incentive according to profits and related performances recorded in quarterly and annual balance sheets. There is, for example, no incentive system for five-year planning.
- Industrial managers confront unpredictable conditions in capital markets and in the fluctuation of prices. An inability to predict the course of

inflation makes any kind of long-term planning extremely difficult. Therefore, the managing of technology and of virtually every other aspect of manufacturing is subject to decisions made over the short term.

- Business schools give their students a lot of techniques for arriving at optimum solutions when making business decisions. The theories and models they use, however, are mainly short-term and marginal, treating the incremental effects of incremental moves. In other words, much of the decision-making that is taught in operations research, management science, accounting, marketing management and operations management is linked to methods of teaching that stress effects of small, short-term, incremental changes. It is hard to apply these theories to long-term situations in which the formally rigorous requirements of the short-term models cannot be satisfied. To be sure, since about 1950, business schools have been teaching capital budgeting, an approach that implies a long-range (or at least longer-range) view. Nevertheless, a lot of the criticism of business schools, like the assessment that appeared in *Business Week* in 1980,[6] remains valid. It is certainly true that Japanese professionals seem to be trained in long-term, team behavior rather than in the American pattern of short-term problem-solving, with its implied emphasis on the success of the individual manager.

- One of the things we noted during 1980–81 was the almost complete failure of executives attending the business schools to comment on the various analyses and criticisms of U.S. managements' short-term decision-making. It wasn't as though these people formally rejected the criticism in *Business Week*. They seemed, rather, just not to understand the short-term/long-term contrast that was being underscored there. After all, short-term decision-making had been a principal feature of both their education and their professional practice.

- One result of the pervasive practice of short-term decision-making is that a course in business strategy which is less quantitative than some others and which looks to more distant horizons may be viewed by students as insufficiently rigorous or coherent. Foreign visitors to our school have said that quarterly financial statements should be outlawed, because they tend to be converted into targets. Also, the pressure to turn in a good report every three months encourages the various devices of creative accounting.

- We are all affected by the disparity between the great speed that is possible in executive exchanges—especially as these are conducted by telecommunications and computers—and the considerable time required for production planning and performance. There are even daily accounting reports. Inflation urges us to set shorter decision times for cash management. A company treasurer, for example, at the end of the day takes account of the cash in hand and must decide what to do overnight with the money, since financial markets operate even within twenty-four-hour time spans.

- Furthermore, the business managers we are training are entering a scene where they must keep an eye on the securities markets, since those are the prime sources of new finance capital. A lot of students obtain jobs with consulting firms—investment banking houses and the like—because they see consulting as a fast track to the senior levels of general management. The two-year training that MBAs get in the techniques of specific modeling and problem-solving is well suited to the needs of such firms. Besides, making money is not so bad. At the same time, management hiring in the production field is relatively thin, and there is higher status to be gained in the head office than out in the boondocks, working at some dirt-under-the-fingernails job.
- The business schools themselves, of course, affect the mind-set of their students. The cases they study deal with the circumstances and problems of potential employers. After all, the business of a business school is to produce a product that the employer wants to buy, and the MBA is hired because he is trained in making money in ways other than production. Before the 1960s, in one major school, about 14 percent of the MBA trainees majored in operations management. By 1980, that was down to 2 percent.*

The foregoing observations come down to saying that the kind of training that the schools of business deliver is strongly influenced by the kinds of managers that earn top salaries and most prestige in the corporate community. Here, then, is a quick view of what goes on in the realms of strategic planning, maximizing money and power, and handling people.

Strategic planning is, without doubt, the highest (that is, best rewarded) management skill. When exercising such functions, the top manager is, above

---

*Of late, it is true, some firms have been asking for MBAs who are also engineering undergraduates, who have some training in manufacturing, or who are prepared to learn an aspect of manufacturing. And by 1982, some business schools were responding to the oft-repeated comment that their MBAs are uninformed about production. Richard Cyert, president of Carnegie-Mellon University, announced: "We are developing courses in our business school that will produce executives as well as engineers who know what manufacturing is all about" (*The New York Times,* January 26, 1982). But a colleague in a neighboring school has not been able to find a publisher for a well-regarded text on production management (designed for the MBA curriculum) because "most business schools don't even offer such a course," and ". . . there are probably not very many instructors who would feel comfortable using it. . . . " Also ". . . its emphasis on the physical aspect of production lies in just the opposite direction of the current trend toward emphasizing strategic and policy considerations in management of the operations function."

all else, the person who gathers and deploys capital for the greatest, fastest return. To that end, he selects the areas for expansion and for contraction, spotting the firms that are the best bet for mergers, and making his decisions according to calculations of market growth, financial resources and tax position. For example, and entirely without reference to the products involved, if a firm has a very large tax loss carry-over (formal losses that can be applied to future profits), then its takeover by a reasonably profitable firm may be strongly indicated, since the much lower tax position of the combined enterprise frees cash for additional investment. Agility and speed are highly prized assets for such operations, as are shrewdness in allocating personnel and devising attractive incentive systems for top executives.[7]

The business press is a handy source of information on the currently fashionable decision-making practices of the strategic planners. One popular mode of analysis compares the money value of a firm's assets with the money value of its outstanding stock. If the assets are worth more than the stock, that is viewed as a reason to sell off the excess so calculated. Then the cash newly in hand may be reinvested in enterprises that promise to yield a higher ratio of dividends to stock price.

A second device is labeled "The Business Portfolio Matrix," and is said to have been invented by the Boston Consulting Group, a well-regarded firm. On one axis a division is made between "low growth" and "high growth"; on the other axis, between "low market share" and "high market share." The four boxes thus created represent the four possible combinations of these factors. The object of the game is to place each component enterprise of, say, a large conglomerate, into one of these classes. Thus the "planners label businesses in each of the four boxes, respectively: stars, question marks, cash cows, and dogs."[8]

This sort of paper work "planning" can be done at a far remove from the actual operation of any enterprise. All one needs is a collection of numbers in the categories that reflect trends in growth, market share, etc. When this style of analysis is applied, "a company's various businesses are viewed as separate investments, much like an investor who owns stock in several companies. And, like that investor, the company's senior executives decide where to make the next investment, not the managers of the operating businesses."[9]

Canny financial decision-making routines of these sorts have contributed to the pattern, catastrophic from a production viewpoint, of factory closings, undermaintenance of plants and equipment, the disposal of assets to raise cash for production elsewhere, and the abrupt abandonment of viable enterprises. Manufacturing competence, product quality, the usefulness of a product, the importance of an enterprise as a source of livelihood for its employees and community—none of these ranks as a primary consideration for strategic planners.

The high status accorded the strategic planner by the business press is exemplified by *Fortune* of June 15, 1981. This issue features "Working Smarter," the first of a series of articles on new techniques for enhancing productivity. Yet, up front in the same issue, the "In the News" section celebrates the career of Edward L. Hennessy, Jr., chief executive officer of Allied Corporation. A photograph shows Mr. Hennessy in black tie as he is whisked by helicopter to a Manhattan social engagement. The news is that during just two years in his post he has shaken the firm to its foundations: got rid of money-losing operations, cut overhead by $30 million, fired 700 people, bought Eltra—a billion-dollar manufacturer of photo-typesetting equipment—changed the name of his firm from Allied Chemical to Allied Corporation, and reportedly entered into hot competition for the purchase of Bunker Ramo, a high-technology electronics firm.

All told, twenty executives star in the various news items of this issue of *Fortune*. Of these, only five are described as having some connection with products or processes. For the rest—and in direct conflict with the message of "Working Smarter"—the news celebrates successful strategic planning.

Hennessy appears also as the principal figure in *The New York Times* story "Migrant Managers: A New Road to the Top."[10] This "think piece" reviews Hennessy's career to date. After getting his bachelor's degree at Fairleigh Dickinson University in New Jersey, he attended New York University Law School. From 1950 to 1979 he was employed by eight firms all told, starting as a staff accountant with Price Waterhouse, one of the larger accounting firms, and moving onward and upward to Textron, Lear Siegler, IT&T, Colgate-Palmolive, Heublein, and United Technologies. At each firm his responsibilities were of a financial character.

When, in 1979, he became the new chairman of Allied Chemical at $250,-000 a year, he could scarcely pretend to knowledge of any aspect of production or research or marketing of the energy and chemicals which have been the major operations of the Allied Chemical Corporation. His immediately preceding post was that of chief financial officer and group vice-president for systems and development at United Technologies Corporation, which is heavily involved in aircraft engines, elevators, helicopters, etc., and before that he concerned himself with financial matters at Heublein, whose products include vodka, wine and fried chicken. The *Times*'s view of the matter is that "Mr. Hennessy's high-level job-hopping . . . provided him with a skill that some companies find more valuable than such traditional business disciplines as marketing, accounting or engineering. The skill is professional management —management as an end in itself."

This kind of strategic planner is especially appreciated by companies that are widely diversified—the conglomerate multinationals with more products, more factories, and more varieties of operations under their capacious wings than any one person could conceivably master. The top management posts of such firms, which now tower above the U.S. industrial landscape, offer alluring money-making opportunities for the strategic planner; whereas the duration of employment in a given management post is often, as in Mr. Hennessy's case, too short to bring any sort of major productive investment to maturity.

Instead of the long-familiar image of a manager whose career is shaped by, and committed to, a particular enterprise, the new breed of strategic planner is, by training, ideological indoctrination and career experience, devoted to enlarging his own wealth, his own power. No conspiratorial purpose is implied by these remarks; they simply describe the professional performance that now prevails. "Today the average corporation can count on losing half its college recruits within five years."[11]

The exploits of the strategic planners who now dominate the main industrial firms in the United States drive home, again and again for the neophytes in the schools of business administration, the point about making money, not ships. Here is an example of money managing at U.S. Steel:

In 1978, U.S. Steel paid only $8 million in taxes on net profits of $250 million and had an effective tax rate of 3.2 percent. In 1977, U.S. Steel paid no taxes and actually received $36 million in tax credits from the Federal Government, while reporting net profits of $135 million. During those years, U.S. Steel continued to pay a constant dividend of $1.60 per share of common stock.[12]

In February 1981, a further celebration of the fortunes of this corporate giant was headlined "The Turnabout in U.S. Steel." The crux of the story was that in 1980 U.S. Steel showed earnings of $504.5 million after 1979 losses of $293 million. The following statistics summed up the situation:[13]

	1979	*1980*
Steel production	29.7 million tons	23.3 million tons
Factories	13	11
Blast furnaces	46	27
Employees	170,000	155,000

From 1979 to 1980, U.S. Steel reduced production more than 10 percent, operated two fewer factories and nineteen fewer blast furnaces, while employing 15,000 fewer people. In short, U.S. Steel produced less steel, but its strategic planners so arranged matters that there was a handsome growth in profit from 1979 to 1980. The lesson to the management trainee is plain enough: the target for him ·is to make money, not steel.

Business schools do not fly a banner over their main gates announcing that strategic planning is the main event, but their internal style of operation obeys that slogan. At Harvard's Graduate School of Business Administration, which probably sets the tone for most of its competitors, students may be required to analyze three company cases a day, each of them requiring the study of a presentation that runs twenty to thirty pages. What sort of data can be reviewed, what kinds of problems can conceivably be solved, at such a pace? Obviously, details of research, of product design, alternative production methods, ways to integrate industrial operations—none of these can be touched in any serious way at that speed. But optimization problems and financial analyses of limited scope—carried out according to fairly set routines—lend themselves readily to rapid-fire analysis. In 1981, an MBA reported: "I was shocked at my fifth reunion, that very few of my classmates were making a product, running a plant or drilling a hole in the ground. Almost everyone was on the finance side."[14]

While it is closely bound up with the short-term business perspective, a general reliance on the dollar as an instrument of measurement in itself carries a number of implications. When the governing criterion for making an investment decision is dollar gain, the use of money for calculating inputs and the output becomes indispensable. There are, of course, other conceivable criteria by which to gauge output: for example, the quality and the usefulness of the product. And, when continuity of employment, thus continuity of production, is made a top criterion of enterprise operation, any accompanying money calculation becomes instrumental and facilitating—but is not the main end in view.

If production were given high value in the operation of an industrial enterprise, then a whole array of criteria that are production-specific would be brought to bear: productivity, efficiency of energy use, product reliability, product quality, etc. But such considerations now play slight-to-zero roles in the training and professional practice of the largest number of MBA graduates.

Another persuasive influence on current business viewpoint is the competitive success of the larger firms. In 1947, multi-unit companies (companies with more than one factory) accounted for 55 percent of all employees engaged in manufacturing, and 59 percent of all value added in manufacturing. By 1972, multi-unit firms employed 75 percent of all people in the manufacturing industries and accounted for 80 percent of all value added. The majority of the multi-unit firms are also conglomerates (firms offering a great variety of products). Top managers of such companies cannot possibly become involved in the details of production decision-making. The mere diversity of the subordinate enterprises under their jurisdiction urges big managers to rely on the dollar as the measure of enterprise success and failure.[15]

Management's concentration on making money and gaining power, with short-term calculations dominating the scene, has had effects probably not anticipated by corporate strategists, or by the business schools that trained them. By mid-1981, the word was out that skilled workers in occupations requiring long training were unexpectedly in very short supply. Expert machinists, for example, are an aging group of workers.[16]

This is, of course, hardly surprising. Financial wizards and brilliant strategists, the movers and shakers of corporate high finance, are not trained either by the MBA program or in professional practice to take responsibility for building up a pool of skilled production workers. For a particular factory or firm, why bother? When more blue-collars are needed, one simply bids up the price and hires them away from someone else.

Top managers necessarily manage people. The chief executive officer selects the managers of the component enterprises of the firm, the first criterion for their selection being their suitability to participate in the main thrust of the corporate design. Here the concern is with qualities of shrewdness, analytical capability, readiness to act boldly, loyalty to the top leadership—attributes that do not lend themselves to clear operational formulation. But unit managers with these most desired attributes are necessarily a minority of the people engaged. The great bulk of employees are middle- and lower-level managers, whose work affects production, and the broad population of technicians and production workers.

Modern managers and the schools that train them are involved in a dilemma of contradictory roles and values with respect to employee relations. It is of the essence of management as a profession that decision-making is reserved to the managerial-administrative occupations: managers manage and workers work. But this grand tradition is increasingly being challenged by a newer understanding that the productivity of single employees and of whole work forces is strongly affected by the degree to which they have a voice in organizing their own work. So managers demand diligence and attention to results measured as productivity of labor and capital, while at the same time holding back employee participation as being incompatible with the tradition of the managerial occupations. It is significant that union contracts are peppered with clauses that affirm "management's right to manage."

In this tradition, management reserves to itself the right to robotize and otherwise automate industrial work, and the right to "move capital," meaning to open and close factories and communities, in accordance with strategic financial calculations, and with the primary aim of getting the optimum profit from both capital and labor. This goal, however, is impeded by the treatment of "workers as a tool,"[17] which elicits predictable defensive responses from the work force.

Public opinion researchers have discovered that as much as 40 percent of the U.S. labor force was composed, by 1981, of workers who subscribe to new work values. Formal job structures are disliked, and money is not prized as an end in itself. The primary objective of these workers is to earn enough money to sustain a given life-style. That being achieved, "more" is deprived of its traditional meaning.

Without formulating any new general theory of production decision-making, managers in the United States have been responding, reluctantly, to pressures from workers for an increased say about their working lives. So new voices are heard at the managerial level. "We're still living in the 1930s world, paying for the use of a worker's hands and not what he can offer mentally." That comes from a new industrial relations vice-president at General Motors. And an official of one of the high-tech industrial firms says, "One of the most dehumanizing assumptions ever made is that workers work and managers think. When we give shop-floor workers control over their work, they are enormously thoughtful."[18]

Since no one has discovered a way to reconcile the contradiction between "management's right to manage" and the workers' control over their work, ambiguity permeates the teaching of the personnel, industrial relations and behavioral science courses in the schools of business administration. Which goal is to have first priority—transferring production work abroad, or trying for higher productivity with greater worker participation at home? Until now, an orientation toward "mobility of capital" has dominated the scene.

The emphasis of the schools of business, and the university systems that surround them, on training for control rather than for production is strongly conditioned by an ideological support system that still mirrors the mainstream popular culture of the United States since World War II. Production seemed to be "solved." Recall that U.S. industry delivered the torrent of weapons and munitions that finally swept away the armed forces of both Germany and Japan. And this was accomplished while the United States experienced the highest level of personal consumption in its history.* When

---

*Average personal consumption expenditures in the United States (in constant 1954 dollars) rose from $1,368 (1939) to $1,606 (1945) per person. More people did production work, for longer hours, than ever before, and a part of the "one third of a nation" that was ill-housed, ill-clothed, and ill-fed entered

the fighting ended in 1945, the United States had the main intact industrial system of the entire world. From 1945 to the early 1960s, the industrialized and the developing countries of the world, almost without exception, looked to the United States as the model for increasing their own productivity. Private firms invested heavily in fresh industrial capacity to satisfy the postwar consumer-goods boom in the United States. Whatever could be produced was sold. Further infusions of federal finance capital occasioned by the U.S. fighting in Korea accelerated investment in basic industry.

Altogether, it was a heady experience, so heady that in 1953 *The New York Times* could publish a dispatch headlined, "U.S. Achieves Aim: 'Guns and Butter.' "[19] The main point of the article was that the country had succeeded in so expanding the output of all its basic industry that the classic choice of "guns *or* butter" no longer obtained. The capacity of the nation's basic industries was in all cases greater than ever before. By January 1, 1953, U.S. steel capacity reached an annual 117.5 million ingot tons, half again as much as the 79.7 million tons available at the close of World War II. Raw material supplies were said to be ample, and civilian market demand remained at a high level.

It was against this background that sociologists began to formulate theories about the United States as an affluent "post-industrial" society, "one indeed in which leisure was becoming at least as central a concern as work."[20] In 1958, David Riesman launched the idea of a post-industrial society in an essay, "Leisure and Work in Post-Industrial Society."[21] And Daniel Bell, Robert Theobald and the Ad Hoc Committee on the Triple Revolution all began discussing various aspects of what they similarly tended to call a post-industrial society.[22]

The common thesis of these writers was that an era of abundance had arrived, and that the problems of production had essentially been solved. Henceforth, production would engage progressively smaller parts of the labor force, major parts of which would be assigned instead to all manner of "service" occupations. The disposition of leisure time would become an increasing preoccupation. Universities would play a central role as the chief enterprises of the "knowledge industry." Whatever industrial work remained in the United States would be concentrated in the "high-technology" industries, while "low-technology" work would increasingly be located abroad and performed by populations with lower wage rates and less ad-

---

the industrial labor force or received higher farm incomes. These effects, it is true, were not necessarily visible to the middle class whose gasoline, tires and meat were rationed while the supply of new consumer durables was cut off. See income and population data in U.S. Department of Commerce, *Historical Statistics of the U.S., Colonial Times to 1957* (Government Printing Office, 1972), pp. 70, 143.

vanced levels of technical development. By the late 1950s, these stimulating notions seemed on the verge of fulfillment when the federal government launched a society-wide panic response to the Soviet Sputnik coup and the universities were called upon to expand their production of scientists and technologists so that the United States might overtake the Russians in space.

Under President Kennedy, all these movements accelerated: government funds flowed into the universities as professors developed closer contacts with government administrators. When Lyndon Johnson launched his War on Poverty, there was suddenly more money for the social sciences as well. A parallel boom occurred in higher education, as student enrollments leaped from 3.8 million in 1960 to 8.6 million in 1970 and 11.1 million by 1975. This created a great enlargement of employment opportunity for faculty, which increased from 236,000 in 1960 to 628,000 by 1975.[23]

The rapid growth of the "knowledge industry" seemed to confirm the post-industrial ideology. Economists, professors of business administration, and deans of burgeoning business schools were all busy reshaping their curricula along lines that would give production—in all its aspects—reduced importance in the training of managers. In the post-industrial society, problems of production were either already solved or about to be dealt with. These ideas are to this day part of the conventional wisdom of MBA students— things that "everybody" knows.

Even engineering schools felt the impact of the new orientation. The funds that flowed into engineering during the 1960s were intended to meet, directly or indirectly, the requirements of the arms race, the space race and the development of the aerospace-electronics industrial base that supported them both. Research and instruction in the many aspects of production enjoyed less attention. Demonstration machine shops, metal foundries, and similar facilities that had given students a taste of hands-on experience with the fabrication of materials, were neglected or abandoned.

The largest increases of engineering employment came in the expanding aerospace and electronics industries that served the federal government's space and arms races. Engineering training for these lavishly subsidized operations no longer required the attention to cost-minimizing that had long been a hallmark of American industrial technology. Accordingly, courses in engineering economy were dropped as degree requirements at many leading schools. In one college after another, engineering was broadened to include "engineering science." That meant basic science research carried out in engineering schools on topics that would directly assist graduates to solve the problems of the newly expanding industries that served the state. Many aspects of civilian product design and production got less attention. In the

1960s, various scholars dismissed production topics as low-level detail that could be "picked up on the job."

In 1971, the president of Textron said when reviewing his company's position, "We're a producing company and we're looking at a trend where the U.S. is less and less a producing country. It's a service country. So in a sense we have some skills that are not really going to be required in the major growth pattern in the United States."[24]

During the previous decade Textron, like other U.S.-based multinationals, had become notorious for exporting capital, which in 1973 nourished their thirty-eight factories outside the United States. The top managers of Textron, and the directorate of America's network of business schools, took from the concept of post-industrial society the ideological justification for making money anywhere in the world where opportunity beckoned, rather than producing goods in the United States.

In interesting contrast to their mainstream colleagues, a few professors in schools of business have criticized the prevailing doctrines of the profession. In their view the schools bear a measure of responsibility for the course taken by U.S. industrial management, and even for the declining competence of U.S. industrial technology and productivity. Their judgment is that modern principles of management may cause rather than cure poor economic performance; that concentration on finance, strategy, short-term market manipulation, and remote finance-based control of far-flung enterprises are a formula for pseudo-professionalism.[25]

Meanwhile, West German and Japanese industrial managers have clearly become far more attentive to production, product quality and the importance of securing worker cooperation.

What has caused these differences? Why is production management assigned the lowest status in most U.S. companies? Why is it that in Western Europe, notably in West Germany, as in Japan, production competence, and technical skill generally, is given greater importance than in many major U.S. industrial firms? Similarly, why is the time allotted for development of an industrial plan typically much longer in those countries than in the United States? And why are managers in those countries more stable in their professional commitment to the enterprises that employ them than are their American counterparts?

Several factors can be identified as sharply differentiating the West German–Japanese experience from that of the United States. The first is the degree of decision-making power exercised in industrial life by production workers and technologists. Since World War II, the development of trade-unionism in West Germany has included the formation of a system of works councils in many enterprises. By formal agreement, these groups must be consulted with respect to decisions on major investments, production methods, plant relocation, and the like. Also, under Bonn's *Mitbestimmung* laws, trade-union representatives comprise up to half the membership of a corporation's board of directors. Obviously, these institutions that represent the work force have a stake in sustaining production and employment and in forestalling the capital runaway strategy that has been extensively employed by many U.S. multinational, conglomerate firms.

At the same time, the trade unions of West Germany and counterpart organizations in Japan have pressed so successfully for income increases that the rate of growth of industrial wages in both countries has far exceeded that in the United States. Confronted by well-organized work forces pressing for better wages, the German and Japanese managers have sought to offset rising labor costs by increased mechanization and more efficient organization of work. There was a time when that pattern prevailed in U.S. industrial firms as well, before cost-minimizing gave way to the cost-maximizing practices in the military economy and the cost pass-along in the rest.

In Japan, the incentive to improve productivity in response to cost increases has been strongly reinforced by the form of social contract between Japanese industry and its workers and technicians. These arrangements, won by Japanese workers and their unions after considerable struggle, include management's commitment, especially in the larger firms, to provide lifetime employment for their permanent employees.[26]

Conditions in both West Germany and Japan strongly dispose industrial management to pay close attention to technological improvement as one approach to the stable production base needed to sustain operations in a given community, despite rising wages and other, heavier expenses. In these economies cost-minimizing has not been compromised by a state-sponsored military industry. Neither West Germany nor Japan was subjected to the exhilarating but obfuscating ideology of post-industrial society. The idea that problems of production were fading away did not become part of the intellectual equipment of managers or of educated people in general.

A further factor that significantly differentiates the U.S. experience from that of West Germany and Japan is the presence, for most U.S. firms, of an enormous domestic market to which they have had priority access. West Germany exports more than 35 percent of its manufactured goods. So does France, and in the Benelux countries the rate rises to 60 percent. It is somewhat less than 10 percent in the United States. So the manufacturing firms situated in Western Europe, as in Japan, can survive only by offering reliable

products at competitively attractive prices. These considerations force attention upon product innovation and product quality.* *Leontief on domestic*

The U.S.-Japanese differences in management orientation include a strik- *profit*
ing contrast in average return on investments. Thus, in 1970 return on invest- *margins*
ment averaged 10.3 percent in Japan and 16.8 percent in the United States.
Calling attention to this difference, Professor Wassily Leontief noted that "if
one excludes the losses of our mismanaged automobile and steel industry the
latter figure would be still higher. In other words, the Japanese companies are
ready to expand so long as they can expect to recover in full the new investment over seven years, while their American counterparts will not move
unless they can count on profits after four and one half years."[27]

In a short but wide-ranging article on aspects of his working life, an
American production worker in the Ford Motor Company mentioned a
comparative study made by his management of a group of foreign cars and
those produced in the Ford plants. The worker reported:

> I asked the supervisor running the comparison, "Isn't 90 percent of the difference
> between their cars and ours not better workmanship but rather better engineering and
> design and better-quality material?"
>
> "Yes," he agreed.
>
> Knowing a case where the same car is made in two countries, I asked him, "Aren't
> the American-made VW Rabbits just as good as the German-made Rabbits?"
>
> "No," he replied. "The American Rabbits are better."
>
> If this is so, then American workers haven't lost pride in their work; those who
> control the workplace have.

German and Japanese industrial managers are better attuned than their
U.S. counterparts to long-term productive investment for assuring production
of desirable products. They make money along the way, but not as a substitute
for "making ships."

---

*Such contrasts with West Germany and Japan apply in good measure to Great Britain as well. British
trade unions have gained significantly less enterprise decision-making power than have their West
German counterparts. Industrial managements in Great Britain have been better able to take the
finance-capital-exporting route than have their opposite numbers in West Germany or Japan. Accordingly, British management has been less attentive to production technology and product quality, less
easily persuaded to increase labor and capital productivity as the basic way to offset cost increases
while maintaining employment and production operations.

4

Managerial Control
Versus Productivity

In order to produce one must decide what is to be made, in what quantity, by what process, to be sold at what price in what market. Nothing in production itself makes these determinations. Therefore, decision-making for production is an indispensable social process. There is a great array of possible systems for making these decisions, whose style can range from authoritarian to democratic. The money costs of a product can be minimized or maximized. Goods can be designed for more or less durability, more or less reliability, more or less safety in use. Production systems can be set up to employ the maximum or minimum number of workers per unit of product. Programs can be chosen to minimize or maximize the amount of capital (machinery, equipment) used in production.

But decision-making that primarily serves production is rarely a preoccupation of managerialism. Instead, the main concern of the managerial occupations is the enlargement of control of their decision-making power.* This characteristic is visible in the performance of single firms and whole economies. During the first half of the twentieth century, the costs of managing grew at similar rates in Britain and the United States (whose economies had similar industrial structures), while productivity growth was far more rapid in the United States.[1] Within firms, managerial activity and costs proliferate independently of their effect on production. Studies of the relation between the costs of managing and the volume of industrial production have shown either a negative correlation or the absence of any significant linkage at all.[2] From 1977 to 1980, for example, the value of goods and services produced in

---

*In the development of managerial control in U.S. manufacturing industry, there is no necessary relation between growth of profit and growth of control. On the evidence, the costs of adding to managerial controls have been absorbed even where that has meant less profit. This does not nullify the role of money gain as an instrumental tool for management. It does say that extension of control has been management's chief goal. (See note 4.)

the United States rose 7.9 percent, while employment of blue-collar and white-collar workers grew 2 and 12 percent respectively. The jobs of the blue-collar people were clearly linked to output; the tasks of the much enlarged white-collar group were mainly undertaken for control rather than production.[3] Such observations contradict the mainstream ideology of the managerial occupations, the schools of business and management journals, all of which play an important part in propagating the belief that intensification of managerial control leads to efficiency in production. The facts of the case even include the absence of positive correlation between intensity of managerial control and profitability. Evidently the extension of such control has been given priority, even over profitability, in the mores of management.[4]

The managerial way of deciding about production is based upon an occupational separation of decision-making from producing. Administrative jobs are typically organized in a hierarchy, and the unspoken goal is wider control.

The greater the number of people engaged in decision-making occupations, the larger is the scale of these operations. But the absolute number of administrative, technical and clerical employees can be a misleading measure of managerial control. For that, one must compare the number engaged in decision-making occupations with those assigned to production activity. By this measure it is possible to gauge the remarkable growth of decision-making occupations during the twentieth century.

In 1899, for every hundred production workers in U.S. manufacturing there were ten administrative employees of all classes. By 1947, this ratio had doubled to twenty-two, and by 1977, it had almost doubled once again—to forty-three administrative employees for every hundred production workers.

In the past, the cost of decision-making was viewed as necessary, but small —an essential fringe activity attached to the main work of an enterprise. But forty-three administrators, clerks and technologists for every hundred producers are hardly a fringe group. And the largest part of the growth has been in the functions that enhance control, not in those that increase production.*

Noting the percentage of administrative, technical and clerical employees in an enterprise is a good way to approximate the burden of administrative cost, but this ratio must be adjusted to the fact that people in administrative positions are paid substantially more, on average, than production workers. Thus, while there were forty-three administrative employees per hundred

---

*The ratio of administrative to production people in manufacturing has an important bearing on the difference between output per production worker and output per employee (production *and* administrative). The difference equals (algebraically) the ratio of administrative to production people. Therefore a ratio of 43:100 in 1977 means a difference of 43 percent between productivity, as output per production worker, as against the lesser productivity, output per production *and* administrative employee. See Seymour Melman, *Dynamic Factors in Industrial Productivity* (New York: John Wiley, 1956), p. 138.

production workers in U.S. manufacturing in 1977, the front office payroll in that year was $68 for every $100 of shop-floor wages.[5] But this equation still understates what firms pay for their administrative operations. A 1980 survey by a firm of personnel consultants reported that "many American executives are seeking, and in many cases receiving, a variety of perquisites as inflation eats away at their salaries." Among 234 U.S. companies with annual sales ranging from $100 million to more than $1 billion, such "perks," not counted as individual salaries received, could amount to as much as $28,000 per year, or about 45 percent of base pay.[6]*

The salaries of top U.S. corporate executives have reached levels that are probably unmatched in any other country. In March 1981, it was reported that an increase of $100,000 had brought the annual salary of General Electric chairman Reginald H. Jones to $1 million.[7]

Executive compensation exceeding $1 million a year has become ordinary. In 1982, *Business Week* identified twenty-six top officials of U.S. firms with total compensation (salary, bonus, long-term income) from $1.4 million to $7.6 million.[8] And growth in higher executive pay can even be independent of profitability.[9]

Substantial "stock options," which are separate from various forms of "perks" accorded to top executive officers, are not uncommon for the chiefs of the top 100 U.S. firms. An interesting issue is involved here. Since the percentage of income that goes for taxes becomes very high at $1 million per year, one may question the reason for running up the cash salary to that level. Is it simply a matter of relative status among chief executive officers of firms whether they are accorded a quarter-million- or a half-million- or a million-dollar salary?

Where engineers and managers are accorded status and privilege to differentiate them from blue-collar workers and are required to occupy administrative offices and never perform hands-on production, strained relations with production workers are to be expected. Arrogance becomes commonplace, reinforced by executive dining rooms, washrooms, parking places, country clubs, and bonuses.†

In the American ethos, occupational status and self-esteem vary directly

---

*"Perks" for top corporate executives refers to nonsalary income that can include such items as free lunches in corporate facilities, medical and other insurance payments, club membership fees, automobiles, credit card payments, homes, vacation facilities, fees for professional training, free legal and accounting services, etc.

†These are conditions that evidently led Akio Morita, president of Sony, to state that "teamwork historically is, I think, the American way. But your managers too often forgot that. They got greedy; they viewed the worker as a tool. That has not been good for American products or American companies, and it has hurt your competitive stature in the world." (Steve Lohr, "Overhauling American Business Management," *The New York Times,* January 4, 1981, p. 42.)

with distance from physical work and the workplace. The more removed an occupation is from the point of production or from physical contact with the product, the higher the status. Hence, production employees, as a group, are paid less than administrative employees, as a group.

Production workers do not ordinarily encourage their children to follow in their footsteps. The young are urged, rather, to seek schooling for business or commerce, or for engineering. And many engineers pursue the Master of Business Administration degree, with the quick entree it offers to upper-bracket managerial jobs.

A principal ideological defense of this value system is that, since a division of labor between decision-making and production is assumed to be essential for industrial well-being, the more evident that distinction and the greater the gap between administration and production, the more beneficial will be the effect on productivity.

Within managerial ranks, the validity of this argument is taken as self-evident. Indeed, it is a core obligation of administration to act for the enlargement of decision-making power—and to affirm that such action improves production and productivity. Factual evidence to the contrary does not temper the zeal with which this belief is maintained.

After World War II, management, especially at the senior level, came to be defined as a set of generalized professional techniques that could be applied without specific reference to any particular product or enterprise. These techniques, which address the manipulation of enterprise capital for maximum rate of investment return, have been declared the most important, the ultimate strategic decisions of any enterprise. And that view of management's supreme function has been used to support the claim that no limit can be set on justified professional income.

By comparison with this virtual adulation of management's mission, the planning for, and accomplishment of, production is scarcely noticed in the suites of American management. Who has ever read a celebration of industrial workers, written in the style of the "manager of the month" sections that appear prominently in business periodicals?

Some have viewed the rise in the ratio of administrative to production employees as an arithmetic artifact: worker productivity has been increasing and, with growing mechanization, fewer workers are needed for a given output. And that, it is assumed, accounts for the rise in the ratio of administrative to productive workers. But office work has also undergone extensive mechanization. The changeover ranges from the electric typewriter to the word processor to computerization of data recording; to filing, retrieval and computation; high-speed duplicating, especially by photocopy machinery with automatic collating and binding; rapid communication of voice and printed text by wire and radio; recording and transmission of digital, text and voice information; and finally, extremely fast search and retrieval of information from computerized data banks.

While many forms of person-to-person relationships are, by their nature, exempt from mechanization, one can say with confidence that the administrative occupations as a group have been transformed since World War II.

The productivity increase for the administrative occupations cannot readily be measured. The input of production man-hours can be computed per unit of product, but the joint product of the administrative occupations is a decision, and that is not a directly observable object. Nevertheless, there can be no doubt that the general trend in the mechanization of functions has vastly increased the average task performance capability of each administrative employee.

Why, then, the growth in the relative cost of decision-making? It is taken for granted in business occupations, and especially in the schools of business administration, that more managerial control raises the level of production. However, the facts do not support the assumption.

Early studies on the growth of administrative overhead in manufacturing industries established that administrative costs have risen along with the rise in industrial productivity.[10] But the two developments have not proceeded in tandem. The intensity of managerial control has increased independently of variations in productivity, and, at particular times, the levels of administrative overhead have not necessarily corresponded to the levels of productivity. The growth of managerial control and its costs, and the fluctuations of industrial productivity, though both were affected by decisions of management, were nevertheless controlled by different decision-making processes, operating from different criteria.

The increase in industrial productivity was mainly the result of plant mechanization undertaken by management to offset the rising relative cost of labor. But the growth of administrative overhead was caused mainly by the elaboration of administrative tasks.

The main direct factor in the expansion of administrative employment has been the broadened scope and heightened intensity of decision-making. This is not a case of more people doing the same work; rather, the amount of work has been multiplied. It has been multiplied so rapidly, in fact, that the sustained mechanization of administrative tasks has failed to offset the rising cost of that growth. An illustration with accounting work is to the point.

Once, there was only general accounting, an activity that produced profit and loss and balance sheet statements. But the record-keeping, data analysis and reporting of the flow of money and money values in today's enterprises has led to a multiplicity of types of accounting. In addition to general accounting, industrial firms of any size now practice cost accounting, budgeting, auditing, tax accounting, inventory accounting, depreciation accounting, wage and salary accounting. The introduction of such specialized accounting geometrically increases the work involved. And it must be emphasized that, despite the elaborate mechanization of accounting, initial entry of data usually requires a direct observation by a person, who writes or otherwise enters the observed data on a record form or into a machine system.

During this century, the trend of accounting practice has resulted in reporting units of diminished size. Whereas the reporting entity was once an entire firm, the development of multi-unit enterprises and then of conglomerates has produced a vast assortment of reporting units. In addition to the firm as a whole, they now include subsidiary firms, divisions of firms, manufacturing establishments of firms, single factories, departments, and designated "profit centers" even within individual departments. A profit center can be a unit as small as the few production operations which are designated a special entity for recording money inputs and outputs.

A third contribution to the amount of accounting activity is the frequency of reporting. Accounting reports once were submitted mainly on an annual basis. At present, accounting practices call for reports annually, semiannually, quarterly, monthly, weekly and even daily.

Let's assume, then, that five forms of accounting have been substituted for the basic type; that there are three times as many reporting units, and that reports are called for three times as often. The result of these innovations in administrative scope and intensity is a series of multiplications: five times as many types of accounting, times three times as many reporting units, times three times the previous frequency ($5 \times 3 \times 3 = 45$). However sweeping the computer revolution in the accounting department, the effect of this equation is a large increase of employees.

Similar developments have occurred in every area of administrative activity. As a teaching exercise in one of my graduate courses I ask the students to report on the information they must provide during an employment interview. Almost always the list of classes of personal information spreads across four blackboards. The data range from name, address and previous employer, to membership in various societies, religious affiliations, subscriptions to magazines, and the results from batteries of psychological tests.

Without doubt, the mechanization and computerization of routine administrative tasks have enormously increased the productivity of such tasks. Computerized computation is now carried out at a speed of millions of operations per second, with results printed at the rate of hundreds of lines per minute. It is therefore the more interesting to know how heavy computerization of the work affects the size of administrative staff.

A group of fifteen major U.S. manufacturing firms that were recently studied had, from 1967 to 1973, increased their budgets for electronic data processing by 176 percent. At the same time the general and administrative expenses of these firms, as a group, had risen 82 percent. There was also a strong correlation (0.8) between the growth in computer data-processing expense and general administrative costs. And, contrary to the conventional wisdom, these fifteen firms showed an increase in the number of administrative employees per hundred production workers (from 50.5 in 1967 to 61.5 in 1973).[11]

The significance of these numbers can be better appreciated if one looks more closely at one part of the administrative activity in a major firm. The ABC Company is a multi-division, multi-product firm with numerous factories, warehouses, research facilities, and a top financial rating for its securities. In 1975 it had net sales of more than $1 billion in four major product areas: pharmaceutical and health care, chemicals, agricultural, and consumer products. One of the accounting operations performed at the ABC Company controls and reports on "accounts receivable," a system for recording and controlling customer indebtedness. The firm keeps track of accounts receivable with daily, monthly and quarterly reports. (For more details, see Appendix II.) There are ten daily reports on aspects of accounts receivable, varying in length from 10 to 1,000 pages. There are six regularly produced monthly reports, ranging from 2 to 15,000 pages. Finally, a quarterly report is also prepared.

The effect of high technology on the personnel and budget assigned to the accounts receivable function can be gauged by comparing figures before computerization (1961) and after (1975). The ABC Company's data processing budget for the accounts receivable function increased over tenfold—from $55,000 to $607,000—while the average number of customer accounts that were kept on file rose from 75,000 to 95,000, or almost 26 percent. And the number of full-time employees assigned to accounts receivable jumped from 30 to 90, while the average number of full-time employees per 10,000 accounts kept on file increased from 4.6 to 9.5.

The increase of manpower and expense for the accounting work on accounts receivable in this firm occurred because of a rapid enlargement of both the scope (kinds of data) and frequency of reporting (many daily printouts) of the information. These demands for work to be performed outpaced the productivity increase made available by introduction of the most modern computerized accounting equipment.

The computer was not used to reduce the costs of administration. Instead, its installation was seized upon as an opportunity to multiply the scope and intensity of accounting, personnel and other administrative functions. This pattern has become characteristic of the way mechanization is applied to administrative work.

The crucial point here is that reduction, or at least minimization, of administrative costs has not been the goal of industrial management. Rather, the managers have been bent on maintaining and enlarging their decision power. One way to do this is to multiply managerial control systems, thus tightening the hold on the work force, on customers and others. It is a procedure that calls for larger administrative staffs, organized into more departments, and justifies promotions for the managers who preside over the increased body of work.

At the firm whose data I cited above, no improvement could be discerned by workaday tests of the performance of the newly computerized and expanded accounting, personnel and other administrative departments. For example, the handling of accounts receivable is ordinarily thought to have been enhanced when customers pay their bills more promptly and fewer of them fall delinquent. In the case of personnel, improvement may be measured by a lower turnover among employees, by less absenteeism, fewer complaints, etc.

Tests of this sort that were applied to the computerized administrative functions of this firm did not reflect these goals. There was no clear improvement in the performance of activities associated with the computerization of routine administrative work. In fact, the contrary was the case. The arrival of the computer had proved a golden opportunity for the expansion of managerial control, but in that respect alone was a clear success.

Among managers strongly committed to the control objective, success in resisting unionism is highly valued. The Human Resources Division of the American Management Association conducts symposia on "The Non-union Employer: Preventive Labor Relations," while warning: "Don't wait for the union to come knocking at your door!"* These goals and attitudes of management breed alienation and distrust, and therefore serve to justify enlargement and intensification of managerial hierarchical controls to assure compliance with top management policy.

The tendency of administrators to push for innovations that yield them wider and stronger control is seen in every aspect of management operation. The following is a memorandum sent to all laboratory managers at the IBM Endicott Laboratories on January 16, 1978:

To prevent the inadvertent disclosure of confidential business or technical information, all material to be presented at non-IBM speaking engagements must be

---

*A 1980 circular offering a course by the American Management Association includes the following principal topics: "Update on recent and pending labor relations; what you should know about unions; how to recognize and resist union organizing early; judging your company's capability for countering a union drive; legal boundaries—how far can you go in resisting unionization?; rounding up available manpower and expertise to plan anti-union campaigns; workshop—how to handle typical organizing incidents; how to build viable election day and post-election strategies; practicing preventive labor relations to make unions unnecessary in your company. . . ."

cleared through Communications prior to the employee making a commitment to speak. This includes not only talks at national technical conferences, but talks given locally at monthly or weekly meetings of various clubs and society chapters. For community relations reasons, clearance is necessary even when in the judgment of the employee the material to be covered in the talk does not directly relate to IBM. Employees invited to give talks should remember that management clearance is required before the employee commits to give the talk.

Clearance can be obtained by submitting a manager's authorization for the release of technical information on form 924-0125, and an outline or abstract of the talk to Information and Technical Communications, Department 775, Building 002-3. Allow 10 working days for clearance. Other types of information that must be approved include trade magazine and professional journal articles, abstracts and papers for outside society meetings and conferences, education theses, and presentation for IBM conferences. For additional detail see Manager's Manual, index 4-13 E, dated 07/29/77, or contact Phil Carapella on Extension 2760.

New Engineer prints such memoranda from industrial firms as a regular feature. They are usually sent in by staff engineers. The expansion of administrative activity by major firms extends from the enlargement of in-house legal departments to intensified efforts by many firms to control employees by devices like monitoring conversations, the use of polygraphs, television cameras in the workplace, etc.[12]

The priority that management gives to administrative functions, as compared with production functions, is repeatedly shown when major layoffs are imposed during periods of business crisis. From 1978 to 1980 the Ford Motor Company reduced its production force in the United States from 179,300 to 118,900, or 33.7 percent; over the same period, administrative and related employees were cut by 21 percent, from 77,300 to 61,000.[13] In response to lagging auto sales, General Motors has laid off the blue-collar work forces of entire plants and divisions; by contrast, at the close of 1981 the corporation announced a possible 7 percent cutback in management staffs.[14]

Management takes great pains to conserve its own staff because these workers are needed to maintain managerial control.

Multi-unit firms and conglomerates have played a strategically important part in the expansion of centralized managerial control. During the 1930s, a number of large multi-division U.S. industrial firms developed a pattern of "decentralized" organizations operating under central office control. The basic idea, as I noted earlier, was that the administrative headquarters would define general policy, the details of which would be carried out by division managers. The central office also performed a policing function—seeing to it that division managements acted in accord with general policy and met various standards set by the top management.

In this scheme, division managements were granted considerable authority to formulate details of policy and practice within the broad outline set by the central office. Division managers were also responsible for reporting their activities to the central office. This corporate structure divided industrial decision-making between those who set policy at the central office and those who implemented it at the division level. When such organizations were established, the usual result was a substantial enlargement of the central administrative office. Major staffs were employed to carry out policy research and to suggest policy formulations. They supported top managements with expert advice. They also did the policing of the component divisions.

One result has been to make the central administrative office the fastest-growing element of organization within the manufacturing industries of the United States. And the growth has been fostered by the tacit belief that centralization of managerial control can expand at a pace limited only by the speed and capacity of computers, communication technology and organizational technique. It is a heady faith, far removed from reality. Neither people nor machines are foolproof. There are limits to the human ability to observe, formulate, transmit, absorb and diagnose data. There is no evidence that the managers who make strategic decisions at national and international central offices can be supplied with the detailed, shop-floor knowledge that is the vital raw material of production decision-making.*

With their compelling and chronic itch for decision-making power, the managers of central administrative offices often blur the qualitative difference between broad policy-making and its detailed implementation. The introduction of computers with enormous data-handling capacity, and of far-ranging communication nets, has given the home-office administrators a new chance to centralize control. Many of them have used computers to bring specific and detailed decision-making, formerly left to the division managers, back to headquarters. As they see it, unlimited central data-handling capability obviates the need for decentralization.

The disasters that can follow from such a policy have been demonstrated by the recent history of General Motors. During his tenure as manager of the Chevrolet Division, and then as a group vice-president working in the main office, John Z. DeLorean saw GM's central managers and staffs trying to design automobiles and estimate costs—for which they were eminently unsuited, being removed by several steps from the point of production. However, the top management and supporting staffs scored a clear win in their seizure of centralized, detailed control over the design, manufacture and marketing

---

*For a pioneering inquiry on these matters, see E. F. Yost, *The Concentration of Management in Central Offices of Industrial Firms: The Limitations of Concentrated Management Decision-Making and Control,* Ph.D. dissertation, Columbia University, 1969 (Ann Arbor, Mich.: University Microfilms, document 70-18875).

of the Vega. A full chapter of DeLorean's professional biography is devoted
to a blow-by-blow account of the succession of blunders that ensued:

> . . . The guiding corporate precept of centralized policy making and decentralized
> decision making was totally and purposefully ignored . . . [The Vega] . . . was being
> put together by people at least one step removed from the marketplace. . . . The
> divisions reported to the 14th floor. But the 14th floor reported only to itself. . . . The
> first prototype was delivered from the central staff to Chevrolet. The first indication
> that this was an unwise way to build a GM car was not long in coming. Chevrolet
> engineers took the prototype Vega to the GM test track in Milford, Mich. After eight
> miles, the front of the Vega broke off. The front end of the car separated from the
> rest of the vehicle. It must have set a record for the shortest time taken for a new car
> to fall apart. The car was sent to Chevy Engineering where the front end was beefed
> up. . . .[15]

And on and on through the rest of the Vega saga as recounted in rich detail
by the former GM executive. The only explanation for the remarkably poor
design of this vehicle was the managers' insistence on using it as an opportunity to extend their managerial control. The cost was exceedingly high, but
they did carry out the managerial imperative.

The multiplication of managerial functions and man-hours, especially in
the operation of central administrative offices, is linked to the increased
prevalence of multi-unit and multi-product firms in the U.S. economy. In
such firms not only the social but also the physical distance between top
managers and the point of production is greatly widened. In a conglomerate
with 100 or more divisions, it is physically impossible for any single person
or small group to acquire knowledgeable judgment and to exert detailed
decision power on far-flung, worldwide operations. Many central offices attempt to bridge the social and physical distances by establishing elaborate,
formal systems of control, with accompanying policing systems. Apart from
their pitfalls and vulnerability (to, for example, faked data), these methods
cost heavily because of the host of people required for track-keeping and
control.*

It is significant, for example, that at the Toyota Motor Company there are
seven levels of organization between the factory floor and the company chairman. At the Ford Motor Company there are twelve such levels.[16] The Ford
managers function in an environment whose values include low status for
production work and pressures on managers to increase their distance from
the factory floor as an essential part of enlarging their status and decision

---

*The very success and expansion of the multi-unit and multi-product conglomerates has had the
collateral effect of encouraging the enlargement of decision-making functions that are a service to
control rather than to production.

power. This attitude is reinforced by a distrust of subordinates within management, leading to intermediate levels of controllers and track-keepers.

The intensification of managerial control mechanisms can even be blamed for unreasonably high costs at the point of production. The major military industry firms are, in every case, large multi-divisional, multi-product organizations. They operate with administrative, technical and allied supporting staffs of a size unmatched anywhere in the civilian economy. In 1978 the B-1 division of Rockwell International was composed of 5,000 production workers, 5,000 engineers and 4,000 administrative and management staff of all ranks. At that time the average ratio of administrative to production employees in manufacturing industry was 43:100. But in that division of Rockwell International the same ratio was 180:100; that is, 180 administrative, technical and clerical employees per hundred production workers. Managing in the cost-maximizing fashion normal to military suppliers, Rockwell that year produced four B-1 bombers at an average price of $4,400 per pound. There was a clear connection between operating on the assumption that cost hardly matters and a readiness to indulge in administrative, technical and other costs to a degree that would ordinarily bankrupt a civilian firm. In this and similar examples from the military economy, assurance of government backing through the cost-plus system of payments guaranteed considerable profits even at ever higher production costs.

U.S. industrial management, on the average, continues to exhibit a powerful trend toward enlargement of administrative costs to levels that weigh heavily on the total operation of the industrial system while exerting a primarily negative effect on production. This development within traditionally private firms is spurred by the formation and operation of a state management.

5

Enter the
State Managers

Since the end of World War II, and notably during the 1960s and 1970s, the
federal government has spent more than half its tax dollars on past, current
and future military operations. While a myriad federal activities affect the
profits and production of the nation's economy (they range from control over
interest rates to the operation of research and development stations in agriculture), the largest single sustaining activity of the government is the operation
of its military economy by its central management. More than 37,000 industrial firms or divisions of firms and over 100,000 subcontractors operate under
the control of a central federal administrative office with a staff of about
50,000—probably the world's largest industrial management.[1]

The firms in the federal government's military economy share unique
conditions of operation. Profits, for example, are effectively guaranteed, since
in most cases the product is sold before it is produced. Furthermore, production is carried out under conditions that have no counterpart in civilian
economy: cost-escalation is institutionalized. Most important, however, the
products of this economy differ fundamentally from civilian manufacture, not
merely because of the destructive or coercive nature of weaponry, but in an
economic sense.

Economists, with rare exceptions, understand an economic product to be
anything with a price. That is one of the core ideas of the various economic
systems that have been offered over the last two centuries. In all these theories
the furthering of production has been seen as an essential managerial self-
interest that also results in a net benefit, however unequal the shares, to
society as a whole. However, the conventional economic wisdom has not dealt
with a situation wherein important parts of the labor force and the means of
manufacture are applied to products that, while having a price, do not, and
cannot, contribute to either ordinary consumption or to further production.
Military goods and services may be useful for political, military and even
aesthetic or religious purposes, but they are no part of what is ordinarily

understood as the goods and services that the citizenry produces and consumes.

That is why it is important to know that the Department of Defense utilizes 17 million acres of land in the United States for its operations and disposes of real property with an inventory value of $339 billion. This includes industrial equipment valued at $3.8 billion that is owned by the Department of Defense but allocated for use by the 642 largest industrial contractors.[2] Furthermore, among the 500 largest industrial corporations in the United States, average assets per employee in 1979 were $49,000; for the U.S. Department of Defense, average physical assets per uniformed and civilian employee exceeded $110,000.[3]

The state managerial industrial organization that serves the military and space operations of the federal government has become a dominant factor in enlarging the scope of profit without production. As in managerialism generally, the extension of managerial control, the acquisition of more power and higher status, is a first priority of the state-managed military economy. As in other managements, an increase in the number of people controlled is both a persistent objective and a conclusive test of managerial success. There is an important difference, however, between managerialism in the private firm and the state economy. For the private firm, profit-making is an intervening, instrumental objective for maintaining and extending managerial control both within and outside the company. (As shown earlier, this pattern is sustained despite the partial contradiction between the administrative costs of enlarging managerial control and the desired profit.)

For the management of the Department of Defense there is no profit and loss, no balance sheet calculation. The Pentagon's central office is not involved in producing goods, selling them for a profit and then using that profit for further investment and production operations. The Pentagon's managers draw their finance capital from taxes, from the whole society. Therefore, as the Department of Defense is only too well aware, its money resources are practically unlimited.* This view among American state managers of their capabilities is well founded in the record and current planning for the military establishment and its industrial base. From 1946 to 1980 the budgets of the Department of Defense came to $2,001 billion.[4]

By 1975, the national wealth of the United States included $4,302 billion as the value of "total reproducible assets," meaning the total money value of everything man-made in the nation, not counting the value of the land itself.[5] By this reckoning, accumulated budgets of the Department of Defense from the end of World War II until 1980 had a money value approximately equal

---

*During 1978, under the Carter administration, an "economic stimulus program" was formulated that gave the Department of Defense a no-ceiling go-ahead for military outlays.

to 46 percent of the direct cost of reproducing the main wealth of American society.[6]

This background of thirty-five years of military expenditures, totalling $2,001 billion and including the Korean and the Vietnam wars, seems moderate in light of the government's planned military spending for 1981 through 1988. That eight-year budget plan for the Department of Defense totals $2,089 billion.[7] But all these estimates of money-valued resources used and to be used by the military establishment are only a first step toward understanding the effects of Pentagon managerialism over U.S. production, productivity and quality of life.

The social cost, the cost to the community, of a continuing military economy is but partially measured by the money value of the resources expended for its operation. That is so because of the economically parasitic character of military goods and services. The individual firm, or any person, employed in the military economy, receives money for the performance of the work. That money, in turn, can be used by the individual to acquire consumer goods and services and by the management of the military-serving enterprise to buy inputs for further military work, or to invest in other enterprises. The point is that for the *individual* employee or for the *single* military-serving firm, the money income that is gained is convertible into real consumers' or producers' goods.

From the standpoint of a larger community, however, the calculation of gain and loss must rest upon different considerations. In the case of the military product, no consumer or producer use value becomes available. Since goods and services for consumption and production are indispensable to the life of the community, the absence of such outcome (otherwise available) from an important part of the community's production capacity is a social cost in addition to the money value of what has been used up for carrying out the military work.

Nor does the matter end there.

One of the crucial characteristics of producer goods is that they can be used to multiply output. Basic machine tools, for example, can fashion more of their own kind as well as manufacturing equipment of many other kinds. Furthermore, by applying increments of knowledge to the design and use of such equipment we can improve the yield, the efficiency, with which these further production operations can be carried out. This ability to create for further production, and at a steadily improved rate, is not present in any military commodity. Thus, whatever the technical complexity and design elegance of a nuclear-powered submarine or a high-performance military airplane, it cannot be used for the further production of any other thing or service. By contrast, a private car contributes to the service of transportation;

a truck may contribute to the construction of a building. In that respect, therefore, military production, by foreclosing any possibility of this additional output at higher productivity, is an end in itself.

In sum: from the standpoint of an entire community the operation of a military economy imposes three classes of costs. First, the cost of the resources that are the assorted inputs for producing military goods and services. Second, the cost represented by the economic use values (for consumption and production) that are unavailable to the community in the case of the production of military goods and services. Third, the cost to the community of the opportunity for, and the results from, productivity improvement that is necessarily forgone by using up resources for military products that might otherwise be used to fabricate and operate new means of production.

Therefore, adding up Defense Department budgets yields a gross understatement of the economic costs from the operation of a permanent war economy. The Department of Defense and its industrial network represent a case of pure service to the extension of power, for economic and political control, which in turn creates no economic product in the precise sense that I have discussed here. It is in the very nature of the military institution to emphasize the expansion of decision power and control. These effects are further amplified by the normal operation of the state managerial apparatus, which adds a series of administrative control strata within the federal government to those of the nominally private firms that serve the military economy.

The post–World War II military economy of the United States had its genesis in a reorganization carried out under General Dwight Eisenhower, when he was Army Chief of Staff in 1946. At that time he issued a memorandum titled "Scientific and Technological Resources as Military Assets." This memorandum by Eisenhower the general was, operationally, the founding document of the collaboration that Eisenhower the president, in his famous farewell address of January 17, 1961, would define as the military-industrial complex.[8]

Eisenhower wrote in 1946 that "the future security of the nation demands that all those civilian resources which by conversion or redirection constitute our main support in time of emergency be associated closely with the activities of the army in time of peace." The memorandum included five major policy recommendations:

1. The Army must have civilian assistance in military planning as well as for the production of weapons. . . .
2. Scientists and industrialists must be given the greatest possible freedom to carry out their research. . . .

3. The possibility of utilizing some of our industrial and technological resources as organic parts of our military structure in time of emergency should be carefully examined. . . .

4. Within the Army we must separate responsibility for research and development from the functions of procurement, purchase, storage and distribution. . . .

5. Officers of all arms and services must become fully aware of the advantages which the Army can derive from the close integration of civilian talent with military plans and developments.

Thus, Eisenhower laid down the policy basis for a military-industrial-scientific collaboration whereby the armed forces and their supporting industrial base became an important and continuing part of the national product, with the money value of military activity being counted as an ordinary part of the gross national product.

Before this permanent war economy was established, military institutions and military industries had played a minor part—both absolutely and proportionately—in the money-valued activity of the American economy. The transformation effected after 1946 was strongly influenced by the assumption, across the political spectrum, that America's resources were so vast as to be sufficient for a "guns and butter" economy on a continuing basis. The significance of the U.S. economic experience during World War II was misunderstood. Economists failed to realize that, in the long run, renewal and improvement of the capital stock of production are essential for any healthy economy. The brief, four-year experience of full-tilt military production was not, therefore, a reliable precedent for predicting the consequences of a thirty-five-year concentration on military economy. After 1945 the press celebrated the efficiency of principal U.S. industries, the abundance of raw materials and the prospect of further growth in the output of consumer goods. The reader of such reports was left unprepared for the industrial incompetence and failure of productivity growth that began to show up two decades later.[9]

Eisenhower, occupying the White House from 1953 until 1961, made no objection to these general assumptions. Indeed, his failure—and the failure of his advisors—to do so made him a political casualty of the military-industrial complex which he himself had set in motion.

In 1960, Eisenhower's designated successor, Richard Nixon, lost to John F. Kennedy in a political race that featured a military scare campaign about a missile gap favoring the Soviet Union, and that was followed by a mobilization of military-industrial and academic-intellectual circles around the new president, who promised military invigoration of all sorts. For Eisenhower it was a bitter pill, since it amounted to an unspoken charge that the old general had failed to guard the military security of the United States. And as president, he had in fact kept tight rein on his "brother officers," using arguments of fiscal responsibility to justify limits on the expansive ambitions of the various armed services. It is therefore important to read Eisenhower's farewell address of January 17, 1961, as a series of warnings against placing excesses of money and power in the hands of the armed services and the military economy—a policy that he feared would be followed by his successor. Note the following in the Eisenhower address:

. . . We annually spend on military security more than the net income of all United States corporations.

This conjunction of an immense military establishment and a large arms industry is new in the American experience. The total influence—economic, political, even spiritual—is felt in every city, every statehouse, every office in the federal government. . . .

Our toil, resources, and livelihood are all involved; so is the very structure of our society. . . .

The prospect of domination of the nation's scholars by federal employment, project allocations, and the power of money is ever present and is gravely to be regarded.

Yet, in holding scientific research and discovery in respect, as we should, we must also be alert to the equal and opposite danger that public policy could itself become the captive of a scientific technological elite. . . .

[We] must avoid the impulse to live only for today, plundering for our own ease and convenience the precious resources of tomorrow. We cannot mortgage the material assets of our grandchildren without risking the loss also of their political and spiritual heritage. We want democracy to survive for all generations to come, not to become the insolvent phantom of tomorrow. . . .[10]

But Eisenhower's forceful and provocative arguments went unheeded, and the military/industrial excesses against which he had warned went into full motion.*

To understand the full consequences for production of a major military budget, one must recognize the relation between that budget and capital.

---

*It is true, of course, that Eisenhower himself engaged in military-political adventurism in the imperial tradition. Under his administration, the Central Intelligence Agency was used to unseat elected governments in Iran and Guatemala that did not suit Washington's political tastes. Eisenhower failed to guard against the possibility that the U-2 reconnaissance flights over the Soviet Union might cause the diplomatic disaster that resulted in Khrushchev's cancellation of their important Paris meeting in 1960. The same Eisenhower handed his successor a military-political bomb in the form of preparations for the Bay of Pigs fiasco. See Blanche W. Cook, *The Declassified Eisenhower* (Doubleday, 1981), pp. 182–83 and pp. 304–306 on corporate investment planning.

When an industrial enterprise makes a major productive investment, the assigned funds are usually classified as contributing to either fixed or working capital. Fixed capital comprises the land, improvements to the land, buildings and machinery. Working capital is the raw materials, energy, small tools, purchased components and payments to workers, technicians and administrators of all classes. A modern military budget is, effectively, a capital fund because its components range across the whole spectrum of things that are labeled elsewhere fixed and working capital. Modern armed forces purchase large numbers of machines of all sizes and complexities, from automatic rifles to fighter planes, bombers, nuclear submarines, and aircraft carriers. Armed forces buy immense quantities of fuel and transportation equipment, and pay for the services of millions of skilled workers and managers, in and out of uniform.

That being so, it is especially interesting to compare the fresh capital resources used by the military with the fresh capital stock generated for all civilian purposes. We can do this because the economic statistics-gathering activity of the United Nations now produces annual data from most countries of the world on military expenditures as well as Gross Fixed Capital Formation. The latter category includes new civilian buildings and other construction, together with the value of new transportation equipment and industrial machinery. From these data I have subtracted the value of new residential buildings (and, for the United States, the value of new passenger cars). The resulting figure more closely approximates producers' gross fixed capital formation. These statistics exclude expenditures on behalf of the military. Therefore the ratio of military spending to producers' fixed capital formation gives us the number of dollars in a particular year devoted to the military per hundred dollars that have been expended for fixed capital purposes in the civilian economy.*

In the United States in 1977, for every $100 of new producers' fixed capital formation, the military spent $46. In West Germany in 1977 the figure was $18.90, and in Japan it was $3.70.[11] On an average, from 1960 to 1978 the United States used up for military purposes $52 of capital resources for every hundred dollars that was assigned to civilian productive purposes. The magnitude of this withdrawal for the military was obviously far greater than that of the West German or Japanese military use of capital.

---

*It should be noted that in making this comparison the denominator consists of fixed capital items as a major part of the civilian output of the economy. The numerator, military budget, consists of various inputs that could be utilized for the production of new fixed capital. This conceptual disparity —the numerator being various inputs for capital goods production, and the denominator representing capital goods output—serves to underscore the idea of the military budget as susceptible to use for alternative outputs, civilian or military. Therefore, this ratio is a measure of the new civilian capital goods forgone.

For twenty-five years the research and development budgets that are centrally managed by the federal government have equalled or exceeded the research and development activities that are funded and controlled by all private managements. By far the largest part of the federally controlled funds is expended in laboratories and development facilities operated by industrial firms and by universities and other "non-profit" institutions; but the Office of Management and Budget, the president's budget control arm, has final say as to the outlays and goals of the government's research and development programs. In 1981, of $35.5 billion of federal R & D funding, 71 percent was absorbed by the Department of Defense, the Space Agency and the military-related R & D of the Department of Energy.[12]

But the government's past disposition to concentrate federal research in the military sector may be only a foretaste of what is to come during the 1980s. President Reagan's science advisor has declared that the government should, and would, focus its support on only those sciences that show a special promise of breakthrough or that are needed for industrial, military and "other essential technologies."[13]

Within the federal government there has been a similar long-standing emphasis on military and military-supporting R & D activities. The National Science Foundation has reported on scientists and engineers who are direct employees of various government agencies. Of 160,988 scientists and engineers employed in all federal departments in 1973, 86,942, or 54 percent, had worked in the Department of Defense, NASA and the AEC.[14]

The federal government's ability to influence the mode of employment of scientists and engineers does not stop with its own payroll. Through the wide-ranging controls of the Department of Defense and its network of supporting enterprises, scientists and engineers are offered superior salaries and conditions of work. It is hard to conceive of a private firm that could match the inducements offered by the federal government, either directly or through one of its subordinate firms, in its effort to employ the desired numbers of scientists and engineers. The results show in the high concentration of technologists in the government-serving (read military-serving) industries. By 1970 the main military-serving industries had, on the average, 7.4 scientists and engineers in research and development for every 100 production workers. In the rest of manufacturing industries that proportion was 1 percent. In other than R & D work scientists and engineers represented 11.2 percent of the production worker force in the military-serving industries, but only 2.3 percent in the rest of manufacturing.[15]

The high starting salaries and rapid promotion available to young engineers and scientists in the federally sponsored economy have become so alluring as to cause a major drain from both the faculty and the graduate-student bodies of American engineering schools. The managers of the federal government's military economy wield their money and political leverage as best they can to get the people needed for the work of the next year's budget. Like many of their industrial counterparts, these managers operate on the short term, on the assumption that the next twelve months is what counts.[16]

As might be expected, technology managers of the Department of Defense are eager to build up their "industrial base." Accordingly, they have designed elaborate manufacturing technology (MAN TECH) projects at the multibillion-dollar level. With enough money, they will no doubt succeed in getting at least part of their desired results—computerized control of production operations that drastically reduce "direct" labor requirements—if not from firms within the United States, then by buying abroad. But by clinging to the existing R & D, design, and manufacturing capabilities, the state managers fail to heed Eisenhower's warning that we ". . . must avoid the impulse to live only for today, plundering for our own ease and convenience the precious resources of tomorrow. . . ." The price of the federal government's short-termism is made highly visible by the operation of its own cost-maximizing economy.[17]

The Department of Defense has never published a policy circular specifying "Thou shalt maximize cost." Cost-maximizing may, at times, be a formal objective, but for the most part it has been and continues to be a sustained effect derived from a series of operating procedures preferred by the state managers and subordinate firms of the military economy. Furthermore, cost-maximizing does not proceed indefinitely: in the end, constraint is imposed by the size of the budgets that Congress will approve. But when these funds are rapidly enlarged, then those budgets become, in effect, targets to be met. The means for doing that are now institutionally well developed under the sponsorship of the Pentagon's state management. When in 1978 I visited the factories outside the Los Angeles airport, where Rockwell International was set up to manufacture the B-1 bomber, I learned that before the contract was cancelled this division had a ratio of administrative (including technical) to production workers of 225 per hundred. This compared with the average A/P ratio of 43 per hundred in manufacturing as a whole in 1977.

At Lockheed's Missile and Space Division in Sunnyvale, California, of its 19,500 personnel, 3,500 were production workers, 8,300 were administrative and clerical employees of all classes, and 7,670 were scientists, engineers and supporting technicians. In 1970, the ratio of administrative (including technical) employees to production workers was 452 per hundred. One might perhaps argue that the technicians, like blue-collar workers, are production employees, but even so defined the ratio of administrative to production employees would be 74 per hundred, or almost twice the aggregate manufacturing A/P ratio of 43 in 1977.

Occasionally one gets an unexpected insight into how one or another aspect of the federal government's industrial system functions. It seems that there is an elite group of Washington lawyers, some 200 in all, who specialize in drawing up and executing lawsuits against the Pentagon on behalf of military-industrial firms. The intriguing point about this activity is that it results in large revenues to the client company, whose legal costs are deemed a proper part of its administrative overhead and thus accounted for in the normal flow of military appropriation money to its management. Three major law firms dominate this scene. Their fees are ordinarily calculated at the rate of $175 per hour of staff time to produce ". . . claims, some running 60 volumes in length, [that] defied realistic challenge on the merits."[18]

The government's Defense Science Board discovered during 1980 that the cost of producing major weapons systems had been growing at an annual rate of 20 percent. This rapid increase was accounted for by the rising cost of various components and materials. For example, during the period 1979–1980 the following price hikes have been noted: aircraft electrical connectors up 170 percent; microwave tubes up 30 percent; nonferrous metals up 86 percent; aircraft radars up 23 percent; aircraft engines up 28 percent; aircraft structures up 34 percent.[19]

Historical costing (a.k.a. parametric costing, statistical cost estimating) is a method for setting prices of future products by extrapolating from costs of similar products in the past. This way of forecasting cost and price rules out any critical assessment of what was done before, and does not involve a consideration of other possible ways to accomplish a given task. Nevertheless, the history of the recent past, all of its practices being accepted, is the preferred baseline from which cost increases for a given class of weapons production are projected. This method of costing was officially sanctioned under the stewardship of Robert McNamara in *Defense Procurement Circular No. 12, 1964,* and has been periodically updated since then. One result of this procedure is the pattern of price increases itemized above—a pattern in the major weapons systems that has been nothing short of remarkable.

Reflecting the current managerial penchant for short-term objectives and short-term gains, the federal government's National Science Foundation, traditionally disposed to support basic research, has been persuaded to place "strong emphasis" on technological problem-solving. This new tack could lead to a reduction of support for basic research in favor of subsidies to various firms in the form of federal research funds.[20]

The managers of the government's industrial empire have made elaborate provision to ensure continuity of operation, even assuming shortages of various materials, tools and machines. The Defense Priorities System "provides the means for exercising production priorities in industry for national defense. When utilized properly, it ensures that defense programs are maintained on schedule providing priority treatment for the purchase of products and materials by defense agencies, contractors, sub-contractors, and their suppliers."[21] This means that when deliveries of important industrial machinery, like certain classes of machine tools, are backed up for periods of one to two years, the Defense Priority System can be invoked to move a government-serving enterprise to the front of the line. One side effect of that would be to press U.S. firms into seeking foreign sources of supply for important production equipment.

The smooth operation of the state managerial control system and its detailed cost-maximizing processes is facilitated by the oscillation of officials between the Defense Department and the largest military-serving "private" firms. From 1970 to 1979 1,942 persons moved between the Defense Department, NASA and eight of the largest military-serving firms.[22]

The domain of the state managers is not restricted to enterprises that directly serve the military. Major parts of the nuclear enterprise, formerly managed under the Department of Energy, are of interest to the Department of Defense and display all the signs of cost-maximizing. On June 30, 1981, a government investigator, who insisted on anonymity, disclosed that a firm "that contracted to supply eleven steam generators to the Clinch River Breeder Reactor project for $57 million renegotiated its agreement to supply just two, but at nearly triple the original price for all eleven." General Electric and Westinghouse had, at the request of the Department of Energy, evaluated various bids for the eleven Clinch River steam generators, and had recommended that Foster Wheeler be awarded the contract, since it had offered to supply the equipment for $20 million, a bid $6 million lower than the one received from Atomics International, to whom the contract was finally awarded. (That firm is a division of Rockwell International Corporation.) After ignoring the GE and Westinghouse recommendations, federal officials "cancelled the bidding process and negotiated a $56.9 million non-competitive contract with Atomics International for the 11 units." In 1981 a congressional investigator observed somewhat despairingly: "Here we are six years later and the estimated cost is $143 million for only two units."[23]

A 1981 report published by the United States Merit Systems Protection Board found that "federal employees have abundant knowledge of illegal and wasteful government activities, but the majority do not report such activity because they believe nothing would be done to correct the situation. . . . Of the 30 percent who did report . . . illegal or wasteful activities, one-fifth believed that they had been victims of reprisal."[24] This report is consistent with common knowledge about the treatment of "whistle blowers" by the top federal managers.[25]

In an unusual letter to the secretary of defense, Senators Barry Goldwater and Howard Metzenbaum wrote (February 25, 1981) that "runaway costs characterized our entire defense procurement program. These vast expenses have nothing to do with maintaining the strength of our military forces. They are, pure and simple, the result of a system that permits DOD officials to operate as though the public purse has no limits." And the senators follow this judgment with the admonition: "It is a system that can and must be changed." But it is doubtful that any fundamental change is possible, inasmuch as these practices have been institutionalized, richly rewarded and carry the promise of larger-than-ever funding.[26]

The control system over the military economy has served as a model for subsidizing, then regulating (effectively, managing) the various firms involved. As this practice was institutionalized it became easier for the federal managers both to extend their control and to guarantee the profits of assorted private firms that turned to the government for special assistance. The procedure was widely publicized when the government became involved in the Chrysler Corporation's financial crisis. (To support the request for a $1.4 billion loan guarantee Lee Iacocca, then president of Chrysler, told a Senate committee on November 15, 1979: "I think laissez-faire free enterprise died a while back.") When it received this loan guarantee Chrysler became, in effect, a state-managed enterprise with surveillance over its affairs exercised by a new layer of management in the executive branch of the government. However, the Chrysler action is but one incident in a wide array of federal subsidies and supporting operations for private firms. In one respect, the government has a long history of making elaborate investments to ensure the creation of an infrastructure. Hence, the networks of canals, railroads, superhighways and airports built at public expense. Less understood is the degree to which the government has become a guarantor of private firm financing. By 1981 federal loans and guaranteed loans exceeded $461 billion.[27]

The state managers' intervention for economic control extends well into the area of marketing itself, a development of ideological interest, since conservatives identify themselves as devout believers in the sanctity of the "free market." Thus the government has, through the secretary of agriculture, been operating a system of marketing orders covering thirty-three commodities in thirty-seven states, or about half the annual crop of fresh fruits, vegetables and nuts that are sold annually in the United States. In 1981 "more than 40 percent of the record California orange crop [was] dumped, fed to cattle or sent to processing plants in a successful effort to keep the prices of oranges from tumbling." In the words of Billy J. Peightel, manager of the Navel Orange Administrative Committee that controls this commodity in California: "There's no doubt that without the order there'd be chaos. The oranges would flood the market at one time, prices would drop; the sellers would back off, prices would rise, and they'd flood the market again. There's no question fewer oranges would be marketed without the order."[28] In other words, to avoid a free-market threat to profit, the government supervises the destruction of 40 percent of the crop. The profit priority is clear. More and more of the same is to be expected when the administration chooses to place control over various federal regulatory agencies in the hands of executives drawn from the industries to be regulated.[29]

Sometimes the zealous quest of the state managers for ways to support the profits of private firms can produce really unusual results. In 1981, James Watt, the secretary of the interior, cut the staff of the Office of Surface Mining by 40 percent. At the same time he let it be known that he was preparing to approve major surface mining of coal in an area immediately adjacent to Bryce Canyon, Utah, one of the great natural spectacles in the U.S. National Parks System. An objection had been raised to the effect that this mining operation would damage a great scenic site. Watt rejected that idea, asking: How will our youth be proud of the surface coal mining industry if they can't see it?[30]

Unlike the management of private firms, a state management can spread its dominion beyond particular firms, labor forces and markets. State management possesses the resources and other means to extend its control over entire territories and their populations. This is precisely what government managers have done by concentrating both fixed and working capital expenditures, especially for the military economy, in the states of the American South and West. On average, from 1965 through 1967 the federal government took, in taxes, from New York State $7.4 billion more than it spent there for all purposes. Illinois suffered the next biggest loss with a net drain of $4.4 billion. But during the same period, California received $2 billion more per year than it paid to the government; Virginia came out ahead by $1.3 billion and Texas by $1 billion net each year.[31]

By the 1970s there was real alarm over this economic imbalance, and a Northeast-Midwest congressional coalition was formed. Further studies sponsored by this group have disclosed that during a five-year period, 1975 to 1979, the eighteen states of the Northeast and the Midwest sent $165 billion more in taxes to Washington than they received in government spending. The heavily industrialized states of the Midwest were particularly hard hit, accounting for three-fourths ($122 billion) of this combined drain. The losses to the Northeast and to the Midwest were translated into concentrated, massive economic cash-flow gains, not only to the national treasury, but also to thirty-two Southern and Western states, which enjoyed a net inflow of $112 billion in federal funds.[32]

By concentrating capital investment, with the attendant new employment opportunity in the Sunbelt states, the federal government has not only encouraged a migration of labor force, but also accelerated the decay of the great cities of the Northeast and Midwest. By failing to make capital investments in the renewal of the infrastructure and productive facilities of the metropolitan centers, the state managers have presided over a process of fiscal crisis and material decay.[33]

One of the sustaining features of state managerial control systems is that they are maintained and enlarged independent of party, personality or ideology. Democrats and Republicans, devotees of Truman, Eisenhower, Kennedy, Nixon, Ford, Carter or Reagan—all have had a hand in carrying out the professionally mandated requirement of all managerial occupations: to extend the scope and raise the intensity of control over people.

The Department of Defense has been steadily enlarging the scale and detail of its control over its prime contractors and subcontractors; in all, more than 137,000 firms. There is little public objection to this operation, whose expense, at the enterprise level, is fully paid for as an allowed cost against the Department of Defense. Indeed, from the standpoint of the profit of the individual firm the more of these costs the better, since the base for calculating profit is thereby enlarged.

During the early 1950s I tried to update my files on managerial control operations in the federal government by asking various departments and bureaus for a set of the forms that individuals and firms had to fill out to meet the data requirements of the particular agency. Soon the file drawers filled up, and keeping track of these forms was beyond my capability. The pages of these questionnaires ranged in size from single sheets to bound volumes containing more than 100 pages of tabular forms. These massive documents were given the formal designation of single report forms. Almost every form of any size was accompanied by explanatory documents to assist the respondents in understanding the meaning of the categories and the boundaries of the reporting requirements. That is why the normal procedure of the military management's control system calls for civilian and uniformed representatives of the Pentagon's central office to be present on the premises of the larger military industry firms.

The Carter administration continued the effort launched under Gerald Ford to curtail the federal paperwork imposed on individuals and firms. Accordingly, the Joint Economic Committee of Congress asked the General Accounting Office to report on the nature and extent of federal reporting and record-keeping requirements imposed on private industry. The GAO was able to identify requirements totalling 69 million man-hours per year (at 2,000 hours for a man-year, the equivalent of 34,000 man-years). The volume of work was generated to satisfy the curiosity of federal agencies whose reporting requirements must be reviewed and passed upon by the Office of Management and Budget. But the Internal Revenue Service was outside that control system and it accounted for about 613 million man-hours per year.[34] Under the Carter administration, despite its pledge to reduce federal paperwork, the number of pages of regulations issued annually jumped from 14,572 in 1977 to more than 20,000 by 1981.[35] The Office of Management and Budget announced that Americans would spend 1,276,000,000 hours filling out 5,000 different kinds of government forms during 1981. The main sources of demand for these reporting activities are the Internal Revenue Service (about 50 percent), the Department of Transportation (about 20 percent), and the Department of Agriculture (10 percent).[36]

The point that emerges here is that government managers are strongly impelled to prefer the most detailed forms of control mechanism that can be devised. Given alternative ways to carry out a particular administrative function, government managers will, characteristically, prefer the one that involves the most minute control and supervision of individuals.

For example, in the cause of reducing "welfare cheating," federal managers have proposed the creation of a data bank whereby one could pinpoint the estimated twenty-five million persons who receive various forms of public assistance. For the first time those twenty-five million names would be consolidated in a single national list.[37] Again, in the campaign against welfare cheating, federal managers have urged that all persons receiving assistance under Aid to Families with Dependent Children be required to file a monthly report. Specialists in these fields predict that "processing a report from each welfare case each month would immobilize Welfare Departments that currently cannot handle even a much smaller volume of paperwork. . . . Massachusetts welfare workers and their supervisors are responsible for more than half of the state's most costly errors. How are they going to process accurately more than ten times the paperwork?"[38]

In the name of national security, federal agencies have attempted to regulate access to, and dissemination of, highly theoretical work in mathematics. The National Security Agency is a top secret federal entity responsible for collecting information, especially by recording and analyzing open and coded communications around the world. That agency has lately become concerned about theoretical work in various universities that might have a bearing on cryptography. After various negotiations a group of mathematicians, computer scientists and university officials agreed to submit voluntarily for prior review by the agency research papers intended for publication in the scientific literature. Francis E. Low, provost at Massachusetts Institute of Technology, stated: "I'm worried about the consequences of this for work in the universities. This represents a kind of control of material and ideas which is very difficult to swallow. What about laser work, robotics, high-speed integration—areas that might have military application?" Indeed, once such rights of control are conceded to military agencies there is no way of drawing a firm line to limit that control.

During the Carter administration the Office of Management and Budget started a new control system that required faculty and supporting staffs of university departments that had accepted government contracts to report on how they spent their working time. This was supposed to help check on the accuracy of the universities' "indirect" cost charges. In correspondence with officials of OMB I wrote that a national system of 100 percent reporting of faculty "effort" is expensive and unnecessary. A sampling system could produce the relevant information at a fraction of the present cost to the Office of Management and Budget and to the universities. I was told that "the new rules . . . were based on recommendations by the Department of Health, Education and Welfare after urging by the House and Senate Appropriations Committees." The exact text of these "recommendations" has never been made public nor could the Office of Management and Budget describe the precise nature of the "urging" by the congressional committees. Congressional committees don't "urge"; they vote money, approve legislation, hold hearings. As for sampling procedures, OMB officials said that "we have proposed a joint research project at selected universities to assess its feasibility." That is, the OMB was going to assess the feasibility of statistical sampling and the interpretation of such results—a remarkable undertaking not remote from an all-out effort to invent the wheel. Meanwhile, the nationwide 100 percent reporting system was set in motion.

The unprecedented expansion of American state managerialism in the military sphere has been undertaken in the name of "protection," and justified on the ground that the Soviets have been outspending the U.S. on armed forces and that U.S. armed forces are militarily weak. These two propositions, repeated endlessly in the media, have rallied major parts of the population and an overwhelming majority of the Congress to support military budgets of a size hitherto never contemplated in the United States. But close examination suggests that the argument is based more on deception than on fact.

The source of the Pentagon's claim that it has been outspent by the Soviets is a set of studies by the Central Intelligence Agency which gauges Soviet military spending by estimating the cost of Soviet armed forces if they were paid for at U.S. dollar prices. Using such methods, the CIA has found that the Soviets outspent the United States in the military sphere during the 1970s by about 50 percent, or some $300 billion. But the basis for measurement is inherently misleading. Never mind the fact that we do not have samples of all Soviet material and cannot gain access to Soviet factories and their costs. Consider only that the "Soviet rates of pay plus upkeep are probably less than one-third of ours, yet the CIA values the Soviet 4.5 million man draft army at U.S. voluntary army pay scales (plus upkeep) reported to average $15,-000–$20,000 annually per soldier. . . . Further, every time the U.S. Congress grants our armed forces a pay increase, Soviet expenditures measured in dollars rise by twice as much as ours because their army is twice as large."

These analyses by Professor Franklyn Holzman, a specialist on the Soviet economy at Tufts University, indicate that a major part of the military spending gap "discovered" by the CIA during the 1970s is accounted for by U.S. pay scales rather than by hikes in actual Soviet spending.[39]

Also, the U.S. state managerial alarmists systematically exclude the military budgets of the NATO countries from the U.S.-U.S.S.R. comparison. Finally, military power does not derive from money spent but from the size and quality of armed forces, including their equipment, morale, training and mode of utilization. The military spending gap invented to unsettle the American people will, in due course, join the ever-growing list of military "gaps" that have been fabricated by the state managers since the end of World War II to justify their budgets and managerial power.

The second assertion commonly made to justify an immense expansion of U.S. military resources is that the United States has become militarily weak. This complaint carries the implication that, with sufficient resolve, it should be possible for the United States to construct and operate a superior, meaning a winning, military combination. But the goal of victory in a major war between nuclear superpowers is not plausible. Each of the superpowers now brandishes a grotesque redundancy of overkill capability, and no present or prospective science or technology is able to evade that limiting condition—people and communities can be destroyed only once.[40]

Present understanding of the limits of military power includes the following propositions:

- In a nuclear war there is no prospect of "winning" because nuclear overkill on both sides guarantees insupportable destruction and death for all.
- Among major nuclear powers, military superiority is undefinable.
- Among nuclear superpowers, even a perfectly executed first strike gives no exemption from the lethal backlash effects of a damaged global eco-structure.
- Major countries can use their armed forces, if permitted by other superpowers, to threaten or assault small countries.
- Small countries, if permitted by superpowers, can use armed forces against each other.

All this is far removed from the idea of wielding superior military force to impose political will on the losing states, as the United States and its allies did at the close of World War II. The revolution in military technology since World War II has severely restricted the traditional possibilities of applying military power for political ends.[41]

After World War II, the managers of the U.S. military establishment organized a worldwide program of military assistance. From 1950 to 1980 it granted $53 billion of military materiel to assorted allies and clients of the United States. However, during the 1970s the program was sharply curtailed in favor of military sales agreements. This change was dictated by the withdrawal of gold cover from the value of the dollar and its consequent collapse in relation to other currencies. The federal government then sought ways to soak up dollars that had accumulated in central banks around the world, and the one given great emphasis under the Nixon administration was intensification of the military sales program. During the 1950s, military sales agreements averaged $162 million per year. In the next decade the annual average was $1,020 million. It rose to $8,540 million per year in the 1970s, and by 1982 promises to attain a level of $25 billion.[42]

The Pentagon has become the middleman in promoting and arranging foreign military sales. In its military advisory groups in fifty-four countries, the Pentagon has its sales teams advising the foreign countries on what arms are available and should be bought. Once the foreign country has picked an item off the shopping list, the Pentagon becomes the contractor arranging with an American manufacturer to produce and deliver the weapons.[43] Thereby the U.S. government arranges and handles these foreign military sales on a government-to-government basis, charging a customary 2 percent administrative fee, while also arranging for credit to finance the purchase.

In 1981 the military sales program was to be supplemented by a $982 million "direct credit" program of low-interest loans that will enable sixteen strategically situated countries to buy American weapons and military training. Federal officials have stated that such credit will be available at rates as low as 3 percent per year. Apart from the various programs for financing expanded military sales, the Reagan administration announced a $350 million "special requirements fund to provide greater flexibility for the United States in responding to direct challenges" in emergency situations. The implication is that the state managers could use this fund to apply the pressure of military assistance at crucial points.[44]

The U.S. state management is heavily committed to extending not only its direct managerial control worldwide but also U.S. military systems and military economy in allied countries. The presence of military-oriented state managements in other, especially smaller, countries makes them more amenable to routine administrative cooperation on a manager-to-manager basis. But the nations that become clients of this military extension operation cannot escape its consequences. Their scarce capital resources are necessarily channelled to the support of enlarged military establishments. Their small pool of skilled manpower is offered exceptional career opportunities through the

armed forces—almost invariably the best financed sections of their governments. Necessarily, civilian economic development is held back.*

America's state managers are committed to the use of military power for
their own aggrandizement—even at the expense of a viable, productive society. They strive to maintain and enlarge the decision-making power of the top
managers in both the private and public "sectors." The foreign investments
of U.S. firms (Appendix I) afford one measure of the private corporate economic power to whose security the state managers are dedicated. In pursuit
of these objectives these managers are, it would seem clear, ready to encourage massive war preparations that endanger the whole society, even the
human race.

---

*Representatives of third world governments met in New Delhi early in 1980, under the auspices of
the United Nations Industrial Development Organization, to plan ways of accelerating their economic
development. The conferees concluded that their countries needed $30 billion of additional annual
capital investment until the year 2000 to narrow the economic gap between third world and industrialized states. Neither during the conference proceedings nor in the formal policy resolutions was it
mentioned that, in the preceding year, 1979, the military budgets of the third world countries totalled
$90 billion—three times the capital fund defined as crucial for accelerated development. And even
if the military extravaganzas of the oil-rich states were excluded, that aggregate military fund would
still be $70 billion.

SHAPING TECHNOLOGY FOR PROFITS/POWER

The engineers who actually design technology get their marching orders from management. That is the crucial link between managing for profits/power and the preferred qualities that are actually built into technology of every sort. The goals and resources of management, private and state, also govern the direction and the pace of research and design efforts. As a result, the profit and power pursuits of the private and state managers have also had effects, unintended but decisive, on the productivity of U.S. industry.

6

Technology Designed
for Profits/Power

Technology is man's creation. It has no direction or movement of its own, and may be defined as the application of man's knowledge of nature to meet a specific social requirement. Once created and set in place, technologies bear significantly on human life, but the source and direction of a decision to make particular use of our knowledge of nature derive from the decision rules (values) that prevail in a given society.

The relation between decision criteria and technology is best seen in the design process. The engineer-designer must select from among the materials, component mechanisms, degrees of precision and reliability that are available to him. The design of a particular technology can vary across a broad range, according to the designer's preferences: simplicity as against complexity, reliability as against a willingness to bear the cost of frequent breakdown, durability against flimsiness, design that minimizes cost of production for a given standard of quality as against design where cost doesn't matter.

Since under industrial capitalism the design of both the means of production and of consumer goods is shaped by the goals of the production decision-maker, management's desire for profit and control is what governs choices in the design of production methods and industrial products. I will illustrate the operation of this process as it affects the design of machine tools, the selection among technologies for energy production and use, and, finally, the consequences of the quest for profits, even at the expense of production, as demonstrated in the operation of the U.S. automobile industry.

Since their earliest invention, the basic machine tools have retained a consistent configuration. This family resemblance is immediately apparent when one compares contemporary machine tools with the drawings and photographs of such machines in use a century ago.[1] The tools have always been designed as general-purpose machines. That is, they have been built to perform a given function, say, drilling, on workpieces of sizes and shapes that are limited only by the size of the drill press and the cutting power of the bit. The positioning of the workpiece, the selection of the bit and rate at which the drill advances into the workpiece all, until very recently, were controlled by the operator. The exceptions to this general rule were certain special-purpose machine tools that performed limited movements on particular, unvarying workpieces.*

After World War II, mechanical and electrical engineers applied a new set of capabilities to the problem of positioning machine tools. These were derived from wartime developments in automatic mechanisms that included computer calculation and feedback control systems. Numerical control was the name given this new technology, which placed the specifications for the movement of cutting tools and workpieces on cards, punched tape or magnetic tape. Thanks to the pathbreaking work of Professor David Noble of MIT, we now know in detail what technological and managerial forces influenced the design of numerical control technology.[2]

The pioneers in the development of numerical control technology, as I noted in the Prologue, were the United States Air Force, a team of technologists at MIT, and various engineers and specialists in major firms of the machine tool industry. Drawing upon the new control technologies, they developed a number of alternative techniques for recording information and controlling machine tools by means of pre-set data. David Noble demonstrates, in a remarkably detailed account, how the prime movers—the Air Force and the MIT technologists—joined forces for mutual advantage and developed those technological options for numerical control that best satisfied their joint requirements, while systematically ruling out alternatives that were less suited to their needs.

The Air Force needed machine tools capable of shaping many large workpieces, such as the main structural members of high-performance aircraft, to close dimensional tolerances. The work could, of course, be performed by conventional, operator-controlled milling machines, but the Air Force wanted production speeds greater than could be had by conventional methods. The military were also attracted by the possibility of production

---

*In these cases the motion of the machine, as well as the placement and removal of the workpiece, could be accomplished in a mechanically controlled sequence. Thus, the work of the machinist who translated desired movements from blueprint to the machine by the turning of appropriate hand wheels and the moving of slides, could be replaced—for a restricted set of movements—by motions that were "stored" in the form of special cams and templates, mechanical stops, and the like. But such special-purpose machines had a narrow capability. Thus a new workpiece, even of a class similar to what had been made before, required new sets of gears, cams, templates, etc., and called for expert and costly retooling by highly skilled designers and machinists.

methods that would give management closer control over operations on the factory floor, even from remote locations.

These interests of the Air Force coincided with those of university-based technologists, who were eager to improve their professional status by developing methods for controlling industrial operations that relied heavily on computer technology. The technologists at MIT designed and demonstrated milling machine controls capable of reproducing to close tolerances complex three-dimensional shapes of large size. The preferred designs to make this possible, including the choice of computer language, assured key positions to mathematicians, programmers and computer operators.

Noble shows, in detail, how other possible technologies were put aside, not developed. These included various methods for "record-playback," whereby a machinist would first put a given machine tool through its paces in fabricating a particular shape. As the machine performed its work, its motions would be recorded. The record could then be "played back," that is, used to control repeated sets of operations with none of the pauses for verification of data and checks of blueprint specifications that would be normal for the machinist-operator. This form of machine control used the skill of the machinist-operator as the baseline for operation and could have served as a transition technology to full numerical control. Also, it did not require a new class of programmers and computer operators, as did the numerical control technology preferred by MIT and the Air Force.

But the directness, relative simplicity and low cost of record-playback were features that did not particularly interest the MIT technologists or the Air Force. MIT's engineers wanted a development that would make their professional skills more important to industry; the Air Force directorate was attracted by the centralized control and greater versatility promised from the more elaborate numerical technology, and cost comparisons were ignored. Noble shows there was no evidence of any interest in cost-minimizing, or in the development of technology that, while improving industrial productivity, would also be most easily adapted by the broad range of metalworking firms in the United States, and so would have introduced them, as early as the 1950s, to the advantages of computer-assisted production.

The preferred numerical control technology, with its complex programming, required the creation of a new occupation, the programmer. Management saw this as an opportunity to move an important part of decision-making in industrial work from the operator-machinist to management's office. Therefore, Air Force managers and MIT technologists were soon joined by top executives of principal machine tool firms, who were eager to share government subsidies, while placing themselves in the front ranks of those using new technology development to fulfill the managerial imperative for extension of control.

Frederick Winslow Taylor, one of the founding theorists of modern industrial management, wrote in his classic *Shop Management* (1911):

As far as possible the workmen, as well as the gang bosses and foremen, should be entirely relieved of the work of planning, and of all work which is more or less clerical in its nature. All possible brain work should be removed from the shop and centered in the planning or laying-out department, leaving for the foremen and gang bosses work strictly executive in its nature. Their duties should be to see that the operations planned and directed from the planning room are promptly carried out in the shop.[3]

The managers of numerical control design tried to fulfill that managerial plan. Indeed, Noble reports that a visiting engineer-manager—after being shown the operation of the continuous-path numerically controlled milling machine —wrote to the developers at MIT that their invention "signals our 'emancipation from human workers.' "

The consequences for the American metalworking industries of the designs fostered under the direction of the MIT–Air Force management team were obvious two decades later. Since 1958, publications of the machine tool industry have been laden with eloquent testimonials to the merits of numerical control technology. But the new ways simply did not catch on—except in the cost-maximizing aerospace industries, where 6 percent of the metal-cutting machines in use were numerically controlled by 1978. In the rest of U.S. manufacturing, 2 percent of the metalworking machines were of this class.[4]

The numerically controlled machines were extraordinarily expensive in themselves and required large overhead costs in the form of supporting computer equipment and programming man-hours. The equipment was therefore unattractive to cost-minimizing industrial managers. To be sure, some managers (disregarding cost) spotted the chance to move decision-initiative from the work force to management, and saw in numerical control an opportunity to "de-skill" the machinist-operator, leaving him with little to do but place and remove the workpiece and the control tape, and press the on-off buttons. However, these dreams of reduced worker decision power, and enhanced managerial control, by the use of NC technology were frustrated in the nonmilitary metalworking industries—first, by limitations of the NC technology itself, and then by worker resistance.

In one respect, an NC machine is like any other: there are limits to its reliability, and incidents of mechanical, electronic and programming (human) failures and errors inevitably occur. That is the nature of machinery. In the case of numerical control technology such mishaps blighted management's hopes, for they made it difficult, if not impossible, really to eliminate the skills of the machinist-operator. As was to be expected, the very complexity of the

NC technology proved a severe limitation on reliability. Accordingly, skilled operator intervention became more significant, as expensive machine downtime could be kept under control only by the presence of an operator who could correct programming errors, tape failures, tool wear; adjust work tolerances; repeat cuts where required; and compensate for variation in the qualities of the workpieces. These requirements blocked the attempts of some managers to reduce the "skill ratings" of NC machine operators. In fact, in a succession of major industrial plants that had installed NC technology, the job ratings of the operators were raised in the interest of keeping the machines running.

The shape given numerically controlled machine tools by the initial Air Force and private managerial design probably had the long-term effect of severely retarding the adoption of advanced technology in the metalworking industry. For NC technology was so fashioned as to put it economically out of reach of the largest number of firms. Thus opportunities for significant productivity advances were withheld from the majority of such firms, even while the requirements of the aerospace industry, operating under cost-maximizing conditions, were amply met. The profit-making and managerial-extension requirements of top government, industry and university managers were also fulfilled at the expense of what could have been a consequential breakthrough in productivity for American industry.

The organization of work is a further aspect of technology that has felt the stamp of management's imperative to maintain and expand its control.

In the cause of advancing work efficiency (output per worker), the theory and practice of industrial engineering, since the first decade of the century, have included the following ideas as virtual axioms: simplification of work is indispensable for productivity improvement; individual work assignments should be broken down into ever-simpler tasks; work assignments should be unchanged over extended periods of time; management's contribution to more efficient work organization includes not only the simplification of tasks but also the coordination of finely divided divisions of labor. These rules for a strategy for the organization of work have rested on the further assumption that production skill is a matter of manual-manipulative capability.

For many decades, almost everyone assumed that these factors were inherent in industrial work. Hence, the assembly line, Taylorism, Fordism, mass production—all have been widely accepted as the essence of industrial work. And the accompanying monotony, boredom, the crushing of spontaneity and initiative—in short, the "modern times" portrayed by Charlie

Chaplin—have been seen as an inescapable condition of industrial work. Only recently, in the 1960s and 1970s, have people begun to question these axioms.

Notably in Western Europe, significant attempts have been made to explore the feasibility and the consequences of alternative methods of work organization. For example, an imaginative set of studies was carried out by the Renault factories in France. The tasks chosen for the purpose were the assembly of automobile front suspensions and engines. Three forms of organization were adopted for the front suspension: first, the standard assembly line with the usual fixed assignment of workers to limited tasks; second, a "continuous assembly line" with each worker "walking" the suspension along a conveyor system while doing each of the necessary, differentiated operations from start to finish; third, a system whereby workers in groups of four performed their tasks at a fixed workbench, controlling the subdivision of labor and its variation among themselves.

The results were striking. In terms of suspensions assembled per worker per day, the conventional work-simplified assembly line produced an average of 26.5; the "continuous assembly line," 30; and the group-workbench system, 33.5. Even more striking results appeared in the studies of engine assembly. There, the transfer from fixed-position assembly lines to the "job enlarged" assembly system showed an average increase of output per worker of 33 percent, and the shift from the classic assembly line to groups of four at a workbench almost doubled the output per person, from 10.5 to 20 engines per person per day. And the methods of work organization that produced more engines and front suspensions also turned out work of higher quality.[5]

The new methods for the organization of work at Renault involved less supervision over individual workers and their simple tasks, and they enlarged the decision power of grouped industrial workers. The worker groups also discovered and demonstrated innovations for work organization—including the grouping and timing of tasks, and ways to vary work assignments and workloads. The former capabilities indicated a reduced requirement for externally formulated work design; the latter capability demonstrated degrees of technical skill among the workers well beyond the manual-manipulative category.

The response of industrial managers to such new ideas has been, understandably, ambivalent. On the one hand, they approve of the production results; on the other, they do not welcome, indeed often view with suspicion, the lessened role of management. These findings and the reactions to them have become important for the organization of work to be done by the rapidly developing computer-controlled machine tools and other industrial equipment.

When the work task of the NC machine operator is defined in terms of work simplification, with severely limited responsibility and initiative, it is to be expected that frequent intervals of downtime will lower the productivity of the equipment. Since mechanisms are subject to failure, and workers to inattention, one problem of the organization of work with the new machines is to structure tasks, responsibilities and incentives in ways that will sustain high-grade preventive maintenance and operator alertness to imminent failure.

In September 1980 I compared characteristics of numerically controlled machining centers* supplied by principal companies in the United States and Japan. These firms, almost without exception, guaranteed their product for as much as 95 percent availability for work under conditions of optimum maintenance and competence in machine operation. That promise of almost perfect performance compares poorly with the finding of expert observers that, in practice, numerically controlled machine tools have often operated as little as 55 percent of the available working time. The difference between optimal and actual performance is large, even if allowance is made for optimism on the part of NC-equipment manufacturers.

To show its managers the potential for de-skilling with NC machines, one firm made a film in which a chimpanzee performs the task of pressing the on-off buttons on an NC controller. Some NC equipment is fitted with locks on the programming capability of the machine, so that the operator, like the chimp, is limited to pressing a button.

Under such conditions production workers have often felt cheapened and degraded, and hence unwilling to take any sort of responsibility. They "work to rule," one aspect of which is to stop the machine on the slightest pretext and call in others—foremen, maintenance men, programmers, etc.—to look after whatever malfunction might be involved or suspected. That is a time-consuming procedure in labor time and, much more costly, machine (capital) time.

The significance of reliability in NC machine operation is illustrated by the cost per hour of downtime for an average NC machining center, about $67.† Assume that there is a reduction in machine uptime from a possible

---

*A machining center is the name given to a class of machine tools with a wide range of work capability, usually including numerical control as well as automatic changing of tools.

†Cost per hour of depreciation (assuming

two-shift operation over ten years)	$ 8.75
Cost of production overhead per hour	10.00
Cost of administrative overhead per hour	3.00
Cost of labor per hour	11.00
Value of production work forgone per hour	35.00

Estimated cost per hour of downtime	$67.75

maximum of 95 percent to a still highly commendable 85 percent. This means that 10 percent of 4,000 hours per year or 400 hours of unscheduled downtime is to be accounted for. The cost per hour of downtime is then multiplied by 400, for a total $27,100 as the cost per year of a 10 percent addition to downtime. This estimate is surely understated, since it includes no allowance for the "ripple effect" caused by the disruption of other production operations, or the cost of larger inventories of work-in-process to cushion against such effects, or the cost of replacing machine parts damaged by neglect.

One implication is clear: high-quality maintenance and a well-educated machine operator with major responsibility and authority for machine planning and operation make a combination that must yield a rich return to an industrial enterprise which uses computer-controlled equipment. Such a work force is trained in computer technology, is motivated to apply this knowledge responsibly and with initiative, and finds individual and group satisfaction in reliable performance of sophisticated work tasks.

That is far removed from the idea of the industrial worker as a manual-manipulative performer whose work management can diminish in both scope and content down to the level of pushing a single button. Locks on numerical controls to prevent any intervention by machinists for correction of error, etc., and penalties for such intervention, are counterproductive in the world of numerical control machining.

Workers observed in one industrial study stated:

"If you treat us like button-pushers, we'll work like button-pushers." . . . Management accused them of "working to rule" and sabotage. Disgusted, the workers increasingly refused to take any initiative—to do minor maintenance (like cleaning lint out of the tape reader), help in diagnosing malfunctions, repair broken tools, or even prevent a smashup. The scrap rate soared (one thing NC can do quickly, efficiently, and automatically, one operator wryly observed, is produce scrap) along with machine downtime and low morale [and] produced the highest absenteeism and turnover rates in the plant. Walkouts were also common and, under constant harassment from supervisors, the workers developed ingenious methods of retaining control over their jobs (and their sense of humor). . . .[6]

There is an inherent incompatibility between the attempt to organize production on the basis of centralized, authoritarian controls over a task-limited (work-simplified) work force, and the potential for optimizing the productivity of labor and capital in computer-controlled operations by entrusting responsibility to the new, well-educated industrial workers of the post–World War II generations.

.   .   .

Social policy on the production and use of energy necessarily influences the choices made among a great array of options. Managerial control and short-term profit-taking dictate a preference for the speedy development of nuclear power and breeder reactors and the production of synthetic fuels. These technologies have strongly attracted private and governmental managers. For private firms, investment in synthetic fuels seemed to bring the prospect of government capital, government guarantees and the ability to utilize the existing petroleum product distribution system on a continuing basis, thus conserving the private capital investment in that network. Then at some point in the future nuclear plants and breeder reactors will plug into already elaborately funded federal programs that are closely linked to principal private firms (General Electric, Westinghouse, Combustion Engineering, Babcock & Wilcox, etc.). These companies have major investments in nuclear technology and their profit positions would benefit from intensified government commitment to energy programs along such lines. Furthermore, private and state managers both would gain from these policies, since the technologies are inherently capital intensive and have been managed thus far by systems of highly centralized control.

But these technology preferences exact a heavy social price. Existing nuclear plants have operated at high costs and have displayed a technical unreliability that has yet to be brought under control. In the early 1980s orders for new nuclear plants had dwindled almost to zero.[7] The characteristics of breeder reactors are not really well known. It is therefore prudent to give attention to the assessment made for the National Academy of Sciences by a study team on nuclear and alternative energy systems.[8] In calculating the consequences of relying on breeder reactors, the report stated that "those who control scarce but necessary resources control the society that depends on those resources." Among other effects, "safety considerations would compel drastic reduction in civil rights, with a general increase in numbers and power of police. The total number of reactors will not affect this general pattern."

This warning arises from the well-established understanding that crucial materials used in nuclear fuels can be converted to weaponry. That raises the prospect of extraordinary police and security measures to safeguard a major network of nuclear plants, including breeder reactors, against unauthorized access to equipment and materials. These considerations are compounded by the increasingly appreciated hazards of radiation leaks caused by equipment failures—even those that are checked far short of catastrophe.

A study team for the National Research Council headed by Professor Laura Nader, at the University of California (Berkeley), examined the social consequences that follow from the choices of energy technology. The Nader group explored the possible consequences for industry, consumption, transportation, etc., that might be expected from a substantial—50 percent per capita—reduction in energy consumption in the United States. Conventional wisdom holds that economic well-being and productivity growth in industry have been linked to increased use of energy per capita. While it is true that these developments have been connected, it is even more important to understand that this has been due, in large part, to cheapness of energy in the United States. American designers of energy-using equipment have given little attention until recently to the energy requirements of mechanisms and processes.

Total energy consumed per person can be stated, for purposes of comparison, in terms of kilograms of coal equivalent per year. In 1978, Americans consumed an average of 11,374 kilograms of coal equivalent energy per person. Compare this with the per capita consumption of energy in the following countries:

Belgium	6,078	Japan	3,825
Canada	9,930	Sweden	5,954
Denmark	5,423	Switzerland	3,690[9]
West Germany	6,015		

Japan has experienced the world's most rapid productivity growth during the last quarter-century. Switzerland pays the highest industrial wages; it is closely followed by West Germany, Belgium and Denmark. Canada is a cousin, economically and culturally, of the United States. The dramatically lower energy consumption in these countries, with standards of living that equal or exceed that of the United States, indicates that the U.S. economy has been something of an energy hog.

A detailed comparison of energy used for all purposes in Sweden and the United States in 1971 shows that Swedes consumed only 60 percent as much per person, while operating a fully sophisticated industrial economy and enjoying a level of living equal to or better than that of Americans.[10]

As of 1978, the United States was consuming 78,256 trillion British thermal units (Btu) of energy per year, from all sources and for all purposes. Of this total, 21 percent was residential, 16 percent commercial, 37 percent industrial and 26 percent for transportation.[11] For each of these main uses of energy I offer the following illustrations for what might be done in terms of available technology. Note the recurring contradiction between managerial imperatives for short-term profit and the needs of the community as a whole for reliable and efficient use of energy.

Staff members of the Department of Energy concerned with energy conservation note that by the year 2000 new houses could easily be made 50 percent more energy-efficient than those now in use. One effect, among others, would be to save 2 billion barrels of oil annually, a quantity imported in 250 days in 1980. "The home building industry is where the American automobile industry was a couple of years ago: making energy hogs and unable to sell them. Home builders are just lucky that Japan doesn't export houses yet." That serious charge comes from James Barron of the New York State Energy Research Development Authority. A wide-ranging assessment of the condition of home building in the United States disclosed that builders on the whole used too little insulation. What they do install is often less than effective because the buildings are poorly caulked and sealed. Heating and cooling equipment is often oversized, with resulting loss of efficiency. Builders tend to ignore inexpensive but technically proven passive solar techniques for storing and circulating energy—the most obvious of them being to orient buildings toward the sun. And builders have neglected various energy-saving devices; for example, vestibules that serve as air locks.

In 1979 a study by the Tennessee Valley Authority of homes built in its area showed 83 percent with less than sufficient attic insulation, 20 percent with none at all and 85 percent without floor insulation. Also, 35 percent lacked storm windows or double-glazed windows. None of this means that buyers of houses are uninterested in energy efficiency. In 1977 and 1978 the National Association of Home Builders reported that 60 percent (or 840) of 1,400 buyers who were questioned said that they had been influenced by the energy-saving features of the homes they purchased.[12]

The technological feasibility for large energy savings in homes and offices is indicated by the results achieved in several locations where designers and builders tried seriously to conserve energy. An office building recently designed for New Jersey will consume annually 27,000 Btus per square foot, as against older, conventional buildings that required 150,000 Btus per square foot per year. The residential drain on energy could also be dramatically reduced by use of long-life, low-energy light bulbs. A General Electric official estimates that installation of the new bulbs in 10 percent of the sockets that are now burning 100-watt and bigger bulbs would lower the demand for electricity by 8 billion kilowatt-hours a year, the equivalent of 40 million barrels of oil.

A visitor to any latter-day shopping mall might well conclude that it had been designed on the assumption that electrical energy is virtually free. The absence of an air supply from other than powered sources and the massive use of electrical illumination during daytime hours call attention to a failure to make the most simple use of skylights and open doors and windows for light and air. But these technological possibilities have been widely ignored, since the higher costs of mall operation justify higher rents and profits to the owners.

The lavish, to the point of profligate, use of power in U.S. industry was sharply revealed when, after the oil shortage of 1973, several large firms told their manufacturing divisions to look around and make a modest attempt—no major investments—to save on energy. One of the largest manufacturing companies in the United States achieved an average 25 percent reduction in energy use with no change in any major equipment or process. It was realized by the simplest means: fixing a valve, insulating a pipe, closing a door, switching off an unneeded light or motor. So it is obvious that very large savings in U.S. industry's energy requirements remain to be made as soon as it becomes painfully unprofitable to waste energy.

If petroleum and coal are regarded as finite resources, to be conserved for uniquely valuable end uses (like chemicals requiring complex hydrocarbons), then the profligate use of petroleum products to power transportation has been an energy disaster in the United States. In terms of energy required per ton-mile, or per passenger-mile, electric-powered railroads are dramatically more efficient than passenger cars, buses or airplanes.[13]

Since the establishment of a mass-producing automobile industry, the combined influence of industrial management, pliant government officials, and cheap gasoline and diesel oil have caused a sequence of displacements that has left the United States with a remarkably expensive and energy-inefficient transportation network. At the turn of the century one of the interesting features of American cities and their surrounding towns was the network of rail lines—urban and interurban trolleys and trains—that linked communities. Buses were used as the first displacement of the electric trolley systems. Then private cars became the displacement for the buses. By the 1980s, American firms manufacturing passenger cars were being rapidly displaced by manufacturers competing from outside the United States, especially from Japan and West Germany.[14]

The same development led to the massive use of public funds for constructing truck-bearing highways, a program that culminated in the 42,500-mile Interstate Highway System. By 1981 that system was deteriorating so rapidly as to require reconstruction of 2,000 miles of roads per year. As sufficient funding for this purpose was withheld during the late 1970s, 8,000 miles of the Interstate Highway System and 13 percent of its bridges were beyond designed service life by 1981 and became candidates for reconstruction. "The costs of rehabilitation and new construction necessary to maintain existing levels of surface on non-urban highways will exceed $700 billion during the 1980s."[15]

While making enormous investments in passenger car and truck traffic, the United States uniformly neglected modern rail technology. Meanwhile, in Western Europe (notably France, Germany and England) and in Japan the technology of high-speed railroads has been systematically put to use. At regular operating speeds above 125 miles per hour, the running costs for advanced passenger trains are projected at .47 cent (1979 values) per seat-kilometer on British Rail, compared with .74 cent for conventional high-speed trains.[16] The French high-speed train began scheduled runs on September 27, 1981, with 156 miles per hour average speed for the Paris-Lyon route. With thirty-eight such trains in frequent operation, the French railroad offers a service that is superior to car and airplane on routes of 300 miles and even longer. (The total land area required for the special rail line—about 5,700 acres—is about the same as the area of one international airport.)[17] That nothing approaching these developments can be foreseen in the United States is evident from the policies of the federal government, which, by 1981, was busily closing down many rail routes.

Since the United States is so heavily committed to the private passenger car, it makes sense to consider ways whereby energy could be saved on the streets and highways. Until very recently, there has been a major conflict between that objective and the short-run profit interest of management in the auto industry. Those firms persisted in mass-producing the gas-guzzler until foreign competitors, notably the Japanese, were moving into the U.S. market at such a rate that Detroit, the capital city of free enterprise, pleaded with the federal government to save its markets and its profits.

American scientists and engineers agree that vehicles accommodating two to five passengers can, with the "current best technology," be built to operate in the range of 58–81 miles per gallon. With new technology, requiring answers to a series of solvable engineering problems, this fuel efficiency could be raised to 82–113 miles per gallon. The technological developments that are required include smaller engines with combustion controlled by microprocessor and turbo-charged, continuously variable transmission, lighter vehicle weight and reduced aerodynamic drag.[18]

These are not "blue sky" projections. In December 1980 an experimental car built at Western Washington State College was driven 4,050 miles from Bellingham, Washington, to Washington, D.C., at an average rate of 87.5 miles per gallon of diesel fuel (fuel cost, $46.75). According to its driver, this entry in a sea-to-sea fuel-economy contest won first place because of "the car's light weight and aerodynamic design . . . one-third aluminum, which makes it lighter than most cars but very safe."[19]

The idea of an electrically powered vehicle has attracted engineers for quite some time. It could eliminate the fumes and noise of an internal-combustion engine, and its inherent simplicity of design—direct drive by electric motors—could have many advantages. But its development has been limited until now by the problem of energy storage. Lead-acid and nickel-zinc batteries can provide only a limited range (15 to 100 miles) and battery replacement costs would be relatively expensive. In 1980 a new development pointed to a possible way out of these difficulties. Gulf & Western Industries demonstrated an "electric engine" based upon a simple chemical reaction employing zinc, chlorine and water. The firm announced that the power unit for automobile use had been tested through more than 1,400 cycles of charge and discharge and was capable of driving a 3,000-pound Fuji van at 55 miles per hour for more than 150 miles on a single charge. The recharging cycle requires six to eight hours.[20]

Since at 50 mph the range of the Gulf & Western "electric engine" is somewhat more than 200 miles, it could be an attractive energy source for, say, a big-city taxi fleet. In New York City, taxis average somewhat less than 150 miles per day. (The recharge cycle could be scheduled late at night, during the hours of lowest demand on the electricity-generating system.)

In response to the ever-clearer apprehension of the earth's limited petroleum resources, some engineers have been giving attention to the technical and economic feasibility of electric-powered (battery) or hybrid (small combustion engine, generator, plus batteries) road vehicles. The prospects are increasingly promising. By 1979 the Copper Development Association fielded an electric Town car with lead-acid batteries, a specially wound electric motor and regenerative braking. The car has a range of 120 miles at a cruising speed of 40 mph and top speed in excess of 55 mph. With this range and speed such a vehicle is a fully competent short-haul vehicle and, with some development, could serve well as a big-city taxi.[21]

The technology of electric cars has been explored in a considerable literature.[22] It includes such strategies as "Biberonnage"—that is, "topping up" the batteries intermittently (as when a city bus turns around at the end of its run).[23] The prospect of electrically powered road vehicles raises the question of the relative efficiency of liquid fuels and electricity generated by power plants (which are themselves largely powered by liquid fuel). A recent study indicates that it is more efficient to obtain power for an electric vehicle from a coal-powered generator than to convert coal to liquid fuel for use in a conventional engine.[24] Clearly, the options for road vehicles extend far beyond the capabilities of internal-combustion engines, however efficient. Thus, where considerations of quietness and absence of fumes are important, we must bear in mind that an array of practical electric-powered vehicles are now only awaiting determined sponsors.*

Finally, it is an important consideration that many measures which save energy in industrial systems and commercial and residential buildings demand substantially lower capital investments per barrel of oil equivalent saved than are required for energy production by conventional thermal and nuclear technologies.[25]

---

*As a small boy during the 1920s I watched large battery-powered trucks picking up and delivering freight for the old Railway Express Company. These trucks hummed softly as they went by, had acceptable city traffic speeds, and had a useful life on the streets of more than twenty years.

In sum, there exists a wide array of workable options that would dramatically reduce energy requirements in all major areas of the American economy and society. But no systematic advantage has been taken of these potentials, because many of them run contrary to the short-term profit and control requirements of private and state managers. Accompanying these constraints, there is, of course, the important fact that Americans have long been habituated to ways of working and living that are based on the passive consumption of very cheap and, it would seem, practically unlimited energy.

As with energy consumption, energy production offers an array of technology options that can be defined and differentiated in terms of renewable versus nonrenewable resources, of decentralized versus centralized organization, of methods that fit into the technologies and distribution systems of present firms as against those that require major innovations. Cutting across all these considerations there is a value choice that was once elegantly formulated by President Eisenhower in his farewell address. Calling attention at one point to problems of "balance" among alternative policy options, he said: "As we peer into society's future, we—you and I, and our government—must avoid the impulse to live only for today, plundering for our own ease and convenience the precious resources of tomorrow. . . ."[26]

Once the main bases of choice and their effects have been identified and explained, anyone interested in the matter can form intelligent opinions about the technology options for generating energy. The National Research Council's study *Energy Choices in a Democratic Society* (1980) would be more aptly titled Energy Choices *for* a Democratic Society. The analyses of that report make a close connection between values and technological preferences by assessing the consequences of particular technologies according to criteria just outlined. Since the United States consumes two to three times as much energy per capita as do other technically sophisticated countries, it is obvious that methods of energy conservation are one of the strategic options, for energy conserved can also be viewed as additional energy generated. The NRC report is sharply detailed in these respects.[27]

Also, the Joint Economic Committee of the U.S. Congress has done a considerable public service by preparing a report on the technical and economic characteristics of the main energy sources.[28]

Recent government preferences have been for nuclear (including breeder) energy and synthetic fuels. These are choices that would continue the "plundering." They include, in the case of synthetic fuels, conversion of coal and oil shale to petroleum products. An investment of $88 billion was committed for this purpose under President Carter, with the federal government taking the lead in research and development, in direct commitment of capital and by encouraging private investments through various forms of capital and loan guarantees. But, as the technical assessments in the Joint Economic Committee report indicate, implementing these technology options would incur very high risks, since "the high-quality U.S. oil shales are located in semi-arid, pristine regions of the country. A large-scale industry, i.e., one producing roughly 100,000 to 200,000 barrels per day, might adversely affect human health and safety, fauna and flora, grazing and agricultural activities and water and air quality."[29]

While the oil shale resources of the United States are indeed large, estimated to contain more than 730 billion barrels of oil equivalent, the extraction of the fuel would draw substantial quantities of water from the Colorado River, a prime water source in a semi-arid region. Furthermore, the process that extracts oil from shale would leave a residue of waste material of literally mountainous proportions.

By way of contrast, it is instructive to read the Joint Committee's detailed assessment of a whole array of renewable energy sources. Photovoltaic energy conversion is almost at the point of general economic feasibility. (Solar cells in sealed panels make a direct conversion of the energy received to electricity.) The state of the art is such that by 1986 photovoltaic systems produced in the United States should be able to generate electricity at 6 to 12 cents per kilowatt-hour. And a sustained drive to reduce costs in the years after 1990 should bring those figures down to 4 to 9 cents per kilowatt-hour.[30] Solar heating and cooling has become cost-effective for many applications and will become more so when the development of the technologies is seriously pursued.[31]

Energy from municipal solid wastes entails a series of technologically feasible processes that can be combined to produce large quantities of low-sulphur fuel, permit the recovery of ferrous and non-ferrous materials, and reduce the land requirement for waste disposal.[32]

The large-scale production of ethyl alcohol (ethanol) from agricultural by-products, including wood, is within technical and economic reach. The same is true for the production of methyl alcohol (methanol), for which there is the serious prospect of utilizing wood and urban wastes as raw material. Either methanol or ethanol can be combined (10 percent) with gasoline to make gasohol, a useful internal-combustion engine fuel.[33]

Low-head hydropower, sometimes called small hydropower, is another substantial energy resource that awaits extensive development in the United States. Virtually no new technology is required here; it is a question merely of selecting and organizing the productive tasks of design, installation and operation for small hydro facilities. These often have the advantage of being able to run almost unattended. The U.S. Army's engineers have identified 5,424 existing dams, some of which are generating power, that could be rebuilt to produce more power. The full exploitation of this incremental potential would yield annual energy generation exceeding 223 billion kilowatt-hours, at an estimated savings in oil consumption of about 1 million barrels per day.[34]

Ocean thermal energy conversion (OTEC) takes advantage of temperature differences between the surface and the depths of the sea. In this process a "working fluid" like a Freon-type refrigerant is put through a closed cycle of condensation (by cooling) and vaporization (by warming). Then the expanded vapor is cooled by the cold sea water that is drawn from the ocean depths, and thereby recondensed to a liquid form. The condensed refrigerant is warmed once again with warm sea water that is drawn from the ocean surface. The refrigerant expands, vaporizes, and the resulting pressure drives the turbine. As this cycle proceeds continuously, the turbine drives a generator to produce electricity.

Research on ocean thermal energy conversion is at the pilot plant stage in the United States, where this work has been sponsored by the Energy Research and Development Administration of the federal government. In Europe a consortium of industrial firms is pursuing development work and the operation of pilot plants. This technology is being brought to operating plant scale in Japan. "Since OTEC plants do not require fuel for plant operation, a major cost component is for amortization of the capital investment . . . estimated cost ranges are comparable to costs projected for other . . . [fossil fuel power] . . . sources in the [U.S.] Gulf Coast electrical market for the years 1990 to 2000." Assuming a modest pace of development and application of this technology in the United States, then by the year 2000 OTEC plants could produce electricity that would otherwise require about 2.7 million barrels of oil per day. With accelerated development this technology could save the U.S. economy up to 11 million barrels per day of imported oil by the year 2000.[35]

These assessments of the technical and economic feasibility of renewable energy resources are confirmed in practice. A division of the Westinghouse Electric Corporation has joined with two California utilities to launch a project aimed at full-scale solar-cell production by about 1986, "using a new low-cost technology developed by Westinghouse for making Silicon material."[36] Enterprising individuals and small firms have been seeking out hydropower sites for rebuilding. "In New York State a state inventory [1979] showed that there were about 300 possible sites for development that could produce as much as 725 megawatts of power if they were brought into production by 1995."[37]

At Petersburg, Virginia, a $160 million plant is being constructed to manufacture ethyl alcohol from "municipal garbage and from agricultural, industrial and forest wastes, using a process developed by the Gulf Oil Chemical Company and the University of Arkansas Biomass Research Center. The plant is expected to produce 50 million gallons of ethanol a year for sale as a gasohol ingredient."[38]

Large-capacity windmills can now be constructed economically and operated to feed power on a substantial scale into existing public utility systems. A Burlington, Massachusetts, firm, U.S. Windpower Inc., is installing twenty windmills on Crotched Mountain, New Hampshire. The power so generated is to be sold under a twenty-year contract to the Public Service Company of New Hampshire. The same firm proposes to start similar windmill farms in California, Oregon and Washington. In San Francisco, Wind Farms Limited is drawing plans for a set of windmills to be erected in Hawaii, the power to be sold to the Hawaiian Electric Company.[39]

Pessimistic analyses of the economics of nuclear power parallel a worldwide falling off of orders for new nuclear power stations caused by the steep, unpredicted increase in the cost of electricity from that source. By 1978 nuclear power in the United States was on average about 7 percent more expensive than coal power. (Only in France and the U.S.S.R., "where bureaucratic power outweighs economic realities," is nuclear power investment being strongly pursued.[40] The strategic situation for energy is that the economics of renewable sources are becoming increasingly attractive. Dr. David R. Inglis, professor emeritus of physics at the University of Massachusetts, has diagnosed the technology and economics of wind power and judges that by 1979 it had become a competent, money-saving alternative to much of the contemplated increase in nuclear power. Inglis believes that "wind power is . . . technically and economically ready to go in a big way now, lacking only decision and financial backing to initiate the needed engineering and industrial effort."[41]

In short, there is now a considerable choice of technical approaches to energy generation from renewable sources. The decision to take advantage of them is clearly a political one, controlled by whether the state managers and citizenry wish to continue "plundering" or to start taking responsibility for community well-being in the days after tomorrow.

By way of further defining how technology is shaped by economic criteria, one may profitably compare the experience of the automobile industry in the United States with technological options that were forgone in design of products and methods of production. Under any circumstances, the mass dependence on automobiles, any kind of automobile, would inevitably have had profound effects on the distribution of population and the associated suburban life-style; these effects would have occurred had motor vehicles been large or small, expensive or inexpensive, energy-efficient or -inefficient, safe or unsafe. However, highways, suburbia and the motor vehicles themselves have in fact been associated with a host of socially destructive consequences that were by no means inevitable. These include unsafe vehicles and highways; grossly expensive, inefficient and air-polluting vehicles; suburban configurations that are unreachable and unusable without the automobile; and the concomitant withdrawal of public capital from metropolitan centers. None of these results sprang inevitably from machine technology. All were conferred upon us by the economic decision-makers who determined, in each instance, which technology was most serviceable to their business advantage.[42]

Throughout its history as a mass-produced product, the design and hence the operating characteristics of the U.S. automobile have been imposed by the requirements of the directing managements of the major auto firms. These managements have sought to maximize the extension of their decision power as gauged by criteria of profit, capital investment, market share and control over workers. However, the strategies used toward these ends have varied, and the changes have been reflected in the technologies of the auto product and of the industry as a production system as well.

In the industry dominated by the Ford Motor Company until the Great Depression, the mass-produced passenger car was simplified, standardized, functional. By the end of World War II, the industry leader was General Motors, whose business strategy, unlike that of early Ford, favored a product technology of growing ornateness, a price-graded product line, and annual model changes that stressed numerous cosmetic alterations and dysfunctional innovations. Product standardization was deemphasized in favor of production variation both in single years and over time. The idea of simplification was almost abandoned. During the period from 1919 to 1929, the average price of a U.S.-produced car actually fell from $830 to $630. From 1949 to 1980, the average price rose from $1,300 to $4,000.[43]

In no sense do these changes in product (and prices) reflect the innate direction and momentum of a technology. All the innovations of auto design were imposed by elaborately developed management strategies. Tail fins, glittering trim, horsepower far beyond what could be used on any public road, failure-prone mechanisms, and quality control at a level to ensure limited component and vehicle life—all these were ordered as part of a top management strategy for profits and expansion of decision power. A special kind of naiveté is required to accept the explanation for tail fins once offered me by a former president of a major auto firm: The consumer, he said, wanted them.

By 1973, one of the Big Three had forty-three models in its "low-cost" line. The cost of auto transportation was raised by the proliferation of body types, engines, transmissions and seat controls; the multiplicity of "options" produced a situation in which a major auto assembly plant could complete a year of work without once building two identical cars. This kind of diversity wiped out the advantages of relatively low-cost quantity production and stable design that earlier had been the trademark of the U.S. auto industry. Instead, vehicle economy gave way to higher price tags and expensive maintenance. Safety considerations that would reduce highway deaths by at least half were forgone. Fuel economy was sacrificed for ever-higher horsepower. Passenger comfort in the form of seating, head room and leg room was sacrificed to the "long, low look."

If product technology had been operating according to a direction and momentum of its own, it is unlikely that product design would have taken on precisely the characteristics that served a particular business strategy rather than the vehicle user. There is no escaping the fact that product technology was selected, managed, ordered. The choices were made (and avoided) according to the criteria of industrial managers and their engineer surrogates. By 1979, 120 million passenger cars were on the road, and 84 percent of U.S. families depended on them. They obtained transportation at an average out-of-pocket operating cost of 24 cents per mile, annual vehicle costs of about $2,400 and a yearly toll of 51,000 highway deaths and 5,681,000 persons injured.[44] The medical and environmental tolls of auto air pollution are unknown, but they are large. All these expenses could have been substantially reduced if the vehicles had been designed by engineers whose work assignments specified cheaper, safer, and less polluting passenger cars. Change the criteria for automobile performance, and you will transform the familiar motor car.

In September 1973, the Porsche management in Germany displayed a prototype of a passenger car designed to last twenty years and run 180,000 miles. The car would cost about 30 percent more at the outset, but over the twenty-year period would accumulate a reduction of 15 percent in full operating expenses. One of the engineers who developed this design stated that it was not based on exotic technology. "The components are either available or manufacturers will have them ready in the next several years." The car body would be aluminum, stainless steel, or recyclable plastic. Larger-than-normal components of many sorts would be used, and the engine would be a modest 75 horsepower, with sophisticated mechanical and electrical features.[45]

Obviously, the production of such a vehicle runs contrary to the U.S. auto industry's long-sustained product and marketing strategy. But it reflects what is technologically feasible if public opinion decides to set limits on the inefficiency of present motor cars. Engineering literature includes an immense number of partial and full designs for motor vehicles that differ dramatically from the conventional products. And, as the Porsche prototype shows, it is management decision and not technological inevitability that determines design.

Thus, several lines of evidence point to the conclusion that auto products have no autonomous genesis or mode of development. Designs that do not advance management policies drop into the limbo of office files, Patent Office drawings, engineering society papers, or science and industry museums. Similar pressures leave their marks on the auto industry's production technologies.

The belief that technology determines its own characteristics includes the assumption that dehumanized and alienating conditions of work are intrinsic to the use of production machinery. Such jobs, it is assumed, are by their nature boring, dirty and dangerous, and cannot fail to turn human beings into appendages of machines. Certainly, existing conditions of work in the U.S. auto industry are consistent with that belief. But are these conditions the inevitable results of automotive production technology? Or, are they perhaps heavily dependent on the choices of economic decision-makers, in which case they might be altered by adopting other criteria and ways of decision-making?

Managements that have long viewed the industrial worker as a replaceable, animated, special-purpose machine have given little, if any, thought to the impact of the physical conditions of the workplace on the men and women employed there. As a result, the environment is often dangerous, or noisy, or dirty, or poorly ventilated, too hot or too cold, or some combination of these. Long exposure to such conditions is bound to have a negative effect on the workers involved, especially when executives may inhabit modern, air-conditioned offices. The production worker may spend the day in a place where, in order to speak to someone during working time, you must shout at the top of your voice, or where you end each day covered with grime.

When external pressures, such as liability for disabilities, compel managers to order the reduction of noise in a factory, for example, ways are quickly found to address the problem. True, there are limits to what is possible in particular places. An iron foundry is certain to be dirty because of the constant handling of large quantities of fine sand. Areas around large presses are bound to be filled with noise and vibration. Batteries of automatic lathes can produce a fearful din. Even after considerable effort, a large amount of residual dirt, vibration and noise is sure to remain in such work areas. Earning one's living there will never be like working in a library or greenhouse.

Nevertheless, much could be done to reduce the monotony of many industrial jobs by redesigning them and, finally, by mechanizing tedious work that need not be done manually. In the auto industry there would also be an economic advantage to mechanizing such jobs, if the mania for annual model changes and meaningless product variety were diminished, thereby increasing the annual demand for many components that could be standardized over several years.

An American visitor to the Saab-Scandia auto factories in Sweden has commented on their four-year attempt to organize automobile assembly work on a small-team basis. Engines, for example, are assembled by three workers acting as a group. He further found that "the noise level of the machinery was far below the decibel level of comparable American machines . . . in contrast to the noisy and dirty conditions of comparable American plants, one could not help but be astonished."[46]

For convenience, the production technology of the auto industry is usually considered in two parts: the physical means of production, and the techniques for organizing and integrating the host of production operations. In fact, these two aspects are intertwined and are separable only analytically.

The industrial manager who is assigned a particular piece of work usually has available to him many alternative tools, devices, and machines capable of accomplishing the task. The richness of choice stems from the accumulated body of science, invention and pragmatic experience.

Consider a very simple task, such as making a hole of specified diameter and position in a one-inch thickness of wood. There is a great array of methods. You can start with a simple instrument such as a knife or chisel, advance to hand drill with exchangeable bits, and move on to the same drill powered by a motor. Furthermore, the device can be held in place on a table or mounted on the floor. The refinements extend to a device that automatically will put the workpiece in place, perform the drilling operation, measure it for an acceptable tolerance, and remove the work to a stack of finished parts.

To be sure, industrial managers and engineers often wish to accomplish a given task in a new manner—for example, by machine instead of human labor. Checking the dimensions of a particular item has long been a manual task, but available knowledge and prior technology open the way to turning this kind of inspection over to a machine. Thus new types of equipment are installed to measure the dimensions of a work in progress and reject those examples that do not conform. The development of new technology for production work enlarges the array of equipment options available for particular tasks. For engineers and managers the typical problem is: Which of the options is most suitable for the job in hand?

This answer is ordinarily found by applying a particular criterion to the range of alternatives, and the criterion most often preferred by cost-minimizing managers is an estimate of the cost of doing the work with any particular machine. In such estimates, two factors have tended to weigh most heavily in mechanical manufacturing operations: the price of the machine and the cost of labor per hour to the management. (In the chemical process industries, including steam-electric power plants, it is the ratio of raw materials to machinery costs.) One can usually rank the alternatives available for the job according to the mix of labor and machinery costs involved—that is, from those using most labor and least machine cost per unit of work to those involving least labor and most machine cost. For a given quantity of work, the method promising the least combined cost will be determined by the prevailing costs of labor and machinery.

During most of the twentieth century a regular pattern of labor and machinery costs developed in the United States. Wages have tended to rise, on the average, more rapidly than the price of machinery. As a result, cost-minimizing managers have favored an ever more intense mechanization of work.[47] Average growth in output per worker man-hour has been the direct result of this process. Indeed, this criterion has been cited to account for the considerable variation in labor productivity from one country to another.

If it were true that technology has a direction and momentum of its own, then it might be expected that the same sort of production methods and equipment would be used throughout the world. After all, the market for production machinery has long been an international one, training in the sciences is similar in every land, and the literature of engineering (except for the secret military type) is universally available. Actually, the methods of mechanical manufacture have varied considerably among economies, and for reasons that are not at all mysterious.

The Ford Motor Company is one of many corporations that owns and operates factories in different countries. During the 1950s I examined aspects of production operations in the Ford factories in Detroit, Michigan, and Dagenham, England.[48] The differences between the two were striking. The Detroit factories were using much more power equipment per worker. The plants at Dagenham, outside London, produced similar products but the work methods required much more muscle power, and more reliance on human sensory-motor capability. In short, the Detroit facilities were much more highly mechanized than those in England. The similarities in the two countries included the same kind of product, the same company, the same underlying scientific knowledge, the same size staffs of engineers and ample access to technological knowledge, the same availability of sufficient capital for designing and operating production facilities.

The differences in degree of mechanization could be accounted for by an accompanying variation in the relative cost of labor to machinery. Thus, in 1950 in the United States it was possible for an employer to buy 157 kilowatt-hours of electricity for what it would cost him to to hire a worker for one hour. In England, the price for a man-hour of work would purchase only 37 kilowatt-hours. Hence, employers interested in minimizing the total cost of particular work were required to buy more electricity and fewer man-hours in Detroit and more man-hours and less electricity in Dagenham.[49] Similar contrasts showed up in the ratio of labor to machine-hour costs.

Making the usual calculations of business cost, Ford managers and their counterparts in other firms made essentially the same decision: less mechanization in England than in Detroit. There is no evidence that production methods technology has a life of its own. No theories of self-actuated machine processes need to be invoked to account for the variation in the means of production, either in one country over time or among countries at a single time. The actual patterns of technological choice lend themselves to fairly straightforward explanation. Industrial managers and their engineer surrogates selected (or developed) those means of production that best satisfied the capitalist economic criteria for the operation of their enterprises. Similar considerations apply to the other major part of production technology—the organization and integration of production work.

A division of labor is inevitable in automobile production, it being inconceivable that one person could fabricate and assemble all the materials and functional components of a motor vehicle. However, there are many possible ways to accomplish the division, with respect both to organizing and integrating the specialized work and to the decision processes needed therefor. One must first put aside the assumption that the division of labor and the accompanying decision processes that have been characteristic of the auto industry are in some way integral to and essential for the employment of any kind of machine technology.

The main elements of division of labor are, for each person, the task to be performed, the physical means to be used, the variability that the task permits, the frequency of performance, and the ways whereby the work of each person is linked to the work of others. In the auto industry (as in mechanical manufacturing generally), the prevailing pattern for division of labor has evolved along three lines: greater simplification, which has meant ever smaller tasks and more finely delimited methods; more detailed specification, which has reduced variability; maximum removal from the worker of responsibility and the authority to integrate his task with that of others. Terms such as "mass production" and "assembly line" have become generalized descriptions of this set of conditions.

The division of labor technology that was chosen for the U.S. auto industries, and which has operated there for many years, was particularly well suited to the objectives of the managers who directed industrial operations. Thus, the microdivision of unchanging work tasks first instituted by Henry Ford lowered production costs by raising the productivity of both capital and labor. More than that, Ford could hire and quickly train workers who were almost entirely without prior industrial experience. A new occupational category was invented: semi-skilled. By using these rigorously controlled workers of limited skill to build its cars, Ford broke the decision power of craft workers and craft unions in the industry. Management reigned supreme and unchallenged (until the CIO organizing movement of the 1930s) in its control of the growing industry, while being hailed as an industrial benefactor for paying the highest industrial wages and mass-producing the cars that transformed the style of American life.

The auto industry's managers were able for many years to draw upon a large, new and industrially inexperienced labor force from the rural states, North and South. As its workers increasingly come from a better educated population, it is more than likely that the managers will be confronted by increased opposition to their ingrained pattern of work simplification, plus mechanization, plus work intensification, plus work discipline policed by an ever-growing supervisory staff. New forms and higher intensities of worker resistance to these conditions manifested themselves in the General Motors factories in Lordstown, Ohio, where in 1972 a young, well-educated work force rebelled against the managers of a much-heralded showplace factory.

So common have work simplification and allied practices become in industry, and so dominant in the literature of industrial engineering, that they are generally assumed to be inevitable. But the progressive restriction of work tasks (work simplification) and the repetition of identical movements are only two of many possible ways to divide work. The jobs can be varied in content, and workers shifted among diverse tasks. Particular tasks can be designed for performance by single workers or by small or large groups. Work methods can allow for variations in the techniques employed. Workers can themselves decide how to integrate their tasks, and that can include varying the assignments.

Work simplification and task repetition have been the strategies preferred by auto industry managers bent on achieving low production costs and maximum control over workers. But there is no evidence that a technological imperative has dictated these choices in division of labor.

Nor is there any assurance that industrial productivity has been maximized by management-controlled work simplification strategies. Little study has been made of alternative ways to divide labor and decision-making within the constraints of given intensities of mechanization.

The prevailing methods of industrial decision-making in the auto industry have stifled in the work force any sense of pride in the product and alienated the workers from management and the workplace. "Pride?" said one auto worker. "Nobody's proud of anything anymore. It's a job they come to because no one else will pay them more money." And further: "I think all blue-collar workers are taken for granted. I think deep down, most workers want to do a good job and take pride in their work, and if they're taken for granted this hurts them. If a car is built good, it's 'GM this and GM that' but if something goes wrong it's always the fault of the workers."[50] One by-product of such management policy is the creation of skill shortages as workers respond with a reluctance to invest time in lengthy training.

Employees report that "General Motors expects two things of a worker: come to work and do what you are told. There is no sense of teamwork or working together to solve common problems. . . . Even now we are not being asked to make sacrifices. We are being told that if we don't, our jobs will be shipped overseas."[51] Independent observers report that under the direction of managements dedicated to profits and power, "workers are frequently slapped down for offering suggestions on improving production . . . [and] . . . auto plant foremen . . . [made] . . . it clear that the foreman's job was to think, the worker's to do what he was told."[52] Spurred by a similar eagerness for profits and power, a team of management consultants, commenting on the Ford Motor Company's 1982 union contract, deplored the "two-year moratorium on closing expensive plants that otherwise would have been shut because components they produce could be more cheaply obtained from other companies or countries." In their view, neither Ford nor the buying public gained anything from this reprieve; the only beneficiary was the United Automobile Workers. The consultants concluded that "the result, unfortunately, appears likely to be further insulation of our auto industry from the advantages it belatedly gained from its purchasing and manufacturing worldwide."[53] In their usage, of course, "our auto industry" means the top managers of the leading firms. (I will discuss alternatives to such policies in Chapter 14.)

According to the technology determinists, worker dissatisfaction derives from the mass-production process. The thrust of the present analysis is to distinguish between the methods of production and the decision processes that govern how they are organized and used. Evidence from communities and industrial situations where workers have a substantial voice in industrial decisions indicates that alienation does not arise from the use of powered equipment in mass production or from a division of labor. Rather, it is traceable to the workers' lack of decision power over their work.

There is nothing intrinsic to industrial products or production processes that vests decision-making over production in the managerial occupations. The idea that there are many ways to divide and organize work permeates a growing literature that seeks to open new options for work in America.[54] An increasing number of industrial consultants have been considering the feasibility and effects of widening and varying work tasks (job enrichment), and of granting workers mutual and democratic control over their own work rather than handing down such decisions through authoritarian managerial hierarchies.

During the 1950s, I examined and reported in some detail on the internal decision-making processes of workers and managers in the factories of the Standard Motor Company in Coventry, England. The company employed thousands of workers and mass-produced passenger cars and tractors. An innovative top management and the local unions agreed upon a "gang system" of production organization, under which responsibility for output was vested in a worker group rather than the individual employee, and workers' earnings varied with the group's output. Under this gang system, the size of particular work tasks was regulated by the given worker group. Management was usually willing to accept the recommendations of workers for modifications of tooling, since the easing and the mechanization of work contributed to higher labor and capital productivity. Management substantially reduced its supervision over the workers; in fact, these factories operated without supervisory foremen.

All these arrangements existed within a framework of an agreed "price" per tractor or per car produced, expressed in the number of man-hours worked in the factory per vehicle completed. Hence, if at the end of the week the output was, say, 50 percent greater than would have been achieved according to the agreed-upon labor time per unit, a wage bonus of 50 percent was paid to all workers and other employees in the bargaining unit. These conditions gave the workers not only high pay but also a substantial voice in the detailed allocation and conduct of their work. Management agreed to this development in return for the high productivity of labor and capital and the lowered administrative costs that accompanied the gang system of production organization.[55]

The successful operation of Standard's factories under these conditions casts doubt on the assumption that work simplification enforced by authoritarian managerial control is a necessary condition for the quantity production of motor vehicles.* More recently, the Swedish Volvo and Saab companies have organized parts of the vehicle-assembly operations on a group responsibility basis, instead of relying on the traditional management-enforced, simplified, repetitive jobs performed along an assembly line.

There is evidence that industrial enterprises do not require a formal separation between final authority over the enterprise and the performance of production work. The evolving industrial development in Israeli kibbutzim represents more than 200 factories in which control over the division of labor and the ways of integrating it is vested finally in the industrial workers themselves. Furthermore, an investigation of the relative efficiency of these enterprises has shown that in terms of productivity of labor and capital, they are as good as or better than conventional managerial enterprises.[56]

This experience from larger and smaller industrial enterprises runs counter to the entrenched belief that mechanized work can be performed only

---

*After several years of operation, with results as summarized, there was a policy split within the top management of this firm. One group, which finally won, rejected this style of operation as leading to a diminution in managerial decision power. This is recounted in chapter 15 of *Decision-Making and Productivity,* op. cit.

under conditions of job simplification, or that a division of labor can be organized and integrated only by managerial controllers.

I have tried to respond to the mystique of technology which holds not only that society is powerfully affected by technology but also that man and society have become the creatures of the autonomously determined machine. Fortunately, the reality is that our machines can be given varying characteristics by our machine designers and builders.[57] Technology, within the limits set by nature, is man-made and hence variable on order. If one wants to alter prevailing technologies, then the place to look is not to molecular structure but to social structure, not to the chemistry of materials but to the rules of man, especially the economic rules of those who decide on technology.

7

Evolving Criteria for Technology of Production

There was a time when it was unthinkable for managers in industry to suppose that they could make money without making goods—that profits could, on a continuing basis, emerge from a system that gave progressively less attention to production. The idea of production as the source of wealth was embedded in the theories of economists and in the organization and teaching of the engineering and the industrial management professions.

Both Adam Smith and Karl Marx pay substantial attention to factory organization, division of labor and the role these play in the choice and use of technology. In Smith's view, the businessman receives for his organization of production a just reward that is determined by the final valuation of the product he sells. Marx emphasized the surplus value that the businessman extracts from his workers by paying them rather less than what he receives in the marketplace. There was, however, a common ground to these divergent analyses: profit was linked to production.

As businessmen became more sophisticated in making money from production, they demanded systematic methods for selecting from among alternative technologies for production and for the computation of cost advantage. This gave rise to two new disciplines—engineering economy and industrial engineering. Engineering economy was developed to work out ways of computing costs of industrial operations and of comparing the costs of alternative production technologies.[1] During the 1920s the engineering schools of American universities began to establish curricula in industrial engineering, courses that offered techniques for organizing all the factors of production into coherent work systems, with special attention being paid to economic selection from among alternative technologies.

Industrial engineering, the twentieth-century technology of production, includes several subfields. The earliest attempt by management's engineers to relate human beings to their work (man-machine systems) was through "time and motion study." Motion study specified manual-manipulative acts, and their sequence, to be performed by the worker. Time study set speeds for the performance of work tasks.[2] These technologies are essentially management control techniques over the industrial work force. Their applications and results have been the focus of dispute and struggle without end between managers and workers. For the standards of work performance were never independent of management's own values and preferences.

After World War II, a new technology was introduced for the design of the man-machine connection. During the war, practitioners of applied psychology had discovered how to design tools, machine controls, data displays, etc., taking into account the sensory and the motor capabilities of human beings. Thereby the technology of human engineering (a.k.a. ergonomics, biomechanics) was swiftly elaborated. "Human factors" laboratories became standard equipment in engineering schools. The new knowledge was increasingly adopted by the designers of tools and machines of many classes.[3]

Fresh research on job characteristics and job design, notably by Professor Robert A. Karasek, Jr., has provided new insights into the design of single work tasks and the organization of industrial production. Karasek has found that when low decision latitude and heavy job demand are combined, the common result is mental strain and an unusually high incidence of stress-related illnesses, including coronary heart disease. Karasek's studies of occupations classified with respect to low and high job demands and low and high job discretion show consistent patterns of psychological and physical effects. His data are drawn from various countries and occupation mixes.[4] These researches produce a major revision of the conventional wisdom stemming from Frederick Taylor: that the largest number of blue-collar workers could not conceivably attain either educational levels, or skill levels, or judgmental sophistication "sufficient to justify significant judgment authority over work task organization and coordination."[5] Karasek calls attention to the dramatic change in the level of formal training of the American industrial work force since Taylor's era. The portion of the work force who had completed high school in 1890 was 3.5 percent; it was 60 percent in 1970. Therefore, late-twentieth-century industrial job design according to the prescriptions of Frederick Taylor results in underutilization of the industrial work force—as when job designs are deliberately "simplified" in order to deskill industrial workers and thus justify wage reductions.

This recent knowledge on alternative work designs and their physical and social effects opens new perspectives for the relation of physical work design, decision-making and productivity. Work tasks and work organization can now be planned to enhance the working experience: a transformation of the factory from a place of drudgery to be endured for the sake of livelihood, to one whose material and social features are devised to elicit the best human capacities in physical tasks and in their shared control.

During the long expansion of American manufacturing industry, which began with the end of the Civil War in 1865, the dominant impulse for designing a new technology and the first criterion for selecting from among available technologies was the minimizing of production costs. Indeed, among industrial managers in western capitalism, cost minimization was generally accepted as the test of efficiency in production. As long as this was the primary goal, engineers were the industrial elite, not only as designers and organizers of production operations, but also as the pool of talent from which general managers were to be drawn.

Under cost-minimizing, alternatives for production, involving choice of design, organization and operation, are major concerns of management. In these operations the major costs of production—and also those most immediately subject to management choice in mechanical manufacturing—were incurred for labor and for machinery. (Costs of machinery, and materials or fuel, have been the main expense in the chemical industries.)

When the managers and engineers of a large industrial system try to minimize their production costs at the same time, an important change occurs in the relation between the wages of labor and the prices of machinery. Wages tend to rise in response to a combination of bargaining and market forces. At the same time, however, machinery prices increase either not at all or less rapidly than wages. At first blush this may seem mysterious, since one must assume that all production is ultimately the result of someone's work. Why, then, do the prices of labor's products lag behind labor's wages?

Under cost-minimizing, the managers and engineers of the firms that produce machinery are also trying to contain their costs of production. So when one of their important input costs—like labor or raw materials—rises sharply, the heads of those enterprises seek ways to offset the increase, thus keeping their machinery products competitive with or more competitive than, those of their rivals.

For this purpose the product may be partly redesigned, changes being made in the materials used. More important, changes are considered not only in the organization of work for turning out the product but also in the tools and machines that are used to make the machines.

Engineers then examine the varieties of equipment available to perform necessary operations. In every case they find that the possibilities can be ranked according to the degree of mechanization, which in turn varies directly with the price of the equipment. Typically, the more mechanized and the more expensive the equipment, the more work it can turn out in a given amount of labor time and machine time. So higher productivity of labor is gained by greater mechanization and larger capital costs. The task of the engineer then is to calculate for each production alternative the cost per unit of work done. For the more expensive, higher-capacity equipment, a low rate of utilization means that the fixed charges of the machine must be divided among fewer units, resulting in a high cost per unit. For this same class of equipment the unit cost drops rapidly as the equipment is used more intensively. Thus the relation of cost to quantity for alternative methods can be compared.

The crucial result of such calculations is that, as the price of labor rises more rapidly than the price of machinery, the cost-minimizing industrial manager is impelled to invest more money in machinery-intensive compensation for higher wages per hour. And that is what industrial managers in the United States and in other industrial economies have done while operating under the imperative of cost-minimizing. The result has been a sustained preference for the more mechanized, more capital-requiring and higher-productivity technologies among the alternatives at hand.

In the machine tool industry of the United States from 1939 to 1947 prices of machines rose, on the average, 39 percent, while average hourly earnings of industrial workers in manufacturing grew 95 percent. That spread of almost 2.5 : 1 was a powerful inducement for investing more heavily in more mechanized industrial equipment.[6] This relationship between wages and machinery prices obtained in U.S. industry for a century after the Civil War.

Then, by the middle of the 1960s, an essential feature of this pattern of industrial operations was short-circuited. Many machinery-producing firms, as in the machine tool industry, had been giving increased attention to the requirements of the state managers and their military-space enterprises. When they sought to serve this market, they confronted buyers for whom price was not a major consideration. Soon thereafter, the cost-minimizing edge became dulled in the machinery-producing industries of the United States.[7]

Prices of many machines rose at least as rapidly as wages of labor. Accordingly, the managers of many industrial firms could no longer apply the cost-offsetting-through-mechanization remedies that they had relied upon during the previous era. The new system was called "cost pass-along." Instead of vigorously combating cost increases, managers simply passed them along in higher prices, thereby enlarging the baseline for profit markups. And they also evaded the hard work and unforeseen problems that necessarily accompany sustained efforts to minimize cost through changes in product designs, production methods, etc. Furthermore, since passing costs along soon became general practice among the managements of industries, the penalties of being noncompetitive did not arise.[8]

A few industries and products did retain the pattern of cost-minimizing after this date. Two striking examples are the industries manufacturing computers and small, hand-held calculators. Indeed, hand-held calculators (main U.S. firms: Texas Instruments, Hewlett-Packard) became markedly less expensive as technical refinements, simplification of design, and mass production were applied to their manufacture.

In addition to cost-minimizing and cost pass-along, a third rule for selecting technology, cost-maximizing, appeared in U.S. industry during the 1950s and has become the dominant criterion among the 37,000 prime contractors and the 100,000 subcontractors that now serve the U.S. government's military-space enterprises.[9]

Cost-maximizing does not mean cost increase without limit. Rather, it means sustained cost increase within the limit set by the size of government subsidy. As machinery-producing industries adopted the process, the prices of what they offered for sale raised no problem for the subsidized military buyers, but were often out of reach for the largest number of civilian-product firms.

When machinery-producing firms operate by cost-maximizing rules, their prices rise more rapidly than the wages of labor. Thus, when the Pentagon and NASA specified that machinery be given "maximum control capability," the important class of numerically controlled machine tools ceased to be attractive to most of the metalworking firms in the United States.

During the 1970s, as I noted in the Prologue, machine tool prices in the United States rose 85 percent, and average hourly earnings of industrial workers grew only 72 percent. The cost incentive to further mechanization disappeared. At this writing, the boundaries of cost-maximizing have yet to be drawn in the economy of the United States. It is significant that the practices established in the Department of Defense have been recommended by successive presidents as models to be applied in other government agencies.[10]

The diagnosis of these divergent criteria is no mere academic-intellectual exercise, for their application significantly affects both the design of machinery products and the operating characteristics of entire production systems.

Machinery of widely differing characteristics can be designed to perform a given task. When tools or machines are desired to ease the burden and reduce the errors of a human operator, the designer must bring to bear knowledge of the sensory-motor capabilities of human beings as studied in the discipline called human factors engineering. The resulting equipment can be operated with less human fatigue, greater reliability and fewer accidents than are to be expected from equipment designed without consideration of these criteria.

Machines of the same general type or function can have quite different operating characteristics and costs, depending on the specific criteria they are meant to satisfy. The helicopter, for example, has been designed according to different specifications to perform different tasks: taking soldiers and munitions into battle, and transporting business executives in comfort. The Sikorsky Division of United Technologies Corporation in 1978 started production for the U.S. Army of 1,107 units of its UH-60 helicopter. At the same time, the firm was manufacturing the S-76 helicopter for commercial sale. Both helicopters would carry a crew of two and similar passenger loads, eleven soldiers in the UH-60, twelve persons in the S-76.

The machines for the military had to transport, in addition to crew and fully equipped soldiers, assorted gear and munitions. It had to fly for at least 2.3 hours at an airspeed of 245 knots. Its key features included an 8,000-pound payload and weight (with payload) of about 16,500 pounds; a structure that could take dense loading (as for cases of munitions); an 8,000-pound capacity hoisting winch; capability for evasive aerobatics to avoid enemy fire; 4,000-foot normal altitude; minimum flight instrumentation; and, finally, easy disassembly for transport in military freight planes.

In contrast, the S-76 had to provide a spacious, airy, colorful, comfortable environment for executive travel. It had to be capable of stable flight for a range of 400 nautical miles, with reserve fuel, at altitudes of 1,000 feet. Its full weight (with payload, including fuel) was 11,549 pounds, with useful load (passenger) weight of 2,900 pounds. This helicopter needed full flight instrumentation according to Federal Aviation Administration regulations. The commercial craft was designed to function at minimum cost per passenger-mile within constraints of desired speed, range, comfort and safety. As of 1978, at a price of approximately $1 million, this craft was being sold competitively in fourteen countries. About 100 per year were being produced in anticipation of sustained marketing campaigns, mainly to corporation buyers.

The UH-60, of which 1,107 were sold before production started under contract to the U.S. Army, cost the Pentagon $2,258,000 apiece, under agreements then in force. Production and deliveries were to be for five years and beyond. No further marketing effort was required. For the military helicopter, "mission requirements drive the design," said Gerald J. Tobias, president of Sikorsky in 1978. "Only then do cost constraints operate," as lesser criteria.

While military products are the main activity at Sikorsky, a parallel organization was set up to produce the civilian craft, perhaps the first of a wider commercial series. Design for the S-76 was turned over to a separate program manager and team of 200 engineers. Tobias explained why "we put them in a separate area of Bridgeport . . . eight miles away from the Sikorsky main plant in Stratford . . . with many management and production functions for the S-76, including design, manufacturing, inspection, purchasing . . . separated out in the Bridgeport plant of Sikorsky." According to Tobias, "we wanted to engender a total commercial philosophy in design without any form of military or government design concept in the designing work. This is not to say that we do not use basic design data. We try to design to cost on the S-76 project."

Per pound of vehicle, the military UH-60 helicopter cost twice the civilian-serving S-76. That is the price of fulfilling the military's requirements, notwithstanding that the military unit will be produced in large quantity and on a stable, scheduled basis that permits many economies in production.

The differences between the military and civilian helicopters reflect characteristic variances between the engineering, production and sales problems of working for the Pentagon and in the civilian economy. The civilian vehicle's requirements are met within the all-important context of minimizing cost and price, the better to maximize profits from sales that must be competitive in a market where other firms offer similar machines. The military vehicle's requirements are met when the designers and builders deliver capabilities that satisfy the military's unique needs. Cost and price are pressed upward to attain that goal, and federal subsidies rise to satisfy them.

A visit to a major American machine tool factory during the spring of 1982 disclosed the following production patterns reflecting the influence of cost-maximizing. About two-thirds of the firm's output consisted of large "special" machines for the aerospace and auto industries. These equipments, with their computer controls, were designed to unique customer specifications and were produced in quantities ranging from one to three.

Since the main products of this machine tool factory had no regular pattern of sequential operations, the arrangement of production machinery was according to class of operations; that is, a lathe department, a milling machine department, a drill press department, etc. With this typical "job shop" arrangement, the cycle time for producing a new machine extended to as much as two years. This was acceptable to management, which was earning a very desirable profit from the sale of these custom-produced machines, mainly to the aerospace market.

At the same time, one-third of this company's sales consisted of smaller computer-controlled machines of fixed design that were produced for the U.S. firm (with its nameplate prominently placed) by Japanese machine tool firms. Thereby this U.S.-based machine tool manufacturer concentrated its own production facilities in the service of markets that could stand high markups and high prices, while "filling out" the line of machines offered under its label with imported equipment. With nothing more innovative than fixed design and a stable production system the imported group of machines could be produced at competitive prices in the U.S. plant. But that would involve a modification in style of machine design and plant operation—implying a substantial change in the work skills of virtually everyone in the firm, from machinist to salesman. Hence, the low-productivity system was kept economically viable by being employed for the production of high-price-tag equipment, mainly for aerospace, while the firm discontinued production of smaller machine sizes and performed a merchandising service to glean a profit from those imports.

The abandonment of cost-minimizing by the managers of American industry is not necessarily permanent. I shall argue later (chapter 13) that certain industrial "conditions of no return," which can be defined, would make a restoration of cost-minimizing rather difficult. But there is no evidence from which to predict the permanent unfeasibility of a major renewal of production competence in the United States. Whenever that is contemplated, new criteria for design of products and for design of production will probably be elaborated in the attempt to reinstate cost-minimizing. These efforts will surely include major attention to new criteria for production design: the productivity of capital, the operation of stable production systems, and enlarged decision-making power by production workers over technology and its utilization.

As industrial managers relied ever more heavily on mechanization, they also reduced the effect of manual labor effort on the rate of output, while requiring greater technical sophistication by the operator for intervening in machine operations. Intensified mechanization of work had the further effect, unintended, of increasing the importance of costs of capital in industrial operations. Indeed, there are strong grounds for identifying the productivity of capital as a new and continuing criterion for managers, workers, and the wider community.

The costs of machinery have long been a major factor in the chemical industries. What is new is their greater importance in mechanical manufacture, as in metalworking. The large fixed capital investments required for numerical control equipment, together with the cost of new technical staffs (programmers, skilled maintenance men) to operate it, have directed attention to the productivity of capital as a vital area for achieving an optimum industrial output from a given input.

This, then, is a new species of cost-minimizing. The traditional strategy was aimed mainly at saving labor cost by substituting machinery for manpower. In the new era of capital-intensive production, capital cost is minimized (or maximized!) by the selection of ways to design and use complex manufacturing and control equipment.

There is no single "correct" set of criteria for the design or mode of applying numerical control and other computer-regulated equipment such as robots. If the main goal is maximum managerial control over the work force, then numerical control and robotics can be used as devices to "simplify" production worker tasks still further, and thus make a case for reducing skill classifications, hence hourly wages. This can be accompanied by restricting programming to a special cadre of programmers who are made a formal part of management, and by a parallel fencing off of maintenance and scheduling tasks, with production workers ordered not to intervene in any way.

A major alternative approach is to educate machinists and other production workers in computer and allied technology to the top of their ability, and to combine responsibilities for oversight of machine performance, first-echelon maintenance, and participation in work scheduling—all in order to maintain stable, high-productivity operation of the large and expensive NC equipment. The worker's job is made more complicated, broadened to include more tasks and more responsibilities. It becomes more interesting and rewarding.

A substantial body of experience accumulated in several countries (England, Sweden, the United States, Japan and Norway) suggests the feasibility of thus employing numerical control equipment to raise the workers' status in, and commitment to, the manufacturing process. The Norwegian experience is especially interesting because it has come about from a collaboration between the Norwegian Computing Center, a government-sponsored research institution in Oslo, and the trade unions of metalworkers and other occupations. The scientific staff of the computing center has provided the team for training production workers in computer technology; specially prepared textbooks and other materials have benefited from an exchange of ideas among scientists, workers and managers.[11]

As the productivity of capital becomes the center of attention for improving efficiency and minimizing costs of production, the idea of a "stable" system takes center stage. Stability in this context means a production system whose output rate, from day to day, or week to week, remains within statistically predictable and acceptable limits. It is important because of the effect that a stable, as against an unstable, system has on productivity. When variation in output rate drops, the average output level tends to rise. For example: a vehicle operates one day at 50 miles per hour, but ranges from 30 to 70 mph; on a second day it moves at the same average speed of 50 mph, but now within the reduced range of 45–55 mph. The second day of travel will be accomplished with *less* fuel, hence greater fuel efficiency, than was attained the first day.

This pattern is characteristic, not only of single mechanisms, but also of entire production facilities, where a stable system yields the gratifying effect of minimizing sources of interference (machine breakdowns, irregularity in the flow of materials, etc.), so that an entire factory can operate in a manner that approximates the performance of a single mechanism with smoothly meshing parts. The stable operation of a factory maximizes the total output of the machines that are used. Automatically, this also results in increased productivity of the people working in the plant.[12]

Analysts of the consequences of numerical control technology have observed that this technology probably offers a substantial opportunity for effecting major capital savings. The potential for raising the productivity of capital and labor through the operation of a stable production system (with major reliance on NC equipment) has been exceptionally well perceived by the managers, engineers and workers of Yamazaki Machinery Works Ltd. in Nagoya, Japan. In the factories of this firm, machining centers and other types of NC equipment are extensively used to produce just such tools. A new computer-controlled flexible manufacturing system went into operation in 1981. The practices of this company over many years have included a sustained effort to achieve a stable operating system, along with standardization in product design and revisions of many methods of production organization. The benefits of the policy have included substantial savings in both fixed and working capital, with automatic productivity increases.

The following is a summary account of principal classes of savings achieved by Yamazaki from reduced variation in output rates:

Fixed Capital Savings
* Machine idle time reduced, therefore capital saved by reducing unneeded capacity.
* Cost of tooling decreased because a smaller variety is needed when programs are standardized.
* Cost of tooling also diminished by the more intensive and better monitored use of fewer tools.
* Fixed capital invested per product reduced by increased output at unit operations and by progressive shortening of the total production cycle time.

Working Capital Savings
* Cost of tooling maintenance decreased by a monitored determination of need for tool replacement.
* Cost of scrap lowered as a result of better condition of tooling and reduced variation in rates of machine utilization.
* Raw materials inventory reduced because production cycle time is reduced.
* Work-in-process inventory reduced, as a function of shortened production cycle time plus smaller lot sizes.

Labor Productivity Increases
* Greater output per production worker owing to lessened machine idle time.

- Reduced emergency maintenance time owing to greater machine reliability, associated with more stable performance.

A stable production system permits the maximum productivity of capital and of labor.

Yamazaki management has used its own experience to show potential customers what capital savings they could make by investing in elaborate computer-controlled manufacturing equipment and adopting modes of maintenance, machine operation and system integration that, together, yield a stable production system. Indeed, this firm has found it possible to sell complex NC-machining systems on the ground that large capital savings could plausibly be generated, whatever the prevailing level of wages in a given industrial economy. This is extraordinary.

For one important class of products, Yamazaki has been able to reduce its production cycle from 5 months to an average of 2.5 months (1980) to 3 weeks (1982). This achieves a sixfold improvement in the productivity of capital alone.

The major improvement in productivity of capital (and automatically of labor) requires a comprehensive approach to the design and operation of computer-controlled equipment, the aim being to attain a stable production system. As machine reliability becomes an increasingly important component of the production process, it underscores the desirability of organizing the work in ways that encourage the greatest possible participation of labor at all levels of planning, maintaining, and operating the relevant equipment. Thus, NC equipment that can be programmed on the shop floor allows appropriately trained machinists to participate in program preparation or program adjustment. The alternative is machines shut down and workers standing idle until foremen, programmers, maintenance men and others can intervene.

The modes of work organization that enlarge and intensify skills, adding to responsibility and authority, are also the modes that can optimize the productivity of capital, and thereby of labor as well. The more traditional approach to the design and use of numerical control and robotics sees them as devices for holding down the skills and wages of working people. That objective, then, is to maintain and extend managerial control over the work force, whatever the costs and other effects on the productivity of capital and labor.

These divergent criteria for the design and use of computer-controlled equipment also have far-reaching effects at the engineering levels. When the enlargement of workers' responsibility is the accepted mode of factory organization, university-trained engineers can help to impart the required knowledge to the production work force. Their own occupations in turn take on a different character. In leading Japanese machine tool firms, university-trained engineers are given hands-on tasks in assembly, production, design, research and other aspects of the enterprise, with job rotation contributing to their broader professional perspective. Thus, well-trained engineers work directly on the assembly of machining centers and their control equipment. Necessarily, the quality of the final product profits from the presence on the shop floor of people who have mastered the mechanical and electronic complexities of the components in question. Enterprises operated in this fashion have enjoyed relatively low administrative costs, along with high growth and high productivity of both capital and labor.[13]

The more traditional policy counts engineers as part of management, requires them to dress appropriately for office work, and bans them from the hands-on activities. An engineer thus insulated from production can make his knowledge of the equipment felt only at second hand.

I have emphasized the consequences that stem from particular criteria for deciding on production and have not discussed the other aspects of organization within which these operate. Actually, a range of decision rules—from cost-minimizing to -maximizing, from rigid managerial controls to important elements of workplace democracy, from production-oriented management to management focused on profits/power—have appeared independently of such variants as private versus public enterprises, large versus small firms, centralized versus decentralized enterprises, state capitalism versus private capitalism, finance capitalism as against industrial capitalism. Evidently, the core features of managerialism (as characterized in chapter 4) can operate even as other aspects of decision-making show considerable variety. Also, highly efficient production is achievable as the classic rules of managerial decision-making are radically revised.

Thus, state capitalism can impose on its managers criteria of cost-minimizing as well as those of cost-maximizing. Indeed, that is one of the important differences between state capitalism in Japan and in the United States. In Japan after World War II, the state used managerial organization to promote productive enterprise on a large scale. In the United States, state capitalism, primarily applying cost-maximizing criteria of operation, has been used to promote an economically unproductive military economy.

Profit with production has resulted from state capitalism in Japan. Profit without production has been the consequence of the American variety.

By way of putting all these variations on the managerial theme in sharper focus, attention should be given to a new American departure in defining criteria for decision-making on technology. In 1981, the International Association of Machinists and Aerospace Workers (IAM) began to circulate, for discussion, a policy formulation called "A Technology Bill of Rights." To introduce it, the following propositions were assembled as a statement of the fundamental values that should shape the criteria for technology:

A TECHNOLOGY BILL OF RIGHTS

1. A community has to produce in order to live. As a result, it is the obligation of an economy to organize people to work.
2. The well-being of working people and their communities must be given the highest priority in determining the way in which production is carried out.
3. Basing technological and production decisions on narrow economic grounds of profitability has made working people and communities the victims rather than the beneficiaries of change.
4. Given the widespread scope and rapid rate of introduction of new technologies, societies require a democratically determined institutional, rather than individual, response to changes taking place. Otherwise, the social cost of technological change will be borne by those least able to pay it: unemployed workers and shattered communities.
5. Those that work have a right to participate in the decisions that govern their work and shape their lives.
6. The new automation technologies and the sciences that underlie them are the product of worldwide, centuries-long accumulation of knowledge. Accordingly, working people and their communities have a right to share in the decisions about, and gains from, new technology.

The choice should not be between new technology or no technology, but the development of technology with social responsibility. Therefore, the precondition for technological change must be compliance with a program that defines and ensures the well-being of working people and the community. The following is the foundation of such a program, a Technology Bill of Rights:

1. *New technology must be used in a way that creates or maintains jobs.* A part of the productivity gains from new technology can translate into fewer working hours at the same pay or into fewer jobs. This is not a technical but a social decision. Given the pervasiveness of new forms of automation, the former approach is vital. The exact mechanisms for accomplishing this—a shorter work week, earlier retirement, longer vacations, or a combination—ought to be a prerogative of the workers involved. In addition, comprehensive training must be provided well before any change takes place to insure that workers have the maximum options to decide their future. Moreover, new industries that produce socially useful products must be created to insure the economic viability of regions that are particularly affected by technological change.
2. *New technology must be used to improve the conditions of work.* Rather than using automation to destroy skills, pace work, and monitor workers, it can be used to enhance skill and expand the responsibility workers have on the job. In addition,

the elimination of hazardous and undesirable jobs should be a first priority, but at the discretion of the workers involved and not at the expense of employment. Production processes can be designed to fully utilize the skill, talent, creativity, initiative, and experience of working people—instead of production designs aimed at controlling workers as if they were robots.

3. *New technology must be used to develop the industrial base and improve the environment.* At the same time corporate America has raised the flag of industrial revitalization, jobs are being exported from communities, regions, and even countries at a record rate. The narrow economic criteria of transnational companies are causing an erosion of the nation's manufacturing base and the collapse of many communities that are dependent on it. While other countries in the world have a pressing need and a legitimate right to develop new industry, it is nonetheless vital that corporations not be allowed to play workers, unions, and countries against each other, seeking the lowest bidder for wages and working conditions. Instead, close cooperation among unions throughout the world and stringent controls over plant closings and capital movement are in order. In addition, the development of technology should not be at the expense of the destruction of the environment.[14]

The Technology Bill of Rights includes decision criteria that are novel to a managerially controlled industrial scene. Technology should be designed and used not only to promote productivity, but also to create opportunity for productive work. Technology should be framed to improve not only the workplace but the environment of the whole community.

8

Opulence in
the State Economy

opulent, *adj.,* having a large estate or
property; wealthy; hence, amply or
plentifully provided or fashioned; luxuriant;
profuse.—**Syn.** See RICH; LUXURIOUS.

The Pentagon's top management in 1978 misplaced, lost track of, or misappro-
priated $30 billion in one of its auxiliary operations. Twenty years earlier,
that amount of money had been two-thirds of the entire budget of the Department of Defense. It's a sum that exceeded the national economic product
of *thirty* (30) countries in 1978.[1] Another view of $30 billion: it would be
the cost of modernizing the main metalworking industries of the United
States.

Apart from limited references in the business press, news of the Pentagon's missing $30 billion got almost no public notice. And this was during
the Carter administration, when the press carried, in detail, every ploy
whereby the president's brother sought to supplement the income from his
gas station. Evidently, the opulence—in both scale and style—of the Pentagon's operations has prevailed so long as to be taken for granted.

To get a rough idea of how the Pentagon performs, it is helpful to familiar-
ize oneself with a few important events in, and aspects of, its operations, but
any attempt at detailed and comprehensive treatment is doomed to failure.
It is a task beyond the capability not merely of any individual researcher-
writer, but even of a large investigative institution like the U.S. government's
General Accounting Office. Here, then, are a few examples, each one important in its own right, to illustrate the opulence in the state economy: first, the
case of the misplaced $30 billion; second, the F-18 aircraft program; then,
lunch.

In July 1978 we learned that

A major scandal may soon be erupting out of the Defense Department's management of the U.S. foreign military-sales program. Defense officials, it appears, have lost track of up to $30 billion in undelivered foreign orders for weapons, equipment, and U.S. support services. What they do not know, because their books are so fouled up, is whether the unaccounted-for money is the result of a series of ghastly accounting errors, whether they have spent a lot of it for something else, or whether they have been undercharging foreign customers—or a combination of all three.[2]

In the event, there was no breath of scandal—federal officials, members of Congress, and the general press all lost track of the misplaced $30-billion item. One person who kept it in mind was Clifford J. Miller, Deputy Controller for Plans and Systems in the Defense Department, and the man in charge of solving the mystery. Said Miller: "This has all the lethal potential of a loose cannon rolling around our deck." The report in *Business Week* explains that

The management failure that lies at the root of the arms-sales shambles apparently stems from the fragmented way in which the Defense Dept. is structured to serve as contractor go-between for foreign arms buyers and U.S. weapons manufacturers. The way it works is that, under the loose supervision of the Defense Security Assistance Agency (DSAA), each military service handles its own foreign military sales requests and makes its own purchases. For example, the Army may get an order from the DSAA for 50 Chrysler-manufactured tanks for sale to Israel. It takes that order to Chrysler Corp. and draws against its account of contracting authority with the foreign sales trust fund to make the tank purchase. . . .

. . . each service is supposed to keep track of how it disposes of its own contracting authority and also of the cash that it siphons from the fund to pay for weapons.

This is where the breakdown has apparently taken place. The accounting task is gargantuan and seems to have swamped the military. Foreign orders for U.S. arms have topped $10 billion in each of the last five years, and this year [1978] they will come to more than $13.2 billion.

"The orders just grew too big too fast," explains one congressional defense budget analyst. . . .[3]

If average hourly earnings of skilled workers are $15 per hour, annual payments amount to $30,000 per man-year. Then, $30 billion would be the cost of setting in motion 1,000,000 man-years of skilled labor. These are enormous magnitudes of work and value. There is no part of the government of the United States, other than the Pentagon, which would conceivably be permitted to record $30 billion as unaccounted for.

In 1980 the Controller General of the United States pointed out, in a report to Congress, that the Department of Defense "could not provide foreign governments with an accurate accounting for their funds deposited in trust accounts. Also, the Department of Defense could not determine the amount of money available for purchases of military goods and services by these countries."[4] The Controller General addressed one aspect of the missing $30 billion:

> GAO found that as of September 30, 1979, detailed accounting records for foreign military sales customers differed by $1.5 billion from trust fund records showing cash on hand. After considering normal processing delays, system deficiencies, and identifiable accounting errors, unexplained differences were still about $390 million.[5]

Again, in no other activity of government is an "unexplained difference" of $390 million unworthy of substantial attention. After all, the executive branch of the U.S. government has been dedicated to minimizing the depredations of welfare chiselers and even to finding ways to reduce federal expenditures by curtailing the delivery of hot lunches to indigent senior citizens.

The F-18 aircraft program was planned during the 1970s to provide the Navy with a fleet of 1,377 airplanes that were supposed to offer superior performance for three military functions: first, as defense of aircraft carriers against airborne attack; second, as fighter aircraft for the Navy or the Marines; third, as ground attack planes. From 1975 to 1980, the cost per plane rocketed from $9.9 million to $33 million, and the end is not in sight. Certain major equipment for the airplane has yet to be designed, tested and installed, and extensive design modification seems to be in the offing to cope with an excess of weight. Two considerations are central for a further discussion of this project: first, the independent judgments of expert analysts concur in the finding that the F-18 is definitely less suited for its stated objectives than are other aircraft already in hand; second, the cost of the plane, already more than three times the initial estimate, makes it dramatically more expensive than the existing aircraft that are functionally superior.

One analysis of the F-18 was performed by Robert Gigliotti, a "well-known defense consultant and navy aircraft analyst," at the request of the Navy's Chief of Naval Materiel. A second analysis comes from Jeffrey Record, an "author of numerous books on military affairs." These knowledgeable men join in the general assessment that in its carrier defense function, fighter function, and ground assault function, the F-18 is inferior to other available and less costly aircraft.[6]

Why, then, is the F-18 program being vigorously pursued? It must be that powerful congressional-political, business enterprise and Pentagon bureaucratic considerations are involved. The engines for the F-18 are to be manufactured in Massachusetts, home state not only of Senator Edward Kennedy, but also of Representative Thomas P. O'Neill, Speaker of the House of Representatives under both the Carter and the Reagan administration. The

McDonnell Douglas Corporation, prime contractor for the F-18, is a very important industrial employer in St. Louis. Further, an elaborate bureaucracy in the Pentagon itself is dedicated to various aspects of the F-18 program. And in the background, there is the belief that a major part of the American public will support any new weapons program, whatever its cost. Parties with a personal interest in the F-18 program have taken full advantage of this alleged popular support, with the result that the Department of Defense has been proceeding with an enormously expensive activity that lacks any perceivable element of even narrowly defined functional usefulness. Only an institution endowed with extraordinary resources and a tradition of opulent expenditure could persist in an error as obvious and as expensive as the F-18.[7]

After these explorations of multibillion-dollar exotica, here's something any taxpayer can more easily grasp. Lunch. Inside the Pentagon are five executive dining rooms: one for each of the services, one for the Joint Chiefs of Staff and one for the 100 "selected senior level members" of the defense secretary's staff. On an average during 1980, the cost per lunch to the users of these dining rooms was $2.64. But funds were appropriated from the Pentagon's budgets at the rate of $14.28 per meal, bringing the average cost per plate to $16.92. All five facilities are overstaffed, "with a ratio of only 4.2 meals per employee served each day." As Representative Les Aspin points out, "The total cost of the dining room is not much when you consider the total defense budget this coming year [1982] will be $222 billion. It is the aura of wastefulness right at the heart of the nation's largest federal agency that is so disturbing."[8]

I remind the reader that (as noted in chapter 5), the military economy of the United States is that part of the national economy which is directly managed by the 50,000 employees in the central administrative office staff of the Department of Defense. From the end of World War II until 1981 the military budgets of the United States amounted to $2,001 billion. The budget plans of the Carter-Reagan administrations provide for additional military expenditures of $1,638 billion over the five years from 1981 through 1986. For 1987–1988 the planned military budgets total $451 billion.[9]

The immense resources devoted to the military community in the United States have been dealt with by mainstream economists mainly according to their ideological preconceptions. To economists of the political center and the right, military expenditure is accounted for mainly as another form of business turnover and thus as an addition to the gross national product. Among economists of Marxist persuasion, the military economy has been seized upon as an area for political attack on capitalism: the state, they say, prefers to engage in military spending rather than civilian activity as a device for maintaining industrial capitalism, because military production yields profit while not competing with goods offered by private firms in the civilian marketplace.

Neither view of the military economy addresses its functional effect on the nation as a system for organizing people to do useful work; that is, the production that is essential for life.

Whatever their political assessment of the desirability of the military economy, economists typically agree that, year by year, military spending adds to the gross national product, as ordinarily understood. By this they mean that the military economy is to be appreciated as adding to the annual output of money-valued goods and services. These comprise the sum of the economically valued activities of the community. More exactly, they are the sum of "economic goods" that have been produced during a given year. What are economic goods? They are things or services that can be had for a price. The fact that something has a price is treated as the test of its usefulness. Clearly, in this way of thinking, military goods and services have prices and are therefore to be classed as economic goods and counted in the gross national product.*

But the idea of using price as the crucial test of "economic goods" is not a part of natural law. It is possible to identify "economic goods" by altogether different criteria. One legitimate purpose of this inquiry is to discover the causes of major decline (or growth) in production competence of industrial systems. To that end, it is more effective to classify economic goods as products or services useful for ordinary consumption or for carrying out further production. If they are thus classified, they qualify as economic goods; if not, they fall outside the category.†

My central interest here is to assess private and state managerialism in the United States from the vantage point of their effect on the level of living and

---

*Which makes it difficult or impossible even to gauge possible effects of a sustained military economy. The Joint Economic Committee of the U.S. Congress reported in 1974 that

> . . . the government's foremost economic experts seem to approve of rising defense budgets at the same time that they discourage studies of the economic consequences of defense spending. They admit to knowing little about these consequences. The Chairman of the Council of Economic Advisors told the Committee that no one on the Council staff is assigned this responsibility. He said in his testimony: "We kept finding that there was nothing in that box so it didn't seem desirable to keep somebody constantly looking in it." Nevertheless, he believes that the defense budget is based on "the minimum requirement of the defense establishment." (*Report of the Joint Economic Committee, Congress of the United States, on the February 1974 Economic Report of the President,* Washington, D.C., March 25, 1974)

This means that the White House and the Congress are kept systematically uninformed about economic consequences of the operation of a military economy, a situation facilitated, as the above report indicates, by an understanding that such economic consequences do not exist.

†Other formulations are also conceivable. For example, in a community that functions as a garrison state, the production of military goods and services can be so highly regarded that they become the centerpiece of desirable production. In societies that feature a fundamentalist state religion, compliance with religious codes and the rulings of clerical bodies can comprise important criteria for defining economic goods.

on capacity for further production. By using these criteria of "economic goods" it is possible to account for many aspects of U.S. economic development that otherwise defy explanation.

What is the cost to the whole American community of the U.S. government's military enterprise? According to the categories of conventional wisdom in which economic value is denoted by price, the social cost is unmistakably defined by the money spent; that is, the sum of all the prices paid for military goods and services.*

The question of the social cost of the U.S. government's military enterprise can be addressed by using another criterion of economic goods: the functional utility of any object or service to meet the demands of consumption or to provide means for further production.

This approach produces a marked change in the way one reckons the social cost of the military enterprise. On the input side there is the same money value for the array of goods and services that have been used up for the military. However, on the output side the matter now takes on a different aspect, because military products serve neither consumption nor further production. By this criterion, therefore, they do not constitute economic goods. Accordingly, a vast quantity of inputs have been utilized to generate zero economic product.

This view of the matter sheds fresh light on the meaning of the military budgets of the United States since World War II. From 1946 to 1981, as I noted in chapter 5, $2,001 billion was spent for military purposes. Therefore the social cost of the military economy of the United States from 1946 to 1981 amounted to not less than $4,000 billion. This is a combined money measure of resources used up and economically useful output forgone. It is an order of magnitude that accounts for what is otherwise inexplicable: the massive physical deterioration in a broad spectrum of American industries and the sustained deterioration of nonmilitary public facilities and services. (I will take up these topics in detail in chapters 10 and 12.)

The economic significance of Pentagon budgets in the forty-two years from 1946 to 1988 can also be gauged in relation to the U.S. national wealth. Excluding the land, it was $4,302 billion in 1975. Therefore the Pentagon's budgets, $2,001 billion, 1946–1981, amounted to 46 percent of the "reproducible assets" of the U.S. (private and public-owned) national wealth; hence about 46 percent of the value of everything man-made in the United States.[10]

---

*A variation on this theme is the idea of opportunity cost, which means that the money value of the military goods and services may also be taken as the money value of some alternative set of goods and services that might have been produced from the resources that were used for the military. In either view of the matter, all manner of inputs are used to produce the military goods and services and the prices of the inputs are reflected in the prices of the military outputs.

From 1981 to 1988 (a mere eight years) the state managers plan fresh military budgets amounting to $2,089 billion—a fund that equals 48 percent of the dollar value of the nation's (1975) reproducible assets.

Without considering the full social cost to the American community, the combined Pentagon budgets of 1946–1988 represent a mass of resources equivalent to the cost of replacing just about all (94 percent) of everything manmade in the United States (excluding the land). But when we take into account both the resources used up by the military as well as the economic product forgone, then we must appreciate the social cost of the military economy, 1946–1988, as amounting to about twice the "reproducible assets" of U.S. national wealth. What has been forgone for American society is a quantity of material wealth sufficient to refurbish the United States, with an enormous surplus to spare.*

The immensity of the resources used for the military enterprise defies comprehension. It is difficult enough to visualize a million of anything, let alone 2,000 billion. One needs, therefore, to translate the resources preempted by the state managers into other categories of approximately equivalent magnitude. One approach is to look at the quantity of resources used for the military not simply as a money magnitude but in terms of their productional importance, as physical capital. A modern military budget (as noted in chapter 5) sets in motion precisely the range of resources that in a civilian industrial enterprise are termed "fixed and working capital." A major military project and a major civilian capital investment both require the same types of resources.

The creation of capital goods has a further importance in this context. It typically takes a long "lead time" to produce them. Inexpensive ball-point pens, for example, are produced within one day for all operations; new industrial facilities and their component equipment take several years to design, fabricate and set in motion. Skilled workers, technicians, engineers and scientists cannot be trained overnight. These are conditions that give capital items a crucially finite character in any society. That condition cannot be altered by even the most extravagant appropriations from the U.S. Congress. Therefore, in periods measured in decades, there is a definite tradeoff for the use of capital between the military and the civilian economy.

The table that follows illustrates the quality and range of this com-

---

*Recalling the analyses of chapter 5, there is a further component of economic loss to the society that stems from the immense concentration of capital-equivalent resources on the military. The part of capital resources that is used for new means of production normally yields a multiplied effect. For production equipment, used systematically, yields an outpouring of new goods, including new production equipment that tends to be increasingly efficient. These incremental gains from the productive use of capital resources are forgone when those resources are applied to the military enterprise on a sustained basis.

MILITARY-CIVILIAN CAPITAL TRADEOFFS

7 percent of the military outlays from fiscal 1981 to 1986	= $100 billion =	the cost of rehabilitating the United States' steel industry so that it is again the most efficient in the world
The cost overrun, to 1981, on the Navy's current submarine, frigate, and destroyer programs	= $42 billion =	for California, a 10-year investment to spur solar energy for space, water, and industrial process heating; this would involve 376,000 new jobs and lead to vast fuel savings
63 percent of the cost overruns, to 1981, on 50 current major weapons systems	= $110 billion =	the 20-year cost of solar devices and energy-conservation equipment in commercial buildings, saving 3.7 million barrels of oil per day
2 B-1 bombers	= $400 million =	the cost of rebuilding Cleveland's water-supply system
Cost overruns, to 1981, on the Navy's Trident and the Air Force's F-16 programs	= $33 billion =	the cost of rehabilitating or reconstructing 1 out of 5 United States bridges
The Navy's F-18 Fighter Program	= $34 billion =	the cost of modernizing America's machine tool stock to bring it up to the average level of Japan's
2 nuclear-powered aircraft carriers	= $5.8 billion =	the cost of converting 77 oil-using power plants to coal, saving 350,000 barrels of oil per day
3 Army AH-64 helicopters	= $82 million =	100 top-quality, energy-efficient electric trolleys (made in West Germany)
1 F-15A airplane	= $29 million =	the cost of training 200 engineers to design and produce electric trolleys in the United States
46 Army heavy (XM-1) tanks	= $120 million =	500 top-quality city buses (West German made)

The cost overrun, to 1981, on Navy Frigates (FFG-7)	=	\$5 billion	= the minimum additional annual investment needed to prevent water pollution in the United States from exceeding present standards
The cost of unjustified non-combat Pentagon aircraft	=	\$6.8 billion	= 6 years of capital investment that is needed to rehabilitate New York City transit
Reactivating 2 World War II mothballed battleships	=	\$376 million	= President Reagan's fiscal 1981 and fiscal 1982 cut in energy conservation investment
The cost overrun, to 1981, on the Navy's F-18 aircraft program	=	\$26.4 billion	= the cost of electrifying 55,000 miles of mainline railroads, and the cost of new locomotives
1 nuclear (SSN-688) attack submarine	=	\$582 million	= the cost of 100 miles of electrified rail right-of-way
10 B-1 bombers	=	\$2 billion	= the cost of dredging 6 Gulf Coast and Atlantic Coast harbors to handle 150,000-ton cargo vessels

petition. Each line shows a military item and its cost, followed by the similar cost of a civilian capital item.[11]

From the standpoint of the viability of the United States as an industrial society, the failure to make the capital investments listed on the civilian side entails a fundamental weakening in direct industrial production as well as in the infrastructure of power, water, transportation and related services that are the underpinning of an industrial system.

The central meaning of this display of military-civilian options is that they really are mutually exclusive alternatives: if the country becomes committed to the military set, then the civilian side must go without. At this writing, the military set enjoys a massive momentum.

There is another side to the preemption of resources by the state management for its preferred objectives. That is the sharp reduction in federal budgets for major classes of civilian service, including energy, education, civilian economic development, transportation, housing, medical care, social welfare, conservation and upkeep of the nation's physical environment, and care of the young and old. All these activities have been short-changed in the attempt to reduce the government's fiscal problems engendered by its priority allocation of federal tax revenues to the military economy. Since these cuts directly erode the economy's infrastructure and reduce the material level of living for important parts of the American population, they are a further indication of the scale and intensity with which resources are corralled for the state management's favorite enterprises.

The Department of Defense absorbs manpower and other resources on a scale without comparison in American economy and society. It also functions as a matter of course in ways that anywhere else would be denounced as corrupt and scandalous.

In 1980, with 987,000 civilian employees, the Department of Defense accounted for 4 out of 10 people working for the executive branch of the government.[12] In the federal budget for 1980, military outlays of all sorts scheduled for the year totalled $194 billion. Of this amount the Department of Defense received $122 billion.[13] The national military outlay planned for 1980 amounted to 51 percent of all the administrative funds allocated by the Congress and the executive branch (this excludes Social Security and other insurance-type funds that are administered by the federal government and whose outlays are based upon payments received from individuals and firms for these purposes).

All told, 5.5 million persons were directly engaged in the operations of the DOD: 2 million in the uniformed armed forces, 1 million civilian employees, and 2.5 million employed by military-serving firms and institutions.[14]

Studying the evident decline in competitiveness of many U.S. industries, economists have noted the apparently small proportion of the American gross domestic product that is invested. "Gross Fixed Capital Formation" is the name given by statisticians to the money value of all civilian "fixed" capital items, including factory buildings, machinery, other private and public structures, including roads. For 1976–1977 the ratio of this civilian investment to the gross domestic product was:

United States	17 percent
West Germany	21 percent
Japan (1976)	31 percent[15]

However, a rather different result is obtained if we examine the effects of the military economy on this proportion of investment to national product. To do so, we must define the military expenditure as a capital fund and see how that affects the ratio. The resources appropriated in a modern military economy are, as I mentioned earlier, the very ones that are classified elsewhere as "fixed" and "working" capital. Therefore it is revealing to note what happens when these items are added to the "gross fixed capital formation" in the United States and other countries.

Using the data available for 1977, we find that the share of gross domestic product devoted to investment would rise by the following percents if the military budgets were directly added to civilian investment: in Japan, 3 percent; West Germany, 13 percent; the United States, 29 percent.[16]

Inasmuch as "planning" is ideological anathema to so many Republicans and Democrats, one of the fascinating aspects of the state management's operations is the intense care with which it applies to the military economy the sort of planning mechanisms that Western European and Japanese governments have applied in varying degrees to encourage civilian industry in their societies. This can be seen in the mobilization exercises and industrial planning conferences convened by the military services. Industrial managers from a cross-section of companies that service the military are brought together to discuss what each service will need from them and what in turn they will require from the services. At these meetings, the air is full of five-year plans and there is no reference at all to quarterly profit-and-loss results. The orientation on both sides is definitely long-term.

The military do a number of things to protect and improve the quality of their industrial base. A "Defense Productivity Program Office" is a regular operation of the assistant secretary of defense for Manpower Reserve Affairs and Logistics. Its concerns include ways to foster capital investment in the military economy.[17]

At a mobilization exercise organized in 1980 by the U.S. Army, with the title "Partners in Preparedness," senior military officers and industrial executives gathered to discuss mutual interests and to review memoranda of policy newly prepared by the Department of Defense to redefine relations between the state management and the managers of their satellite firms. The exercise even took up the question, What sort of war are we preparing for? (A short war was defined as one enduring up to six months; a long war, as anything beyond that.) These discussions took on particular importance because of conflicts in the Middle East, especially during the 1973 war. For in that operation, closely watched by the U.S. high command, the human casualties and attrition rates in armored materiel reached levels of 50 percent in two weeks of operations, a rate of loss hitherto thought to apply only to nuclear war.

In another area, the Industrial College of the Armed Forces—a section of the Defense University—conducts an annual Issues Conference on Mobilization. These exercises undertaken by the state management are a far cry from the conservative ideal, which holds that the design and mode of operation of U.S. industrial work should be left to the managements of individual firms. Obviously the state management pays less heed to doctrine than to the requirements for organizing its own economy.

The U.S. Army's November 1980 mobilization exercise produced a report that recommended ways for improving the responsiveness of the industrial base and for planning with industry. The recommendations included the following:

[Formulate] a clear statement of policy regarding the . . . [effect of] . . . war reserves [on] the responsiveness of the industrial base . . .

[Expand] . . . military hardware production as a political signal to the world of our national resolve. . . .

. . . Provide industry with clear planning guidance based on stable, believable, and properly funded requirements. . . .

[Arrange] . . . regular interaction between industry's senior executive level and the army's top leaders. . . .

Essential U.S. industries should be identified and monitored for possible assistance or remedial action in the event they may become war-producers. . . .

Planning staff should be provided. Centralized policy with decentralized planning and execution is preferred. . . .

[Establish] . . . an industrial preparedness board composed of government, industry, and labor representation that reports to the NSC. . . .

The industrial preparedness planning system must be revised, improved, and adequately funded. . . .

[Increase] federal stockpiling of critical raw materials. . . .

[Increase] the emphasis on research and development of substitute materials. . . .

[Schedule] . . . continual modernization of reserve production equipment. . . .

[Install] . . . state-of-the-art machines [to] assist in improving productivity and repairability. . . .

The army should be willing to pay for sub-tier and vendor analyses toward developing more flexible tooling which could be used for commercial or industrial production. . . .

[Accelerate] depreciation/amortization. . . . Credits will provide improved cash flow and investment incentives. . . .

[Open] federal land for exploration and development of scarce minerals to help lessen dependency on foreign sources. . . .

[Establish] . . . a top-down triggering mechanism [to] provide automatic waivers of governmental regulatory/statutory provisions which adversely affect the ability of the base to react to a crisis situation. . . .[18]

The proposals for improving industry's incentive to work for the military do not go as far as lending out the currency plates from the U.S. Bureau of Printing and Engraving, but they come close.

The scale of the Army's forward planning for the industrial base is strongly conditioned by the type and length of the wars being planned. Here are two of the possible options: first, a war like that in Vietnam; second, a war between nuclear superpowers. The Vietnam war cost American society—apart from the killed and wounded—about $676 billion.[19] The cost of a general nuclear war is unplannable.

While the quality of the means of production has deteriorated steadily in civilian industry, the directorate of state management has taken steps designed to check parallel erosion in the military industry. Conferences with the managers of Pentagon-serving firms have helped to formulate state management plans to replace in their plants about 25 percent of the 115,000 machine tools that are owned by the Department of Defense. This general updating of equipment is to be followed by selective modernization thereafter at 5 percent per year.[20] Such steps are designed to guarantee a flow of money that will have the effect of integrating civilian industries within the framework of state managerial control. They are but the most recent development in a long process that began in 1946 when General Eisenhower, then chief of staff of the U.S. Army, issued a memorandum, which I summarized in chapter 5, on "Scientific and Technological Resources as Military Assets."[21]

One of the pervasive qualities of the military's technical-industrial planning is an emphasis on mechanization and high technology for prospective war production. This involves lots of subsidy money to develop, produce, and operate high-tech types of machinery. However, reports of the military-industrial conferences on these matters omit reference to the training of workers, technicians and others. Thus, the Pentagon has fallen in with management's scheme to apply computerized technology in a way to fight the unions. The consequences have included restrictions on the optimal use of computer-controlled machinery in the metalworking industries—by contrast with the rapid pace of production and application in countries of Western Europe and Japan. (See Prologue and chapter 6.) Hence, the Pentagon's policy has been, effectively, one of accelerating the industrial backwardness of the United States.

The aerospace industry, a principal component of the state management's industrial empire, maintains a large excess of industrial capacity. Essentially, the "aircraft industry is roughly twice as large as it needs to be in order to produce all the commercial and military airplanes needed between now and 1990." The cost of this excess capacity amounts to $300–500 million a year—payment for unneeded employees, for idle factories and depots, for the inflated cost of airplanes and helicopters that are manufactured at inefficiently low production rates. The excess capacity is equivalent to 30,000,000 square feet, or about 700 football fields, one-third of it government owned. So large is the potential production capacity of the aerospace industry that during the "surge production of the Vietnam war, when both military and commercial orders reached simultaneous peaks, the industry was still operating below its nominal one shift capacity."[22] This massive excess capacity reflects the competition among aerospace managers for decision power and the readiness of the Pentagon's top managers to subsidize the extravaganza. No civilian industry or set of firms could conceivably sustain economic viability with practices of that kind. The state management can do so because it draws upon the income flow of the entire society for an annual fresh capital fund.

Lavish use of research and development talent and other resources is also a trademark of U.S. state management. For 1976 the estimated proportion of total U.S. R & D funds that was used for the military compares as follows to the percentages in West Germany and in Japan:

United States	31	percent
West Germany	8	percent
Japan	1	percent[23]

As might be expected, there is also a substantial difference among these countries in the "estimated ratio of civilian research and development expenditures to Gross National Product." These percentages are also for 1976:

United States	1.57	percent
Japan	1.93	percent
West Germany	2.09	percent[24]

While low levels of research and development have prevailed in the many U.S. industries that are progressively less able to hold even their U.S. markets, in the military-serving industry there is no such restriction. In the fiscal years 1981 and 1982, for example, the Pentagon's research budgets include science and technology programs of $2.8 and $3.3 billion. In addition, "manufacturing technology" programs are provided—at a cost of $158 million in 1980 and $150 million in 1981. These programs are directed specifically toward development of new manufacturing technologies for military products and industries.[25] Similar conditions apply in the opulence of the military's funding of research and development in the universities.

In civilian industry, administrative methods and management organizations are often expanded to achieve greater scope and intensity for managerial control, independently of effect on production or productivity (the theme of chapter 4). The state management's industrial empire is an outstanding performer in this respect. Thus, in 1977 for every 100 production workers in the principal military-serving industries, there were, on the average, 50 administrative, technical and clerical employees. In the rest of manufacturing industries the ratio was 41 per 100 production workers.[26]

The jumbo size of administrative staffs in military industry is an important factor in the high costs and prices of military industry. The aircraft firms have become notorious for their heavy concentrations of nonproduction employees. In 1975 they outnumbered the production employees.[27]

As a result of the opulent mode of operation in virtually every aspect of state management, the prices of the weaponry produced from the military industry network have shot up at unprecedented rates. In the last quarter of 1980, the price of forty-seven of the Pentagon's major weapons systems rose by more than $47 billion, an increase of 18 percent during the three-month period. If such a rate remained constant, it would yield a staggering annual price growth of about 93 percent. But even that would not necessarily alarm the state management. An authoritative report states that "Budget Director David Stockman has promised Defense Secretary Caspar Weinberger that if the administration's optimistic inflation forecasts for each of the next five years proves too low, any shortfall in the defense budget will be made up with additional money."[28]

Profitability in military industry is endowed with special conditions. In the classic ideology of business economists, profit is at least in part a reward for taking risks. But firms serving the state management take little risk, since their goods are sold before they are produced. Nevertheless, there is sustained evidence of a solicitude for the "adequate" profits of military-serving firms that puts them in a unique position. *Business Week,* in no sense an unfriendly critic of management, has noted that "defense companies have long complained about their low profit levels, often with little justification. The defense industry's return on sales, currently [1977] around 5 percent before taxes, is admittedly low. But the figure is not a fair yardstick because much of the industry's plant and equipment is owned by the government and risk is often less than in commercial business."[29] Nevertheless, in the search for a "spirit of cooperation," proposals have been made to assure a 20 percent profit for military industry firms. And all sorts of special "incentives" have been invented to boost their profits—as when they invest some of their own money for new plant and equipment.

Another aspect of state management's opulence may be seen in the scale and characteristics of its moves to extend its decision power around the world. The "General Purpose Forces" of the U.S. Armed Forces have been set up mainly for military operations in relation to smaller, non-nuclear states. The last military budget prepared by President Jimmy Carter settled 37 percent of total Pentagon expenditures on these forces. But the first Reagan budget showed a sharp increase both absolutely and proportionately, with the General Purpose Forces being allotted $89.5 billion, or 40 percent of the total military budget planned for fiscal year 1982.[30]

The worldwide sale of weapons on an increasing scale has become a part of the military-political power game of government management. Over a thirty-year period, 1950–1980, the foreign military sales arranged by the Pentagon amounted to $110 billion. (N.B. To be compared with the $30 billion "missing" item discussed at the start of this chapter.) But then, in 1980 alone, $15 billion of sales agreements were concluded.[31] The Pentagon's worldwide military sales and assistance program operates out of the Pentagon with a central staff of 106 persons. Another 6,000 people are engaged in this work at various embassies and military assistance offices around the world. It is a formidable sales organization and can be counted on to accelerate military equipment and military training "sales," especially since the Security Assistance Agency can arrange a variety of credits, guaranteed loans, etc., for favored client states.

But the true measure of opulence in the state economy is the parallel restriction of production resources and the breakdown of productivity and competence in the rest of the economy and society.

9

The Collapse
of Productivity

Until about 1979, productivity was an esoteric topic for people concerned with American public affairs. It took a fifteen-year decline in the rate of productivity growth in U.S. manufacturing, and in other aspects of the economy, to put the word on the front pages of serious journals of opinion.[1]

This is not to say that economists and others have been unaware of the importance of productivity levels and their rates of change. Output per man-hour has long been known to set a definite limit to the ability of a society to support with goods and services a given standard of living. Also, the rate of increase in productivity has been a key factor in the historic ability of U.S. firms to offset increases in wage and other costs. It enabled them to pay the world's highest wages for manufacturing occupations while producing goods that were competitive in American and other markets.

A 3 percent annual increase in output per person in the manufacturing industries had long been taken for granted, as though it were a natural condition of American society. Economists and others were simply not prepared, by schooling or experience, to cope with the 1965–1980 figures for average annual rise in productivity per man-hour in manufacturing: for the United States, 2.0 percent; for West Germany, 5.2 percent; for Japan, 8.1 percent.

The economic doctrine of American intellectuals had reached the point where the conditions discussed earlier were seized upon as reasons for celebration, not for concern. The export of capital (chapter 1) had been judged a source of increasing strength, and short-term profit-taking (chapter 2) a strategy for accumulating the finance capital needed for further investment at home and abroad. The business schools were turning out exactly the sort of graduates needed to operate such enterprises successfully. They in turn played a key role in the expansion of managerial control (chapter 4), the assumption being that this would necessarily contribute to an improved productivity. Given this perspective, the ascendancy of the state managers and their new permanent military economy were welcomed as a further stimulus to the system as a whole. Altogether, the influences of these managerial groups, and especially their decision criteria for technology (chapters 6 and 7), were judged to be inherent consequences of the development of technology itself, while the deterioration of many basic industries (as discussed in the Prologue) was shrugged off as merely a side-effect of the surge toward a post-industrial society that would be dominated by the knowledge industry and high technology, as illustrated by the operation of the state economy (chapter 8).

Obviously, anyone holding this overall view of economic relationships is ill equipped to diagnose, or prescribe for, the decline in U.S. productivity growth. Instead, dominant factors in the causal chain producing U.S. industrial depletion have been treated by conventional wisdom as reasons for self-congratulation. It is little wonder, then, that so many attempts to account for the U.S. productivity debacle have been exercises in confusion.

In the manufacturing industries, productivity is directly controlled by the degree to which work is mechanized; that is, by the amount of powered machinery placed under the command of industrial workers and technicians. For example, the options lying between the least and the most mechanized methods for performing a routine materials-handling task permit a range of output per worker-hour of 1 to 10. That is, the most mechanized of the available methods will handle ten times as much material per man-hour as will the least mechanized. Similar comparisons can be made for every sort of industrial operation.*

When the mechanization of work is accompanied by ways of organizing work that encourage the stabilization of output rates, then optimum conditions can be obtained for productivity growth.

With that as background one can identify the main factors that control the movement from less to more mechanized, less to more productive ways of performing industrial work. First, when machinery makers themselves practice cost-minimizing, the relative cost of labor to machinery rises, making the use of additional powered equipment increasingly attractive to cost-minimizing users. Second, the users of machinery must themselves work out the least costly combination of work methods, thereby taking maximum advantage of mechanization under the conditions noted. Third, the move to more mechanization is as a rule induced by the greater rise of worker wages

---

*Since 1952, graduate industrial engineers in my classes have been comparing alternative costs and methods for performing particular work tasks. In all this time, no one has discovered a job for which there are no alternatives available in equipment and work methods. In every case it has been possible to identify a range of less to more mechanized ways to perform particular tasks.

compared to machinery prices; therefore, the operation of a worker decision-making process plays its part. Fourth, buyers of machinery need finance capital for the investment. Fifth, a research and development process is required, because it contributes to new and more effective designs of production equipment. Sixth, manufacturing machinery is most productive when it runs at a steady pace in a factory that operates with the least possible fluctuation of output rates. Seventh, all these considerations are best served when the administration of an enterprise operates primarily as a service to production, and is not directed primarily toward enlargement of managerial control. Finally, the whole set of essential conditions for advancing the mechanization of work requires a supporting infrastructure of power, transportation, communication, water supply, housing, etc.

Of the necessary conditions here enumerated, <u>cost-minimizing managements and the rising relative cost of labor to machinery are the critically active variables among the other necessary conditions</u>. The decline of productivity growth in U.S. manufacturing and other industries will lose whatever mystery it may possess as we examine what has happened to each of the main conditions necessary for that growth.

During the first fifty years of the twentieth century, the mechanization of work proceeded so rapidly in the manufacturing industries of the United States that by 1950 the average hourly output per production worker was almost four times what it had been in 1899. The average annual increase in industrial output per worker man-hour exceeded 5 percent.[2] This long period of rapid productivity growth in manufacturing created after World War II a dramatic contrast between the average productivity of industry in the United States and in many other countries. Throughout postwar Western Europe extensive studies were made of differences in the production methods of European and U.S. industries. In Great Britain, for example, the average productivity of the industrial work force was widely agreed to be one-half to one-third that of its American counterpart and this difference was treated as a central political-economic issue.[3] And for the next decades U.S. productivity growth continued at a traditionally satisfactory rate.

Then, after 1965, there came a sudden and dramatic change, shown in the annual percent increase in U.S. manufacturing productivity:

1965–1970	2.1 percent
1970–1975	1.8 percent
1975–1980	1.7 percent[4]

This extended decline is without precedent in U.S. industrial history, and contrasts sharply with the picture of the American economy obtained by focusing on measures like gross national product, a monetary figure derived from the prices of all goods and services that are produced.

Similar effects are obtained when other parts of the U.S. economy are included in the calculation. Across the entire "private business economy" of the United States the average annual growth of productivity declined as follows:

1948–1965	3.2 percent
1965–1972	2.3 percent
1972–1978	1.1 percent[5]

And productivity rates similarly slowed among the larger population of businesses comprising all the nonfinancial corporations (that is, other than banks, etc.) in the United States. From 1975 to 1980 their output per employee showed an average annual growth of only 1.6 percent.

The collapse is especially alarming when contrasted with the rapid improvement (in annual output of manufacturing per employee-hour) in Germany and Japan from 1965 to 1979:

United States	2.3 percent
West Germany	7.3 percent
Japan	13.7 percent

Since 1965, productivity growth in U.S. manufacturing has been at the lowest rate of all industrialized countries for which such data are available.[6] These sustained differences are bound to have their effect on the total output of goods per person. In 1981, the European-based Organization for Economic Cooperation and Development ranked the United States tenth in terms of per capita gross national product.[7]

The relative level and rate of growth of a country's productivity has important effects on the pattern of its relationships with other economies. In 1979, the top ten Japanese imports from the United States were:

soya beans	wheat
corn for fodder and feeds	cotton
saw logs and veneer logs (Douglas fir)	turbojet airplanes
saw logs and veneer logs (hemlock)	rawhide and skins of bovine animals
coking coal	waste and scrap metal, for smelting other than alloy steel

In the same year, these were the top U.S. imports from Japan:

passenger cars	nails, screws, and other
iron and steel plates and	fasteners
sheets	TV receivers
radio receivers	office machines
motorcycles	metal-cutting machine tools
audiotape and videotape	calculating machines
players and recorders	automotive trucks
iron and steel pipes, tubes	microphones, speakers, and
and blanks	audio amplifiers
still cameras and parts	iron and steel angles,
	shapes, sections

Reviewing these data, a committee of the U.S. Congress commented:

A comparison of our leading exports to Japan versus our imports from her is devastating. The data seem to indicate that (aircraft excluded) we are a developing nation supplying a more advanced nation—we are Japan's plantation: haulers of wood and growers of crops, in exchange for high technology, value-added products.[8]

Observers of the American scene during the early nineteenth century noted that "in Europe work is often wanting for the hands; here [that is, in the United States] hands are wanting for the work" (Michael Chevalier). Writing in 1833, E. G. Wakefield noted that "where land is very cheap and all men are free, where everyone who so pleases can easily obtain a piece of land for himself, not only is labor very dear, . . . but the difficulty is to obtain combined labor at any price."[9]

Responding to the high relative cost of labor, American designers and industrial artisans developed the method of interchangeable parts called the "American system." One of the most important applications of the "American system" was to the design and fabrication of new classes of machine tools during the latter half of the nineteenth century. Thus new classes of milling machines and turret lathes, designed for fast production of specialized parts, were not only developed but first produced in the United States. Indeed, " . . . in the 1850s and 60s . . . firms of specialized machine tool builders multiplied their number, until by the 1880s, it has been said, the price of American machine tools had fallen to half that of the equivalent British tools."[10]

All this happened in the United States because

. . . The U.S.A. was in a better position than the U.K. to make . . . labor-saving developments in the making of machines for exactly the same reasons as it was in a better position to make them in the using of machines. . . . The Americans had to develop tools which would replace labor. The methods specifically designed to replace labor in one operation, for example, the system of interchangeable parts, were widely applicable to other operations and, to some extent, they were applicable to the manufacture of machines themselves.[11]

These processes continued into the twentieth century, so that from 1915 to 1950 labor's hourly earnings in manufacturing increased fivefold, while the prices of metals and metal products only doubled. From 1939 to 1947 average hourly earnings of workers in manufacturing industries rose 95 percent, but general machinery prices increased only 26 percent and machine tool prices 39 percent.[12]

Over a long period, it was the practice of U.S. machinery manufacturers to stress productivity improvement on their own premises, the better to offset rising costs and to restrain increases in the prices of their products. As a result, the machinery-using firms were served by suppliers who offered products that were progressively more attractive to cost-minimizing industrial managers.

Finance capital was, generally speaking, abundantly available for U.S. industrial investment during the nineteenth century and first half of the twentieth. Capital accumulated from the profits of the firms was readily supplemented with money supplied by the banking system at attractive, stable rates, and similarly through the securities exchanges. With respect to physical plant and equipment, U.S. industry was in a privileged position at the end of World War II; its physical plant was intact and able to serve a worldwide market for every class of industrial goods.

Scientific and engineering research and development contribute substantially to the development and application of new technology, which in turn creates improved production processes and products. Until the mid-1960s, the economy of the United States employed a proportionately larger force of scientists and engineers than did any other major industrial country. As recently as 1965, the United States had more scientists and engineers per 10,000 persons in the labor force than West Germany or Japan:

West Germany	22.6
Japan	24.6
United States	64.1[13]

The United States excelled in this respect even if one makes substantial allowance for employment by the military. Assume, for example, that as many as half of American scientists and engineers were in the service of the military economy. Even so, the U.S. ratio for the civilian sector would have been 32 per 10,000 in 1965, still a third higher than the German or Japanese figure.

Also, in 1964 the United States spent by far the most for R & D, measured as a percentage of gross national product. In that year the Japanese ratio was 1:48, West Germany 1:57, and the United States 2:97.[14] Again, even if one assumes that as much as half the U.S. R & D went into military projects, the United States was still at no apparent disadvantage to Germany and Japan.

Recall that a stable production system is crucial to the most efficient use of industrial production facilities. In this respect the industrial system of the United States, and its machinery industries in particular, have operated under far less than optimum conditions. Studies of the U.S. machine tool industry have disclosed that its long history of unstable operations has played an important part in restraining its own internal productivity.[15]

Finally, there is the role of management in American industry. At least until the middle of the twentieth century industrial management operated on the assumption that serving production was an essential part of its function. Then in the 1960s, as shown in chapters 3 and 4, there began a strong ideological swing from the premise that serving production was a necessary condition for profits and power, to the idea that production was no longer a primary requirement of American economy and society. The latter notion, which introduced the image of a post-industrial society, justified the rapid expansion of schools of business and steered managements toward finance and pure administration, thus displacing the production orientation.

All the necessary conditions for mechanization of work and productivity growth were supported by an American infrastructure that provided unequaled central power, transportation, communications, water supply and similar needs. These were available to American industry and their surrounding communities in relative abundance and acceptable quality.

What had happened, by the mid-1960s, to this group of factors, the majority of which had hitherto spurred and supported a high level of productivity growth in the United States? I have already shown how the machine tool industry was brought into close relations with the Pentagon and its network of aerospace and other military-serving industries. Management and technical staffs then became adept in the ways of cost-maximizing that were appropriate to the Pentagon customer. By so doing, they abandoned the design and production practices and traditions that were integral to cost-minimizing. In their internal operations the machinery producers became less able to offset

their own wage and other cost increases. Their products became less technically innovative, especially after 1965.[16]

After World War II, U.S. machine tool firms also began an active program
of foreign investment. Managements found that they could make money by
transferring their tools and techniques to Western European countries and
could take advantage of rapidly expanding machinery markets there. These
new major sources of gain reduced the pressure on U.S. managers to pursue
profits by the more burdensome practice of revising product designs and
internal production methods.

The long period when American machinery prices rose at a rate slower
than the wages of labor came to an end. From 1965 to 1977, the average prices
of metalworking machine tools produced in the United States increased by
116 percent. That matched the 115 percent rise of hourly earnings of workers
in manufacturing during the same period.[17] Thus, U.S. machine tool firms
could no longer offer American customers new equipment at prices that were
clearly cost-attractive. The special role of the Air Force in this process was
noted in the Prologue and chapter 6.

This loss of the labor-saving sales argument is crucial to the collapse of
U.S. productivity growth. Therefore, it is important to record that the reversal of the tendency of wages to outstrip the cost of machinery (capital) is
confirmed by several independent parties, who base their calculations on
diverse data.

The economic research firm Data Resources, Inc., has compiled an index
of capital costs that takes into account prices of machinery, as well as the
interest rate for borrowing finance capital. The *Wall Street Journal* has
compared that index of capital costs with unit labor costs as computed by the
U.S. Bureau of Labor Statistics. The finding is clear: after 1965, the index of
capital costs rose more each year than did the index of unit labor costs.[18]
A second estimate shows the annual rate of change in the relative prices
of labor to capital as experienced by manufacturing firms in the United
States.

1945–1965	1.1 percent
1965–1972	−4.5 percent
1972–1978	−4.2 percent

In this comparison, the "price" of labor includes money wages plus fringe
benefits; the price of capital is a composite of the purchase price of new capital
equipment, energy needed to operate machinery, and interest paid to finance
the purchase of new machinery. In these terms, "while total capital costs fell
1.1 percent per year relative to total labor costs in the first period, total capital
costs rose 4.2 percent per year relative to total labor costs in the third

period."[19] In separate computations of the relation of labor's wages to machinery prices Thomas Boucher records for the 1970s a sharp drop in the changing relative cost of manpower to machinery.[20]

Design improvements that translated directly into enhanced machine productivity had proceeded at a rapid pace across the main range of metalworking machinery from World War II until the early 1960s. After that came a distinct slowdown in the rate at which new, productivity-improving features were introduced into the stock of U.S. metalworking machinery.[21]

During the 1960s, the movement of machinery prices closely paralleled the growth of wages, but during the 1970s prices of metalworking machinery and equipment rose much more rapidly than did the wages of labor. Boucher found that from 1973 to 1977 U.S. machinery prices rose 58 percent while wages of industrial workers increased 39 percent. For cost-minimizing managements such a development induces a reluctance to purchase new machinery, and, above all, marked resistance to attempts to mechanize work previously done by more manual means.[22] It was especially important that during the 1970s the prices of the new computer-controlled machine tools also showed a pattern of price increases more rapid than the wage gains of labor. This put a sharp brake on the introduction of computer-controlled machine tools in U.S. manufacturing industries.

Meanwhile, during the 1960s and 1970s the machine tool industries of Japan and West Germany were proceeding full tilt with new strategies of production that increased the productivity of their capital and labor. In particular, the machinery-producing industries of those countries took advantage of the productivity improvement to be achieved by the stabilization of output rates. The result was a great leap in production competence, whereas in the United States the industry remained tradition-bound to a pattern of unstable, erratic production. The results should have been predictable, though few observers made the prediction: by the 1980s many U.S. machinery-producing firms had been pushed out of the international market and even from the U.S. domestic market.

As machinery users felt less incentive for further mechanization, they lost their main traditional opportunity to improve productivity. As a result they were less able to utilize productivity to offset cost increases of every sort. American industrial managers turned instead to a new strategy for coping with cost increases: cost pass-along. Instead of trying, vigorously and variously, to counteract cost increases, they merely added them to prices—with appropriate markups.[23]

With the loss of incentive to replace plant and equipment, the average age of U.S. industrial facilities escalated. By 1981 it stood at about twenty years, about double the figure for Japan.[24] As part of this development the average age of the metalworking industries' machine tool stock increased steadily, so that by 1978 the proportion of metalworking machinery ten years old and older was substantially higher in America than in West Germany and Japan:

United States	69 percent (1978)
West Germany	63 percent (1977)
Japan	39 percent (1973)[25]

Diverse measures of the age of U.S. industry's plant and equipment confirm these results, which define a physical brake on the growth of productivity.[26]

As noted earlier, for more than a century the high and rapidly rising wages paid to American industrial workers impelled American managers to seek ways of easing the payroll burden. From the 1960s on, however, wages to American industrial workers increased at a much slower rate than the wages to workers in other major industrial countries. From 1965 to 1979, the average annual increase in hourly compensation (money plus fringes) to industrial workers was 13 percent in the U.S., 19 percent in West Germany, and 43 percent in Japan.[27]

During 1975 there came a historic turning point: for the first time, hourly compensation to U.S. industrial workers was exceeded by workers' wages in Belgium, the Netherlands, and Sweden. Thereafter, the relative position of U.S. wages declined progressively, so that by 1980 the United States had become a medium-wage industrial country.[28] The change in the wage position of the United States was accompanied by a shift in average per capita income. In 1975, the United States became third in the world in average per capita income, behind Switzerland and Sweden.[29]

In parallel with the reduced incentive for mechanization of work (and the export of capital from the United States by major industrial firms), the United States showed from 1960 to 1973 the smallest percentage of fixed investment to the national product of any major industrial country.[30] At the same time, American manufacturing industry entered the 1980s with a declining proportion of its outlay for new machinery being spent on automation equipment (defined as "advanced mechanical equipment, especially in combination with self-regulating controls and/or high-speed computers.")[31] All this spells a poor prospect for productivity growth in U.S. industry, as there is a weight of evidence that productivity growth depends importantly on increased capital investment.[32]

Growth in productivity is also strongly affected by the ability of an industrial system to produce new knowledge in science and technology and to apply it to industrial work. This capability is directly affected by the number of scientists and engineers serving civilian industry. As shown earlier, in 1965

American industry had the use of a proportionately much larger population of scientists and engineers compared with other major industrial countries. But this advantage had been wiped out by 1977, when Japan had 50 scientists and engineers serving civilian industry per 10,000 in the labor force, West Germany 40, and the United States an estimated 38.[33]

Especially because of the large scale of military research and development activity in the United States, it is useful to compare the *civilian* R & D expenditures, expressed as a percentage of gross national product, in several countries. In 1976 these percentages were:

United States	1.39
Japan	1.91 (1974)
West Germany	2.09[34]

Even though the United States has had a much larger total R & D activity as compared to either Western Europe as a whole or Japan, the civilian proportion of the U.S. R & D has been much smaller than in the other major industrial areas.

Another way of looking at the effectiveness of R & D on behalf of productivity growth is to trace to its source the funding for R & D that is actually carried out in business enterprise. In Japan, during 1975, 98 percent of R & D in the "business enterprise sector" was funded by the firms themselves. That same year the figure was 79 percent for West Germany, and 64 percent for the United States.[35] This means that in Japan virtually all the R & D carried on by industrial firms was presumably used for these firms' ordinary industrial civilian purposes. The portion was less in West Germany and markedly less in the United States, where 36 percent of the R & D in industrial firms was done on behalf of projects (mainly military-serving) of the federal government.

These three important industrial systems also show a considerable contrast in the purposes for which their respective governments used public R & D money in the 1970s: In Japan during 1974–1975, 78 percent of public research funds were applied to "the advancement of knowledge" and "economic development"; in West Germany (1976), these interests were supported by 64 percent of public research activity; while in the United States, they received but 13 percent of public R & D expenditures.[36]

In West Germany and Japan, the state has proved to be an important organizing instrument for spurring economic development; in the United States the national government has deployed its large R & D resources primarily on behalf of its military and related enterprises.

The fundamental importance of stable operating conditions for optimum industrial productivity was recognized long ago (as noted in chapter 7). A stable production system can operate at close approximation to the planned capacities of single machines and work sections, and is inherently more predictable, hence plannable. By the same token, an unstable operation—be it a single machine or a factory or an enterprise—cannot be planned; its functioning cannot be forecast. Its instability, therefore, largely precludes the possibility of obtaining maximum productivity from either labor or the capital investments involved.*

But though these considerations were known in the United States, they were first applied widely and systematically in the manufacturing industries of Japan. This came about as the derived effect of an intensive and sustained effort to improve the quality of product while striving to minimize industrial costs. If single work tasks, and then combined operations, are refined in order to reduce defects and other waste, production goes forward in a progressively more predictable fashion.

When management serves production, its decision-making can contribute substantially to the improvement of productivity. But management in the service of control has been the prestige- and money-rewarded style in the United States. Then the ultimate product is no longer goods, but money— in pursuit of which U.S. managers have been willing to reduce domestic production, the better to operate in the context of short-term profits and evade the long-term calculations of product and process improvement. Even the potentials of new industrial technologies, like computer control of machine operations and robotics, are often viewed mainly as instruments to extend managerial control, with emphasis on work simplification, and removal of decision-making responsibility and discretion from the work force. Therefore, management has been ready to accept much less than optimum productivity from the new technology, if by so doing it gains further control over the work force.

Administrative functions of every sort have been expanded in scope and intensity, at very high costs in salaries, office equipment, floor space and supporting activity. Thereby, managerial control functions have been extended without regard to their negative effect on productivity. When managers exert themselves primarily to strengthen their control over other people, details of equipment selection, product design, age of equipment, and productivity are bound to get short shrift. The president of Sony, a sophisticated manager, has summed it up:

---

*It is grimly fascinating to read a report done in 1948 by the Machinery and Allied Products Institute (Washington, D.C.) called *Technological Stagnation in Great Britain.* Paragraph after paragraph describes conditions that now exist in the machine tool and other industries in the United States.

A lot of American companies know they have old machines. But the manager figures he'll keep the old machines as long as they still run, make a big profit one year, and take that record as an advertisement to get a job elsewhere. So productivity here declines.[37]

Finally, this agenda of factors crucial to productivity growth must take into account the quality of the infrastructure of the American industrial economy. During the 1960s and '70s, when capital was lavished upon every aspect of the military economy, the underpinnings for a competent industrial system eroded. Major deterioration can be seen today in such vital services as clean water, roads, railroad transportation, ports, waste disposal, bridges and other facilities indispensable for an industrial system. (See details in chapter 12.)

The impact of the military economy has of course registered on all the "average" data that I have presented on the U.S. industrial system. However, its effect on productivity has been especially unhappy and should be examined in some detail. In this review I do not emphasize how internal operations affect the economy of the military class of products. Rather, the focus is on the effects of the total military operation on the rest of the economic system.

In the 37,000 firms that are prime contractors to the U.S. Department of Defense, the Pentagon has effectively displaced cost-minimizing with a system of cost- and subsidy-maximizing. By doing so, the state management has been instrumental in destroying a decision-making process that operated for more than a century in the United States to spur the mechanization of work and thus improve productivity.*

For engineers or industrial managers who have been trained to minimize cost in the design and production of industrial goods, the normal operation of a military industry firm is a professional nightmare. With rare exception, such firms operate according to an upside-down version of the engineers' and production managers' handbook of preferred practices for minimizing industrial costs. And close analyses of the military economy indicate that the cost-plus relationship prevails, no matter what formally detailed language appears in the contract arrangement.[38]

A considerable literature is now available on the nature of the U.S. military economy, including the escalation of costs. Only rarely, however, are we

---

*The impact of the management styles preferred by the military economy directorate is probably less intense among the 100,000 "subcontractors." The effects are surely felt there as well, but the prime contractors maintain the closest relationships with the Pentagon's top management, including the presence in their plants of permanent teams of civilian and military personnel, who assure the firms' compliance with the general policies laid down by the Pentagon's central office.

given an insider's account of military industry operations. One such view has been delineated by J. Ronald Fox, professor at the Harvard Graduate School of Business Administration and onetime Assistant Secretary of Defense for the U.S. Army. In *Arming America: How the U.S. Buys Weapons* (Graduate School of Business Administration, Harvard University, 1974), Fox carefully notes that "this study is not an exposé. It is an attempt to pinpoint the most fundamental reasons for breakdowns in the acquisition process." Nevertheless, in the course of attempting to identify the facts of what he terms "problems of cost growth, schedule slippage, and technical performance shortfalls," Fox has provided an ample body of information for understanding how the military industry system operates to maximize cost. (See Appendix III for substantial excerpts of a review essay written by the present author on Fox's volume.)

Since the state military economy has been an important customer for firms in the machinery-producing industry, its specifications for machinery products and the prices it is prepared to pay for them bear heavily on the operation of the supplying firms. The effect on the strategically important industry has been decisive. During the 1970s the characteristic pattern of cost-maximizing within industrial firms appeared in U.S. machinery production, prices of machinery rising more rapidly than the wages of labor. By contrast, during the same decade, prices of German- and Japanese-made machine tools relative to industrial wages demonstrated that cost-minimizing was alive and well in Japan and West Germany during the 1970s.

Here, in summary, are the percent changes in labor costs compared to machine tool prices in three countries, 1971–1978:

	Worker Earnings/Hour	*Machine Tool Prices*
United States	+72	+85
West Germany	+72	+59
Japan	+177	+51

These data mark the end of a way of industrial life in the United States.

The state managers have also wielded their decision power on behalf of their nuclear enterprise, with the result that they have impaired the productivity of the extremely important electricity-generating industry. Until the mid-1960s low prices to industrial users of electrical energy were an important spur to the mechanization of work. That cheap energy was made possible by a persistent productivity growth within the electric utility industry, a process that ended well before OPEC was invented.

During the first two-thirds of the twentieth century, the price of electrical energy to industrial users in the United States declined year by year. Improvements in the efficiency of converting fuel to energy, and of transmitting electricity, made it possible to offset increases in the wages of labor, prices of fuels and costs of machinery. As a result, electrical energy became a spectacular bargain in the United States, when compared to the cost of industrial labor. In 1909, when industrial hourly earnings averaged 19.3 cents and the price of electricity to industrial users was 2.2 cents per kilowatt-hour, manufacturers could buy 8.8 kilowatt-hours at the cost of one man-hour of factory labor. By 1925, that figure was up to 39.1 kwh and by 1950 American manufacturers could buy 157 kilowatt-hours at the cost of an average man-hour of labor. This reduction in both the absolute and the relative price of electrical energy to U.S. industry continued until 1966, when for the first time in the century the electric utility industry could no longer compensate for cost increases by improving its internal efficiency. That happened just seven years before OPEC's "oil shock" in 1973.

The remarkable record of the electricity-generating industry for two-thirds of a century was achieved by persistent reduction in the fuel consumed per kilowatt-hour, by reduction in labor requirements, and by increased output per unit of capital assigned to production and distribution. Among these factors, efficiency in the conversion of fuel was central. This is ordinarily expressed as a "heat rate," the number of British thermal units contained in the fuel per kilowatt-hour of electricity produced. Thus the heat rate in 1925 in the United States averaged 25,000 Btu per kilowatt-hour; by 1965 it had been reduced to 10,400 Btu per kilowatt-hour. The electricity-manufacturing industry maintained this steady improvement in fuel efficiency thanks in large part to the general progress in science and technology, but, specifically, it benefited from the persistent research and development carried out by the manufacturers of major power plant equipment.

It was in the 1950s that a new factor entered the scene. The federal managers, centered in the Atomic Energy Commission and the Department of Defense, had embarked on a major campaign to outstrip the rest of the world in nuclear technology for military and allied purposes. The main allied purpose was the generation of electrical energy, and since atomic power plants required nuclear fuel from the facilities of the AEC, the state managers had in their control the primary instruments that would be needed for a nuclear electricity enterprise in the United States and elsewhere.

Accordingly, the government, through the Atomic Energy Commission, became a principal subsidizer, manager, advocate, research director and regulator of a new nuclear power industry in the United States. From 1954 to 1967 the AEC spent $2 billion on civilian application of nuclear power, a sum supplemented by one-half that amount from private sources. In combination, these private and public capital allotments marked a shift in finance capital away from the fossil-fueled steam-electric technologies. To protect them from disastrous losses in the event of major accidents, the Price-Anderson Act of 1958 guaranteed to indemnify the owners of nuclear plants at a maximum of $500 million for any single nuclear accident.

As is now known, the early promise of virtually free electrical energy from nuclear power has never been fulfilled. The construction time for nuclear plants lengthened, it sometimes has seemed almost interminably, as design requirements became increasingly complex to meet reasonable standards of safety and reliability. At the same time, costs for nuclear plant construction escalated to levels that made inevitable a price for electricity well above that of fossil fuel plants. Most dismaying, perhaps, was the persistently higher down time of nuclear plants, as compared to coal-fired stations. The nuclear technology simply could not match the levels of reliability that had long since been attained in the electricity-generating industry. But none of these disappointments deterred the federal government's state managers from their enthusiastic pursuit of the new power industry. Thus a technical advisory committee on research and development for the Federal Power Commission recommended in its *Report on R and D for the Electric Utility Industry* (1974) that $25 billion be spent for R & D during the period 1974–1985, of which 50 percent should be for nuclear power and 18 percent for fossil fuel technology and various new conversion techniques.

As the state managers marshalled capital investment, government and private, to expand their new nuclear industry, they generated a series of collateral effects that combined to raise the price of electric power in the United States. The manufacturers of generating equipment, scrambling to expand in the new nuclear industry, with its federal subsidies and prospects for international expansion, gave priority of research and of general manufacturing attention to the new nuclear technology and neglected the established fossil fuel equipment.

During 1963–1975, the number of engineers, technicians and scientists working on design and engineering of nuclear facilities, including reactors, increased more than threefold, from 16,786 to 61,318.[39] The recruitment of a large national contingent of scientists, engineers and technicians for the new nuclear enterprise necessarily required a major transfer of such people from their R & D, design and production responsibilities in firms producing fossil fuel equipment of all classes.

At the same time, industry informants say, prices of nuclear conversion equipment were favored over advanced fossil fuel equipment. That is, the major manufacturers were less interested in making the prices of fossil fuel equipment attractive to electric utility customers. The state management's subsidies to the nuclear enterprise also induced railroads and coal operators to lessen their long-sustained efforts to continue as major suppliers of the coal-using electric utility industry. They were discouraged by the massive federal assistance to the new nuclear industry.

During the long history of the electric utility industry, the steady introduction of new power plants with improved fuel efficiencies permitted the retirement of older, less efficient plants, thus raising the average fuel efficiency of the industry. This process was abridged as the electric utility industry concentrated its money and technical talent on nuclear technology.

The net effect of these factors has been to create in the electricity-generating industry a pattern of unimproved heat rates, of lower capacity performance by major plant and equipment, and of larger reserve margins dictated by the increased maintenance time required for the less reliable nuclear plant.

On the consumer side, the federal managers and the state regulatory commissions have joined in approving various price adjustment clauses that permit utilities to pass along to their customers the rising cost of fuel. Thus the incentive to offset costs has been substantially removed. The industry's successful cost-minimizing led in the past to a remarkably productive pattern of steadily falling electricity prices. That has now been replaced by cost pass-along and consequent price escalation.

The government managers, eager to expand their decision power over production at almost any price, persuaded the country and Congress to provide them with unprecedented capital funds for research and subsidy in the nuclear electricity industry. That technical and industrial-economic venture has failed, and as a result the American industrial economy pays in higher electricity costs, and thus in diminished productivity growth, to maintain and enlarge the decision power of state management's nuclear branch.

The normal operation of the military economy also depresses productivity in the rest of the American industrial system by preempting trained workers, technicians and engineers. The military firms can attract the skills they require because they are able to outbid other employers with financing guaranteed by the federal treasury. Military managers in the aerospace industry, for example, scoop up trained workers, production materials and special equipment with an intensity that produces critical shortages of personnel and supplies in the civilian sections of the same industry. Lockheed Corporation discovered in 1980 that production costs for its L-1011 passenger plane were soaring because of intense competition for workers and components from the military part of the aerospace industry.[40]

During the 1980s, the planned military budgets require the application of more than $2,089 billion of fresh capital resources for military purposes. This

will surely raise the ratio of military spending to civilian fixed capital formation to unprecedented heights, with far-ranging effects in limiting capital
resources for all civilian purposes and causing an escalation in interest rates.
For the civilian economy this promises depressed rates of fresh capital investment and further restraint on productivity growth.*

By its command of the largest single block of research and development
resources in the American economy, the federal military enterprise, whether
intentionally or not, exerts a major restraining effect on productivity growth.
That is because the largest part of the military's R & D funds are for applied
research and development; that is, they are directed to the design and development of particular military products rather than to the accumulation of new
knowledge that may have wide application. For 1982 and 1983 the state
management, as part of the general military escalation, earmarked increased
research spending for military and related operations. This will intensify the
priority accorded the military in the federal government's R & D activities
of the last three decades. The importance of this trend is underscored by the
substantial consensus among scholars in the field that the social "cost of
federal R & D contracts in defense-space programs has been slower growth,
reduced productivity, and lower quality of output in the civilian sector."[41]

The siphoning of R & D money into the military economy has direct effect
on the availability of technical resources for the civilian economy. Thus, in
1970 the military-serving manufacturing industries employed an average of
7.4 scientists and engineers in research and development for every hundred
production workers. For the rest, the larger part of manufacturing industry,
this percentage was 1.0.[42]

Notwithstanding the accumulating evidence to the contrary, many
Americans continue to believe that, by a process of spinoff, the technical work
done for the military yields great benefits to civilian economy. The fact is that
such benefits are severely limited by the applied and product development
character of much of the military work. Indeed, a formal inquiry into the
possible percentage of spinoff effect from military research expenditures has
found that perhaps 5 percent, but not more than 10 percent, of spinoff for each
military research dollar may have occurred.[43]

As might be expected from a cost-maximizing economy, the productivity
of research on behalf of the Pentagon and NASA is modest. " . . . the U.S.
Department of Commerce has estimated that ten man-years of industrial
R & D produce a commercializable patent, but that it takes a thousand
man-years to produce such a patent from either in-house or contract R & D

---

*At this writing, my estimate is that by 1988 the military use of capital in the United States will be
about $87 per $100 of (civilian) fixed capital formation.

work from DOD or NASA."[44] The military use of R & D resources is clearly a prescription for withdrawing vital technological assistance from attempts to improve productivity.

The government's military directorate also hinders productivity by its propensity to encourage unstable rates of production. Conferences convened in Washington by the managers of the military economy show a sustained interest in such factors as "surge capability"—the ability of plant managers to expand output very quickly in response to military demand. But that requires the existence of large, mainly idle, production facilities, as well as access to a pool of labor, all skills, that can be tapped at will. In this way military planning institutionalizes industrial instability.

In chapter 8 I called attention to the massive size of the capital funds that have been preempted for the military economy, and gave some examples of equivalent civilian capital investments. An important part of the civilian investments forgone includes provisions for rail and road transportation, water supply, bridges, sewers, dams on major rivers, and the set of public buildings and facilities in the nation's large cities. In 1981 the Council of State Planning Agencies, comprising the planning and policy staffs of the nation's governors, found that "America's public facilities are wearing out faster than they are being replaced. . . . the maintenance of public facilities essential to national economic renewal has been deferred, replacement of obsolescent public works has been postponed. New construction has been cancelled. The deteriorated condition of basic facilities that underpin the economy will prove a critical bottleneck to national economic renewal during this decade unless we can find ways to finance public works."[45] By making all sorts of productive industrial investment more costly or impossible to achieve, the preemption of capital that has cost the United States the deterioration of its infrastructure translates into substantial counterproductivity.

It is generally acknowledged that the vanguard of mechanization for industrial work, worldwide, will henceforth include a major component of computers, allied electronic devices and robots. In the United States, developments in these fields are strongly affected by the interests of state management. By noting the overall style of the Pentagon's operations, we can anticipate the productivity consequences for the United States that will be traceable to the military's dominant position.

Since the Pentagon awards its contracts without competitive bidding and encourages cost-maximization, the resulting products will necessarily lack the cost-minimizing characteristics that might attract commercial buyers and encourage widespread installation. Delays in production and a further contribution to high costs will be the result of the Pentagon's practice of awarding contracts to preferred industrial firms, which often operate within severe infrastructure limitations—limited labor force, scarce housing, inadequate transportation, etc. Furthermore, the Pentagon's allocation of R & D and production contracts is habitually short-term-oriented, hence necessarily unstable. This means that instability is automatically imposed on the scientists and engineers it employs. Also, the Pentagon is biased against free commercial exploitation of technologies developed for its own purposes, and therefore imposes export and related controls which seriously impede the prospects for marketing such high-technology products.

All this contrasts markedly with Japanese and Western European practice, wherein the state is used as an instrument to encourage productivity, productive employment and marketing success.

Inasmuch as the Pentagon has been granted major increased control over capital resources during the 1980s, the prognosis for industrial productivity in the United States is somber.[46]

At the outset of this chapter, we identified a set of conditions that are favorable to productivity growth: Cost-minimizing within the machinery-producing industries; cost-minimizing among machinery users; rising wages of labor relative to machinery prices; availability of finance capital at modest interest rates; research and development to innovate new means of production; operation of a stable production system; management oriented to production, and availability of a competent infrastructure. In the normal pursuit of their profits/power, the private and state managers of the U.S. have created circumstances that are, in every major respect, detrimental to productivity growth.

INCOMPETENCE IN PRODUCTION

As a consequence of the evolution of managerial guidance of technology and other capital resources for profits/power, the classic productivity mechanism in U.S. industry broke down. In another era, the failure of particular managements was often an opportunity for fresh entrepreneurs to undertake the management of production. The present condition is different in that incompetence in production in the United States has become epidemic. Fresh production that replaces the failed factories in the United States comes typically from other economies. Meanwhile, the American community becomes the scene of a deterioration without precedent: a shabby infrastructure for the economy and society, and massed, permanent unemployment owing to deindustrialization.

10

Deterioration in the Industrial System

For a decade after World War II, the automobile industry in the United States not only paid the highest wages in the world to its industrial workers but also produced the lowest-priced cars in the world, measured in price per pound of vehicle. Detroit pay scales were two to three times those of auto workers in Western Europe. But the average productivity of labor in the U.S. auto industry, thanks to greater mechanization and more refined organization of work, was about three times that of Western Europe. As a result, the Detroit product was so attractively priced that it not only dominated the U.S. market but was also exported to markets around the world.

By 1980, twenty-five years later, the situation had been transformed. The U.S. auto industry was able to sell only 73 percent of the cars appearing on the roads of America. The remaining 27 percent were imported from Western Europe and, especially, from Japan.

The automobile industry has been the flagship enterprise of the mass-producing, high-productivity economy. During the twentieth century its methods have been the model for other industries worldwide. Therefore the loss by this industry of one customer out of four within the U.S. home market is proof of a massive industrial breakdown.

The air has been full of recriminations about who is at fault. Everyone knows, of course, that the auto industry's "Big Three" firms clung far too long to the production and selling of big cars for big profits; but the main issue here is competence in production. The top managers of the Big Three have singled out the high wages of U.S. auto workers as the prime cause of their noncompetitiveness in the marketplace. In fact, however, in 1980 the average hourly payment to U.S. auto workers ($15.02) was less than the earnings of their German ($15.46) and Belgian ($15.30) counterparts.[1] To be sure, average hourly earnings of U.S. auto workers in that year were more than twice those of Japanese workers ($7.16), but it is important to recall that, during the 1950s, when the wages of U.S. auto workers were two to three times those of Western European workers, that proved no barrier to the U.S. industry's holding its domestic market, as well as sizable markets abroad. At that time, Detroit offset the wage differential with high productivity of labor and capital. What, then, happened to the productivity of labor and capital in the 1980s? Why is the U.S. auto industry unable today to compensate, as it once did so effectively, for differences in labor and other costs?

No comprehensive comparison has been made of productivity in the Japanese, U.S. and Western European auto industries. From 1980 to 1982, however, there have been several independent estimates of aspects of productivity in the U.S. and Japanese auto industries.[2] The consensus of these estimates is that Japanese manufacturers of subcompact autos have been able to offer them for sale in the United States at a cost advantage of $1,200 to $1,700 per 1980 vehicle. Again, what is the source of this new inability among the U.S. firms? The place to begin is with the quality of the means of production themselves, and then the methods of production organization.

Machine tools are the basic production equipment of the auto industries. In 1978, 76 percent of the machine tools used in the U.S. auto industry were ten years old or older. Its production equipment was older than the average for all U.S. manufacturing (69 percent ten years old and older).[3] The managers of the Big Three failed to modernize and upgrade their basic production equipment. Many production divisions were treated as "cash cows," being milked of their assets. The failure to upgrade production methods is also reflected in large productivity differences among the various factories. When auto factories were ranked by productivity per employee during the late 1960s, the top quarter was two and a half times as productive as the lowest quarter. This signalled a pattern of neglected maintenance and withholding of fresh investment in important parts of the industry.[4]

But the development of major differences in the organization of production between the U.S. and the Japanese auto industries has probably had the major effect on productivity. The core of the matter is this: major Japanese auto firms have discovered the connection between stabilization of production rates and increased productivity of labor and capital, as well as the wide range of cost savings that are made possible when a production system is operated in a sustained, stable pattern.

Two ideas are crucial here: stable operation of a single machine means working at rates within predictable and acceptable limits. The average output (productivity) of the machine improves automatically as it approaches stability. For example, when a power plant is operated in a stable manner, more electricity is produced for each ton of fuel that is consumed. The rolls in steel rolling mills last longer when they are used at more even speeds.[5]

The second underlying idea is that stabilization of output rate in an entire factory raises the productivity of the system as a whole. This results from the ramified effects caused by the removal of interferences with the steady operation of single machines and with the flow of work through many operations.

When output is stabilized in an entire factory, there are fewer breakdowns, and the average life of machines and metal-cutting tools is increased, resulting in a higher degree of utilization of the production machines (the actual operating time increases as a proportion of the available time). At the same time, stabilization lowers scrap rates and improves the quality of product. Under these conditions it becomes possible to operate an entire factory with a substantially reduced inventory of work in process, since "buffers" are not required between operations as insurance against breakdowns. For similar reasons inventories of raw materials and purchased components can also be reduced. Those reductions, in turn, make possible a larger output in proportion to the working capital invested in the plant. Also, owing to the higher productivity of individual machines, and lessened requirement for factory floor space for in-process storage, a smaller fixed investment is possible in machines and factory buildings. All told, the stabilization of output in a factory as a whole makes possible substantial improvement in the productivity of capital.

Under these conditions there is, necessarily, an increased productivity per production worker man-hour. The productivity of labor is increased by the higher degree of machine utilization, reduction of scrap rates, and reduction of materials-handling work.

As must be obvious, more is involved here than a simple statistical harmony between machines and materials. Stabilization of output in an entire production system requires a method of organization of work, of decision-making on production, that encourages sustained cooperation among workers, technicians, engineers and administrators. Such cooperation is the vital element that permits a production system to respond to the requirements of stable operation. And there is little evidence to support the prevailing idea that a managerially imposed supervisory system can produce in an auto factory the fine integration of operations made possible by a cooperating work force.

An early description and diagnosis of a stabilized system of work organization in an auto factory appeared in my 1958 book *Decision-Making and Productivity.*[6] There I described and analyzed the operation of the automobile- and tractor-producing factories of the Standard Motor Company in

Coventry, England. The main effects of the stable production system were all there: reduced variation in output rates; unusually high productivity of capital and labor; strikingly low inventories of work in process per vehicle produced; close attention to preventive maintenance and markedly efficient performance of emergency maintenance to prevent downtime; a sharp increase in average output per worker and output per unit of capital investment that corresponded with the stabilization of output rate in the factory as a whole; very high product quality.*

In the Standard Motor Company the production-oriented management defined itself, saying "we try to give a service to the factory." With respect to the familiar process of expansion of managerial control and costs, the top management at Standard said: "We just don't want to have people who do empire building. We make it a point of going after a person who attempts to enlarge his staff."[7] As might be expected, the Standard Motor Company operated with substantially lower administrative costs than did other automobile firms of Great Britain, which included Ford and General Motors.[8] The stabilized production system comprises, together with a congruent mode of work organization that induces cooperation in production, the optimum productivity system for any given degree of mechanization of work.

All this is necessary background for appreciating the contrast between the 1970s' and 1980s' productivity in the American and Japanese automobile industries. In 1977 four engineers of the Toyota Motor Company presented a joint paper on the Toyota production system at the Fourth International Conference on Production Research (Tokyo), August 1977.[9] Here is the text of the summary of this paper as presented:

The Toyota Production System and Kanban System introduced in this paper were developed by the Vice-President of Toyota Motor Company, Mr. Taiichi Ohno, and it was under his guidance that these unique production systems have become deeply rooted in Toyota Motor Company in the past 20 years. There are two major distinctive features in these systems. One of these is "just-in-time production" [inventory minimizing—S.M.], a specially important factor in an assembly industry such as automotive manufacturing. In this type of production, "only the necessary products,

---

*The system of work organization that operated in the factories of the Standard Motor Company involved a management-union agreement on a "gang system" whereby worker groups took responsibility for the detailed allocation of work tasks. Production bonuses were paid to the gang's members on the basis of the output of the group as a whole. In the tractor factory, the entire factory formed one gang, with output measured by quality-accepted tractors at the end of the line. Every worker, technician, engineer and administrator in the factory knew the production targets for the day and the week and could therefore gauge every individual work performance in accordance with the requirement of the factory's goals. There are, of course, alternative possible ways of inducing cooperation for the detailed performance of production work.

at the necessary time, in necessary quantity" are manufactured, and in addition, the stock on hand is held down to a minimum. Second, the system is the "respect-for-human" system where the workers are allowed to display in full their capabilities through active participation in running and improving their own workshops.

The Toyota engineers emphasize that in order to minimize inventories throughout the auto plant it is essential "to level the production at the final assembly line, the most important line," that sets the pace for all the other production divisions of the factory. Levelling production means stabilizing production.

Y. Sugimori and his associates have touched in this paper on the principal features of the stable production system and the cooperation-inducing method of work organization as developed at Toyota. Their data show a much higher productivity of fixed and working capital compared with other Japanese and principal U.S. firms, fewer man-hours required for "completion of a vehicle in automotive assembly plants" of Toyota as against factories in the United States, Sweden, and West Germany, high productivity in the press shops of the Toyota factories as against comparable units in these countries. The Toyota engineers also reported a frequency rate of injuries in the factory for 1974 that was almost one-half the average in U.S. auto plants.

Sugimori and his colleagues did not refer to the cost of managing under these conditions. That information is available to us from an officer of the Ford Motor Company. As I noted earlier, Ford has twelve layers of organization "from the factory floor to the chairman's office, compared with only seven layers at Toyota. At Toyota a foreman reports directly to the plant manager. In a typical Ford plant . . . the foreman must struggle through three layers of in-plant management to get to the plant manager."[10] The same Ford official estimates that halving the white-collar staff "in Ford's North American automotive operations alone would lower Ford's costs from $4 billion to $2 billion per year." Informed observers of the auto industry in the United States and Japan estimate that the average of top official salaries in General Motors, compared to Toyota, is about five to one.

In sum: as the U.S. auto industry managers have stressed their goals of short-term profits/power, they have operated production facilities by methods that are the obverse of those required for a stable production system, thus debasing the productivity of both labor and capital. The product quality, cost and price noncompetitiveness of U.S. auto firms are derived effects of these conditions.

.   .   .

For a century after the Civil War, the manufacture of steel occupied a central position in the industry and economy of the United States. The prices set by steel's managements became costs for the rest of the industrial system. Similarly, the pay scales prevailing in the steel industry, including those negotiated with the United Steelworkers of America after the 1930s, became a standard for wages in the rest of the industrial work force. With easy access to abundant and cheap coal and iron ore, and sitting in the middle of the world's largest market for steel, U.S. producers held key advantages over steelmakers in Western Europe and Japan.

Soon after World War II, new technologies made possible a revolution in steelmaking. The basic oxygen furnace superseded the open-hearth furnace. Continuous casting of steel shapes replaced the traditional rolling mill. These new production methods, plus ever more refined control systems, yielded great economies in the use of raw materials and fuel, raising the productivity of capital and, as always, that of labor.

The diligent pursuit of the new technologies in Europe and Japan—plus, in Japan, the economies derived from large-scale plants and equipment—finally gave these countries a competitive edge for many steel products that extended even to the American market. By the end of the 1970s, the steelmakers of Japan and Western Europe were supplying between 15 and 20 percent of the requirements of American steel-using firms. By 1978, one out of five jobs in the U.S. steel industry had been suspended or terminated.

But the underlying science and the attendant technology for the revolution in steel production was known around the world. Why didn't the managers of U.S. steel firms order their development and application in their own plants? What policies and practices inhibited them? A diagnosis of production costs is the place to start.

By 1978, the "[average production] cost of Japanese steel (F.O.B. Japan) was about $385/ton (materials, labor, capital costs)—some 10 to 20 percent below U.S. production costs."[11] One forecast is that during the 1980s production costs in major steel-producing countries will tend to even out, "with an approximate 15 percent margin between the highest (France) and lowest-cost (Japan). . . . West Germany and Japan are expected to continue as leaders in the more efficient use of raw materials, with cost increases at only about half the U.S. rate."[12]

For basic *carbon* steel, we have comparative information about production costs in the U.S., West Germany and Japan.

First, the total production costs per ton of *carbon* steel in 1978:[13]

United States	$395.65
West Germany	438.12
Japan	410.51

Three categories of cost dominate this scene: materials, employment, and financial. Here are the materials costs per ton, which in each country amount to more than half the total:[14]

United States	$237.66
West Germany	243.87
Japan	227.03

Both West Germany and Japan have paid higher prices for raw materials (coal, iron ore, electricity) than the steel industry of the United States. But they use those materials more efficiently. Therefore the materials component of total production costs, notably in Japan, is less than in the United States. Energy-saving equipment is given high priority in Japan. By contrast, in the factories of the American steel industry, equipment is older and therefore less efficient in extracting the energy potential of fuels and the metal content of ores.

By 1979, 33 percent of U.S. steel production facilities were more than 20 years old and 12 percent were more than 30 years old.[15] That age of U.S. steel industry equipment must be set against the 11 years required to recover (depreciate) the cost of new plant and equipment in the U.S. industry. In West Germany, the cost-recovery period is 10 years; in Japan it is 11 years.[16]

Since there is a substantial discrepancy between an 11-year period of amortization of U.S. steel plant and equipment and the 17.5-year average age of domestic steel production facilities, one wonders what happened to the revenue available after the 11-year amortization period. It would seem that the steel-making facilities of the major U.S. steel firms were milked for cash flow that was accumulated and used for investment elsewhere, for dividends and for large senior executive salaries. Notwithstanding this record, top managers of the U.S. Steel Corporation complain about being disadvantaged by "the world's slowest capital recovery times" and the increase in "wages faster than output per man-hour."[17] Apparently, steel company executives, often without firsthand experience in production, are prone to believe their own rhetoric.

After World War II the basic oxygen furnace was, on grounds of energy and material savings, the clearly desirable successor to the open-hearth furnace. By 1980 the following were the percentages of steel output from the new process:[18]

United States	62
West Germany	75
France	75
Japan	80

By 1978, a similar pattern was visible in the use of continuous casting—which also permits large savings in energy and materials, as well as labor, over older methods. The respective percentages of raw steel output using continuous casting were:[19]

United States	15
European Community	29
Japan	50

The backwardness of the U.S. steelmakers with respect to the use of continuous casting is striking when one considers that the process eliminates energy-intensive and materials-wasting methods that involve the pouring of hot steel into ingots, reheating the ingots in soaking pits, and finally rolling them to desired shape in massive rolling mills. The continuous caster takes hot metal into a mold and draws it through a curved, water-cooled channel so that within four minutes a continuous stream of shaped semi-finished steel emerges, ready to be cut to the desired length. "U.S. steelmakers will increase their continuous casting output to 41.2 million tons within two years. That will be about 25 percent of their steel-making capacity, up from only 18 percent in 1980."[20] With that addition, the United States will still be well behind the Europeans, with about 43 percent of their output continuously cast, and the Japanese with 65 percent. Indeed, F. K. Iverson, president of Nucor Corporation, a small, technically sophisticated "mini-mill" steelmaker at Norfolk, Nebraska, believes that "if a U.S. steel company doesn't have continuous-cast production in the next five or six years, it won't be in the steel business."[21] The backwardness is the more deplorable because of the large energy savings to be gained by the use of continuous casting (about $15 per ton) and the reduction of waste by at least 10 percent in the finished material.

From time to time, management spokesmen in the U.S. steel industry have pleaded that the high costs of the made-in-U.S.A. equipment have prevented investment in the new technology. There is little evidence, however, that the industry has grappled with its major suppliers on the cost issue. Neither has there been any concerted effort by companies to do research and development on problems of equipment and facilities design. On the whole, the companies have accepted the relative cost of machinery to labor, or the cost of machinery relative to materials, as a given, limiting condition. By tacitly agreeing to this condition, management has permitted equipment costs to rise while seeking opportunities for profitable investment outside the industry. Industry managers have under-invested in equipment, general plant, technical research and process innovation.

The Office of Technology Assessment concluded, in its wide-ranging and sober report to Congress, that "More often than not, steel industry executives express a desire to be second with proven technology not first with new technology . . . domestic firms also tend to sell whatever innovative technology they do create as quickly as possible, in order to maximize immediate profits, instead of keeping the technology proprietary and thereby gaining a competitive advantage. . . . One explanation for these and other such shortcomings is a lack of dedicated, long-range strategic planning by domestic steel companies, particularly by integrated producers."[22]

In the absence of a substantial commitment to research and development by steel management, it is unreasonable to expect much ability among these firms either to innovate technology, or to make timely use of innovations developed elsewhere.

In addition to the dominant cost of materials, carbon steel production requires large doses of manpower and capital. The average employment costs per ton of carbon steel show the Japanese industry at advantage. Again, for 1978:[23]

United States	$127.18
West Germany	134.23
Japan	101.60

The lower Japanese employment cost, however, is offset by high financial costs per ton; these include interest charges for financing (particularly heavy in Japan and West Germany), amortization of plant and equipment:[24]

United States	$30.91
West Germany	60.02
Japan	81.87

In the U.S. steel industry, the cost of materials has accounted for 60 percent of average cost per ton of carbon steel, employment 32 percent, and financial costs 8 percent. This means, for example, that a 10 percent efficiency gain in the use of materials and energy would yield twice the cost saving of a 10 percent wage reduction. Since it is often held that U.S. wage rates are a sufficient explanation for the growing inability of American firms to compete, it is worth shedding further light on wages.

Here, in 1978 dollars, are the steel industry employment costs per hour (wages plus fringe benefits) for the United States, West Germany and Japan:

United States	$14.73
West Germany	11.34
Japan	10.42

Even more interesting are the average annual percent increases in the dollar cost of employment from 1969 to 1978:[25]

United States	18.4
West Germany	42.3
Japan	55.8

Obviously, the long-established lower wages of West Germany and Japan have been rising swiftly and, assuming the continuance of anything like these rates of increase, will exceed U.S. wage levels within a few years.*

Up to this point, the focus has been on components of production cost. But price must, of course, include administrative costs and profits. The costs of managing, though an important factor in the total picture of modern industry, are seldom mentioned in analyses of the steel industry. By 1977, for every 100 production workers in the U.S. steel industry, 26 people were employed in administrative, technical and clerical occupations. Studies of the steel industry in the United States and other countries have established that there is a *negative* correlation between administrative employment and steel industry output.[26] Administrative costs in this industry have been rising. The ratio of administrative to production employees in the steel industry was 14 in 1947 and had risen to 26 by 1977.

Within the management of steel industry firms, the tendency has been to improve the position of accounting and financial executives. The steel industry "employs only about 60 percent as many scientists and engineers as the average manufacturing industry."[27] Of these technical personnel only about 5 percent are in the top management organizations of the industry. In the operation of steel firms "financial considerations are given priority, operating considerations are secondary, and technology is at best ranked third. . . . Technological change per se is generally not a primary concern of steel executives."[28]

Independent observers judge that in the larger "integrated" firms (from mines to finished steel products) that have long dominated the industry, management tradition has favored the adoption of " 'off the shelf' solutions, while maximizing the performance of existing technology. . . . In the process a whole cadre of engineers (in effect 'craftsmen') has been displaced by 'unit'

---

*The rising value of the U.S. dollar relative to other currencies can have an important countervailing effect on the relative dollar-cost growth in steel that is owing to the rising wages of Germany and Japan, measured in their own currencies. Thus, as the high interest rates in U.S. financial markets attracted large blocks of finance-capital, the relative value of the dollar was bid up compared to the mark and yen. Hence when American, German and Japanese wage costs are compared in dollars, the lessened exchange values of the mark and yen cause an apparent decline in German and Japanese wages. This effect has been operative in the period 1979–1982.

managers, MBAs with little or no technical understanding, who have difficulties in fitting the off the shelf 'unit' into an organic whole. . . . Technological competence in the U.S. steel industry has been depleted, while managerial 'know-how,' its intended substitute, has not been capable of filling the gap."[29]

The managements of the major U.S. steel firms have focused on short-term profit, and in these terms they have succeeded admirably: "Despite major technological and economic difficulties, domestic steel industry profit levels have been higher than those of foreign steel industries, although they are only about half the U.S. manufacturing average."[30]

A comparison of profit rates in the U.S. and the West German/Japanese steel industries is complicated by differences in the sources of capital. "Japanese companies are about 83 percent debt-financed compared to an average of 44 percent for U.S. steelmakers."[31] This means that U.S. firms derive the major part of their capital from the sale of stock, which is encouraged by a high level of dividends. The Japanese firms are financed mainly by loans from banks, with fixed rates of interest. Therefore, part of what appears as "profit" for a U.S. firm appears as interest "cost" for a Japanese firm. Nevertheless, the comparison of steel industry net income as a percent of net fixed assets (for 1969–1977) is instructive:[32]

United States	6.7
West Germany	2.9
Japan	1.7

For 1978 we can compare the pre-tax profit per ton of steel shipped:[33]

United States	$31.00
West Germany	−2.00
Japan	9.00

Indeed, this record has been a source of pride to the top managers in the industry. Thomas C. Graham, president of Jones and Laughlin Steel Corporation, says that the U.S. steel industry is the most "economically efficient" in the world, by which he means the most profitable.[34] But this kind of "efficiency" has been achieved at the price of serious technological obsolescence which has finally led to the inability of the industry to serve about one-fifth of the U.S. market.

How could the steel industry of the United States produce basic steel at a lower average cost per ton, earn higher profits than chief competitors and, at the same time, experience major plant closings during the late 1970s, with many managements bewailing their inability to compete—even in the United States domestic market? What appears as a contradiction is resolved when one understands that the industry-wide performance data that have been reviewed here are *averages* for many firms and factories. The efficiency of steel mills has, in fact, been highly varied. A unique tabulation for 1967 of productivity for separate blast furnaces and steel mills shows that, when ranked by productivity, the top 25 percent of factories had 2.3 times the productivity of the lowest quarter.*

Obviously, the wave of steel mill closings was concentrated in the lowest quarter of factories, ranked by productivity. This reflects the pattern of management neglect of renewal, by reinvestment, of production facilities, and the preference of top managers for moving profits out of the steel industry.

In many countries, including West Germany and Japan, whose steel industries are mostly privately owned, the managements operate within the framework of a national policy administered by the government for the purpose of making sure that the local steel industry is a fully competent supplier of products for the rest of the economy. In these countries the steel enterprises are not merely organizations for production and profits. They are subject to a governmental determination to sustain employment levels and the technical economic vitality of key components of the industrial system.

One might well ask: Where has the U.S. government been during this period when the U.S. steel industry fell steadily behind, until, in the years 1977 to 1979, there were wholesale closings of entire steel plants? Government managers, it seems, have been busy with enlarging and managing their own economy, the military economy. That is where resources and administrative attention have been lavished without stint, as shown in chapter 8.

In the very important realm of research and development, one steel industry R & D executive has concluded that: "There is a trend toward more defensive type of research . . . more time being spent on shorter-ranged projects and projects designed to meet government mandates and regulations, and less time being spent on the kinds of long-term, high-risk, innovative projects which will lead to the new ways of making steel in the future."[35]

What is crucial is not only the character of what the U.S. steel industry calls R & D—focused on short-range, quick-payoff operations—but also the relatively impoverished level of this activity. In 1972, the average R & D expenditures amounted to $1.30 per ton of raw steel produced. At the same

---

*Michael Boretsky, *U.S. Technology: Trends and Policy Issues,* U.S. Department of Commerce (Washington, D.C., October 1973). Productivity is measured here as Value Added per Employee for each steel mill. The factory data were ranked, then grouped by quarters, and the average of the top quarter was compared with that of the lowest quarter. The average Value Added per Employee of the top quarter was 2.3 times the average Value Added per Employee of the lowest-ranked quarter of steel mills.

time the European Community spent \$1.46 per ton, and Japan \$2.26 per ton.[36] More than that: during the 1960s and 1970s there was a continuous decline in the U.S. industry's R & D activity.

R & D personnel in the industry have little voice in strategic planning, even when it pertains to major new technology. The R & D function, such as it is, is often linked closer to sales and marketing than to production or corporate planning. By contrast, in European and Japanese steel industries, there tends to be a close association between production and R & D staffs. Furthermore, the European steel industries observe a tradition of mobility for engineering and scientific staff, who move about among firms, universities and government facilities. Working in R & D has high prestige, and attracts top-grade scientists and engineers.

Moreover, in those countries, managements in steel and in government see research and development as a valuable instrument for developing innovative solutions to competitive problems. Thus, "much of R & D effort in European universities and research institutes is government funded; in the United States, there has been a decline in academic steelmaking programs, largely because of a lack of government support. There are no national institutes for steel R & D, such as those in West Germany, in which companies join with university personnel in long-range R & D projects, including a great deal of basic research."[37] In the United States "the training and development of technical staff are geared to managerial and executive development rather than to on-going education in technical specialties. These are the areas viewed by management as the industry's backbone, an orientation reflected in mobility patterns that generally de-emphasize R & D."[38]

Given this background, it should come as no surprise that during the 1970s the U.S. steel industry reduced the average annual employee hours required per ton of carbon steel shipped by only 1.87 percent. In West Germany during the same period the average annual productivity improvement was .9 percent, but in Japan it was 3.7 percent. In 1980 the United States still showed a slight margin of advantage in total man-hours required per ton of steel shipped compared to Japan: U.S., 8.37 hours; Japan, 8.54 hours. But the rate of Japanese productivity improvement promises to reverse that pattern swiftly enough. Given a continuation of the previous trend, by 1985 the U.S. steel industry would use 7.19 hours per ton of steel produced compared with 6.48 hours for Japan.[39]

The steel industry has accounted for about one-fifth of all domestic industrial pollution, and independent observers note that it has unusually high rates of occupational illness and injury. This is an important part of the hostile management-labor relations that have long prevailed in the industry.

At the turn of the century and after, the great organizers of the major firms—Henry Frick, Andrew Carnegie, and the others—maintained a sternly authoritarian and often violent control over the largely immigrant work force. The industry resisted the wave of industrial unionism during the 1930s with methods that included the infamous Republic Steel Massacre. Management typically saw steel workers as inferior beings.

In 1911, Frederick Winslow Taylor published his proposals for setting industrial work standards, based upon his experience as a manager in the Midvale Steel Works. He emphasized the importance of removing all planning of work from the workers. As one justification for this general policy, he offered the following: " . . . the pig-iron handler is not an extraordinary man difficult to find; he is merely a man more or less of the type of the ox, heavy both mentally and physically. . . . The work which this man does tires him no more than any healthy normal laborer is tired by a proper day's work. . . ."[40]

Despite the formalization of relationships between the managements of the steel industry and the United Steelworkers of America, the traditions of the early steel masters still weigh heavily. When a reporter inquired about aspects of plant modernization at the Gary Works of the U.S. Steel Corporation, a steelworker said to him, "Our eight foremen don't have fifteen years experience between them. You can understand a man not knowing, but they walk around with their heads in the air and won't even speak to us. It's costing them millions, mostly in spare parts going to waste. The supervisors don't know what to do with them."[41]

At the nation's number two steel company, Bethlehem, reporters for the *Wall Street Journal* learned from a local union official that "The steel industry's biggest problem is management's attitude toward the workers. Last year, when Local 6787 asked to be allowed to use the Sand Creek Club, a Bethlehem golf and swimming club for management, 'we were turned down flat,' he says. 'They told us, we don't want you people using the Sand Creek Club.' As Mr. Wilborn, the Local's president said: 'You could just sense the discrimination in the way they turned us down. They offended a lot of people with that one.' "[42]

The U.S. Steel Corporation, after closing its Ohio works in 1979, was confronted by a new kind of problem in relation to the trade union. In cooperation with various community groups, the union had developed plans for buying the Ohio facilities, the financing to be a combination of private funds, community funds, and federal loans or grants. The management of U.S. Steel refused to consider the proposal, saying that, on principle, it did not wish to sell to any party that would use federal funds to compete against U.S. Steel. A local union official reported: "The company wouldn't even let any of our members walk through the plants with our engineers and bankers."[43]

Suppose the proposed reorganization, re-equipping and reopening had been achieved, under the control of a union-community-based ownership. The way would have been open to operating with lower profit margins and lower administrative costs than are acceptable to the managers of U.S. Steel. Those factors, plus the cooperation induced by shared controls over operations, could have made possible a steel plant producing a saleable, quality product, while maintaining employment and assuring long-term economic viability. The strategies for those objectives would be rather different from the short-term profit maximizing, enlargement of managerial controls, and maximum return on investments from whatever enterprise seems handy for the purpose.

Virtually assured of a healthy domestic market, the managers of U.S. steel firms agreed after World War II to steel wages well above those of any other manufacturing industry. In return for a 1959 no-strike agreement, steel management offered wages linked to the cost of living. By 1979, inflation had escalated steel wages to 56 percent above the average for manufacturing workers overall. Steel management, however, was ill equipped to offset that cost increase with productivity growth.

Steel industry management has been aggressive in seeking out major financial concessions from the federal government. Unembarrassed by any appearance of contradiction with free-enterprise ideology, they had, by August 1981, extracted a series of major concessions:

- Tax law was revised to permit the write-off of steel plant in five years instead of the previous eleven.
- Tax credits on steel investments were raised.
- Rules governing the leasing of equipment were changed, making that strategy more advantageous to the steel companies.
- Pollution-control standards were relaxed for three years, saving the industry $170 million a year.
- "Trigger price" mechanisms,* administered by the federal government, had the effect of increasing steel prices and raising profits.

The first three of these changes in federal regulations could add about $500 million a year to the treasuries of steel industry firms. However, steel

---

*The federal government monitors the prices of imported steel mill products. When any of these prices falls below a level judged to be the cost of production in the exporting country, the government can limit the quantity of imports.

industry managers indicated that these gifts from the federal government were still not sufficient incentive to encourage major investments in really new, integrated steel plants.

In their search for short-term profits, regardless of source, steel industry managers have relied increasingly on diversification. The 1980 annual report of the United States Steel Corporation showed that of its total "identifiable assets" only 51 percent remained in the steel industry. There is more of that to come. U.S. Steel and Armco have announced a continuation of the strategy; in 1980 the National Steel Corporation paid $241 million for a savings and loan company.[44]

From 1977 to 1980 the non-steel assets of U.S. Steel grew by 80 percent, while steel assets increased 13 percent. In 1979 and 1980 the corporation showed the way for profit-making with less steel production. It lowered steel production from 29.7 to 23.3 million tons while reducing its blast furnaces from forty-six to twenty-seven, and its employees from 170,000 to 155,000.[45]

Meanwhile, the superintendent of U.S. Steel's Fairless Works reportedly "dreams of the time when he can replace his outdated open-hearth furnaces with modern basic oxygen furnaces that produce steel faster and cheaper. Such a shop, however, would cost more than $300 million, an investment that the company is unlikely to make under the present return." Accordingly, the superintendent has chosen to seek out methods of improving quality and efficiency by sending several managers to Japan to study their technology and production methods.[46] But the Japanese have been the world leaders in scrapping open-hearth furnaces in favor of the basic oxygen method. Sending U.S. managers to Japan to study efficiency with open-hearth furnaces is something like a developing country sending a team of managers to the United States to study the making of automobiles by handicraft methods.

Observers of the steel industry note that U.S. Steel, which controls about 20 percent of the domestic market, also operates a concentration of the most obsolete facilities in the industry. In the industry as a whole, 20 percent of steel production is from open-hearth furnaces; in U.S. Steel's plants, the percentage is 30.[47]

According to steel management, the sharp increase in imports as a percent of U.S. steel consumption hurt them mainly because of unfair pricing by foreign competitors. However, industry analysts judge that the saleability of steel products from Western Europe and from Japan in the United States is more related to efficient technology (as in Japan) and the high quality of the Japanese and Western European steel products.[48]

A continuation of the policies and practices exhibited by the U.S. steel industry's managers during the last quarter-century will assuredly force deterioration to a point where, by the end of the 1980s, imports of steel could account for about one-third of U.S. industry's requirements, while employment would decline "by about 20 percent, or some 90,000 workers from the 1978 level."[49] Meanwhile, the major U.S. steel firms, having protected themselves financially with investments of all sorts outside their own industry, would still be able to maintain levels of profitability that were sufficiently attractive to investors and to financially oriented top managers.

Brushing aside all these considerations of steel and autos, many people believe that the future of U.S. prosperity depends on the newer high-technology industries. That, they say, is where the United States can and should excel. How, then, is it doing in the realm, for example, of integrated circuit production?

In the spring of 1979 Richard W. Anderson, general manager of Hewlett-Packard's Computer Systems Division, caused a considerable stir when he disclosed that, in his firm's experience, integrated circuits delivered by U.S. manufacturers had five to six times the failure rate of comparable products available from Japanese firms. In October 1980 he reported an improvement among the U.S. firms amounting to a 50 percent reduction in the failure rate for the U.S. products.

What caused this quality difference between U.S. and Japanese producers of electronic components? In response to higher wage rates in the United States "American integrated circuit vendors typically moved their labor-intensive operations offshore, to areas of low technology and low labor rates where it's very hard to exercise the control that's required to maintain a high level of quality. What the Japanese did was automate these operations, and surround them with highly trained supervision."[50] The Japanese approach to cost reduction was once the classic American pattern. It was the one that gave American industry its world supremacy in productivity.

The solution adopted by the American firms secured immediate short-term cost reduction without the long-term commitment associated with investment in new facilities. The Japanese firms, by contrast, secured cost reduction in their own factories by making a long-range commitment to new production equipment and to the training of a more sophisticated work force.

The U.S. producers of micro-chips and the computers that use them must expect a gathering storm of Japanese competition. The chief citadels of U.S. leadership in the world computer industry are now under challenge. Will the American managers of Silicon Valley and the great computer firms marshal the research, design and production competence that is needed to hold a front-rank position? Or will they too slip into the familiar patterns of industrial decay which have spelled catastrophe for major parts of the consumer electronics and other industries in the U.S.? (This matter will be taken up further in chapter 14.)

. . .

One test of production deterioration is the inability of U.S.-based factories to hold on to the home market. This has come about from the inability of managements to design, produce and market competitively in terms of technology (quality of product) and economy (cost and price). The following table shows the extent of this declining competence, giving for each product the proportion of U.S. purchases that was supplied from production outside the United States during 1979–1980. In each case, the imports displaced former U.S. production. For each class of product, the percentage of imports implies a substantial, for the most part permanent, loss of employment opportunity in the domestic industry.

PERCENTAGE OF U.S. CONSUMPTION PRODUCED ABROAD (1979–80)

Product	%	Product	%
Automobiles	27	Integrated microcircuits	34
Machine tools	25*	X-ray and other irradiation	
Steel mill products	15	equipment	24
TV sets, black and white	87	Motion-picture cameras	
Calculating machines,		(1977)	74
hand-held	47	Sewing machines (1978)	51
Calculating machines,		Tape recorders and dictation	
desk-top and printing	39	machines, office type	100
Microwave ranges and		Bicycles	22
ovens	22	Apparel	20
Communications systems		Leather gloves	37
and equipment	16	Footwear (non-rubber)	45
		Flatware	50

*As of 1982, this figure is 42%.

This list of products and industries, while a small sampling, includes a number of industries whose basic importance is obvious (steel, machine tools, electronics). It also shows that the decline of production competence has not been limited to any particular class of product. The disabling of U.S. industry has proceeded in both producers' and in consumer goods, in hardware and in software, in "traditional" and in newer "high-tech" industries. By 1980, it is clear, the U.S. industrial economy had suffered a debacle.

Many individual industries, to be sure, have been holding their own, and then some, in both the U.S. and world markets. These include a number of important machinery industries—electrical industrial apparatus, construction and mining machinery, miscellaneous mechanical equipment—as well as large chemical industries (industrial, pharmaceutical, plastics). Other U.S. industries that have maintained strong positions, technical and economic, abroad as well as at home, are ones that have received massive government subsidies for research and development and for capital investment—mainly as part of the military-space economy. These industries include the manufacturing of aircraft, electrical equipment, engines, communications equipment, ordnance, and professional and scientific instruments.[51] The group of deteriorating industries identified above have not shared in state managerial largesse that, since World War II, has flowed to participants in the guaranteed military-space markets.

During 1978, there was a marked change in the composition of U.S. imports. Petroleum, long this country's leading import item, dropped to third place behind machinery and transportation equipment, and manufactured goods. The machinery ranged from machine tools and electronic equipment to motor vehicles, railroad equipment and ships. The manufactured goods included iron and steel, non-ferrous metals, alloys, plastics, medical and other instruments. The suppliers for both categories were located mainly in Japan and Europe.[52]

European and Japanese exporters to the United States have relied increasingly on offering quality products. For example, a senior officer of Japan's Canon Company reports that his company regularly commits 10 percent of its annual sales to research and development and depends on sophisticated technology to produce quality products such as precision 35mm cameras and allied optics and equipment at relatively low cost and price. The strategy of designing for quality and acceptable cost has produced a steady flow of European-made household appliances, a field in which U.S. firms were once preeminent in both design and price.

By 1977, Mitsubishi Aircraft International had captured about 15 percent of the U.S. executive aircraft market.[53]

Also in 1981, a classic American industry, the manufacture of sewing machines, made a probably irreversible decision when the Singer Company closed its 107-year-old factory in Elizabeth, New Jersey, thus ending the U.S. production of sewing machines for home use. Singer will retain and operate factories in a number of other countries, but the only sewing machines to be produced here will be for industrial users.

In response to the epidemic closing of factories and the concentrated unemployment resulting from the replacement of U.S. production by imports, the federal government established a Trade Adjustment Assistance Program for workers and for firms that could demonstrate injury from displacement of work, or sales, by imported goods. In 1979, the Department of Labor reported that 2,545 firms and 561,000 workers had been certified to receive federal adjustment assistance payments. (Claims by another 3,200 firms were denied.) These workers and their firms were concentrated in industries listed in the tabulation supplied above.[54]

These depleted industries reflect a development that is unprecedented in the American economy. The history of industrial capitalism records a succession of "business cycles," of booms and busts, but no instances of massed production incompetence. Until the present era no American manufacturing industry ever died from an inability to produce competent products at acceptable prices.[55] A pattern emerges, in which each industry's decay may be likened to a particular production of a classic drama. In each production the actors wear different costumes, the stage settings vary according to industry and locale; as in the theater, the quality of the performance varies from one presentation to the next. But all these differences exist within essentially the same framework of plot and action:

The top management becomes increasingly finance- and short-term-profit-oriented; research and development activity is limited; investment in new equipment is deferred, and the age of manufacturing facilities increases; product variety is enlarged and opportunities for meaningful standardization are avoided; production equipment is pushed beyond limits of reliable performance; quality is controlled in a way to set acceptable percentages of defective products; work and workers are accorded low status, and therefore the organization of work is of secondary importance; decision-making by workers is resisted as diminishing the decision power and effectiveness of management; profits are maintained by seeking investment opportunities outside the original product sphere of the firm; production facilities are abandoned after systematic withholding of maintenance and equipment replacement; management seeks improvement in overall efficiency by intensifying administrative controls and supervision; wage rates are described as the prime cause of noncompetitiveness; opportunities for productivity of capital and labor through stabilization of operations are characteristically ignored, being mainly unknown to industry management; management attempts to pass along cost increases to customers. When all else fails, and profits as well as management's position are in peril, management turns to government for subsidy and rescue. All the while, as these processes unfold, management seeks its self-justification in pronouncements about post-industrial society, "sunset" industries and the like.

I have referred repeatedly to data from West Germany and Japan in order to establish that the conditions in U.S. industry are not without alternatives. There is, of course, a considerable body of literature that contrasts the United States with these countries. Japan, especially, is seen as moving, as if by magic, from junk production before World War II to top-quality high-tech products, with swift productivity growth, after World War II. In fact, there is nothing mysterious here. Furthermore, if Japan were not in the picture, it would be West Germany that would be viewed as offering the embarrassing contrast to U.S. industry in terms of product quality, product tradition, high-tech product design and productivity growth. For the purposes of this book, it is far more important to focus on the common features of West Germany and Japan vis-à-vis the United States.

To begin with, all three are industrial capitalist countries. In all of them, management has the main decision power and is hierarchically organized. Management tries for profit-making and for the enlargement of its sphere of control. Finally, the U.S., German and Japanese economies use the state as an instrument for decision-making. But these common features are accompanied by substantial differences in mode of operation and ideology.

In the United States, management typically claims a sole "right to manage," even as unions have been recognized as the representatives of workers —thereby making effective decision processes bilateral in character. In West Germany/Japan, management concedes the worker some part in decision-making. The way of doing so differs widely, according to the different cultures of the two societies. In West Germany, a network of laws includes those providing for *Mitbestimmung,* for the functioning of works councils and the relation of these institutions to trade unions. In Japan, a network of hard-fought management-labor agreements, institutions and usages defines rights and obligations of workers and managers, against a background of strongly production-oriented management.[56]

In the American industrial pattern, a real effort is made to effect a sharp separation between the decision-making and the production occupations. Engineers are strongly oriented toward management careers and typically have no part in direct production operations. The German/Japanese pattern creates less separation between decision-making and producing. Engineers often participate directly in production. German and Japanese management systems are more congruent with modern technology than the U.S. Taylorite managerial model.

In all the above contrasts, the controlling difference is the attitude of these societies to workers and work. The other elements defined in this overview are consistent with and linked to the differences in that fundamental area.

At the close of World War II, American managers were laden with self-confidence: they were victors over the ruling hierarchies of Germany and Japan, and custodian of the world's largest industrial system. German and Japanese managers were faced with physically shattered industrial plants. Organizing talents, technical competence and production skills were the main economic assets of the German and Japanese economies. These were marshalled for work by managers who had no time for theories about "post-industrial society," about the problems of production being solved.

Production of every sort was obviously the basic requirement for national reconstruction. With this in mind, German and Japanese managers (and the surrounding community) had to assign first importance to work and to workers. These managers were also prepared to modify the classic managerial claim to total decision-making authority.

The consequences of these essential differences of managerial posture are necessarily far-reaching. Here is an illustration from the problems of the automobile industry. Japanese and American auto firms both experienced the "oil shock" of 1973. It's instructive to contrast the response in the number-three firm of each industry: Chrysler in the United States and Mazda in Japan. The Mazda management had invested heavily in the Wankel engine, an innovative mechanical design which also had high fuel consumption. Therefore, Mazda sales dropped sharply after 1973, changing hundred-million-dollar profits into equal losses, while the firm also faced indebtedness of about a billion dollars.

The Mazda management started a vigorous campaign to redesign product and production methods toward more fuel-efficient engines and the drastic mechanization of work (especially through installation of robots). The program was supported by financing from banks, no help coming from government. At the same time, the management gave notice that the jobs of its workers were protected: attrition and early retirement would be the only methods used to reduce employment. During the period of major changeover and lowest production rate, management arranged for 5,000 of its workers to be deployed to Mazda dealers, working there as salesmen and maintenance men. There were pay cuts at Mazda—the largest, 20 percent, among the senior managers—and elimination of bonuses for four years. Middle managers had their salaries and other income frozen. There were no reductions of pay or bonuses for factory workers.

By 1981, Mazda's indebtedness had been cut almost in half and the firm was profitable once again. Its labor productivity was almost doubled.

At Chrysler, the response to OPEC oil pricing did not really start seriously until 1979, when the company was on the verge of bankruptcy. Chrysler turned to the U.S. government to guarantee its future financing, and management discharged 28 percent of its workers and 7 percent of white-collar employees. About two weeks before Chrysler management applied for federal loan guarantees, the top managers announced pay cuts for their levels of 2 to 10 percent.

At Mazda the management extends to the work force an implicit understanding that they, production workers, have a major stake in the enterprise and that it is the obligation of management to make sure that that stake is protected. By contrast, the Chrysler management treated its production worker force as "commodities," tossing the ones not needed for management's plans onto "the market." The Chrysler pattern contains the idea that management has a far greater stake in the firm than the production workers, and that the presence of management employees is of greater importance for the competence of the enterprise. Mazda policy was oriented toward conserving the work force as a prime productive asset.

The effects of these contrasting policies are obvious enough. At Mazda, management was virtually assured of full support from the work force, including cooperation in the introduction and utilization of new technology. In the Chrysler case, that was hardly to be expected against the long background of management-union confrontationism.[57]

Among Americans with a strong nationalist tradition, the spectacle of industrial decline has evoked a barrage of mainly irrelevant "explanations."

High wages is the explanation usually advanced first.

For two centuries, workshops, then manufacturing industries, in the United States prospered while paying the highest wages in the world. This was notably so during the twentieth century, when there was no question about the ease of transporting industrial goods, even across oceans. Product design and productivity in manufacturing in the United States were fully adequate to offset the lower wage costs enjoyed by manufacturers in all the other industrialized countries. Therefore one must ask why U.S. design and production competence faltered even as American managements no longer had to overcome a wage cost handicap.

Could the United States be suffering the consequences of having spurred the industrial reconstruction of Japan and West Germany after World War II? The fact is that from 1948 to 1971 Japan received $21.8 million in economic assistance from the United States. U.S. private investment in Japan was negligible. Under the Marshall Plan, West Germany received $1.6 billion of economic assistance from the United States. "By way of comparison, during the period 1967–1969 the average annual new capital investment within the West German economy was $35.6 billion and in Japan $51.2 billion."[58] There is no escaping the fact that the spectacular industrial and other economic developments in Japan and West Germany after World War II were homemade.

But didn't Germany and Japan get the benefit of building and operating new industrial facilities just because the U.S. had destroyed them during the war? On average, manufacturing equipment (except for certain units like power plants, railroad roadbeds) have been depreciated in the United States, West Germany and Japan in cycles of about ten years. By this reckoning the period 1945–1980 represents three and one-half machinery replacement cycles. This points to the importance of the decision processes of industrial management that operated over this period, rather than to the unique event of new facilities construction some time after World War II.

Perhaps the United States just doesn't have "comparative advantage" with respect to industries that have suffered major losses in the U.S. market? The economists' idea of comparative advantage has solid meaning when referring, for example, to the natural head start that the United States has in the growing of wheat, corn and cotton, or that Quebec has in the production of electricity from water power. But comparative advantage loses clear meaning when one considers the array of products in which West Germany and Japan have come to excel. What is particularly "German" about many classes of machine tools, or of the electric trolleys ("light rail vehicles") that enjoy a world market? Nor has anyone discovered an inherently "Japanese" quality in precision 35 mm cameras, hi-fi electronics or electron microscopes. National culture, geography and history, per se, do not account for either their industrial excellence or the U.S. industrial decline.

11

Coming Home to Roost: Breakdown in Military Technology

"Proud Spirit" was the name of a twenty-day war mobilization exercise conducted by the U.S. Department of Defense in November 1980. What showed up was a platoon of conditions in the military sphere that are mirror images of civilian industrial developments. Overcentralized control, priority for gains in profits/power, dysfunctional design of mechanisms, and major deficiencies in U.S. industrial capability were all on display, with correspondingly catastrophic results.

The Worldwide Military Command and Control System (WIMEX), set up by the Pentagon and intended to do what the name says, is probably the world's largest and most expensive information-gathering system, a vast network of computers, satellites, control centers, etc. During Proud Spirit it was supposed to give generals and admirals detailed, up-to-the-minute data on the readiness of their military formations. What happened, however, was that WIMEX became "overloaded," and updated information was temporarily stored in an interim memory bank called a "buffer." Then the buffer wouldn't release the information and the whole system was down for twelve hours while programmers unsnarled the software of the computer net and extracted the necessary information to set the system operating once again.

Another principal outcome of Proud Spirit was an appraisal of the degree to which U.S. production capability was unable to replenish military hardware and munitions. "One way Proud Spirit planners considered to meet a shortage of M-16 rifles was to order them from a plant in South Korea."[1] The M-16 is the standard infantry rifle.

In 1977 an extended test of WIMEX found that messages put into the system were lost in breakdowns 62 percent of the time. "One part of the network, the Readiness Command, broke down 85 percent of the time." James Fallows has discovered that

One study of the NATO central command bunker in Europe pointed out that to keep up with the flow of information and orders coming in over its communications system, the commanders would have to keep reading 790 words a minute, around the clock.[2]

Observing criteria that emphasize more money and power, and with technical design governed by these rules, American private and state managers have created a military technology and industry that is biased toward producing ever more complex, more costly and less reliable military hardware. A common streak runs through the military industrial endeavor: widespread and sustained production of "crackpot technology." By this I mean devices, procedures and modes of organization that yield results which contradict the ostensible purpose. The military are provided with communication systems that block communication, with weapons that either don't work or work the wrong way (like killing their own men), with control systems that cannot conceivably control. I will outline these characteristics in three parts: first, the competence of American military industry as a production system; second, key factors that affect the design of military products and the ways of producing them; third, operating characteristics of several key military systems and weapons.

During 1980, the Pentagon's Defense Science Board and the House of Representatives' Committee on Armed Services reported on the shortcomings of the defense industrial base.[3] Both groups issued assessments of depleted industrial competence—of the sort earlier disclosed by the diagnosis of production failures in the civilian economy. In a word, the massive resources funneled into the "defense industrial base" have not protected that part of the American economy from types of deterioration that have become endemic elsewhere.*

During the 1970s, the aerospace industry invested about 2 percent of its sales in new capital. This compared with a 4 percent average for U.S. manufacturing firms as a whole and 8 percent for all firms in the U.S. economy. Apparently the managers of the military-serving firms have preferred to emphasize either profits (often used to invest in other industries) or other classes of cost—like lavish administration or R & D staffs to make a display of "competence" for the Pentagon. Given the nature of the control system operated from the Pentagon's central office, none of this can happen without approval by the top levels of the state management.

---

*The House Armed Services Committee notes that "although a precise definition does not exist, the defense industrial base is broadly viewed as encompassing those elements of American industry that contribute to defense-related work and whose production capacity and technical expertise are required to meet national security requirements." House Armed Services Committee, *op. cit.*, p. 7.

One immediate consequence of this investment policy was an aging stock of metalworking machinery. By 1980 60 percent of the metalworking equipment used on military work was more than twenty years old. Only about 7 percent of the government-owned machine-tool base is less than ten years old. While formal Pentagon policy specifies that production equipment should be modernized at the rate of 5 percent per year (implying an average twenty-year life for machinery), actual replacement "has never exceeded 2 to 3 percent per year."

Shortage of skilled manpower is described as a serious and continuing problem for the military economy. In Pentagon circles the talk is about a shortfall of a quarter-million machinists from 1980 to 1985 and the lack of any government or company programs to train that many people. Witnesses before the House Armed Services Committee recalled that during World War II, farmers, clerks and housewives "were trained in a matter of weeks to build aircraft engines. And they built thousands of them. Today, however, you can't just take someone off a farm or out of a kitchen and expect him or her to build aircraft engines. The technology is too advanced, the tolerances too tight, the equipment too sophisticated. It takes three years for a machinist apprentice to complete his rigorous course. It takes the better part of a year to retrain someone from producing autos, for example, to work on high-technology aerospace parts."

Neither the congressional nor the Pentagon studies cited here comment on the fact that many industrial firms seize on the introduction of sophisticated computer-controlled machine tools as an opportunity to downgrade the skill classifications and wage rates of highly trained machinists. These managements try to use the new equipment as a way to produce "without workers." However absurd this may appear, it has nevertheless been serious policy in leading firms. Obviously, when that sort of behavior is noised around in the high schools, able young people are not powerfully attracted. Why go through three to four years of machinist apprenticeship training, not to say learning computer technology, to be told that, since operating a computer-controlled machine tool involves less manual work, the job should pay less.

While the productivity growth rate for the manufacturing industry as a whole in the United States has been for some time the lowest among industrialized countries, "the productivity growth rate of the defense sector is lower than the overall manufacturing sector. . . ." The House and Defense Science Board reports are laden with detail on the ever lengthening lead time between ordering and delivery of equipment components and complete products. "For example, from 1976 to 1980, the typical delivery span of aluminum forgings increased from 20 to 120 weeks. From 1977 to 1980 the delivery span for aircraft landing gears grew from 52 to 120 weeks. In just the last two years the delivery span for integrated circuits more than doubled, from 25 to 62 weeks. . . . In 1978 normal lead times for one of our military jet engines was 19 months. Today the Air Force has to order that engine 41 months before delivery." The witnesses who testified before these official groups called attention to the closing of numerous industrial facilities in the forging, foundry and metalworking industries.

The House committee reported that "the majority of assembly work done on United States–manufactured semiconductor devices is carried on in Malaysia, Singapore, Taiwan, the Philippines, Korea, and Hong Kong. . . . The panel finds this dependence on offshore labor for assembly of critical defense-related components as troublesome as our offshore dependence for critical materials." The Defense Science Board "estimated that from 80 to 90 percent of military semiconductors are assembled and tested outside the United States. . . . In addition, most ceramic packages and a significant amount of lead frames are supplied from Japan as are certain high-technology electronic components."

The House committee concluded that "if solutions are not developed to address the myriad problems that plague the defense industrial base and, indeed, the total industrial base, the United States is in danger of losing its position as the industrial leader of the world. General Alton D. Slay (Commander, Air Force Systems Command) told the panel, '. . . it is a gross contradiction to think that we can maintain our position as a first-rate military power with a second-rate industrial base. It has never been done in the history of the modern world.' "

Production capability on behalf of the military is further constrained by short-term, therefore unstable, operations. Thus, annual contracts may be drawn for military aircraft products with changing production rates and qualities. One of the important effects of Reagan administration budgeting, starting in January 1981, was a destabilization of the industrial system as a result of helter-skelter changes in military budget items. During the period of budget revisions carried forward by the Office of Management and Budget, the hectic rush of the operation was indicated by the fact that the Carter budget was revised with black marker pens, then photocopied and widely circulated. There was no opportunity for the input-output studies that are indispensable for assembling a large industrial program without causing major upsets in parts of the system.

As noted earlier, another pervasive feature of the military industry enterprise is the unusually high intensity of administrative controls and associated paper work. One subcontracting firm reported to the House committee that "when bidding on government contracts, we factor in the regulatory and administrative requirements, and increase the price quite substantially." Other witnesses reported that the prices charged for performing government contracts range from 25 to 100 percent more than would be asked for comparable commercial work. The Defense Science Board received a briefing that underscored the large amount of paper work and complex contracting procedures, especially in relation to small production runs.

Finally, both the House panel and the Defense Science Board agreed that the military economy had been significantly impaired by the effects of high inflation and high interest rates—the former limiting purchases of its products and the latter limiting access to capital that might have been available for further investment by military industry firms. In the military economy as a whole, costs of systems increased during 1980 at a rate approaching 20 percent, a rise far more rapid than the consumer price index of 14.3 percent. The following are illustrations from a long list given by the Defense Science Board of annual percent price increases, 1979–1980:

PRICE INCREASE PERCENTAGES, 1979–1980

Selected Parts	%	*Selected Materials*	%
Aircraft electrical		Non-ferrous metals	86
connectors	170	Petrochemical products	43
Aircraft semiconductors	18	Titanium products	38
EMI filters	35	Copper	92
Torque motors	106	Molybdenum	267
Hydraulic actuator	68		
Aircraft elevator		*Aggregated Parts and Materials*	
indicator	57	Missile	21
Aircraft landing gear	48	Aircraft radar	23
Microwave tubes	30	Electronic system	16
Missile wire	35	Aircraft material	37
Capacitors	87	Satellite material	34

During the 1960s an unusually competent and widely experienced industrial engineer accepted a senior post as cost analyst with the U.S. Air Force. Trained and devoted to the goal of minimizing cost and improving efficiency of operations, A. Ernest Fitzgerald applied his engineering talents to relations between the Air Force and its myriad supplier firms. He was soon on a collision course, not only with the managements of subfirms but, more important, with the larger part of the Air Force's central office staff. One of the thorniest issues was Fitzgerald's insistence that industrial firms serving the Pentagon be required to develop justifications for their proposed products in terms of "engineering costing" or "should cost" calculations. The point here is that alternative designs, materials and production methods should be explored to discover what combination of design features will most economically achieve the desired product characteristics.

Opposing Fitzgerald's engineering point of view were the administrators, who favored "historical costing." This method requires the contractor to display on a graph the past history of costs or price for the class of product in question. If a new fighter plane is proposed, the first thing to show is a pattern that plots the price per pound of fighter planes over, say, the previous fifteen years. The second part of this method is to compute the average trend line that best "fits" the pattern of development of price per pound in fighter planes. The third operation extrapolates into the future the trend line so calculated. Thus, if the proposed aircraft is to be constructed during a ten-year period, the estimated price shown on the extrapolated line during the fifth year from now would represent the average price to be expected during the average life of the plane. This assumes that costs (and therefore prices) will continue to grow during the next ten years at the same average rate as in the past fifteen years. The weakness in this method is that it takes as given factors the previous product design, materials and production methods, as well as the causes of all cost growth incurred for them. Such uncritical acceptance of the behavior of the past assures an escalation of costs and prices.

Fitzgerald fought, and lost, the battle of engineering costing versus historical costing. In October 1964, Robert McNamara, the Secretary of Defense, issued a directive that included the precise instruction that "forecasting future trends in costs from historical cost experience is of primary importance."[4] Thereafter, historical costing (sometimes called parametric costing) became holy writ in Pentagon managerial procedure, with inflationary effects exactly what Fitzgerald expected.

Concurrency is another managerial invention of the Pentagon. In industrial and other enterprises it has long been standard practice to prepare schedules for the steps to be taken from the inception of a new product to its introduction on the market. Typically, a product schedule includes a research and development phase, followed by product design and the preparation and testing of a prototype. Modifications are then made to eliminate undesirable features and a revised design is drawn up for further testing. This process repeats until a prototype has withstood operational tests that satisfy the management as to the adequacy of the product. Not until then does the new model go into production. The idea of concurrency is to perform various of these steps simultaneously. In one case, which I shall describe in chapter 13 in some detail, a major product was moved from early blueprint stage straight into production. The implication of describing this as concurrency is that the intervening functional operations can all be carried out at the same time.

In practice, that is rarely the case. What usually happens is that defects in the products are discovered either at the factory or while in use by the customer. Then modifications are made on the already produced and delivered equipment. This is the most expensive way known to carry out revisions in industrial design, but it is a procedure ordained as standard practice in the regulations of the Department of Defense. During 1980 the top managers of the Pentagon ruled that sections of the Department of Defense "should give consideration to minimizing acquisition cycle time by planned concurrency. This may include increasing funding, overlapping, combining, or omitting the phases of the acquisition process or overlapping or combining development, test, and evaluation with operational test and evaluation. . . ."[5]

Concurrency imposes costs of unpredictable magnitude on the producing enterprise. As I will show later in this chapter, it was a primary source of the remarkable cost increases in the Army's XM-1 heavy tank program, for which production orders were being executed at the very time the tank was going through the testing process to ascertain its acceptability to the Army.

Complexity of product design has become another characteristic of U.S. military technology. There is now an abundance of evidence to support the charge that functionally meaningless, and even performance-degrading, attributes are being designed into military products, in the hope of giving them improved "capability" over a wide range of situations. When a large, fast airplane is required to penetrate enemy territory at a height of 200 feet, under automatic control, it must rely on the flawless functioning of a very complex set of mechanisms. But the complexity that is intended to bestow greater capability has the characteristic effect of setting limits on reliability. The general formula is that the reliability of a system is not greater than the product of the individual reliabilities of its linked components.*

The point that complexity affects reliability is lost in the Pentagon's desire for more capability and the contractors' enthusiasm for enhancing profits by selling more intricate, hence more expensive, products. Thus there has been delivered a Niagara of ever more complicated weapons systems of necessarily lower reliability and higher costs. Consider one example: U.S. high-performance aircraft like the F-14 and the F-15 are capable of carrying and firing the Phoenix missile, a complex device theoretically competent to attack multiple targets beyond visual range. Actually, no way has been found to differentiate without error between unseen friendlies and unfriendlies. Furthermore, the vivid experience of the 1973 Middle East war includes evidence that each combatant attacked its own planes in significant numbers, even as targets were within visual range. "Israel, Egypt, and Syria all shot down large

---

*On the assumption that the failure rate of a component of a mechanism is in each case independent of the other components. It often happens, however, that the failure of one element in a system, or mechanism, affects the performance of other elements, in which case the reliability of the system is much lower than is projected by the assumption of independent failure rates.

numbers of their own planes with surface-to-air missiles during last October's war. . . . Syria on a single day downed nearly twenty Soviet-built MiG fighters that had been supplied to her by Iraq. . . . Israel shot down a large number of her Mirages with both SAMs and air-to-air missiles from other Israeli fighters. . . . Dr. Malcolm R. Currie, director of defense research at the Pentagon . . . said that the United States could not be confident it would be able to operate its own missiles much better and that builders of tactical missiles must give priority to consideration of this problem."[6] Also, the price of a Phoenix missile has risen to about $1,000,000, so any extensive use of them for target practice could strain even the escalated Pentagon budgets.

Part of our military's new look is a self-guided missile that supposedly can distinguish its particular target from surrounding terrain or other moving objects. Reports, especially in the business press, are glowing on this subject,[7] but experience thus far fails to confirm the reliability acclaimed by the electronics enthusiasts. We do know that the Falcon "smart" missile was introduced during the Vietnam war, after it had run up a production cost of $2 billion. Its theoretical "probability of kill" was 99 percent; in practice it performed at 7 percent.[8]

All these aspects of military procurement are accompanied and amplified by a steady thrust toward centralization of managerial operations. Since centralism and hierarchical control are core features of large military organizations, these criteria govern the selective preference for centralizing "command and control" without apparent limit. The same criteria shape the design of communications and production equipment (as in numerical control), as well as enterprise-level production information systems that are designed to Air Force order. Thus, the Air Force project for Integrated Computer-Assisted Manufacturing Systems is designed to contribute to greater centralism in management control of industrial work.

An interesting development in civilian industrial management has been the widespread attempt to use the huge data-handling capacity of computers as justification for great concentration of decision-making at the central offices of far-flung enterprises. But that is an abuse of computer capability because the machines cannot read the printouts and make judgments about the flows of resources and responsive activity. That was one of the limits on centralism of managerial control noted in chapter 4.

The military managerial domain is permeated with the notion of using technology to displace people. In step with their civilian counterparts, military managers have been downgrading the employees who do the hands-on work. Meanwhile, devices are produced to amplify overkill, to destroy unidentifiable planes beyond visual range, to fly hundred-million-dollar bombers at 200 feet above the ground. And the same state managerial institutions have installed a production technology with built-in schemes of historical costing, concurrency, rising complexity and rising costs.

What are the results? How well do the elaborate weapons systems and managerial control networks set up by the Pentagon actually work? Here I will omit data from wars and substantial military operations—like, for example, the misconceived and mishandled attempt to rescue the U.S. hostages in Tehran in April 1980. Instead, I will concentrate on the narrower information available on the functional operations of organizations, control systems and weapons. What sort of output is being obtained in weapons and organization in return for the very large capital input? A basic measure of the quality of an international military control system is its ability to communicate. The Pentagon's Worldwide Military Command and Control System has been put to that test on a series of critical occasions:

On the afternoon of 8 June 1967, the U.S.S. *Liberty* cruised some 12 miles off the Sinai Peninsula, eavesdropping on battlefield communications in the 1967 Arab-Israeli war. During the previous 13 hours, six urgent messages had been sent to the ship by U.S. command forces, messages ordering the *Liberty* out of the area, telling it to pull 100 miles offshore. [It did not do so and was attacked and sunk by Israeli planes.—S.M.]

Due to a series of human and computer errors, however, none of the messages reached the ship in time. Two were misrouted to a U.S. communications station in the Philippines and one went to Greece. One was never addressed to the *Liberty*. One was lost in the electronic labyrinth at the Army Communications Station at Pirmasens, Germany. The final message, marked urgent and "Top Secret" by the Joint Chiefs of Staff, spent the morning of 8 June passing from ship to ship in the U.S. Mediterranean fleet, never reaching the *Liberty* at all. The Joint Chiefs, it turns out, had overlooked the fact that the *Liberty* could not receive Top Secret messages.[9]

[A] . . . communications snafu led to the shooting down of a U.S. spy plane off the coast of North Korea. And in 1968, the U.S.S. *Pueblo* was seized by the Koreans and its crew held captive for 11 months—a crisis that could have been avoided if the message warning the *Pueblo* of potential trouble had not been misrouted by a computer. . . .[10]

And the computers of WIMEX are not the only machines that bedevil the Pentagon. Take the Air Force's Advanced Logistics System (ALS). It was intended to provide central, computerized management of a global parts inventory of more than 6 million items. For example, during the 1973 Yom Kippur war, Israel early on needed new cockpit canopies for several damaged F-4 Phantom jets. Logistics Command headquarters at Wright-Patterson Air Force Base near Dayton, Ohio, searched in vain for 12 hours through its vast computerized inventory. Finally, a warehouse-by-warehouse search was started, involving hundreds of personnel at dozens of centers worldwide. By the time the canopies were located, the war was over.[11]

One of the crucial responsibilities of the Department of Defense's early warning, command and control, and communications systems is to monitor possible attacks on the United States and to facilitate appropriate evaluation, military assessment and possible military or political response. It should therefore be a cause for grave concern that WIMEX has displayed a pattern of repeated failures. We have learned that

. . . the giant NORAD site in Colorado, one of the twenty-seven WIMEX sites, has been plagued by false warnings of nuclear attacks, some of them computer generated. Over one eighteen-month period, 147 "missile display conferences"—the first of three alert levels to evaluate threats to North America—were called at NORAD as the result of the pickup of some physical phenomenon by warning sensors. And sometimes a computer or a piece of communications equipment simply transmits false data. "This happens with some frequency," Senators Barry Goldwater and Gary Hart reported to the Senate Armed Services Committee [in 1980]. . . .

Five times during 1979 and 1980, NORAD went to the second state of readiness and called "threat assessment conferences." One of these was the June 3, 1980 alert; another occurred in November 1979, when a computer war games tape was misidentified as the real thing. The Defense Department is still unable to explain how that happened.

The final stage of alert—a "missile attack conference"—has never been reached.[12]

Limits of reliability are also visible in the modes of organization and the personnel practices of American armed forces. Deficiencies in officer performance increased as short-termism and a focus on individual career advancement were borrowed from civilian management and installed as preferred patterns of the U.S. Army's officer corps. Frequent changes in organizations and stations (job-hopping) became normal, and costly ($3 billion a year), while contributing to failures of leadership and the breakdown of morale.[13]

The relationship of reliability to complexity among Pentagon weapons is studied in a remarkable "brief," *Defense Facts of Life,* prepared by Franklin C. Spinney of the Pentagon's Program Analysis and Evaluation Division. He has analyzed the principal functional characteristics of a series of tactical fighter planes purchased by the U.S. Air Force and Navy. These airplanes are listed on the facing page in order of increasing complexity, along with the average percentage of each type of aircraft that was found to be "not mission capable," that is, unable to perform, during 1979.

There is an evident relationship between greater complexity of aircraft and increased percentage of unavailability. The complex aircraft break down more often because they contain many more devices subject to failure. Not surprisingly, the more complex aircraft also require significantly more maintenance man-hours.

Air Force	Percent "Not Mission Capable"	Navy	Percent "Not Mission Capable"
A-10	32.6	A-4M	31.2
A-70	38.6	AV-8A	40.0
F-4E	34.1	A-7E	36.8
F-15	44.3	F-4J	33.4
F-111F	36.9	A-6E	39.5
F-111D	65.6	F-14A	47.5

These data are confirmed by independent observations from many places in the world where U.S. Armed Forces operate. At an Air Force base in West Germany equipped with seventy-five F-15s, the Air Force's first line fighter, only 60 percent are considered "fully mission capable on a typical day."[14]

Reliability is also a continuing problem in NATO military planning. "One of the most serious and longstanding operational problems in air defense involves aircraft identification so that a distinction can be made between enemy forces and friendly forces."[15] It seems that the problem which had proved so serious during the 1973 war was not solved by 1981.

The XM-1 is the U.S. Army's latest heavy-tank project. It weighs 54 tons and is driven by a 1,500-horsepower turbine engine to speeds greater than 45 miles an hour. The tank's sophisticated design includes elaborate stabilizing and fire-control equipment. However, by April 1981, the XM-1, though being produced by the Chrysler Corporation on a regular schedule, was also failing to meet the Army's official requirements for durability and reliability. In January 1980 the General Accounting Office reported that the tank, at last testing, "was achieving only 145 mean miles between failures in operation and development testing. This compared unfavorably with the 272 mean-mile goal the Army had hoped to reach. . . ." The tank tended to throw its track in certain types of soil. Also, the precision-built turbine engine was easily damaged by the dust it ingested.

Testing observations proceeded even after May 1979, when the secretary of defense approved an initial production run. The Army plans eventually to procure 7,000 of these mammoth tanks. However, "because of the compressed development schedule established for the XM-1, operational testing was performed concurrently with development testing." The testing program itself ran into a host of complications, including such matters as whether particular malfunctions and maintenance events should or should not be included in the scoring whereby the Army decides whether a vehicle has met or failed its requirements.

Because of complicated design, the XM-1's turret has been described as "a maintenance nightmare." The Army's goal is to achieve no more than 1.25 hours of maintenance for every hour of operation, but that has yet to be approached.

Critical to the XM-1's performance is the reliability of its engine. The desired performance level is about 1,000 hours between overhauls, but by 1980 the level achieved was only 316 hours. At the 1980 state of testing, incidents reported included losses of power and difficulties with the power train, among them an inability to move the vehicle either forward or backward.[16]

By the time the XM-1 testing program had proceeded to the point of discussing such radical changes as, for example, substituting a diesel engine for the turbine, a firm that had been manufacturing the previous heavy tank (the M-60-A1) offered the Army an improved model, also with a top speed of 45 miles per hour, that contained a number of modifications—new engine, new armor, lower silhouette, etc. Notably, the cost of the "super M-60," about $525,000 (1982) would be one-third that of the new XM-1. At last report "the Army has shown very little interest."[17] The XM-1 is said to consume 3.86 gallons of fuel to the mile.[18]

One of the most spectacular examples of modern technology in the U.S. Armed Forces was the production and deployment during the late 1960s of the C-5A cargo plane. This plane, though the largest regularly produced aircraft in the world, was nevertheless supposed to be able to take off and land, even on short, unimproved runways, thus serving as a forward base freighter. To give it the short runway capability, each wing of the C-5A was lightened by at least 10,000 pounds. One result was that metal fatigue and cracks developed quickly and the plane has been kept to limited loads and, of course, away from short, unimproved runways. In 1980 the Air Force approved replacement of the C-5A's wings, at a cost of $1.4 billion, the work to be done once again by the Lockheed Corporation. The long history of this aircraft has been elaborately reported; it demonstrates mismanagement of virtually every conceivable kind.[19]

Seeking greater capability, the Air Force has entered into a major contract with a private company for servicing of the supercomplex F-15 fighter. The plane contains 127 individual electronic units, 45 of which must be evaluated by computer. An F-15 "wing" of 72 aircraft has, therefore, 3,240 line replacement units, "boxes," to be computer serviced as needed by the Avionics Intermediate Shop. But the three AIS computers assigned to the job can each check only one electronic "box" at a time and it takes about eight hours to test a unit. Moreover, the equipment of the AIS is itself quite complicated. Electronic failures are quickly signaled on the F-15 and a new unit can then be plugged in. But these line replacement units are costly devices and require servicing by the limited AIS facilities. The result: a major maintenance bottleneck associated with the soaring complexity of this fighter plane.[20]

The Navy's F/A-18 is a $34 billion investment in a new, highly complex twin-jet to serve as a fighter, attack plane, etc. The plane is now in production, and already major defects have been discovered in the durability of the jet engine.[21] The plane's radar and built-in test systems have been objects of major concern. These and other aspects of the plane require further testing and redesigning—to be carried out, according to the principle of concurrency, while the plane is "in production."[22]

The Army has begun to worry because the new, ever more complex equipment it is ordering requires special test equipment that is enormously expensive and itself has problems of reliability. For example, "there are estimates that development of special test equipment for the M-1 tank and M-2 and M-3 fighting vehicles will require about $2 billion." In the other services as well, significant underestimation of failure rates of components and of the maintenance effort thus required has resulted in long turnabout times, shortages of spare parts, high rates of cannibalization of existing equipment and lower availability rates of various weapons.[23]

The famous AWACS plane, designed to detect aircraft at a great distance and permit control of an air war over a large area, has developed the familiar symptoms of poor reliability associated with high complexity:

... In fiscal 1979, U.S. AWACS planes were "mission ready" 15 percent of the time. In fiscal 1980 they were mission ready 54 percent of the time. The breakthrough was achieved by lowering the readiness standards. . . .

The AWACS is childishly easy to jam. In a Pacific test whose results were revealed by James Coates in *The Chicago Tribune,* a Navy EA-6B plane, fitted with a device similar to one described in a Soviet textbook acquired by U.S. intelligence, successfully jammed the AWACS' radar at a distance of 350 miles and then guided two F-106 fighters to within 150 feet of the AWACS—at which point, a participant in the test told Coates, "We didn't need a missile to kill the AWACS. We could have used a rifle."[24]

Again, organizations and individuals have limits of reliability. For instance, it has become widely known that in an attempt to provide more rapid threat assessment and speedier response to potential nuclear attack, the personnel assigned to nuclear programs are put under heavy stress while being required to function flawlessly. Therefore, the Air Force operates a "Personnel Reliability Program" which keeps tabs on about 100,000 people.

In 1975, 5,128 personnel were removed from access to nuclear weapons because of violations of the PRP; in 1976, 4,966 and in 1977, 4,973—an annual rate exceeding 4 percent. Reasons for removal in 1977 included alcohol and drug abuse; the primary drug abused was marijuana, but more than 250 were removed for abuse of drugs such as heroin and LSD. In the same year 1,289 were removed for a "significant physical, mental or character trait or aberrant behavior, substantiated by competent medical authority," which might "prejudice reliable performance of the duties of a particular critical or controlled position."[25]

The percentages cited are probably lower than would be found in a like number of the general public, but the point is that they have cropped up among people assigned to detect promptly and react properly to an all-out nuclear attack.

The Navy employs an MK-86 fire-control system as the primary weapons control on its most advanced combat ships. When the system is inoperative, "the ship is virtually defenseless." During 1979, it functioned only 60 percent of the time. "[A] primary reason for this low availability [was] the large number of random failures among the 40,000+ parts in the system. . . ."[26]

A study performed by the Navy found that

> The MK-13 launcher for the *Tartar*, the Navy's principal air defense missile used aboard at least 50 guided missile cruisers, destroyers and frigates, operates only 28 percent of the time. . . . An older *Tartar* launcher (MK-11) operates only 15 percent of the time. And the MK-115 fire-control system for the *Sea Sparrow*, the air defense missile which is supposed to shoot down Soviet aircraft and cruise missiles, works only 67 percent of the time, according to the report.[27]

The Navy has also developed a highly sophisticated anti-air warfare system called Aegis, composed of "phased array radars, high-power illuminators to guide missiles, advanced missile guidance, high fire power missile launchers, and a fast reaction command and control system." The Aegis system is carried on large destroyers, and a vessel so equipped has a price in excess of $1 billion. However, "the Navy expects that the actual level of operational availability will be 43 percent or less. . . ." Aegis requires an elaborate computer software input. "The software was planned to operate continuously for five hours before failing, but less than 50 percent of this goal was achieved during operational tests conducted in May 1979."[28] The Aegis vessel needs an elaborate detection and guidance system for its weapons performance; when it fails, the vessel is effectively "disarmed."

Aegis is another example of the consequences of concurrency. The General Accounting Office noted in its assessment of weapons systems that "experience has shown that this management approach can frequently increase the risk in a program to an unacceptable degree, often leads to higher costs and lower performance, and is generally undesirable in the absence of an overriding immediate military requirement."

One of the characteristic and ingrained features of the U.S. Armed Forces higher command is a stubborn reluctance on the part of well-informed people to give serious attention to ordinary workaday considerations of practicality, reliability, ordinary competence. It seems apparent that the officer corps, and notably those responsible at all levels for procurement relationship with Pentagon suppliers, are under unspoken but substantial pressure to play the game, to cooperate, not to rock the boat. A definite element of this pressure is the expectation, or hope, held by many officers that they will find a career after their military retirement in the civilian firms associated with the Pentagon. Recent studies suggest that the number of officers who take this career route has been increasing.[29]

Given the background of the management imperative to enlarge decision power, and the special availability of resources for a cost-maximizing military economy, it is hardly surprising that we have produced idiosyncratic military technology.

It should not be assumed from this discussion that these characteristics of the military system are unique to the United States. In significant testimony during 1980 hearings on the research and development budget, W. J. Perry, Undersecretary of Defense for Research and Engineering, stated, in part:

A related myth—and I consider it a myth, or rather, a conception which is no longer valid—is that everything would be all right if we were just as smart as the Russians and built our equipment simple, and cheap, and rugged, and reliable like they do, and I submit to you that that is a misconception of what the Soviet Union's acquisition program is. That might have been a true concept 10 to 15 years ago. It wasn't even true 5 years ago, and it is not true today. For better or for worse, the Soviet Union is using the same acquisition schedule that we use. They are introducing, as fast as they know how to introduce, the same kinds of technologies that we are embodying in our system. In effect, the great virtue which people attribute to their systems of being simple, cheap, and reliable the Soviets are moving away from as fast as they get the capability to move away from them. They are, in effect, emulating us in all of our systems. We see this now in the evolution from the Mig-19 and 21 to the Mig-23 and 27, where the Mig-23 costs two to three times what the Mig-19 did, and it is a comparable cost to the F-16.

We see the evolution to the AAX-9 air-to-air missile, which is a more sophisticated, more technically complex missile than our Sparrow is. We see the evolution to a whole family of naval cruisers they're building, all of which are of equal or greater complexity than Aegis. We see a new surface-to-air missile system, the SA-X-10 coming along, which is equally sophisticated to the Patriot, maybe even somewhat more complex and sophisticated.

So, for better or worse, they are doing the same thing that we are doing in introducing technology in systems. . . .[30]

On certain narrow military grounds, it may be a source of comfort to Pentagon officials that particular Soviet weapons are as costly and as unreliable as their own. Whatever the case, that in no way alters the combined effects of the profits/power drive on the quality of technology and on priorities for the use of the society's finite capital resources. These effects, intended or not, cast a pall without precedent on the ability of the United States to operate a modern industrial system.

12

Eroding the Production Support Base

The first panacea for a mismanaged nation is the inflation
of the currency; the second is war. Both bring a temporary
prosperity; both bring permanent ruin. But both are the
refuge of political and economic opportunists.

ERNEST HEMINGWAY
Esquire, September 1935

Sustained high productivity in a modern industrial system needs a dependable
support network of varied services and facilities. A currency of stable, predictable value makes possible private and public economic planning of future
exchanges. A competent infrastructure delivers essential transportation,
water, power, waste disposal, housing and allied services. A sophisticated
labor force is a core requirement for high productivity of labor and capital.
Altogether, these are the major components of a modern production support
base.

Although deterioration in each sector of this base has some unique causal
explanations, they share a common foundation in the normal operation of
managing for profits/power and its accompanying ideological rationales. The
decline of productivity growth disabled traditional cost-minimizing and
spurred inflation, hence debasing the currency. Infrastructure decay followed
the export of private capital from the United States and the concentration of
public capital on the military. Hostility to any economic planning other than
the Pentagon's five-year plans contributes to neglect of public resources. A
castoff labor force has been enlarged by industrial deterioration, by the creation of a permanent big city underclass, by the deliberate use of technology
to create "workerless factories," and by the sustained use of capital for the
military economy.

As in a closed-loop network, the erosion of production competence in the
United States has consequences that feed back on themselves. Thus, manag-

ing for profits/power has led to deterioration in the production support base, which, in turn, further weakens production competence in the economy.

In the personal experience of most Americans, inflation is felt as a higher cost of living, reduced value of savings (including insurance, pensions, long-term bonds) and remarkably higher costs of education, medical services and housing. However, unseen from the "consumer's" vantage point is the destructive role of inflation on industrial planning of every sort.

Almost two decades of price inflation in the United States cannot be dismissed as a momentary crisis, a passing incident. Nor can the undermining of the dollar as a reliable symbol of value be attributed to the OPEC "oil shock," or the Vietnam war. General price inflation began in the United States just after 1965, well before OPEC's 1973 price escalation. The inflation continued long after the United States war in Vietnam had ended. Without question, the OPEC price increases and the enormous economic waste of the Vietnam war spurred sharp price increases; but they do not account for the onset and long endurance of U.S. inflation.[1] To get a handle on the price inflation that has endured for almost twenty years, one must uncover its connection with industrial productivity and with the fundamental changes in managerial attitudes toward cost and price, as displayed in the manufacturing industries of the United States.

Until 1965, industrial managements in U.S. industries could respond to all manner of cost increases with productivity improvements within their enterprises that were sufficient to offset all or a large part of cost increase. That was the core of the cost-minimizing process characteristic of manufacturing firms during the history of U.S. industry, 1865–1965. Furthermore, the hard work of changing production methods, product designs, etc., was facilitated by the ability of managements to find alternative, more mechanized ways of producing. This, in turn, was made possible by the aggressive application of the cost-minimizing process within the machinery-producing firms themselves. During the latter part of the nineteenth century, as we have seen, new machine tools with advanced production capabilities were produced more cheaply in the United States than in Great Britain, even though the American wage rate was much higher.

The whole scene was transformed by 1965, when the main instrument of cost-minimizing—productivity growth by cost-attractive mechanization—became conspicuously less utilized. That is the significance of the considerable fall in the rate of productivity increase in U.S. industry that has prevailed since 1965. American managers began to seek other ways of responding to cost increases. When the inability to offset cost increases became characteristic of manufacturing industries, managers saw that they could pass these increases along to price without risking a loss of market position to cost-minimizing competitors. After 1965, cost pass-along became the prevailing custom among the managements of American industrial firms. As the process continued, the pace of price increase advanced until the annual rates of price increase clearly exceeded the savings bank rate of interest. Under this condition, when leaving money in the bank meant a loss of its value, the pace of price increase was deservedly called inflation.*

The inflation process in manufactured goods is further accelerated by the normal operation of the cost-maximizing military economy. During the fourth quarter of 1980 the prices to be paid for forty-five major weapons systems increased by $47 billion.[2] The Pentagon's Defense Science Board has reported that the prices of military goods have been rising 50 percent faster than the general price index (which, of course, includes the military items).[3]

The full range of the effect of sustained price inflation is seen not only in the living standards of most Americans but also in the transformed operating conditions of industrial firms. A disparity is growing between textbook-theoretical formulations and the operational realities in the U.S. industrial economy.

Persistent inflation has had a massive effect on the mode of operation of industrial firms in the United States. As an alternative to making money by producing, managements can now score substantial profits by judicious handling of inventories of materials as these rise in price. A principal trend in the internal economy of industrial firms had been the increasing importance of the "fixed" costs represented by plant and equipment. With sharp price increases in raw materials and purchased components, as well as wages and salaries, these "variable" costs of production rise in relative importance. This forces a major alteration in the classic industrial strategy of producing at a larger percent of capacity, so that the "fixed" plant and equipment charges can be distributed over more product units. As sustained price increase raises the money value of materials and manpower, the opportunity for implementing this strategy is diminished. That, in turn, counters the incentive to invest in enhanced mechanization of work.

As the price of new machinery and allied equipment rises rapidly, many managers are reluctant to buy new equipment. For the most part, the manag-

---

*An unusual statistical analysis that established the validity and predictive power of this cost pass-along inflation mechanism was carried out by Dr. Byung Hong, and is reported by him in *Inflation under Cost Pass Along Management* (Praeger, 1979). Lloyd J. Dumas has diagnosed "Productivity and the Roots of Stagflation" in a paper, *Proceedings of the American Institute of Industrial Engineers,* May 1979. The special importance of the analyses by Hong and Dumas is that they describe the nature of the fundamental change that has taken place in the internal operations of the decision-making institutions of American industrial firms. Thus, the post-1965 inflation is exposed as no mere price aberration, but rather the consequence of a fundamental institutional change in the American industrial economy.

ers in question are those who receive bonuses calculated on the ratio of profits to assets. If one effect of purchasing expensive new production equipment is sharply to increase the money value of assets, it reduces the profit percent on assets, also known as "return on investment." As a result, industrial consultants have observed resistance to new investment among many industrial managers.

One of the great strengths of the American industrial economy has been the existence of a finance capital market that made available long-term funds at a fixed rate. This facilitated investment planning by industrial firms. The high and unstable interest rates that have accompanied price inflation since 1965 frustrate this classic form of financing. Indeed, the very size of interest rates during inflation is a severe deterrent to new productive investment.

Consider, for example, the effect of interest rates on the conditions for buying and using a new computer-controlled machine tool whose price is $350,000. Assuming that an interest rate of 17 percent must be paid on the capital borrowed for this purchase, then over a period of five years the compounded cost of interest would amount to $417,357, or 119 percent as much as the price of the machine itself. The combined cost to the purchaser then becomes the price of the machine ($350,000), plus the compounded interest to be paid ($417,357), for a combined cost of $767,357. If we assume that this can be charged off in five years, during which the machine is run on two shifts (4,000 hours a year), and at 75 percent of maximum capacity, then the fixed charges traceable to the price of the machine, and the interest charge, amount to not less than $51 per hour of anticipated use. Let us assume further that the new machine is a replacement for some existing equipment. Therefore, this estimated cost per hour of use of the new machine represents the minimum savings that would have to be made, as against the present costs with older machinery. That is a considerable requirement of cost reduction per hour, the largest part of which is owing to the interest charge rather than the price of the machine.*

There is a close connection between high costs of finance capital under continuing inflation and a soaring bankruptcy rate. Small firms are particularly vulnerable, as they have less favorable access to finance capital and hesitate to raise their prices. By contrast

---

*By contrast, if interest rates were at 6 percent for the borrowing of $350,000 for five years, then the interest charge would be $118,378 and the total fixed outlay to the firm for interest and equipment would be $468,378, with a requirement for hourly savings of $31 per hour during a five-year period of use. This illustration emphasizes the important effect of interest rates on the readiness of firms to invest in new machinery, even when the predictable rate of utilization is high.

Fortune 500 companies understand how to pass along the high cost of borrowing. They are sure enough of their market share that by raising their prices they won't be pricing themselves out of business. The small manufacturer thinks that if he starts to pass along the cost of 24 percent borrowing he will price himself out of a market in which he's a very small piece.[4]

Wall Street has come to recognize the link between high interest rates charged for finance capital and massive federal borrowing to pay for the expanding military economy. The size of the federal government's credit demand, as the economy's largest borrower, in relation to the total supply of market credit, dominates the nation's finance markets and has a controlling effect on interest rates.[5]

Inflated interest rates and machinery prices that increase as much as or more than wages of labor combine to discourage capital investment in new manufacturing equipment, especially for replacement purposes. When this restriction persists, it necessarily depresses the rate of productivity growth.

In 1958, John Kenneth Galbraith published his landmark diagnosis, *The Affluent Society*. His central argument was that American industrial capitalism now combined private affluence with squalor in publicly supported services.[6] The book's thesis was widely noted and debated, but the deterioration in infrastructure was not yet so visible or painful as to stimulate reform of the decay-producing system. Mainstream economists and their students (most college graduates) brushed aside Galbraith's warnings about the limited efficacy of the "market system" as a corrective for public domain (nonmarket) conditions.

In 1965, I published an analysis and forecast of the role of the war economy as a prime cause of industrial and infrastructure decay.[7] At that time, not even the facts of depletion were conceded, let alone their probable causes. Why? Many American intellectuals then supported public policies cast in terms of "post-industrial society," a "guns and butter" economy, military spending as a path to prosperity, and a vision of America that included a permanent frontier of indefinitely large resources. These beliefs functioned as a blinder, obscuring the reality that things wear out and must be replaced, that the United States was no longer a "new" country and was fast ceasing to be the most modern.

Gradually, through the 1970s, many Americans were surprised as they traveled abroad and experienced shiny, modern, well-maintained cities like Toronto, Frankfurt, Tokyo, Stockholm, Paris, Berlin. While there was still little readiness in the media to recognize the role of management's profits/

power drive in causing American decay, there was at least fresh attention to the facts of deterioration in the infrastructure of the economy.

America in Ruins is both the title and the forecast of a 1981 report issued by the Council of State Planning Agencies, an organization of the planning and policy staffs of the nation's governors.[8] The Council finds major deterioration in parts of the country's infrastructure—that is, vital services such as clean water, reliable transportation, efficient ports and competent waste disposal. It warns that "America's public facilities are wearing out faster than they are being replaced. The deteriorated condition of the basic public facilities that underpin the economy presents a major structural barrier to the renewal of our national economy. In hundreds of communities, deteriorated public facilities threaten the continuation of basic community services. . . ."[9] The council reports that, "despite a number of recent analyses, the precise condition of the nation's public works inventory—and the future investments we face— remains unknown." The following items from the council's report illustrate the scale and scope of what is at issue:

The nation's 42,500-mile Interstate Highway System, only now approaching completion, is deteriorating at a rate requiring reconstruction of 2,000 miles of road per year. Because adequate funding for rehabilitation and reconstruction was not forthcoming in the late 1970s, over 8,000 miles of this system and 13 percent of its bridges are now beyond their designed service life and must be rebuilt. . . .

The costs of rehabilitation and new construction necessary to maintain existing levels of service on non-urban highways will exceed $700 billion during the 1980s. Even excluding the estimated $75 billion required to complete the unconstructed final 1,500 miles of the Interstate System, the balance required for rehabilitation and reconstruction is still greater than *all* the public works investments made by *all* units of government in the 1970s. . . .

One of every five bridges in the United States requires either major rehabilitation or reconstruction. The Department of Transportation has estimated the costs of this task to be as high as $33 billion. Yet in Fiscal Year 1981 Federal Highway Authorizations, only $1.3 billion was allocated to repair bridge deficiencies . . .

The nation's municipal water supply needs will make heavy demands upon capital markets in the 1980s. The 756 urban areas with populations of over 50,000 will require between $75 billion and $110 billion to maintain their urban water systems over the next 20 years. . . .

Over $25 billion in government funds will be required during the next five years to meet existing water pollution control standards.

Over $40 billion must be invested in New York City alone over the next nine years to repair, service, and rebuild basic public works facilities that include: . . . two aqueducts, one large water tunnel, several reservoirs, 6,200 miles of paved streets, 6,000 miles of sewers, 6,000 miles of water lines, 6,700 subway cars, 4,500 buses, 25,000 acres of parks, 17 hospitals, 19 city university campuses, 950 schools, 200 libraries, and hundreds of fire houses and police stations. Because of its fiscal condition, New York City will be able to invest only $1.4 billion per year to repair, service, and rebuild these facilities.

At least $1 billion will be required to rebuild Cleveland's basic public works—$250 to $500 million is needed to replace and renovate the publicly-owned water system; over $150 million is required for major repairs of city bridges; and over $340 million must be spent for flood control facilities. In addition to these expenditures, Cleveland must find additional funds to rebuild or resurface 30 percent of its streets, now in a state of advanced deterioration, and to reconstruct the city's sewer collection system, which frequently floods commercial and residential buildings.

Even fiscally healthy cities face large public works investment requirements. For example, Dallas must raise almost $700 million for investment in water and sewerage treatment systems in the next nine years. More than $109 million must be generated to repair deteriorating city streets. . . .

Rural facility needs, as yet unknown, are the subject of a major survey by the U.S. Department of Agriculture currently under way.

Water resource development will require major investments in *all* regions of the nation in the 1980s. The agricultural base in the old "Dustbowl" will be in jeopardy toward the end of the decade unless new water sources can be developed. After the Second World War, vast underground water resources close to the surface were tapped for irrigation. Today, this area in the Texas and Oklahoma panhandles and surrounding states has over 10 million acres under irrigation (23 percent of the nation's total irrigated farmland). This irrigated production produces over 40 percent of the nation's processed beef and major portions of wheat, sorghums, and other crops that supply much of America's agricultural exports. The region's water source is being depleted. At present rates it will be gone by the year 2000. The reversion of the region's agricultural production . . . to low-yield dryland farming would have a devastating effect on the economies of six states. It would seriously harm the nation's balance of payments and ultimately reduce the value of the dollar in international markets. If this production is to be retained, major public works to bring surplus water from adjacent regions are required. . . .

A large number of the nation's 43,500 dams require investment to reduce hazardous deficiencies. The Corps of Engineers has already inspected 9,000 of these facilities and found many of them in need of safety improvements. The funds to inspect even the balance of these dams have not been available. A majority of the dams that are potentially hazardous are privately owned and the dam owners lack the financial resources, willingness, or understanding to take remedial measures. Nor do the states have the legislative authority, funds or trained personnel to conduct their own inspection and remedial efforts.

. . . Despite unmistakable evidence of such deterioration, the nation's public works investments, measured in constant dollars, fell from $38.6 billion in 1965 to less than

$31 billion in 1977—a 21 percent decline. On a per capita basis, public works invest-
ments in constant dollars dropped from $198 per person in 1965 to $140 in 1977—a
29 percent decline . . .[10]

In 1981, the editors of *Business Week* discovered "a nationwide need to
build and repair the infrastructure of the American economy."[11] They judged
that "industry cannot expand without adequate water and sewage systems
and well-maintained roads, bridges, and mass transit systems to get its employees to work and its goods to market." The same editors, however, could
not discover exactly why the infrastructure had so decayed. Nevertheless,
their enumeration of the facts of the case adds something to our understanding of the extent and scope of the infrastructure decay.

Poor roadways and bridges restrict growth possibilities for about 25 percent of America's cities.

In New York City, where street repair slowed to a near standstill in the late 1970s,
streets, which engineers say have about a 25-year life, are being replaced at a 700-year
rate; the replacement rate is 49 years in Cleveland, 50 years in Baltimore, and 100 years
in Oakland. . . .

Inadequate and dilapidated sewer lines and wastewater treatment plants are also
stalling economic activity both in stagnating cities that have to bring their systems
up to congressionally mandated standards and in growing areas that need additional
capacity. Wastewater treatment plants in 47% of the communities surveyed by the
Commerce Dept. in 1978 were operating at 80% or more of capacity, while the
generally accepted effective full capacity utilization rate is 70 percent. That means that
new plants and homes could not be hooked up to those systems.

. . . in the Chicago area, where the sewer systems overflow raw sewage into homes
and lakes and rivers alike with a disturbing regularity, the Metropolitan Sanitary
District is less likely to get the funds it wants to build a $3.4 billion, 131-mi. "deep
tunnel" to upgrade its system.[12]

In the absence of a comprehensive national assessment of the condition
of infrastructure, I have assembled the following illustrations to give a realistic view of the scene.

Underground Networks   Under the streets of large and especially old
cities lie remarkable networks, all uncharted, of "aging water mains, sewer
lines, and other subterranean facilities that have deteriorated to the point
where they threaten public health and safety. . . . Many cities do not know
what is in the complex of wires, pipes, cables, tunnels, and conduits under
their busiest arteries or exactly where that complex is. The original plans have
been lost in some cases and have grown inaccurate in others as facilities were
expanded haphazardly." Many cities' water mains have weakened to the point
that Boston, for example, "which began laying iron water mains in the 1840s,

has a system that carries 150 million gallons of water a day, but loses 78 million gallons a day through leakage." While this condition is well known to Boston's administrators, they find that they "can replace only ten miles, or about 1 percent, of the 1,100-mile system each year."[13]

Water Pollution   In July 1981 the federal government's Environmental Protection Agency, pursuant to the Clean Water Act, identified thirty-four streams and rivers in various parts of the United States where waters were so contaminated, mainly by toxic chemicals, as to require extraordinary technical measures to protect human health. All these "hot spots" are in or near major cities. The contaminants in these thirty-four bodies of water include the following chemicals or heavy metals: "arsenic, cadmium, chromium, copper, cyanide, lead, silver, mercury, polychlorinated biphenyls, phenols and cresols and phthalate esters."[14]

To be grasped on a human scale, the enormous social costs of power and profit accumulation at the expense of production competence and the quality of life need illustration in the experience of a particular community.

On June 20, 1980, New York City Councilman Gilberto Gerena-Valentin escorted a delegation of the Soviet Peace Committee on a tour through the South Bronx, pausing at Charlotte Street, where President Carter in October 1977 had promised to use his good offices for reconstruction. Standing against the background of what looks like a bombed-out area, the councilman said, "What I am doing is asking the Soviet government, through the Soviet Peace Committee, for $5 billion in foreign aid to rebuild the South Bronx."[15] Neither at the time nor thereafter has there been any public discussion about why a New York City councilman would seek publicity by asking for $5 billion from the Soviet government. The explanation is plain enough: neither he nor any other New York City official has been able to get serious funding from the United States government for the reconstruction of an important part of New York City. As already shown in chapter 5, during the whole period when information was readily available on the matter (after 1965) the main economic relation between the federal government and New York (state and city) has been a form of imperial exploitation.[16]

That pattern continued. By 1976, the federal government had collected in income taxes from New York State $10.6 billion more than it spent in the area. By 1979, this drain on the state had risen to $12 billion.[17]

The federal government has been milking the economy of New York State (and of Illinois, Michigan, Pennsylvania, Ohio, Indiana, Wisconsin—all of them centers of civilian industry) and transferring capital and purchasing power to the states where military industry and bases are concentrated.

Since 1945, the federal government has subsidized the development of suburban communities by the tax deduction allowed on home mortgage interest, and by the federal highway network that links the suburbias of the country and gives easy access to central cities. Meanwhile, urban renewal has been neglected. So the cities of New York State developed blighted areas, and metropolitan transit was allowed to decay, being deemed unworthy of federal largesse.

These federal attitudes apply to all the major urban centers. The troubles of New York City, therefore, should be read as an early warning of what awaits the others. The federal government's net take from New York State averaged $412 per person during the late 1960s. For the 7.8 million residents of New York City, this was a loss of $3.2 billion per year—more than enough to have avoided any deficiency in the city's budget and to fund at least some of the economic development for New York City residents that successive federal administrations have avoided in order to finance the military economy.* This extraction of finance capital killed any possibility of doing something effective to maintain and renew the infrastructure of New York City.[18]

Various estimates have been made of the capital expenditures needed to maintain and reconstruct the main support facilities of New York City. The city government has placed the cost at $30 billion over a ten-year period, starting in 1981.[19] A privately commissioned study projects an annual need of $4.7 billion.[20] Neither estimate can be fulfilled as long as the federal government persists in exploiting for its own purposes the population of New York City and state.

In 1977, New York's Senator Daniel Moynihan pointed out that "If New York got the proportionate amount California got, we should have received $32.3 billion more than we did. Such a surplus could retire all the debt owed by state and local government in New York in fifteen months. I conclude from this that the federal government is, however unintentionally, deflating the economy of New York in order to sustain expansion elsewhere. . . ."[21]

Here are some highlights of the condition of infrastructure in New York City.

Mass Transit The New York City subway system is the world's largest urban underground network. Until the late 1960s, when maintenance and replacement began to be neglected, the trains, however crowded and noisy, were fast, frequent and convenient. But conditions altered sharply as the system endured more than a decade of withheld maintenance and sparse new investment. In July 1981, 8,400 trains in the system "either failed to get into service or were pulled out of service. There were 7,900 such failures, known as abandonments, in July of [1980] and 4,900 in July 1979."[22] And these

---

*As New York City approached bankruptcy in 1975–1976, President Gerald Ford declined to grant any loan-guarantee support to the city, similar to that given the Chrysler and Lockheed corporations, for example. The New York *Daily News* captured the tone of the proceeding with its memorable page-one headline FORD TO CITY, DROP DEAD (October 30, 1975).

performances were really not so bad, considering that in January 1981, abandonments reached the unprecedented level of 10,500. Meanwhile, on-time performance was suffering badly. From 1979 to 1981, the proportion of late trains leaped from 3.2 to 11.3 percent of the approximately 6,500 subway runs scheduled each day.

Veteran subway workers report that, as equipment has deteriorated, they have been repeatedly directed to operate trains with faulty lights, horns, windshield wipers—even cars with dead motors. They point out that the management has been breaking its own rules in order, somehow, to keep the system in motion. Failing doors, failing lights, failing motors, burning brakes and motors, failures of air conditioning, have imposed major delays and severe discomfort on the millions who must ride the subway to and from work. The Federal Reserve Bank of New York has estimated that deterioration in the subway service has cost businessmen and their employees between $165 million and $330 million a year in lost time.[23]

The commuter lines around New York City have experienced "frequent malfunctions of poorly maintained equipment . . . shortening trains and causing overcrowding. Fires on undercarriages, cars without air conditioning, and ruptured brake lines and air hoses have intensified fears among veteran commuters. . . ."[24] Difficult conditions like overcrowding and late trains are no longer confined to rush-hour periods on various commuter lines.

Bridges   The New York City comptroller's office has reported that many of the city's bridges are in danger of failing structurally because "normal maintenance has been almost nonexistent." The same report notes that the East River Drive in Manhattan is "beginning to exhibit deterioration similar to that which closed the West Side Highway." A year earlier, the City Planning Commission had called for a major program to rehabilitate decaying bridges, repave worn streets, saying, generally, "we are losing the battle to keep up the city's lifelines." And the city's own transportation department completed a survey "of all the city's bridges, rating thirteen of 133 waterway bridges and 120 others as being in 'poor' condition."[25]

Garbage   As the city government has cut back sharply on the manpower and money available to the Department of Sanitation, the streets have become increasingly filthy. Manual sweeping was cut to the lowest level in the Sanitation Department's 100-year history, and street-sweeping machines wore out and were not replaced. Morale and management at the Department of Sanitation have suffered dramatically, with the attendant result of sloppy waste removal.[26]

Water   New York City's water system, designed 120 years ago and drawing water from as far as 125 miles away, has proved to be remarkably efficient. It has delivered 1.5 billion gallons a day, distributing it through 6,000 miles of water mains. But the arteries laid out long ago require replacement. The incidence of breaks was 234 in 1947, rising to 476 in 1976. Following a survey by the U.S. Army Corps of Engineers, a report recommended spending $90.5 million over ten years to replace 11 percent of the city's water distribution network, especially in Manhattan, where 28 to 35 percent of the breaks occur. But this 1980 recommendation has yet to be implemented.[27]

Libraries   When I was in public school in New York City, the once- or twice-weekly visit to the public library was an adventure I looked forward to. So I am no impartial observer when, some fifty years later, I read the judgment of the director of the city's branch libraries that "it is the worst library service in New York State." Cuts in budgets, cuts in librarian staffs, cuts in funds to buy books, fewer hours, less building maintenance—all these reductions add up to the adult community's rejection of its own young.[28]

The scope and depth of decay in the infrastructure of the United States can only be the result of powerful, sustained causes. Government-controlled capital has been used with priority for the state managers' military economy. Private managers declined responsibility for conditions of infrastructure, even adding to public burdens by practices like widespread unsafe disposal of hazardous industrial wastes. The devotion of private managers to short-termism and their role as exporters of capital precluded concern for the general welfare over a long term. Furthermore, the combined neglect of the quality of infrastructure by private and state managers was congruent with post–World War II mainstream American ideologies.

A labor force of high quality is the single most valuable production asset of an industrial society. This was demonstrated beyond doubt by the dramatic rise of Japanese and German industry from the ashes of World War II bombardments. The main available resource that remained was the brains and hands of the Japanese and German working people. But American managers who focus on their profits/power have been creating a castoff American labor force as a by-product of their successes. They have done this in a variety of ways: by their preference for investing abroad rather than in the United States, by presiding over industrial deterioration, and by their deployment of new technologies in ways that emphasize the de-skilling of working people or their displacement altogether. I have already shown the degree to which imported goods supply U.S. consumption in a sample of industries. For each of these industries, or particular products, I have estimated, in the accompanying table, the degree of U.S. unemployment that is directly represented by those imported goods. These unemployed are strategically important, because they do not reflect a temporary cutback in the operations of particular factories. They are jobless because U.S. production has been terminated and replaced with production abroad. For some products (like household radios and audiovisual recorders) there is no remaining U.S. production on which to base a statistical comparison; in these cases, I have estimated the total employment represented by the importation of these products. Furthermore, even the direct unemployment effects are probably understated. For example, federal officials have testified that the U.S. auto industry (including parts suppliers), which employed 2.8 million in 1978, would employ 550,000 fewer people after it had been "revitalized" as planned.[29]

ESTIMATED NUMBER OF U.S. JOBS DIRECTLY DISPLACED BY IMPORTS
IN A SAMPLE OF INDUSTRIES (1977–79)

Industry	Jobs Displaced	Industry	Jobs Displaced
Autos	131,000	Bicycles	5,000
Machine tools	29,000	Leather gloves	3,000
Steel	81,000	Shoes (non-rubber)	118,000
Calculators	22,000	Flatwear	6,000
Microwave ranges and ovens	8,000	Cameras (still)	26,000
Communications systems and equipment	73,000	Motorcycles	68,000
		Videotape recorders and players	27,000
Semiconductors and related devices	67,000	Home radios	37,000
		TV—black and white	26,000
X-ray and related equipment	11,000	TV—color	23,000
Motion-picture cameras	5,000	Audio recorders and players	98,000
Sewing machines	9,000	Apparel	328,000

Such estimates of the number of jobs lost tell only a part of the story. What has been lost to the American community is not simply a sum of individual jobs. These people were parts of production organizations that have been dissolved—entirely or in large part. An organization is a major asset in its own right, apart from a single person or small group. Work time, diligent effort and a variety of skills must be applied in profusion in order to create a production system. The loss of entire production organizations multiplies the castoff effect that is measured in numbers of jobs lost.

Apart from the unemployment caused by the export of capital (jobs) and industrial deterioration, the creation of a further castoff population is assured if American managers proceed to apply computer technology with priority to the pursuit of profits/power. Informal reports from major industrial firms disclose an intention to eliminate half or more of their production jobs by the end of the 1980s. There is no historical precedent for such speed and scope of job displacement. At one time, new tools and machines had relatively limited application within and across industries. Most of the impacted skills were manual-manipulative in character. In time, new industries and new products enlarged the total demand for labor. Now no new industries and products are likely to offset the job impact of the computer technologies wielded for management's profits/power. I have not been able to identify an occupation or industry whose functioning is exempt from change by the new technologies. After all, they include capability for varied sensing, for storing, processing and retrieving information, and for programmed physical manipulation of everything from pencils to multi-ton workloads.

The present perspective includes the rapid development of sensors and small special-purpose and ever cheaper computers (as microprocessors). This is paralleled by a full array of computer sizes, from the size of this book to banks of large standing cabinets. The applications of the new sensing and control technologies include present machines and processes, as modified with self-diagnostic devices and computer regulation of performance; a range of quite new devices, like robots with varied capabilities; computer-assisted design (CAD) and computer-assisted manufacturing (CAM); and computerized systems for production integration to control the pace and flow of work through an entire factory.*

The reader has received the cues for suspecting that there are limits to reliability that must constrain the use of such inherently complex manufacturing systems. Acceptable reliability requires sustained skilled maintenance of all functional elements. High reliability cannot result from the fantasy of the "workerless factory." Indeed, if improperly attended by skilled technicians, poor reliability can be the Achilles' heel of such technologies.

Yet the American managerial lust for the workerless factory, or at least the union-less factory, is not likely to be constrained by workaday considerations. The U.S. Air Force has been pressing the development of a costly Integrated Computer Assisted Manufacturing (ICAM) project designed to generate prototypes of a workerless factory. As in the past, earliest applications may be expected in the military economy, where cost does not matter. Then, managers in all sectors who yearn for "emancipation from human

---

*With CAD, a design can start as an electronic sketch on a screen, be translated into precise dimensional information that is magnetically stored, then be converted into instructions for a numerically controlled machine tool by CAM. Both the CAD and CAM information can be readily transmitted by telephone—including satellite—linkage, hence theoretically permitting control of manufacturing operations from a great distance.

workers" will be able to centralize their control by optimizing the goal of eliminating blue-collar workers.

Meanwhile, civilian industry managers have been moving swiftly to install proven robotics and allied small-computer devices all over the manufacturing scene. A 1980 estimate reckoned a U.S. market for industrial robots at $800 million by 1990.[30] By 1982, informed opinion anticipated a U.S. robot market worth $2 billion in 1990. Thus, a major firm that once planned to install 10,000 robots during the 1980s is expected to put in not fewer than 20,000 and as many as 30,000.

Here is an example of what is in motion. Knowledgeable architects predict that by 1988 "nearly all draftsmen will be out of work." Inexpensive ($80,000 a copy) CAD machines can be used by architects to swiftly show the precise shape and proportions of a structure, following instructions drawn by an electronic pen, or directed from a keyboard. Retrieving designs from a stored "menu" of structural, decorative, electrical, plumbing, and other features, the architect-operator can visualize a proposed design which the CAD machine will, on command, render in the form of a drawing within a few minutes. For a time, more programmers will be required while they and the architects "write" the software packages that contain the array of design options which architects would like to wield. Not only draftsmen are due for this scrap heap. The CAD machines do the detail work that traditionally took about 60 percent of the architect's time.[31]

Managers are appropriating technologies (and their embodied knowledge) that are the product of a great social heritage in science and technology and applying them to the familiar goals of maximizing quarterly returns on investment and managerial power. Once upon a time, mechanization in production was associated with price decreases. But there is not much talk of such a prospect for the 1980s. Instead of reducing the work week or work year across the board—one way of sharing the fruits of higher productivity—the prospect is for massive discharge of working people (of all skill levels), paralleled by modest increases in demand for certain occupations, like programmers and equipment-trouble-shooting technologists. The same managers who claim for themselves the fruit of man's greater mastery of nature take no responsibility for the further participation in useful work by millions of displaced workers. These castoff workers are consigned to an increasingly nonexistent "labor market."

The state managers of the federal government administer the largest single capital fund in the American economy. Therefore, changes in their policies on the deployment of capital can have major impact on job creation or dissolution. As federal officials implemented the policies of President Reagan they shifted the uses of federal funds in ways that directly created a new castoff population.

For example, the AFL-CIO examined the Reagan 1982 budget and calculated the job loss for each case where it was predictable. Thus the 69 percent cut in solar energy research development and demonstration projects, a reduction of $380 million, would eliminate about 2,500 jobs. However, the reduction in federal payments for child nutrition, amounting to $1.5 billion, has no directly traceable effect on jobs. The list of 1,259,200 jobs marked for elimination (see Appendix IV) takes no account of the multiplier effects that such unemployment has on the rest of society. Therefore, the itemization of the Reagan budget's toll on jobs in fiscal 1982 is a modest estimate of the human castoff effect.

The most significant, persistent, direct contribution of state management to the ranks of the unemployed is through the normal operation of its military economy. When money, and the resources it sets in motion, are invested in the state management's military enterprise, the same resources are not available for investment and working operations in other aspects of the economy. Typically, military spending has been more capital-intensive, therefore generating less direct employment than civilian spending. Thanks to the enterprise of Marion Anderson of East Lansing, Michigan, we have estimates of the effect of military spending on employment, with separate figures for each state. The question asked in each state was: What employment would have been generated if the resources spent on the military in that state had been expended on the civilian economy? From this number one deducts the employment created by the military spending actually carried out in the state, to arrive at an estimate of the number of jobs lost or gained in each state. The list is shown in Appendix V.

All told for the United States, 1,015,000 man-years of employment were forgone annually in 1977–1978 by the application of federal funds to the military enterprise. This estimate does not account for secondary effects from the concentration of capital on the military, like further productivity forgone owing to the economically nonproductive character of military goods and services.

In a way that ordinarily escapes attention, the long-enduring employment of millions of people in the service of the military *appears* to produce something. On closer examination, the military product lacks the ordinary economic usefulness for consumption or for production. Hence there is compensated activity but no production of economically useful goods. More important for the present discussion: the very skill in applying cost-maximizing and allied criteria for acceptable performance in the engineering and administrative jobs that serve the military "disables" the people so experienced for ordinary civilian work.[32] The disabling effect of military work is particularly true of the administrative and engineering occupations, and less so for production workers. Nevertheless, there is no escaping the fact that sustained service in the military economy weakens or destroys competence for civilian production work.

There is a second, indirect route by which the state managers deplete production competence. They subsidize the university faculties to do military research and development, and graduate students who participate as research assistants in military-serving projects. Thereby graduate students are taught early on how to "make it" professionally in the service of the state managers. All this while the state managers run down civilian-oriented education, notably in engineering and the basic sciences by concentrating research and related funds for servicing their own economy.

Permanent unemployment, a growing castoff population, has become integral to the economy of profits without production. The estimates of the parts of castoff population created by the normal operation of private and state managerialism are clearly incomplete. Nevertheless, they sketch a chain of processes whose humanly destructive effect, individually and socially, is incalculable.

A 1976 study by the Joint Economic Committee of the U.S. Congress found that "at least 26,000 deaths from stress-related diseases of stroke, kidney, and heart ailments, at least 1,500 of the suicides and 1,700 of the homicides during a five-year period [1970–1975] were related to unemployment. The stress-related deaths were 2.7 percent of the total deaths from those diseases, the suicides 5.7 percent of the total and the homicides 8 percent."[33] These results were derived from the research of Professor M. Harvey Brenner of Johns Hopkins University, who had been studying relationships between unemployment and particular health indicators for about fifteen years. The cumulative effect of an increase of 1.4 percent in unemployment in 1970 was estimated to have "cost American society some $21 billion in the form of lost income, mortality, and institutionalization." The increased unemployment accounted for:

- about 5.7 percent, or 1,540, of the 26,960 suicides;
- about 4.7 percent, or 5,520, of the 117,480 mental hospital admissions;
- about 5.6 percent, or 7,660, of the 136,875 state prison admissions;
- about 8 percent, or 1,740, of 21,730 homicides;
- about 2.7 percent, or 870, of 32,080 deaths from liver cirrhosis;
- about 2.7 percent, or 26,440, of the 979,180 deaths from cardiovascular and renal disease.

These findings are reinforced by the fact that the data examined came not only from parts of the United States but also from England, Wales and Sweden, and disclosed a consistent relationship with unemployment rates, independent of age, sex, or race.[34]

Malnutrition is predictable for the permanently unemployed, because unemployment insurance funds have been designed to cope with temporary layoffs, not with the termination of enterprises or the displacement of whole occupations.

When the Reagan administration proposed its various reductions of social programs, committees of Congress heard testimony on the consequences of the food-stamp cuts. Speaking for the Illinois Consortium on Governmental Concerns (a church organization), Richard Wood testified that "more than a thousand families had to be turned away from church-run food kitchens in Illinois in January [1981] because supplies had run out." All such testimony was resisted by the chairman of the Senate Agricultural Committee, Jesse Helms of North Carolina, who feared that "great harm" might come to the recipients of food stamps from accepting a largesse that would "destroy their initiative."[35]

For the jobless automobile workers of Detroit, and for others made unemployed by the ripple effect from the auto industry, food lines have already become a normal part of life. According to an article in *The New York Times,* the Salvation Army and church workers in the Detroit area report that "The men and women who have lost their jobs in the area's worst industrial slide in decades are coming in ever greater numbers to sit on the worn benches of steamy soup kitchens in churches and community centers. . . . The Capuchin Brothers Soup Kitchen here in Detroit served 135,483 hot lunches in 1980. The figure for 1981, calculated only through November, was 145,645. . . . The Capuchin Kitchen . . . also gives destitute families emergency food packages worth about $60. . . . Five years ago it was safe to say that 95 percent of the street people we saw were chemically addicted to drugs or alcohol or whatever. . . . Today 70 percent of our guests are just homeless and jobless people, not addicts. . . . Among our guests today, being out of work is the reality, not the exception anymore. . . . We are getting a lot of young men. . . . The most common thing we hear nowadays is that they just cannot make their [welfare] check stretch anymore. At the beginning of the month we probably average 600 meals a day. Beginning with the 26th or 27th of the month, we begin to exceed 1,000. The money just runs out."[36]

Being a castoff means being unneeded, unwanted, and that contributes to hopelessness and loss of pride and self-esteem. When that is made into a permanent condition, then social disintegration is set in motion: the castoff population becomes a concentration area for mental depression and illness, alcoholism and other drug addiction, family disintegration and abandonment, emotional and behavioral breakdowns among children, juvenile delinquency, school dropout, social violence, child abuse, prostitution, and soaring crime rates that have given rise to entirely new industries selling fancy locks, personal defense equipment and electronic security devices. (Paradoxically, the preoccupation with military aspects of national security has contributed to a domestic security problem.)

A castoff nation is created when its working people—all grades—are progressively discarded by decision-makers determined to make money outside production, outside the country, and by military work that contributes no life-serving product.

ECONOMIC FUTURES FOR THE UNITED STATES

The assessment of futures that follows is guided by the assumption that a community must produce in order to live. I lean on the previous chapters to help answer an unusual question: Could a set of conditions develop that would make a constructive renewal of U.S. production capability so difficult as to be unfeasible in any near future?

Short of such a prospect, what are the changes in decision-making by managers, engineers and workers that would spur a renewal of production competence?

13

Reaching a Point
of No Return

If the goals of decision-making that I have called "profits without production" continue to be characteristic of the American economy, the only future in prospect is further decay of productivity and production competence. But the implications of this decline go well beyond a simple continuation of what has occurred thus far. Even if we rule out dangerous military adventurism and nuclear war as part of America's future, the continued decay inherent in profit without production must one day reach a point of no return.

Let's assume that sometime soon there arises in the United States a great popular consensus committed to restoring production competence. Such a movement would, for a start, need to take stock of the assets indispensable for the task. Four conditions would have to be satisfied: First, it would be necessary to lay bare the true cause of the production incompetence, and thereby to establish the areas for priority action. Second, a list would have to be drawn up of resources that are crucial for carrying out the renewal of industry and infrastructure. Third, since an important part of industrial and other renewal would require reorienting the resources of the military economy, it would be vital to know how widely dispersed is the capability for carrying out this economic conversion. Finally, a far-reaching and sustained industrial effort for reconstruction requires a firm ideological commitment, to assure people that the desired economic renewal can actually be achieved, and so to maintain the will and drive necessary to carry it through. In the event that these conditions are not met, the process of decay may be irreversible. The situation could be such that production renewal would be extraordinarily difficult, if not impossible, to achieve.

The single most influential attempt to explain the collapse of U.S. competence in production has been offered in "The Reindustrialization of America," a special issue of *Business Week* (June 30, 1980) that grapples with the problem in more than fifty pages of text. The attempt, however, is less than satisfactory. The magazine's editors deserve credit for at least identifying many of the major issues involved, and for assembling an imposing array of data on many aspects of the U.S. economy; but their analysis is fundamentally flawed by their failure to come to grips with the underlying causes of the problem.

Thus, *Business Week* recognizes that industrial productivity growth is down, but nowhere refers to the mechanism that has made cost-attractive new machinery less available to American industry. Neither is there mention of the transformation whereby firms have forsaken cost-minimizing techniques in favor of cost pass-along and cost-maximizing. Technical innovation is said to be flagging, and the availability of finance capital from savings is said to have shrunk. But there is no acknowledgment of the presence and operating characteristics of the military economy as a massive institution that has preempted finance capital and technical talent. The editors fail to discover, when they gauge the prospects for "the reindustrialization of America," that finite resources of technical talent, and capital in all its aspects, if preempted by the military, deprive the society of consumption and production use values that would otherwise be available. Indeed, there is no reference, even in the most ordinary financial terms, to the size of the military budget and its possible effect on the economy at large.

The *Business Week* analysis deplores inflation as skewing the profit incentive, but makes no connection between its persistence and the permanent war economy.

The editors of *Business Week* condemn short-term corporate decision-making and the decline in entrepreneurship of the classic production-oriented variety. But the picture they offer of the industrial firm is seriously muddied by their contention that collective bargaining is a factor which induces industrial decline. The discussion lacks data on the substantially more influential role of unions in collective bargaining throughout most of Western Europe. Thus, the allegedly depressing effect of American unions' wage agreements hardly survives as a serious explanation of flagging productivity, especially when one notes the relative decline of wages to American workers as compared with current rates in Western Europe and the swift rise in Japan.

"The Reindustrialization of America" is in the main an appeal to nationalism, pride and team spirit. Its tone is set by the figure of Uncle Sam on the front cover—here holding a wrench, as though to admonish us that it's time to get to work. Therefore the analysis concludes with warnings against unreasonable expectations, and calls on management, labor and academics to confer together and draft a new kind of social contract, attention being paid to the post-industrial thesis that in our era making information (high technology) is more important than the mere making of goods. Ways should be found, the editors say, to advance some industries while others are cut back.

But *Business Week* offers no explanation as to just why so many U.S. industries have developed the lethal combination of technical/economic incompetence. We are apparently given to understand that some unnamed external force determines which are the "sunrise" industries, and which the "sunset."

The editors of *Business Week* are not alone in their vision. From the other side of the collective bargaining table, the AFL-CIO has produced a popular pamphlet, *Blueprint for a Working America: Rebuilding Our Economy in the 1980s.*[1] It describes inflation as the core defect in the U.S. economy, but does not account for the occurrence, duration and particular causes of the dollar's decline. Plant closings and the export of capital and jobs are singled out as ills to be cured, but the causal system underlying these developments is not suggested. The entire discussion proceeds without reference to the establishment in the United States of a permanent war economy or to the consequences that flow from that condition.

In similar fashion, the editors of *Business Week* have addressed the troubles of state and local governments.[2] Again, there is no indication that the fiscal and material problems of states and cities might be by-products of the long-term operation of a major military economy. An extensive data-based discussion of infrastructure elements that badly need repair is presented with no mention of where the finance-capital and material resources have actually gone during a quarter-century of infrastructure neglect.

Elsewhere, astute and respected individual economists and institutions have been discussing such topics as the uses of capital, capital formation, and finance-capital shortages in the American economy without calling attention to the fact that enormous military budgets have the quality of capital funds. The Chase Manhattan Bank bought a full-page newspaper ad to advise Americans that they should "Scream!" What we were supposed to scream about was the meager proportion of American income flow that has been applied to productive capacity, as compared to the allotments made in Japan, West Germany, France and Canada.[3] Said the Chase: "Failure to close this capital gap could result in significantly higher unemployment and a higher inflation rate ten years from now. Both unacceptable conditions, in our opinion." What to do? Says Chase: "Encourage an ever-growing base of personal savings. Establish more realistic depreciation allowances. . . ." The Chase's agenda in 1975 closely resembles the Reaganomics package of 1982 and suffers from a similar deficiency: the largest single block of capital in the American economy—that is, the military slice of the pie—is simply omitted. This oversight has also diminished the usually sophisticated analyses of the Machinery and Allied Products Institute, which exists to represent the interests of the machinery-producing industries of the United States.[4]

Many economists, alert to the decline of U.S. productivity growth, have recommended major new capital investments in means of production and technical research. But such proposals are almost always accompanied by the warning that sustained fresh investment requires a reduction in the living standards of important parts of the population, so that their consumption money may be gathered up and converted into finance capital for industrial redevelopment. Again, this approach neglects the nonproductive function of the largest single block of capital in the American economy, does not allude to the acceleration of productivity growth that would result if it were applied to productive undertakings of every sort, and assumes the ready transferability of consumer to production resources.[5]

One version of the less-consumption-for-more-capital theme is that if only the American middle class were resolved to consume less today in order to invest more for tomorrow, money could be found to multiply productive investment in the American economy.[6] The argument is that since payments to individuals in the form of Social Security, Medicare, unemployment compensation, civil service and military pensions amounted to 36.2 percent of total federal spending in 1980, those funds, properly cut, can supply the financing for new productive investment. That recommendation supposes that the goods and services bought with Social Security and similar payments can be reduced without causing any real hardship. The further and more important assumption is that those consumer goods, or the money payments that represent them, are readily transformed into industrial production resources. This is absurd: Packages of food and the work of food preparation are not convertible to machine tools. The trained technical brains and hands that are a vital production resource cannot be marshalled overnight by the announcement of more expenditures for such work. After all, a good high school and college preparation is required to produce even an apprentice engineer. There is no basis for assuming some magic quality in money that makes possible swift conversions from dollar units to industrial production resources.

A variant of this view is that an industrial economy generates a homogeneous mass of money-valued outputs and that everyone in the society serves his or her own well-being, and thus the well-being of all, by striving for a maximum share of the money-valued pie. But that presupposes a competent production system underlying the competitive struggle for a share of money, a condition which no longer obtains as private and state management in the United States becomes less competent to organize people for work. As late as 1964 it seemed reasonable to thoughtful people that "an adequate distribution of the potential abundance of goods and services will be achieved only when it is understood that the major economic problem is not how to increase production but how to distribute the abundance that is the great potential of cybernation."[7] By then, the decline of production competence in American industry was already well established though still concealed from those who clung confidently to established economic wisdom.[8]

Thus, virtually the full range of conventional theory and ideology falls sadly short of accounting for the deterioration in the American production system. Across the spectrum, the full social cost of a sustained military economy is unappreciated. That is not just a technical economic error, like the typical failure to take into account the change in management's basis for decision-making from cost-minimizing to new priorities that suppress the growth of productivity. The focus remains on money, and therefore the flow of money is taken to be a measure of economic benefit—an assumption that fails to explain what happens when the money sponsors work that yields no consumption or production usefulness at all.

In short, valid explanations for the cause of American production incompetence are in very short supply.

A definite set of material and human resources is indispensable for successful industrial renewal in the United States on a large scale. It includes specialized work capability, finance capital, technical knowledge and criteria for decision-making.

Because the process of depletion has been so extensive in many industrial fields, it will often be necessary to develop entire industries that have either disappeared or never operated in the United States. Electron microscopes and household sewing machines are examples of items that were once produced in the United States, but for which there no longer exist skilled workers or a cadre of experienced administrators. Capital investment planning for such industries will have to include time and money to train teams of administrators, engineers and production workers. For this task, it may prove useful to draw upon the methods employed in Western Europe after World War II, when every country in that region established productivity centers, which for about twenty years cooperated with U.S. industrial, university and trade union groups to transfer technology and to train key persons in many industries.

Almost all the depleted industries in the United States (see the sampled list in chapter 12) severely lack the engineering and allied skills needed to design products to world standard and to operate production systems at high technical and economic competence. For example, the design, production and operation of modern high-speed railroad equipment and systems are unknown in the United States. Therefore, to introduce such technology it will first be necessary to train substantial numbers of engineers, administrators, technicians and blue-collar workers—all grades. It can be done either by sending them to work abroad or by bringing teams of specialists to the United States for the purpose.

For the rest of this century, many American industries face the prospect of shortages of skilled workers, notably in occupations that require long periods of theoretical as well as practical training. In the structure of American institutions there is no point of responsibility for seeing to it that the school systems are properly equipped and trained to produce a steady flow of highly competent workers. Such a lack makes sense in terms of the long period in which work and especially production work has been assigned inferior status, all this reinforced by the background fantasy of post-industrial society. Therefore, economists report on shortages of skilled workers in many key industries,[9] and trade union officials tell of the aging population of skilled workers in industries like shipbuilding that have had a long history of unstable employment.[10]

For many industries, the development of skilled workers will require cooperation with industrial, technical institutes, and trade union groups abroad. The Scandinavian countries, for example, have made notable progress in acquainting metalworking machinists with computer technology, thus enhancing their skills as operators of computer-controlled equipment.

There will be much need for management personnel of all grades who have a strong bias toward production planning and the operation of production facilities to supply useful goods of high quality. American industry is short of such people, because it has drawn a large percentage of its managers from the pool of business-school graduates or from those with allied finance and legal training, while neglecting to train managers who will be primarily disposed to serve production.

A federal institution, set up to plan capital investment, is essential for major industrial renewal. Such an agency must employ a technical staff trained in Leontief-type input-output analysis. It would need access to a fairly detailed (say, 600 × 600) input-output table that is reasonably up to date.*

A substantial input-output table is vital for any large-scale industrial renewal effort because not everything can be done at once. It would be necessary to schedule a sequence of classes of capital investment so that they might proceed in a way to build up cumulative production capability. And

---

*An input-output table and accompanying analysis is a method formulated by Professor Wassily Leontief to show the interrelations among industries and activities in the economy—that is, how the output of each industry has a place in the input of many others. This method of quantifying the interdependence of principal economic activities is a strategic tool for capital investment planning.

There is a fine explanation and illustration of the Leontief system, especially for the nonspecialist reader, in "The 1980 Input-Output Chart," with accompanying booklet, from *Scientific American*. A fundamental statement is by Wassily Leontief, *The Structure of the American Economy, 1919–1939*, 2d ed. (Oxford University Press, 1951).

these operations must be carried out by the federal government because it alone has the formal power to demand the relevant data from all the enterprises whose activities must be accounted for in an adequate input-output table.

Many industries need new technical knowledge if they are to design up-to-date general products and production systems. In the crucial machinery-producing industries, for example, such knowledge is required if industry is to be supplied with equipment using standardized components and modular units for machine construction. The technical and economic problems inherent in the design and operation of stable production systems have to be explored, so that newly created facilities can be operated at high levels of labor and capital productivity. At present, no departments of American industrial firms, universities, technical institutes or government agencies are prepared to supply such knowledge. Indeed, until recently, the need for it has been generally denied.

Decision processes in industrial enterprises require fundamental restructuring to give important weights to the morale of shop employees, for that is the only way to guarantee the sustained interest in methods of operation that will deliver both technical and economic competence, as well as the prospect of sustained employment. Workers and production-oriented engineers are precisely the people who have a stake in a viable production system. Unlike top managers, who can see a future for themselves in an enterprise that moves away from production, the production-related occupations are, by definition, dependent on competent output of useful goods. The requirement here is for participation by working people in decision-making at all levels of the enterprise. That degree of participation has not yet been reached in various management moves designed to elicit worker involvement in matters of product, quality, economy of operations, and so forth.

Administrators, engineers and workers all require training in cost-minimizing the design and use of industrial facilities. Such instruction is little stressed in the present array of professional and occupational training institutions.*

This brief sampling of resource requirements for carrying out major industrial renewal exposes the limitations in each of these spheres within the economy of the United States. For example, the managements of principal American industries, marshalling the services of their engineers and administrative subordinates, "have been fighting tooth and nail over consumer protection, [while] other nations have been using consumer protection as a means

---

*A young man receiving a degree in mechanical engineering at a major American university informed me (fall 1982) that during his four years of training he had not had a single lecture on how to design anything cost-effectively.

of improving industry performance and enhancing national reputation for commercial quality."[11]

American engineering societies are beginning to show renewed concern for the state of engineering competence in many fields. We are told that in the case of technically related breakdowns,

the record indicates that many of these mishaps are directly attributable to defective engineering and its supporting research and development activities—for which management clearly is ultimately responsible. For example, testimony before the President's Commission to investigate the Three Mile Island nuclear accident reveals (in addition to the many nontechnical problems) malfunctioning valves, unreliable instruments, control panels that heightened the chance of operator error, and failure to make essential thermodynamic analyses that could probably have anticipated the disaster. To cite another instance, Federal Highway and Safety Administration reports show that over 60 percent of the automobile recalls in 1977 were traceable to faulty engineering.[12]

In a word, American industry is short of the technical skills that are indispensable for industrial renewal.

Even the most carefully prepared industrial renewal operations will have a quota of failures. Therefore, capability for turning failed organizations around, or for taking them apart and regrouping their people and equipment, is a vital part of what is needed to carry out industrial renewal on a large scale.

With 37,000 industrial firms serving the Pentagon as prime contractors and at least three times that many working as subcontractors, there can be no dispute about the need to draw on the resources of this vast industrial system for carrying out a far-reaching industrial renewal in the United States. Since these military firms have been an important factor in the country's industrial production decline, the ability and willingness to convert from a military to a civilian economy is an important part of the larger problem.

Economic conversion means changing over the physical resources, the skills of all employees, and the ways of organizing work to serve civilian rather than military goals. Organization is a problem area because of certain characteristics of military industry. The decision goals and occupational practices of that industry encourage cost escalation. Cost-maximizing is feasible because subsidies from the federal government offset extraordinary increases. Military products are often designed to deliver increased military "capability," regardless of cost. Given that priority, reliability takes second place, as do such considerations as ease of maintenance and minimum cost for accomplishing a given function. As I noted in chapter II, military industry managements are encouraged to compress production schedules, even to the extent of skipping important stages, in order to meet arbitrary target dates. Extraordinarily high costs of maintaining military equipment are not tolerable in civilian practice.[13] In short, economic conversion means retraining managers, engineers and production workers to abandon the job practices that are accepted, even desired, within the military economy and to abide by conditions that are essential for competent functioning in the civilian economy. Economic conversion also means the physical redesign and re-equipment of military production facilities for civilian purposes.

During the 1970s, two military industry contractors attempted to change over part of their production facilities and labor forces to civilian work: the Rohr Corporation of Chula Vista, California, and Boeing-Vertol, a division of the Boeing Company located near Philadelphia, Pennsylvania. Rohr built the BART (Bay Area Rapid Transit) system for San Francisco, as well as the Washington, D.C., subway system, acting as general contractor for the rolling stock and the control equipment. Boeing-Vertol, starting in 1971, undertook to design and then produce electric trolley cars and subway cars. Both firms displayed a severely limited competence in the manufacture of civilian vehicles. I shall discuss the Boeing-Vertol experience, since many of the key problems are similar, and the Rohr Corporation case has been extensively reported.[14]

Stimulated by potential subsidies from the federal government's Urban Mass Transportation Administration, Boeing-Vertol bid, in 1971 and thereafter, won orders for electric trolleys and subway cars in the United States. The company was, in fact, the frontrunner in a national competition to design such vehicles, and its management hoped that its product would set the national standard. Boeing-Vertol had reached a peak of production during the Vietnam war, when its 13,500 employees were producing helicopters for the military. But this business had dropped off and by 1978 4,300 workers, engineers and administrators were operating the design, production and assembly shops that spread across a 180-acre tract along the Delaware River. Two-thirds of Boeing-Vertol's employees were then still on helicopter production, but the remainder were working on light-rail vehicles and stainless steel rapid-transit cars. The firm had received orders for 275 trolleys from the transportation agencies of Boston and San Francisco. Also, 200 stainless steel rapid-transit cars were on order for Chicago. The seventy-one-foot trolleys are of particular interest in this discussion, since their design and production involved many innovations.

No trolley cars were built in the United States after 1952. Thus, by 1978, all such vehicles in use in the United States, about 1,200, were of vintage design, the majority being more than thirty years old. The hope was that these represented a definite replacement market, with prospects for a lot more orders when the worth of a modern electric-powered light-rail vehicle had been demonstrated.

The electric public carrier designed by Boeing-Vertol was downright handsome: sleek, articulated at the center to permit easy negotiation of sharp curves. Its windows were large; it was well lit, had comfortable seats, air-conditioned interior; it was quiet and speedy. The motorman's console was comfortably designed, with radiotelephone linkage for easy system control. Riders and motormen were pleased with the new vehicles. The Boston press carried comments from riders and operators who welcomed the elegant successor to the noisy, jerky, drafty and slow trolley cars of an earlier era.

· To design and construct the vehicles, Boeing-Vertol assembled a team of eighty engineers who, with one exception, came from the aerospace departments of the firm. These professionals and their managers saw themselves as transferees from the high technology of aerospace to a field of comparatively low technology. Deciding that the technical transition should be easy enough, these sophisticates of high technology proceeded to conduct the project on a "systems engineering" pattern. Design tasks were subdivided among the engineering group and a small team was dispatched on brief visits to European plants that were manufacturing rail vehicles. The Boeing engineers sought to make a major technological leap by assigning key components to a network of seventeen subcontractors in the United States and other countries. They thus established themselves as system designers and assemblers, leaving the principal functional work to specialized subcontractors. German firms supplied electrical equipment and a company in Yokohama supplied not only the "truck" frames carrying the driving motors, brakes, etc., but also the welded steel car body. In that way the Boeing-Vertol engineers arranged a "transfer of technology" in the form of the detailed know-how embodied in the equipment supplied by the various contractors. In other words, the engineering staff attempted to skip an otherwise long learning period and to dodge the manufacturing problems they might have encountered if they had tried to design and produce many of these components themselves.

However, as the Boeing-Vertol engineers became involved in other aspects of the design and subsequent tasks, they ran into some of the specific and unique requirements of this class of equipment. For example, trolley-car doors, which, unlike those on airplanes, are opened and closed thousands of times a week, impose special design criteria of simplicity and durability. However, there was no way to learn the art of trolley-car design from other American firms, or from engineers who might be hired away from them. Also —such was the boundless self-confidence of the aerospace team that took charge of this project—it seemed unnecessary to call on anyone else to advise them on how to "bring automation" to an area long neglected in the United States. Finally, no American university had been training engineers for this long-dead industry.

Starting in 1976, thirty-three of the new light-rail vehicles were put in operation on the "Green Line" of the Massachusetts Bay Transportation Authority. A succession of difficulties began to show up rather quickly, and by December 1977 about seventy-two essential modifications had been recognized and were agreed by both MBTA and Boeing-Vertol to be the responsibility of the vendor. Most of the changes were minor, but there were some major, intractable problems. The cars derailed repeatedly on tight curves, and successive modifications of the truck and wheel adjustment in the center section of the vehicle failed to achieve a durable "fix." The doors on the original cars, designed and built abroad, had 1,300 parts and failed repeatedly. Boeing-Vertol did its own redesign, scaling down the complexity of the door mechanism to about 600 parts. The vehicle was subject to repeated delays under certain emergency conditions. For example, when air pressure was lost, the brakes went on in emergency pattern. But to release the brakes, maintenance men had to unwind six sets of brakes mechanically with a special tool, a job that took twenty minutes or more, often in a cramped subway area. Certain maintenance requirements had been overlooked. The car batteries were not arranged for easy roll-out and required time-consuming physical disconnection for servicing. Similarly, no provision had been made for "quick disconnects" to allow servicing of the air-conditioning system without cutting and then resoldering piping, a long and costly process.

In their first year and a half of operation, the new vehicles were involved in more than 100 reported derailments. The MBTA reported that it had been forced to assign more maintenance personnel to keep "fifty-odd LRVs going on the Green Line than . . . to maintain 220 rapid transit cars on the Red, Blue and Orange Lines." MBTA's director of operations said, "Everybody was taken by surprise by the LRV's rate of failure. They were supposed to be reliable, but it just wasn't true."[15]

Boeing-Vertol made a solid showing of responsibility under the warranty terms of its contract and dispatched a team of thirty engineers and skilled workers to the MBTA shops to take charge of modifying the cars that had been delivered. By June 27, 1979, the MBTA gave the following accounting of the 175 vehicles that had been ordered from Boeing-Vertol in 1973. On the previous day 30 of these vehicles were in service. Of the rest: 40 were never delivered, 35 were returned to Boeing, 19 were extensively damaged, 5 were under modification, 24 were awaiting maintenance, 5 were awaiting parts, 3 were awaiting inspection, and 14 were in maintenance.

Difficulties with the light-rail vehicles piled up. The propulsion-control circuitry proved unreliable. The cooling motors and fans for the traction motors burned out rapidly and were expensive to replace. Spare parts proved difficult to obtain. Proper operation of a spare parts maintenance inventory requires a baseline of records of reliability in performance, but there had been no systematic prototype testing on which to compile a record. The far-flung network of parts suppliers was not always responsive to the user, and some parts required lead times of eight to nine months.

By November 1979, following extended negotiation, the MBTA and Boeing-Vertol arranged a legal settlement under which Boeing-Vertol agreed to pay MBTA $40 million as final settlement of its responsibilities for these vehicles. And 40 cars of the original 175-car fleet would not be delivered. Of the remainder, 100 of the vehicles were to be repaired and modified by MBTA personnel at Boeing expense. Another 35 were to be stripped for parts or brought into service by the MBTA or returned to Boeing-Vertol.

The legal settlement, however, did not resolve technical problems. By February 1980, it appeared to be the judgment of many MBTA managers and workers that the entire fleet of light-rail vehicles might have to be taken out of service within two or three years because of "prohibitive corrective costs." The flexible center section had never been made to function reliably and replacement units were estimated to cost $100,000 apiece. The cooling mechanisms for the main traction motors were failing repeatedly and were estimated to cost, at three motors per vehicle, about $720,000 for fleet replacement. Major gearboxes, 47 in number, were leaking their lubricant and no "fix" for this had been devised. New gearboxes for the fleet would cost an estimated million dollars. Major adjustments were known to be required on axle assemblies. Finally, problems developed with respect to spare parts availability, since the Boeing-Vertol Company had decided to abandon the light-rail vehicle business and the MBTA was left to deal with the makers of principal vehicle components. Meanwhile, the MBTA, needing new vehicles to replace its aging fleet, was negotiating with Canadian, Belgian and German manufacturers.

What went wrong? What were the crucial elements of the Boeing-Vertol failure to produce a competent vehicle? The answer is important, because Boeing-Vertol's practices reflected normal operation procedure in much of military industry.

Boeing-Vertol applied "state-of-the-art" technology to the separate components, which they then matched together in their design. Design practice was somewhat tempered by the brief visits abroad, but on the premises of Boeing-Vertol there was no senior engineering staff with long experience in this class of vehicle design or production. The idea of sending a team to be trained abroad, or engaging foreign experts to train the staff outside Philadelphia, was evidently unthinkable. So the Boeing-Vertol staff got the benefit of "on-the-job" training without the benefit of direction by experienced hands. It accepted the new vehicle assignment as a case of low technology, by comparison with the aerospace high technology with which it was familiar. This technological chauvinism blinded the Boeing-Vertol staff to the need for a definition of the difference between criteria appropriate in aerospace and in civilian vehicle design. Subcontractors were relied upon for primary functional components on the assumption that the quality of individual parts would assure their competent function in combination—an idea that makes no sense on theoretical grounds, nor in varied engineering experience.

The Boeing-Vertol management/engineering team was prepared to accept "sophisticated" designs in many components, when what was needed was rugged simplicity. In many aspects of the vehicle design Boeing-Vertol overlooked ease and economy of maintenance, major issues in mass transit vehicles intended for long lives of reliable service. The firm assumed spare parts would be as readily available in the future as they had been in conjunction with original orders. There was no clear justification for that optimism, especially with respect to vendors scattered all over the world.

Boeing-Vertol, believing that full service testing of prototype equipment was dispensable, practiced the familiar military strategy of "concurrency." Indeed, the light-rail vehicles were put into production straight from the drawing board.

Working for the Department of Defense, military contractors have had repeated experience of major maintenance and reliability problems with complex military products. These difficulties have been smoothed over by redesign, retrofitting of new components, assigning extensive maintenance time and equipment, retiring the equipment earlier than planned, or by some combination of these expedients. In the military market, equipment failures customarily occur under conditions of restricted access—behind barbed wire, on ships at sea, at remote air bases. Boeing-Vertol's light-rail vehicles sailed in full public view and to the inconvenience of a great many passengers. The press soon discovered that there was a real story in "the cars that couldn't."

From the civilian technology and civilian service viewpoint, the Boeing-Vertol experience is a saga of managerial and engineering arrogance and incompetence. It also closely resembles the performance of aerospace firms on military contracts. The C-5A and missile programs come immediately to mind. That is why it is so important to estimate accurately the capability for weaning military industry engineers, managers and blue-collar workers from their accustomed professional ways. And that also is why it is cause for very serious concern that, until now, no major military-serving enterprise has demonstrated an autonomous ability to carry out the sort of occupational switch that is needed to go civilian. Economic conversion is therefore an important policy idea that has yet to be proved in operation by American industry. If such capability can be shown, there may be at least a fighting chance to turn the vast resources of the military economy to productive use. If it cannot be shown, there is no prospect for success without a complete dismantling of military-serving firms and a regrouping of people in order to break the military industry pattern.

The federal government's Urban Mass Transportation Administration (UMTA) played a key role in two major aspects of the Boeing-Vertol contract: the practice of "concurrency" in the production system, and the failure to draw upon the technical knowledge of other countries for making a trolley car.

UMTA provided 80 percent of the $300,000 purchase price of each vehicle that was delivered to Boston. Since the agency had reserved the right to approve the contract between the Boston unit and Boeing-Vertol, it had effective power of veto. It did nothing to enforce a requirement for prototype testing, and indeed approved a schedule so short as to preclude the possibility of such testing in any serious way.

The administrators of UMTA also had a hand in making sure that American high-technology aerospace engineering teams would not be disturbed by the advice of foreigners, who were no doubt alien to the "systems approach" as practiced in aerospace. In March 1975 George K. Isaacs, an electrical design engineer, wrote a letter in the public interest to a research administrator of UMTA. He said in part:

Let me suggest an approach that would allow the United States to once again become a leader in electrically powered transit and, as a bonus, railroad electrification. Because private enterprise is hesitant to commit manpower and capital to design and manufacture vehicles considered anachronisms by the public, the impetus for such development must come from federal and state transit administrations. UMTA should inaugurate a center for electric vehicle technology that will offer two-year fellowships for engineers and manufacturing personnel to live abroad and study European, as well as Japanese, transit technology and manufacturing methods. This group would become a cadre of experienced personnel (to the point that all would have learned to service the various vehicles) that could be placed with those manufacturers who might wish to enter the field of electric transit vehicles. This would be a continuous process until such time as we have developed our own technology and the personnel to apply it.

Isaacs soon had his reply, in which the UMTA administrator called attention to the rail cars and light-rail vehicles already on order, saying

. . . When these orders, and additional ones we can reasonably expect, are completed, the nation may find itself with a surfeit rather than a deficit of engineering expertise in the field of manufacturing electric rail cars. . . .

While we consider it important to keep abreast of achievements in mass transportation technology abroad, and attempt to do so, we do not consider it necessary to assign engineers and other personnel overseas for the purpose of gaining experience. . . .

George K. Isaacs persevered. In May 1977, he repeated to the Secretary of Transportation his recommendation for a "program of grants to American engineers, production managers and service personnel to study abroad the European and Japanese transit-car technology, manufacturing processes, and service programs. These people, in turn, can help in renewing America's ability to produce economical and reliable electric vehicles for our energy conservation effort." A month later, Isaacs received a letter from the DOT, in which the writer advised that "I do not feel it is necessary for the *Federal Government* to become involved in the transfer of specific technologies because our *private sector* is perfectly capable of acting on its own to cope with foreign competition. . . ."* (N.B. Emphases in original—S.M.)

The story of Boeing-Vertol's light-rail vehicle program in Boston is also the story of the Morgantown, West Virginia, people mover; the BART system of San Francisco; the Washington, D.C., subway; and the Grumman venture in city buses.[16]

The occupational and institutional ways that generate profit without production in all its aspects are strongly reinforced by an ideology that "explains" and endorses those practices. The implication of this is that a significant measure of ideological flexibility is required to accomplish industrial and general economic renewal.

Perhaps the single most important and powerful ideological reinforcement of the status quo is founded on American conceit and what that implies of arrogance and self-deception. It is indicative of this self-deception when a leading management journal pronounces that "the U.S. still remains the unquestioned leader in worldwide technology, and there is little doubt that it will continue to play a leading role—despite the growing intensity of competition from Japan and Europe."[17] A few months later the authoritative industrial journal *Electronics* produced the judgment that

with President Reagan's fiscal 1983 budget now in the congressional hopper, the nation's electronics industries must honestly ask themselves if the U.S. is becoming a weapons welfare state. The record military spending plan of close to $216 billion— more, if the supporting programs of the Department of Energy and the National Aeronautics and Space Administration are included—is a confirmation of earlier predictions (*Electronics,* January 13, p. 63).

The weapons spending proposals also confirm the various views of some Reagan

---

*I am indebted to George K. Isaacs, P.E., of St. Paul, Minnesota, for permission to quote from his correspondence with the Department of Transportation, Urban Mass Transportation Administration.

critics. . . . the nation's electronics industries do not have the technological skills and experience to meet military requirements and at the same time cope successfully with competition from corporations in West Europe and Japan—allies all—in the burgeoning consumer, computer, telecommunications, and test equipment markets. . . .

In the last dozen years or so, the world electronics markets have changed almost as rapidly as the semiconductor, computer, and communications advances that produced them. Sony Corp. leader Akio Morita recalled some years ago in private conversation that American Telephone & Telegraph Co. engineering executives laughed when he told them of Sony's plan to use transistor patents licensed from AT&T to make radios. Morita smiled as he added, "The rest is history."

It is also history that most of the recent and important advances in electronic technology during the past decade have come despite the Department of Defense and the Federal agencies, not because of them. Indeed, the military services are steadily falling behind in their ability to field systems with state-of-the-art electronics, notably computers. . . . Yet President Reagan's steadily rising military budgets offer so many opportunities for electronics manufacturers, that their ability to compete in other markets is strained.

Is there a relationship between the historical dependence of the U.S. electronics industries on weapons markets and their relative loss of world market share in the private sector? That should be part of the renewed guns-versus-butter debate that is sure to resound once more in Congress in an election year. It is time for the electronics industries' leaders, too—engineers as well as managers—to consider the issues and come up with some answers.[18]

The presumption of unlimited resources encourages a general abdication of responsibility when state managers preempt every sort of production resource for their enterprise. And the alibi of no responsibility clearly extends to the realm of engineering research. "The federal government views it as primarily an industrial responsibility, although most industrial companies limit their research to relatively short-term objectives. The technical areas in which engineering schools carry on research are largely determined by the federal funding agencies."[19] In the absence of agreed, defined responsibility, no one is charged with testing the justification for and consequences of the preemption of technology resources by the state managers.

In the prevailing American ideology what is important is that money be earned. In this view, money earned is spent in the stores or put in the bank, or invested in securities. So the nature of the work that yielded the dollars, or the purposes for which they are subsequently spent, are matters of secondary importance.

In conventional theory, the amount of money spent on the nonproductive military enterprise is not important by itself. What counts is the proportion of the gross national product that is utilized for this or for any other purpose. In a recent analysis I wrote that using the G.N.P. as a baseline for assessing military spending is perfectly sensible if your objective is to examine the flow of money to various segments of the population or different institutions. But if you seek to determine how capital resources are employed in the economy for production, the G.N.P. total is wide of the mark because it encompasses the money value of movie tickets, vacations, the military and all manner of consumer goods and services. The relevant economic category for perceiving the effect of military spending on the entire economy's production capability is its ratio to total fixed capital formation. Thus, in 1977 the U.S. military budget was $4.90 per $100 of gross national product, while comprising $46 per $100 of (producers') fixed capital formation.

The small ratio of military spending to total G.N.P. encourages the view that it is a modest overhead charge on the economy as a whole, and the argument is made that an enlargement of the ratio by 2 percent [the Reagan military budget] "is far more a question of political priorities than of economic resources." One implication is that economic resources are readily interchangeable, that retail clerks, office workers and other burgeoning white-collar occupations—and their equipment—are readily convertible to the production of fixed and working capital. This expectation is absurd on its face. A ten-to-twenty-year major effort to enlarge the labor force and equipment of the industries directly responsible for the society's fixed capital formation would be needed to accomplish such a conversion.[20]

From the standpoint of G.N.P.-ism, "the scale of the Reagan defense buildup is relatively modest."[21] If, by contrast, one chooses to address the production consequences of U.S. military spending, viewing the military budget as a capital fund, then the military budget appears as a major drain on the production capabilities of the society.

Further, in conventional wisdom a sharp separation of managerialism from production is entirely acceptable. That follows from the assumption that making money, not things, is the main event. This bias is reinforced by the belief that for production decision-making there is no alternative to managerialism as we have known it.

To this day, countless Americans assume that military spending is not only generally "good" for the economy, but especially valuable as a job creator. I know of no systematic opinion polls that test the degree of adherence to these ideas, but I repeatedly come upon evidence that they are exceedingly potent myths.

For reasons that are not systematically defined, the ideology of post-industrial society has become enormously influential among educated Americans, including the young. During recent visits to several universities, I was impressed by the degree to which "everybody" takes for granted the main propositions of the post-industrial society thesis.

Schools of international affairs are important institutions in the major American universities. With rare exceptions, their training in public affairs encourages students to regard alternatives to the arms race and the associated military economy as essentially unthinkable. Accordingly, the economic concomitants of the arms race are made to appear as inevitable policy systems.

The retention of these conventional beliefs engenders support for the private and state managers whose "successes" have set the American economy on a course toward a point of no return.

14

Economic Futures

One way to project an economic future for the United States is to assume that the processes of decision-making and production diagnosed in this book will continue essentially unchanged. These have caused technical/economic incompetence of a quality and scope unprecedented in American history. Private and state managers have been schooled to an inability to carry out the basic task of organizing people for work. At the same time, production competence is a shunned or secondary goal for private managers oriented toward profit-making by whatever means and for state managers who seek power over the military economy.

If continued, these two aspects of American management will surely produce a second-rate industrial system that exhibits sustained economic crises and continuing decay. Moreover, they will do so independently of variations in personality, party, or ideology of political leaderships. That is a reasonable inference from the experience of almost four decades of development since World War II, during which time the processes defined here have spread without regard for substantial variations of personality and ideology in administrations of both major parties.

Consider but one aspect of the matter: the consequences of the Carter-Reagan military budgets, $2,089 billion from 1981 to 1988. If implemented, this appropriation will sharply raise the ratio of military to civilian use of the country's production resources to $87 (military) : $100 (civilian) by 1988. With some variation among industries and firms, the overall effect, one may be certain, will be further technical/economic deterioration in the competence of American industry, in the capacity of the whole infrastructure, and in the quality of ordinary life.*

---

*In its issue of February 8, 1982, *Business Week* presented a forecast, 1981–1987, for the growth of military business in thirty industries, as compared to the expected rise in ordinary civilian business. With one exception (water transportation) in the twenty-nine enumerated industries—ranging from

Look back to the network of tradeoffs between military and civilian capital investment areas that were defined in chapter 8. In the foreseeable future, say until the end of the twentieth century, it is most improbable that the United States could fulfill both its military and its civilian capital agenda. To the degree that the one is accomplished the other will fall short. Any serious attempt to fulfill the military programs projected to 1988 will entail a further looting of the means of production of the American industrial system. Plant and equipment will continue to deteriorate and industrial incompetence will spread, with consequent rapid price increases, unemployment, etc. One important factor that operates to fulfill this prognosis is the concentration of research and development talent and laboratory resources on parasitic—that is, military—economic growth.

To break out of the relentless system of cause and effect that has produced the deterioration of American industrial economy, we must begin by clearing away a series of ideological misconceptions that have confused us as to the nature of America's economic debacle. These false assumptions are as follows:

1. *Modern industrial economies tend to have "sunrise" and "sunset" industries.* Thus, solid-state electronic components, computers and aircraft are viewed as "sunrise" industries in the United States, while steel, automobiles and shoes are relegated to the "sunset" category. Strategists of "reindustrialization" and "industrial policy" argue that the course of political-economic wisdom in the United States is to press strongly for investment in sunrise industries while letting the sunset enterprises wither away, even as the community facilitates the transfer of resources from their products. Why does an industry fade into the sunset? The sunrise/sunset strategists never really face that question, except to suggest that the decline is caused by external factors like "technological change" and the less onerous wage rates of other countries.[1]

But the sunrise/sunset thesis ran into trouble when it was discovered, in 1981, that the leading Japanese electronics firms had seized 80 percent of the world market in a crucial class of semiconductors—the random-access memory chips that are major building blocks for modern computers.[2] The shift in the relative position of the United States and Japanese electronics industries as the world's leading producers of the microchips occurred between 1979 and 1982.[3] The major Japanese electronics firms have concentrated on the interna-

---

radio and TV equipment and aerospace products to motor vehicles, chemicals and petroleum products —the predicted increase in military business was some multiple of the growth forecast for civilian activity. This means that in those industries managers, technologists and industrial workers will find their livelihoods increasingly dependent upon continuation and expansion of the military economy.

tional commercial market, while their American counterparts have long relied on Pentagon subsidies for their research budgets and for guidance on new-product development. The Japanese firms, evidently addressing the production side of these technologies, have been able to produce better, and cheaper, integrated circuits. At the same time there are serious fears in the U.S. electronics industry that it lacks "the technological skills and experience to meet military requirements and at the same time cope successfully with competition from corporations in West Europe and Japan. . . ."[4] All this bears on the U.S. position in the worldwide electronics industry. If the Japanese firms take a major lead in developing and manufacturing the "fifth generation" computers of the 1990s they would, inevitably, command a dominant position, with advantages that could be pressed in many areas. The concerted Japanese drive in that direction, organized by the Ministry of International Trade and Industry, is countered by a U.S. effort in research, product development and manufacturing technique organized by a consortium of U.S. firms (microelectronics and computer technology enterprises) and jointly financed. If the U.S. firms are to hold position as innovators and competent producers of computers, they must at least match Japan's already well-developed capability for sophisticated design and operation of manufacturing processes, including quality control. These have been areas of major weakness in various U.S. industries.[5] The question at issue is: Will the sun set for this U.S. industry even before the predicted worldwide explosion of computer technology occurs?

2. *The technical and economic troubles of U.S. industries, especially in relation to West Germany and Japan, are bound to be a passing phase.* After all, the United States rebuilt West Germany and Japan after World War II, so the competitive difficulties of U.S. industries are merely the consequence of American generosity. But the facts don't support this optimism. As shown in chapter 10, from 1948 to 1971 U.S. economic assistance to Japan was trivial; the Marshall Plan aid to West Germany was $1.6 billion; in both countries the U.S. aid was overshadowed by the rapid pace of homemade capital formation.[6] Such beliefs about the role of the United States in the industrial reconstruction of West Germany and Japan are significant primarily as evidence of unwillingness to confront the causes of technical/economic decay.

3. *The capital fund that has been serving the U.S. military enterprise is not conceivably available for civilian use.* "Short of unilateral disarmament, we are never going to find enough 'defense cuts' to finance large increases in productive investment."[7]

This opinion rests on the belief that there is no conceivable way to design and implement a multilateral, mutually agreed reversal of the arms race. But the arms race is not ordained by natural law; it is a social artifact, and so addressable in the appropriate categories of politics and economics.*

4. *The reason why American industries cannot compete is because the Japanese, and others, have "caught up" with the U.S. in technological sophistication.* This belief rests on the assumption that there is one and only one technological road to follow. It is not true that different economies are simply at different positions on the same road; different roads are being traveled. American corporate managers have preferred the path of short-term profits, capital exports and the priority of making money rather than making goods. The leading industrial firms of Japan have concentrated on producing goods as their path to business success. In America the state has been used primarily to manage a nonproductive military economy, while in Japan the state has worked to spur new civilian products and new production technology. As shown in chapter 9, the Japanese industrial economy enjoys the services of a greater density of science and engineering brains compared with the U.S. civilian economy because the latter has such a large contingent of technologists working for the military.

These differences show up sharply in the way Japanese firms have advanced production methods and product designs. By introducing a stable production system (termed a "Just-in-Time and Respect for Human System") the Toyota Company did not "catch up" with America's Big Three auto firms. Toyota took a different course. In the multitude of product innovations that Japanese firms made in radio, television, photography, sound and video recorders, computer controls of machine tools, they have advanced the state of the art as would be expected from the concentration of technical brains and hands that were applied to these tasks. For similar reasons, there is no

---

*The idea of reversing the entire arms race was an explicit subject of international and individual governmental discussion until the Cuban missile crisis of October 1962. Just six months earlier, in April of that year, the United States had submitted elaborately detailed plans for a phased reversal of the arms race to be mutually agreed upon by the United States and the Soviet Union, with accompanying provision for inspection and other safeguards. The Soviets presented a parallel proposal in September 1962. (For the full text of these documents, see S. Melman, *Disarmament, Its Politics and Economics,* Boston: American Academy of Arts and Sciences, 1962.) After the near-nuclear brinksmanship of the following month, however, both proposals fell by the wayside. Thereafter, American authorities, confident in their ability to win games of nuclear chicken, put aside all serious planning to reverse the military build-up and turned their attention to new ways of using armed force for the extension of their decision power. The war in Vietnam was just such an exercise. The 1962 proposals, it should be noted, had been strongly backed by major establishment groups led by John J. McCloy, then recently retired as president of the Chase Manhattan Bank. McCloy, known to the press as a key figure in the American establishment, rallied support for the disarmament proposal from business and other groups. All this is set forth in a series of documents that make absorbing reading twenty years later. See the following from the U.S. Arms Control and Disarmament Agency: *Blueprint for the Peace Race: Outline of Basic Provisions of a Treaty on General and Complete Disarmament in a Peaceful World* (May 1962); *Toward a World Without War: A Summary of U.S. Disarmament Efforts—Past and Present* (October 1962); *Disarmament: The New U.S. Initiative* (September 1962).

Japanese counterpart to U.S. developments in military electronics, rocketry, military aircraft, nuclear submarines, and aircraft carriers.

The prospects for any serious attack upon the decline of the American industrial economy require an examination of possible options for decision-making among managers, workers and others. Are there potentials for competent production-oriented decision-making in the American society?

There is no single aspect of the American industrial economy which, if changed, would suffice to correct the processes that generate technical/economic incompetence. However, it is possible to define major alternatives for management, for workers and for engineers. In each case the emphasis here is on direction of change.

Management, as an entity for decision-making, has developed a number of sustaining, core features which I identified in chapter 4. Decision-making activities have been separated from production, so that occupations have steadily taken on either a primarily decision-making or a primarily production content. Under managerialism the decision-making occupations have been organized in a hierarchy, and permeated by the professional imperative that every manager, high and low, must strive to become more important by acquiring greater decision power. Income is a function of position in the hierarchy. These characteristics of managerialism have been found in private and state capitalism, private firms and corporations, small and large enterprises, and in economies variously described as industrial capitalism, finance capitalism, or mercantile capitalism.

Nevertheless, there have been substantial variations in the ways the characteristics are fulfilled. For our present purpose the most interesting differentiation is between the idea of management as primarily a service to production (with profit as a result) or as primarily a service to control and thus to profit and power. In the distinctions that are to be drawn here, recognition should be given to the fact that we are not contrasting absolutes, that the variants, while significantly different, nevertheless overlap—hence, are "primarily" in one or the other category.

I have referred repeatedly in this book to conditions in the U.S. steel industry for illustrations of the characteristics of management that operates for profits without production. Therefore it is important to show that, with respect to steel, management with primary emphasis on production is really workable.

F. K. Iverson, president of the Nucor Corporation, a "mini-steel" plant at Norfolk, Nebraska, produces "steel at a lower cost than any steel company in the world, including the Japanese. . . . We build plants very economically and, secondly, we run them very, very efficiently; the primary thanks to that goes to the employees themselves and the incentive production systems."

Nucor has invested heavily in modern steelmaking technology, profits being ploughed back for new equipment and experimentation with new methods. Management believes that the performance of the whole work force is the most important factor. Said Iverson: "Our production workers work on a production incentive system. They are groups of about thirty people who are doing some complete task, such as producing a certain number of rolled tons. If they exceed that standard in a week, then they receive extra pay based upon how much they exceeded the standard. It's not unusual for the bonuses to run over 100 percent. The bonus is paid the next week. There's no maximum on it. The average hourly worker in this plant earned about $22,000 last year (1979); we had melters who earned about $35,000. . . . If they produce again twice as much, the bonus would go to 200 percent. We never change the standard."[8]

Production workers at the Nucor plant had the following comments: "It's the people's attitudes here. You look around and you talk to everybody, it's all production. . . . If we break down or break out ever on the caster, everybody is kind of running around trying to get things going. . . . Job security is another big, big item to me." Iverson reports that not a single employee has been laid off for lack of work in more than ten years. Also, from 1976 to 1980 the price of steel from this plant "has been equal to or less than the Japanese price of steel landed dockside in the United States. Actually, most of our market has come from taking that market that used to belong to foreign steel producers."[9]

When managers are oriented to serve production and reject the idea that a workingman is ". . . more or less of the type of the ox," then the way is open to viewing production work as important and honorable. Engineers and technicians may spend part of their time or careers in hands-on participation in production. Even managers, as in training programs, can be required to gain experience in the actual manufacturing process. A union official reported what happened when Sanyo of Japan took over a unionized and failing American electronics firm in Arkansas in 1975:

The International Union of Electrical Workers has represented the production force for several years. This is a union in the U.A.W. tradition—militant and responsible. The first thing Sanyo did was to assign Japanese managers, who quickly called the union committee in for a meeting.

The Sanyo people said they had two requests: they wanted the committee to talk with them about production policies, methods and goals and they wanted it to join in a start-to-finish quality control program that would guarantee that not a single defective TV set left the plant.

The union committee was shocked by the first proposal and overwhelmed by the second. The old American management never missed the chance to remind the committee that production policy was the prerogative of the boss, all the while winking as imperfect TV sets were slipped into the market.

Today, employment at the plant has risen to more than 2,000. Sanyo, despite intensive "foreign" competition and apparently bearing up well under its union "burden," seems to have profitably made its way in the tough TV industry. . . .[10]

When management is oriented toward rendering a service to production there tend to be easier relations and a closer dialogue between blue-collar and white-collar workers.[11] One of a group of U.S.-based Japanese managers interviewed notes that such relations are "not the case in the U.S. In this respect we may even be more advanced in the concept of democracy than Americans."

When blue-collar employees are regarded as vital to the prosperity of a production-oriented enterprise, management finds it appropriate to announce: "We will endeavor not to lay employees off. If we face difficulty, we first proportionately reduce the wages of all employees from general manager down to the lowest-paid employee, other than probationary workers. Only if we can't manage do we resort to a layoff."[12]

By contrast, when a management operates primarily as a service to profits and power, it is prepared to resort to the whole array of devices that I have identified.

The steel industry provides some illuminating contrasts between the two main management styles. From 1980 to 1982 the U.S. Steel Corporation refused to deal with the labor-community consortium that was set up in Youngstown, Ohio, in an attempt to purchase the former Youngstown Sheet and Tube plants of the corporation. U.S. Steel's top management declined to do anything that would facilitate a union-community ownership, which, it held, could receive some form of government subsidy. The issue was irrevocably closed on April 28, 1982, when four blast furnaces at the Youngstown plant were blown up at management's direction, with full media coverage of the spectacle.

This episode bears out the judgment of Thomas C. Graham of Jones and Laughlin Steel Corporation, that "you don't overstate the case when you say that this business used to be more totalitarian than the Prussian army."[13]

In the factories of his own firm, Graham has set a new tone for management's relation to workers. In a move that would have been "foreign to the U.S. steel industry only a decade ago," the chief executive of a major J&L plant invited the workers to a meeting at which the plant manager "convinced them that he wanted them to help management improve the production rate."[14]

While a measure of hierarchy is to be found in all management organizations, those oriented primarily to serve production seem able to operate with significantly fewer layers. In the production-oriented management, status is gained by doing useful work. Such managers are prepared to cooperate with trade unions in various forms of "employee participation" schemes, hierarchical lines being relaxed to secure production-enhancing cooperation. In these organizations, the managers responsible for production typically have high status.

Among managements dedicated primarily to the profits/power combination, status is obtained primarily from being in charge of people, from asserting authority over them. There is little dissent from the proposition that "production management is the lowest status function in most U.S. companies."[15]

The managerial imperative to enlarge decision power can take various forms. Some managements have been able to specify service to production as a guiding justification for performing particular administrative functions. Students of international management observe that it is not unusual for Japanese executives to have had blue-collar experience on the factory floor or apprenticeship in the performance of lesser administrative tasks.[16] Managers in that tradition can recognize and cooperate with worker decision-making processes, as in trade unions, without fear of losing status. They are also prepared to examine possible reductions in the cost and complexity of management organizations. For example, the president of Ford Motor Company, Donald E. Petersen, has attributed the growth of corporate staff in America to top management's distrust of middle managers. From his study of Toyota's management, he concludes that "Japan's top executives trust their workers and assume they will do the best job they can. In the U.S., on the other hand, top executives assume they cannot trust their subordinates, so they added layers of staff to check on line operators. The result is confrontation, delay in decision-making, exploding costs, and a deterioration of the business. In their struggle for power the staff people too often ignore the problems of the business, seeking what is best for themselves instead of what is best for the company."[17]

In production-guided enterprise the management-worker wage spread is smaller than in companies primarily concerned with profit and power. The president of Sony has suggested "that American chief executives be paid more modest salaries. I have read in *Fortune* that among the top one hundred companies, presidents earn something in the area of $600,000 a year, on average, including bonus. Such salaries may be appropriate for singers or movie actors but not business executives."[18] Production-oriented managements are prepared to pay bonuses to everyone in the firm, production workers and top managements alike. In such organizations pay cuts or layoffs for workers do not occur without parallel burdens falling on management. During 1981 the Maruzen Oil Company of Japan "announced that it would discharge 1,200 of its 4,600 workers." However, before the layoff, "the company had taken several other economizing steps, such as cutting the pay of its corporate officers in half."[19] We are told, further, that the "willingness of Japanese corporations to keep workers on the payroll is often viewed as a social peculiarity, a remnant of the feudal era, similar to the liege's obligation to his samurai. But, in fact, it is a relatively modern invention that results from the concern of Japanese employers with attracting and retaining skilled laborers."[20]

The contrast with the practice of managements addicted to profits/power is often dramatic. A few weeks after General Motors signed with the United Auto Workers a 1982 contract that included an array of substantial wage and other union concessions, the corporation announced a plan to change the basis for granting management bonuses so that they would be payable at lower rates of profit.[21] Apart from money payments and fringe benefits, managers can obtain "psychic income" from serving the profits/power objective—mainly from the privileges of status and from controlling people. By contrast, managers engaged primarily in rendering a service to production are eligible for the "psychic income" of contributing to useful work.

There is yet another way to differentiate the performances characteristic of the two kinds of management aspiration. Industrial managers must constantly make decisions on what to produce, how to do the work, and the pricing and distribution of the product. There is a sharp difference in the ways these problems are addressed, even though both management styles depend on the market system to recoup investments and operating costs.

Managements engaged primarily in service to production select products with an eye to long-term market position. This means choosing and designing items that will attract a more or less permanent pool of buyers and give them an acceptable service. Such products, offered at competitive price, assure a long-term, stable market position. That, in turn, becomes a basis for planning and operating a stable manufacturing system dedicated to minimizing cost for quality products. Sustained evaluation and replacement of manufacturing equipment is encouraged by applying a relatively long payback period. Shop conditions are regularly examined for improvement, on the understanding that the workers are a species of "human capital" and that the enterprise can only benefit from their cooperation and improved skills. Quality control is geared increasingly to the idea of "zero defect," a goal never to be attained, but serving as an incentive for sustained improvement in manufacturing methods and products as it is ever more closely approximated. Emphasis on a stable production system opens up opportunities for major gains in the productivity of capital as well as labor. In such a framework production equipment and modes of organization are revised and upgraded in the interest of improved productivity and reduced costs.

In a regime primarily directed toward service to profits/power a contrasting set of production criteria prevails. Cost pass-along and cost-maximizing are favored as ways to garner fast return on both fixed and working capital outlays, while pricing and distribution methods are adapted to fast returns on capital and sales and to maximize short-term profit. From this approach comes the marketing strategy of sell, sell, sell, and ignore the possibility of dramatically dysfunctional product multiplication as propagated, for example, by the managers of the U.S. auto companies.

Managements oriented to profits/power goals are typically prepared to lay off production work forces and limit capital investment, the better to minimize money outlays. At the same time such managements are quick to declare particular production facilities "uneconomic," shutting them down and moving their finance capital elsewhere, thereby avoiding the hard work entailed in redesigning production methods and organizations.

By way of contrast, Professor Robert H. Hayes of the Harvard Business School examined operations in a range of Japanese factories and reported his findings in "Why Japanese Factories Work."[22] Hayes found that "the modern Japanese factory is not, as many Americans believe, a prototype of the factory of the future. . . . Instead, it is something much more difficult for us to copy; it is the factory of today running as it should." The details of the Hayes report illustrate the systematic attention given in Japanese factories to quality of product, minimization of inventories, operation of a stable production system, meticulous housekeeping, profit-sharing, and pervasive cooperation in production among managers, engineers and production workers. Hayes confirms, once again, that production methods in the large industrial firms of Japan reflect management priority to production.

The Harbour report on the auto industry (chapter 10) and the Hayes report are important because they make it clear that the striking development of productivity and allied production goals in Japanese industrial capitalism is altogether explicable in terms of straightforward methods used in production and, above all, management criteria for decision-making on production. The latter and not some special "Japanese" cultural feature is what accounts for the development. It follows, then, that similar production methods and results are clearly attainable by U.S. firms whose managements will assign first priority to production. One example is found in the operating style of Texas Instruments. The Dallas-based electronics firm has been a world leader in the research, design and manufacture of semiconductors, calculators, digital watches and a host of other imaginative electronics products. Texas Instruments organizes its employees in teams that participate "in the planning and control of their own work to improve productivity." This company has given a classic demonstration of technological innovations in both product design and production, with the result that hand-held calculators of steadily improving quality and capability have been offered at successively reduced prices.[23]

The evidence coming from major American industries that have developed severe production problems indicates that there is little pressure to move decisively and on a broad front toward management that is of service to production. When moves in that direction are made, they are for the most part carried out as emergency measures to improve productivity at particular facilities. General Motors, for example, did that sort of thing in the early 1980s. Employee participation teams and quality-of-working-life groups were set up at manufacturing locations that were clearly in trouble. At this writing, the word from these locations is that management's initiative for cooperation with workers has produced positive results in production and productivity. However, such localized shifts of emphasis toward production have not affected the overall strategy of top managements, at GM or elsewhere. At those levels the profits/power pattern continues, unimpaired. This is extremely important, for it shows with what tenacity the top executives have held to their style of operation, even when confronted by dramatic setbacks in the marketplace.

This is not to say that the concept of management for production has entirely disappeared from the American scene. Texas Instruments and the mini-steel firms are impressive examples of its survival.[24]

Furthermore, several hundred American firms have made formal arrangements for sharing the income gained from growth of productivity among managers, engineers and workers.[25] Such programs reflect a solicitude for production in at least a part of the management class. There is evidence that more U.S. firms than ever before are experimenting with "participative management" in an attempt to improve product quality and productivity.[26] "Participative management" is a broad term that covers a considerable array of arrangements designed to open communications between decision-makers and production workers. It seems evident that management for production can be made to work wherever it is tried. In 1974, when Matsushita Electric of Japan took over a former Motorola TV factory in Franklin Park, Illinois, an average of 1.4 adjustments or repairs per TV set were required to meet quality standards. By 1981, the figure was down to about 7 adjustments per 100 sets.[27] A similar transformation occurred at a TV factory taken over in Wales by the Sony Corporation. There, too, in industrial surroundings characterized by relatively low productivity (and profits), Sony's production-dedicated management has outpaced the British companies. But the Japanese have no secret ingredient. They merely established the sort of atmosphere wherein management and workers share the same cafeteria, while at nearby plants, operated according to the usual profits/power criteria, "employees are separated into as many as a half-dozen groups according to rank." In the words of one Sony worker: "The management here is more worker-oriented. You can treat them like normal people rather than like bosses."[28]

The introduction of quality-of-working-life groups in many factories and offices is one management attempt to improve productivity by recognizing that people prefer to work in self-directed teams, that factory hands have useful ideas about their own work and enjoy the challenge of solving problems together. But experienced consultants in this class of management practice have observed that participation often "turns out to be what the top of the organization tells the middle to do for the bottom. But nothing is done for the middle person—the manager—who in turn defeats the program."[29] Resistance by middle managers to any sharing of authority continues, despite efforts by consultants to be reassuring in their advice that "quality-of-working-life groups should create a new kind of 'parallel organization' that can function alongside the conventional hierarchical, multilevel line organization which has proved to be a perfectly good vehicle for carrying out routine tasks where knowledge is certain. The parallel organization provides a framework for worker involvement in problem-solving and does not interfere with the established organization that carries out routine operations."[30] Despite such admonitions and the likelihood that cooperative decision-making can contribute to productivity, this "democratic" broadening of the process is anathema to managers who remain committed to the sharp separation of decision-making from producing.

From experienced American worker-unionists and local union officials I have learned that in many American companies quality-of-working-life groups have been formed by management as a device for organizing workers in groupings separate from trade unions. When such groups are used as fresh devices for an ongoing management struggle against the decision power of trade unions, the union response is predictable, and it is not likely that they will produce durable improvement in either working life or productivity.

In the Japanese automobile industry the elaborately organized quality circles, the formalized consultation between labor and management, the high-productivity stable production system did not come about spontaneously or easily. After World War II, there was a long period of intense struggle between management and workers in the industry. Strikes, lockouts and production sabotage were commonplace. Then, at a moment of crisis in 1954, labor and management formed consultation groups while hard bargaining proceeded. In the view of one union official: "The consultation system is to increase the pie, the fruit of the company, [while] collective bargaining is for cutting up the pie for the good of the union members."[31]

The idea and the practice of so conducting industrial enterprises as to give first attention to production is clearly cross-cultural, not unique to any nation. But in those postwar years when Japanese industry was finding ways of managing that could optimize the productivity of labor and capital, the managers of American industry, seemingly on the threshold of material abundance, sought and found their status by accumulating money and power. It is no great surprise, then, that by 1982 it is impossible to identify a single major American industrial firm that has embraced the fundamental changes of policy required to move from the ambitions of profit and power to the service of production. And as long as finance capital can be kept mobile, the top managers of major U.S. industrial firms have a secure escape route: they can move their hoard of money to other industries, other locations, other forms of investment that involve no production. They can ship their money out of the United States altogether.

But production workers and engineers (including some close-to-production managers) have no such options. Their skills, useful for production, are valueless in its absence. Therefore, management policies that generate incompetence in production and include the termination of U.S. manufacture and the movement of capital funds to offshore sites leave production workers and engineers with no economic prospect whatsoever.

The weight of evidence is that a shift of management toward production priority cannot reasonably be expected to come from within management itself. When people are trained to see the whole world as an arena for the maintenance and enlargement of their decision power, a shift of viewpoint involves a major human transformation. Status, self-image and particular work capabilities are all intertwined. A major reinforcing effect comes into play when large groups operate in a given way over a long period of time and when organizational-institutional support is given this style of operation by awards for conforming, by the prestige of dominant training schools and by the journals and other literature that endlessly invoke and reaffirm the goals and criteria of managing for profits and power. That being the situation, fresh attention to production and productivity goals in American industry will have to come primarily from outside industrial management itself.

American workers and their trade unions have typically functioned according to rules set for them by industrial management. Managers gathered capital, made the decisions on when and where to invest, chose the products and production methods, set the prices and arranged the methods of distribution. Within the limits of these decisions individual and organized workers dealt with management on wages and conditions of work. To be sure, the agreements thus reached became important limits on management as well. However, management has been the initiator of decisions as to investment, location, product and price. Indeed, and especially since the 1940s, union contracts have included "management prerogatives" clauses, stipulating that nothing in the contract should be understood as impairing management's right to manage.

This "right to manage" has not been challenged by any of the quality-of-working-life or participative management arrangements that have been made. These innovations, however constructive, in the relation of workers to managers have been confined to problem-solving on or close to the factory floor. Decisions on capital investment, starting or shutting down factories, hiring or laying off workers have typically been kept out of the hands of plant managers. Observers have noted, for example, that at General Motors "the goal of shared problem-solving is limited mostly to assembling cars." The larger, framework-setting decisions have been reserved to the managers who preside over the central administrative office at G.M. and kindred firms.[32]

Yet when it comes to setting appropriate goals for operating industrial facilities, the ideas of organized American workers differ markedly from those of management. This emerged rather sharply when the workers of Youngstown Sheet and Tube joined with representatives of the local community in an attempt to buy and operate the plant owned, and closed, by U.S. Steel. Robert Vasquez, chairman of Local 1130, United Steelworkers of America, stated the union position:

> Why do we think we will be able to run a mill successfully in Youngstown when U.S. Steel gave up on the idea?
> First, we believe our workers will be more productive because each worker will own part of the business and because management will listen closely to the workers. No one knows more about steelmaking than a steelworker, and we will follow worker suggestions about how to improve efficiency—something corporate managements rarely do.
> Second, we won't feel any compulsion to close just because we're not making a 15 percent return on investment. Since our chief concern is creating jobs, not maximizing profits, our shareholders will be satisfied with more modest profits.
> Third, we will maintain and modernize our plants—something U.S. Steel refused to do here because it worried far more about showing its shareholders short-term profits than about reinvesting to maintain long-term competitiveness. We won't be investing in chemicals and real estate—as U.S. Steel has done—we'll put our capital into making sure our mills can compete with Europe's and Japan's.[33]

As one union after another, across the country and in many industries, faces the prospect of permanent unemployment traceable to the technical/economic inability of management to organize work, or the preference of management to make money with no production, the trade unions are compelled to broaden their view. They can no longer leave production decision-making to management on the assumption that management will surely do the job in its own self-interest. By 1982 trade union officers were driven to declare that the "unions can no longer afford the luxury of protecting their virtue by staying out of management. The welfare of their members now demands that unions know enough about management's business to recognize management's motives and options and to present alternatives. Like it or not, management has become labor's business."[34]

That being so, it is predictable that industrial workers, through their unions, will increasingly demand responsibility and authority for the larger decisions of industry. The fact that the president of the United Automobile Workers is sitting on the board of the Chrysler Corporation is more than a trivial concession to gain union support for the top management of a failing firm. The International Association of Machinists and Aerospace Workers has begun to offer its members instruction in computer technology and methods of enterprise planning.

The building trades unions, traditionally the most conservative in the AFL-CIO, are joining with industrial unions to affect public policy on interest rates; since every type of private construction is depressed by the high cost of renting money, the unions are working together to seat representatives of workers, farmers and consumers on the Federal Reserve Board, whose policies directly affect interest rates.

The unions are learning that whoever controls finance capital holds a key to production decision-making. Having observed the ease with which managers close factories and transfer finance capital from industry to industry, state to state, country to country, workers and their unions have been asking questions about how finance capital is controlled and, closer to home, how the finance capital represented by their own pension funds is controlled.

Altogether, the pension funds of American employees, private and governmental, unionized and nonunionized, workers and administrators, had grown to about $600 billion by 1982. In 1978 $200 billion of these funds were invested in the stocks of American corporations, and accounted for 20 to 25 percent of the securities of firms listed on the major stock exchanges. Evidently, pension-fund finance capital—the money of American workers— owns a large share of giant corporations, but has no share in their control. The $200 billion in nonfederal pension funds, the savings of 19 million trade unionists, and the public pension funds of government employees in northeastern and midwestern states, is controlled primarily by banks and investment-managing firms that act as trustees for the funds, or by the managements of firms whose employees are the future recipients of the pensions. What is new is that trade unions have become increasingly interested in the decision power that derives from these funds, and which is now often used to bolster anti-union firms, or to move finance capital out of the United States, thereby destroying opportunities for livelihood here. Public officials in the Northeast and Midwest have become alert to the practices of banks that deploy the pension funds of workers in their areas to fresh capital investment in the Sunbelt states.

At issue here is political and economic power on a vast scale. As far back as 1946, during a Senate debate on legislation designed to restrict union control over pension funds, Senator Harry Byrd declared: "I am endeavoring to strike at the attempt of representatives of labor to use such payments in establishing funds over which no one but the labor representative would have any control. I assert that if such a condition were allowed to take place, labor unions would become so powerful that no organized government would be able to deal with them."[35]

Specialists in this field estimate that the pension funds representing 60 percent of private firm employees who are also trade union members account for "at least 45 percent of all private pension assets."[36] This amount of finance capital represents enormous potential decision power. The desire of trade unions to acquire this control will surely intensify as managements continue to show themselves incompetent for, or indifferent to, the task of organizing production work.

When and if unions acquire decision power over important blocks of finance capital, it may be expected that there will be innovations in concepts like "return on investment." For industrial workers with a growing voice in all levels of decision-making on production, the "return" is bound to include good working conditions, equitable wages, a share in decision-making on production, an appreciation of cash flow to the surrounding community and its consequences for economic well-being. Workers, organized workers in particular, are well situated to appreciate the social "return on investment."

Moves in this direction also imply a fundamental alteration in the opportunistic "mobility of capital" now engaged in by conglomerate, multinational corporations. It is improbable, for example, that an otherwise excellent production facility, offering a livelihood to workers, would be shut down simply because its percentage "return on investment" was smaller than the market interest rate obtainable at the time.

In the presence of a continuing large-scale military economy, the federal government is likely to remain the country's largest borrower, thereby maintaining high interest rates in the finance capital markets. One result thus far has been a virtual termination of the secure and stable bond market, which for a long time provided capital for private and public investment at relatively modest rates. Economists have noted that the absence of that reliable pool of investment capital has had a seriously depressing effect on private and public investment. This is where finance capital funds under trade union control could conceivably play a historic role. Since their concept of acceptable return on investment includes employment in useful work and all its collateral effects, the interest rate earned on their funds ceases to be the controlling criterion. Thus worker pension funds are potentially a finance capital base for fresh productive investment in the American economy.

Assuming worker interest in productive employment, and the wider community's interest in restoring lost capability for organizing work, it is hard to escape the conclusion that the spread of workplace democracy is indispensable for restoration of industrial productivity, and that worker control over finance capital, along with a stronger voice in production decisions, is a prerequisite for the acceleration of productive capital investment.

As designers of products and of production systems, engineers are vital to the manufacturing industries of the United States. Nevertheless their position vis-à-vis managers and workers is ambiguous. The prevailing corporate culture has it that engineers are "part of management." That is what they are taught in engineering school and what they expect when they go to work. If employed in manufacturing firms, young engineers discover soon enough that definite barriers have been placed between them and blue-collar workers. One basis for differentiation is the high school diploma as against the college diploma. In part, there is an average and real difference in knowledge, especially in ability to wield the data of mathematics and the physical sciences. However, the lines are drawn deeper yet by the desire of management to keep the engineers within its own camp. Union rules and traditions, moreover, often deny access to "hands-on" work except to persons of specifically designated occupations.

The career prospects of engineering work are often uncomfortably equivocal. Although declared "part of management," engineers are seldom actually within the management hierarchy. They are therefore apt to discover few vertical lines for possible promotion, and as a rule, they have little direct decision-making power over production technologies or products, final decision being reserved to the straight-management occupations. Thus, engineers find themselves alienated from both the blue-collar workers and the mainline management occupations. This isolation is to a degree overcome by engineers who concentrate in the staffs of large R & D and design departments. In such cases, however, they are often organized into fine subdivisions of labor. One result, especially noticeable in the aerospace and related industries, is the spectacle of ordered ranks and files of engineers crouched over their drawing boards in acres of floor space. Many engineers have sought an escape from these conditions by a flight to business.

The outlook for an engineer is much brighter in enterprises that give priority to production and where a master's degree does not ban him from the shop floor. Under these conditions some share in production work becomes possible, making the formal engineering tasks more interesting. Horizontal job variation can offer a diversity of challenges and satisfactions, whether or not one rises through the managerial hierarchies. The prospect for engineers is substantially improved when they become involved in implementing criteria like those of the Technology Bill of Rights (chapter 7). In that case the engineer is challenged to innovate improvements in the quality of work, of workplaces and of products. At the same time, his technical training becomes of increased value to the entire work force, since he can take responsibility for technical education that upgrades the whole work force. Also, his special knowledge is bound to be needed when workers and unions participate in production decision-making.

Can workplace democracy work? When working people have a part in making decisions about their own work, will the result be a reduction or an increase of productivity? Here are some reports, independently gathered, on the experience of several firms in widely separated locations, handling unrelated products.

Back in the early 1970s, the General Foods Corporation tried to operate a dog-food factory in Topeka, Kansas, according to a system of work organization and decision-making that eliminated several ranks of management and supervisory employees and divided the whole work force into three major groups: processing, packaging and shipping, and office work. Each area was assigned to a team of workers that was jointly fully responsible for decision-making on the conduct of operations, and could rotate the various jobs among its members. Attached to each team was a "team leader," who functioned more like a coach than a foreman. All sorts of status differentiations were eliminated: everybody used the same entrance, there were no specially reserved parking places for individual managers, etc.

The system worked. During four years unit costs were reduced by 5 percent, an annual saving to the firm of $1 million. Employee turnover fell sharply and the plant ran for three years and eight months before suffering its first lost-time accident. Obviously, the system was a success economically, "but it became a power struggle; it was too threatening to too many people." A former employee stated, "There were pressures almost from the inception, and not because the system didn't work. The basic reason was power." It soon became apparent that "some management and staff personnel saw their own positions threatened because the workers performed almost too well. . . . Lawyers, fearing reaction from the National Labor Relations Board, opposed the idea of allowing team members to vote on pay raises. Personnel managers objected because team members made hiring decisions. Engineers resented workers doing engineering work."[37] Finally, the firm's central office put an end to this "experiment" where workers made job assignments, scheduled their coffee breaks, interviewed prospective employees, and made decisions on pay increases. By 1977 General Foods management was discouraging further publicity about its Topeka enterprise and would not let reporters from the business press into the plant.

Thanks to the research of James O'Toole, we have a series of interesting accounts of arrangements for workplace democracy in several firms. The following is based upon his account of the record, starting in 1977, at a chemical-processing division of a large industrial firm.[38]

As one of America's larger corporations was opening a new chemical plant in Texas in 1977, the managers estimated that for optimum productivity it was essential that the 300 workers involved be prepared to be flexible in their job assignments. But job flexibility was not consistent with long-established craft and job classification traditions and rules that had been guarded by the workers' union, the United Steelworkers of America.

Evidently, company executives and union officials surprised each other as they exchanged views on possible ways of meeting this problem. After substantial discussion a contract arrangement was negotiated, which, in the eyes of the union, was an advance in industrial democracy ("the elimination of the master/servant relationship"), including "the right of workers to participate in managerial decisions and in company profits."

The terms of the agreement included "provisions that have scant precedent in the adversarial history of American labor relations:

- There is a no-layoff agreement.
- There are no time clocks.
- There are no company rules.
- Foremen have no authority to assign or to discipline workers.
- The only discipline available to the company is to send a worker home (but it must continue to pay his salary, and he is presumed innocent until proven guilty). . . .
- There is a single wage classification for all production workers and a single classification for all maintenance workers."

The contract included provisions for technical and organizational problem-solving.

Conventional grievance and related procedures seemed to be inappropriate, as the plant is "governed democratically by a series of joint worker-manager committees." There are problem-solving committees in each section of the plant and plant-wide units that are empowered to address issues of their choice. "The plant safety committee not only sets rules but has authority to make expenditures to improve physical working conditions." There is even provision for a "hotline" linking union and corporate headquarters for use in addressing "unusual problems."

From management's standpoint, the organization of work with each "self-managing crew" responsible for its task has produced an extraordinary level of productivity, far greater than "the predictions engineers had made based on the capability of the technology employed." Mr. O'Toole reports that "the company nevertheless has a policy of full disclosure to the workers and the union of all managerial and financial information."

All this has apparently pleased both the working people and the management. After two and a half years of such functioning, absenteeism and turnover rates became negligible, despite the presence of a very young work force.

By mid-1981, the workers and managers at General Motors' Buick Division had chalked up clear gains from the operation of what management called a quality-of-working-life program. To the auto workers this meant a transformation from being mere instruments of a foreman's instructions to exercising responsibility for and authority over many details of their working lives. Machine operators could adjust machine settings without awaiting the intervention of special employees. They could reject faulty materials and products, and could stop assembly and other lines to prevent faulty products from proceeding through the system. Detailed supervision of their work by foremen was curtailed, as was the use of time clocks. Furthermore, workers could make group decisions on varying their work assignments. Many of the workers felt there had been a major transformation in their lives. One employee preferred to stay on the job rather than take retirement for which he was eligible, in order to participate in the new regime. This man said that after thirty-two years of "never having any say in how my job is done," he found the new arrangement "fantastic."[39] At the same time Buick management got the benefit of drastically reduced absenteeism and a near-disappearance of union grievances in the plant, coupled with substantial cost reduction that made this division's factories a preferred location for parts production intended for other General Motors Divisions.*

---

*The much admired quality control circles in major Japanese industries ". . . did not originate with senior management. They spring rather from a voluntary, grass-roots movement of workers and middle managers from across the nation.

"The spearhead has been the Union of Japanese Scientists and Engineers, or Nikka-Giren. In 1962, it began publishing a magazine, later named FQC, which called for quality control circles among factory workers and foremen and helped precipitate a change from the Western concept of quality control as the prerogative of technical experts. The magazine circulated widely among industrial workers, who bought it themselves (it cost them about the same as a pack of cigarets) rather than receiving it through their employers, and read it together—in a circle. The magazine, together with a generation of supervisors familiar with QC concepts from the '50s, helped initiate massive training of non-supervisors.

"The Nikka-Giren Union continues to have great influence. It publishes case histories of success-

These brief accounts illustrate a general characteristic of factories where the working people acquire a measure of decision power over the details of their employment. Almost without exception, the reports from diverse enterprises, industries and countries converge on one point: productivity of both labor and capital tend to increase. These effects are typically accompanied by improvement in morale, as shown in expressions of job satisfaction and the objective evidence of lowered turnover rates, reduced absenteeism and sharply diminished work grievances. A substantial literature now supports these conclusions.[40]

In 1982 there were 5,000 worker-owned enterprises in the United States. One of the latest and most important to come under worker ownership is Hyatt-Clark Industries, called Hyatt Bearings when it was a division of General Motors. Since January 1982 the employees, mainly blue-collar workers, have owned this factory, which they bought for $53 million. The new management functions without the old-fashioned management perquisites, and there is also a twenty-five-member committee of blue-collar and white-collar employees responsible for training supervisors and helping solve on-going problems. The new president has lunch each day with a different group of workers.

Management announced in April 1982 that productivity was up 80 percent and "the number of defective products manufactured is down from about 10 percent to 7 percent." Production workers took a pay cut from about $12 to $9 per hour, and many traditional work rules were scrapped. At the same time, however, the new company set up a system of incentive bonuses, which have ranged from $110 to $160 per month.

The financing for the $53 million purchase was arranged through loans from a consortium of banks and insurance companies. The transfer of ownership was much facilitated by agreement of General Motors top management to purchase 70 to 80 percent of its bearings from the new enterprise for three years. Reportedly, a crucial move in the financial takeover was the initiative of several Hyatt executives who, in January 1981, "distributed leaflets at the plant gate asking whether workers would be interested in joint white-collar and blue-collar efforts to establish a form of worker ownership; 1,530 workers said they were interested; 4 said no. The interest of management people was a turning point. Employees were asked to contribute $100 apiece for a feasibility study and legal fees; $125,000 was gathered . . ." to finance a consultant's report.[41]

---

ful QC circles and sponsors regional and national conferences, where circle participants from different companies share their experiences." (K. Ohmae, "Quality Control Circles: They Work and Don't Work," *The Wall Street Journal,* March 29, 1982.)

The Chicago and Northwestern Transportation Company is an unusually prosperous Midwest railroad that has been owned by its employees since 1972.[42] In August 1980, employees of Dayton Press, Inc., "one of the nation's largest magazine printing plants," voted to buy the company from its corporate owners at a quoted price of $135 million.[43] In Waterloo, Ohio, the stockholders of the Rath Packing Company agreed to sell the firm to its employees in 1980. The workers, organized in Local 46 of the United Food and Commercial Workers, were slated to hold 60 percent of the company's stock in the immediate future and would appoint ten of the sixteen company directors.

Organized workers must face the problem of making finance capital arrangements to take over ownership of productive enterprises whose conventional managements do not find an adequate rate of return on investment to justify their further participation. The problem is bound to accelerate as interest rates in the finance markets are sustained at a level far higher than the profit rates achievable by many industrial enterprises. The National Steel Corporation, for example, announced in March 1982 that it was considering sale to the employees of its Weirton Steel Division in West Virginia. Management indicated that this was part of its general plan to channel its finance capital "into areas of highest return." At the same time, the president of Weirton Steel approved such a sale on the grounds that "not only could it result in the preservation of jobs and maintaining the economic viability of the entire Weirton community; it also could provide employees with a share of the profits earned by the steel mill and is the best alternative for obtaining the capital needed to stay modern." At this time, the Weirton Division employed 8,900 workers, and a further 2,000 were on layoff.[44]

As managers attracted by fast profits have closed many New England and midwestern factories and moved their finance capital elsewhere, they have created economic crises not only for former employees but also for entire communities. In a search for effective responses, unions, managers and community leaders in Jamestown, New York, found a way to encourage labor-management cooperation in industrial problem-solving. A panel of representatives from management, labor and local government has aided plant-level committees in about thirty enterprises to resolve issues extending from factory layouts and methods of manufacture to technical training for new workers. In some plants, the labor-management committee system effected major reductions in energy consumption and improved the utilization of raw materials. When the introduction of new technology was addressed by joint committees, union approval cleared the way for installation of industrial robots, which improved productivity and relieved workers from dirty, monotonous jobs. Net employment in Jamestown, a city of 37,000, increased during the late 1970s as a result of the community-labor-management cooperation system. Observers report that the "Jamestown concept" has been picked up in other small cities.[45]

The advance of workplace democracy will have major effects on the design of production equipment, job definition and the shape of entire production systems. Single tools and equipments will increasingly be designed in accordance with the sensory-motor capabilities of the human beings who will use them.[46] Managements planning for production will surely be guided by the new factors in job design discovered by Professor Robert A. Karasek, Jr., and his coworkers. The aim is to vary job demands and allow for individual discretion, so that work becomes an enhancement of, rather than a drain on, the worker's physical and mental health.

At the same time the design of production systems is sure to be restudied, particularly close attention being given to the ever more important issue of gaining the maximum productivity from capital. As this problem is addressed it will be discovered—everywhere—that productivity of capital (and of labor) is markedly improved when unstable production systems are made stable—that is, when variation of output is held (and reduced) within predictable and acceptable limits. The goal of the overall approach to performance standards is that, as industrial operations are refined and controlled so that the incidence of accidents and of defective products approaches zero, all aspects of even the most complex production system will be operated with an elegance that truly approximates the smooth intermeshing of precisely fitted machine parts. But such a result is not achieved by people acting like machines. Sustained high productivity of capital and labor is obtained by the deliberately cooperative activity of people.

All these contributions to a technically sophisticated workplace require extensive cooperation among the administrative, planning, engineering and production groups engaged in the enterprise. For this purpose increasing doses of workplace democracy is the best available prescription. In combination, these factors can (and will) comprise the main elements of the high-tech production system.

What are the prospects for Americans to find and hold useful jobs in the years ahead? As the causes of depletion in the American economy and society are more widely appreciated, there is bound to come a greater readiness to move in fresh, constructive directions. The main consideration is the nature and direction of change.

Institutions like authoritarian managerialism and a military economy are not dismantled by the wave of a wand. However, as the crisis of production in the United States comes to be better understood, it will be seen that it cannot be dealt with by mere allocations of money. Real resources will have to be redirected, with appreciation of the fact that, even in the bounteous United States, their limits are finite. That is why conversion of resources from military to civilian economy (and a parallel reversal of the arms race) is essential to the reconstitution of production competence in the United States.*

Major redirection of resources for productive use in the United States will engage a gamut of economic planning. Local, extending to regional, responsibility and initiative are technically and economically the most effective style for planning and operating productive undertakings of every sort. National planning should be limited to calculating the availability of resources and finance capital, and to setting broad national priorities as required for energy policy, conservation of natural resources, education policy, limits on characteristics of technology and the like. For the rest, the community is best served by local authority, as by labor management groups in enterprises, and by community planning bodies that set policy and encourage development in accord with local problems, priorities and resources.

In order to carry out industrial renewal on a large scale, major industrial decisions must emphasize long-term investment in useful work. A second criterion concerns the boundary of the decision-making unit. For example: the high-speed railways that now represent the world state of the art as applied in Japan, France, Germany, and Britain do not necessarily break even or show a profit within the boundary of the ordinary enterprise profit and loss statement. The same activities, however, show substantial net gain when the accounting for cost and income is altered to measure social cost as against social gain for the whole community that is served.

In previous discussions of American economic problems and development, I have called attention to the existence of rather detailed plans for productive capital investment that could be substitutes for the use of production resources by a permanent military economy.[47] However, we have overwhelming evidence of widespread decay both in particular U.S. industries and

---

*The prerequisites for competent economic conversion include the following: alternative-use committees of administrators and workers to be set up in every military-serving factory and base; contingency plans to be made for civilian use of military and industrial base facilities; income support to be appropriated for former military industry and base employees during periods of retraining, reorganization of enterprise and relocation of personnel; retraining for civilian competence to be supplied, especially to engineers and administrators in the military economy; a national economic conversion commission to be established for allocations of finance capital for major civilian investments, public and private. These and other components of competent economic conversion capability have been detailed elsewhere. See Seymour Melman, *The Permanent War Economy* (Simon & Schuster, 1974), chs. 8, 9, 10. An excellent bibliography on economic conversion topics is found in Cary Wong, *Economic Consequences of Armament and Disarmament (A Bibliography),* Center for the Study of Armament and Disarmament, California State University, Los Angeles, Calif. 90032, 1981.

in many aspects of the infrastructure of American economy and society. At least 70 percent of the basic metalworking machinery of U.S. industry is old-fashioned, outdated. Furthermore, the steady, unbroken trend of the last thirty-five years is toward increasing obsolescence because managers, finding new machinery prices less attractive, have moved investment capital out of basic manufacturing industries. As this process continues, one may expect that by 1985 at least 75 percent of the U.S. metalworking machinery stock will be outdated.

Similar conditions are found in the infrastructure: railroads, roads, water supplies, waste-disposal systems, bridges, libraries, housing, etc. The largest part of the "fixed capital" stock of American economy is severely depleted. That is the thrust of the sober 1981 report *America in Ruins.* [48] The deterioration it describes is nationwide and proceeding continuously as even routine maintenance is skimped.

The political/economic turnabout required for a major economic rebuilding effort is unlikely to occur before 1985. If a new executive and a revitalized Congress are elected, and if they are committed to economic rebuilding, it is prudent to assume that not less than two years must elapse before even a start is made on the lead-time aspects of blueprinting and organizing that are required for major constructive operations. Thereafter, a gradually increasing tempo of work may be expected. Under the most favorable conditions, including a major start toward reversing the arms race, it is reasonable to predict that processes of industrial and infrastructure decay will prevail until at least 1988. Accordingly, there is little point to venturing detailed estimates of the condition of depletion in particular industries and public services. The scale of such a task now exceeds the capabilities of any single investigator.

Since depletion has become the most characteristic condition, it seems appropriate to attempt a large-scale comprehensive estimate of the possible cost of rebuilding the portion of American industry's means of production, and associated infrastructure, that have deteriorated. For this purpose, we must assume that not less than two-thirds of the nation's fixed capital stock will be eligible for replacement or major rebuilding. I include here all structures, fixed equipment and machinery (also roads and railroads), private and public; I exclude from this count military equipment and consumer durables (cars, refrigerators, etc.).

What can that rebuilding or replacement cost? What will it require in terms of man-years of work? The published data that measure the national wealth of the United States supplied in 1979 an overall figure of $5,700 billion as the value of fixed reproducible tangible wealth (excluding military and consumer durables). This includes business, government and household structures and equipment. [49]

Assuming that about 66 percent of the main capital equipment and infrastructure will have to be replaced if production competence and allied facilities and services are to be brought up to a first-class technical standard, then a capital outlay of $3,800 billion will be required. In 1979 an average man-year of industrial labor cost $13,380. Translated into man-years of work, such rebuilding will require direct employment of 14 million man-years each year for at least twenty years. It is also interesting, possibly coincidental, that the estimated 14 million work force required for rebuilding corresponds to the sum of unemployed (9 million) plus the military economy personnel (5 million) as of 1982.

If we are to deal with the myriad problems of industries, occupations and regions of the country, it will be essential that everyone who identifies his or her future with productive competence begin to address the question: how to rebuild America.* Means must be found to cope with new technology in every workplace. The criteria of the Technology Bill of Rights are critically important because they combine a thrust for advancing technology in the service of productivity with a recognition of the importance of designing and applying technology in ways that serve the goals of making useful work available and improving conditions of work.

A series of national policy and technical innovations are needed for a competent rebuilding effort. Two fundamental requirements pertain to capital. First, as discussed in chapter 13, the country must have an up-to-date and elaborated rendition of Professor Wassily Leontief's input-output table and analysis. This is indispensable for setting the limits within which industrial and other particular decision-making can be made, and to establish the outside limits for scheduling the production and use of real capital (production) resources.

Second, and for similar reasons, control over the finance capital required to encourage major new productive undertakings cannot be entrusted to private banks and the workings of a "free" finance capital market which, for example, is fully capable of setting interest rates at levels that profoundly discourage productive capital investment. Measures of government control over banks and banking will be required to forestall such possibilities. As workplace democracy is increasingly institutionalized among American firms, the control of capital will more accurately reflect the requirements of working people and communities for productive use of resources.

The education of skilled workers, technologists and engineers has been neglected in the United States for some time. Computer-controlled equipment of every sort is best used when overseen by people who are competent in both

---

*The International Association of Machinists and Aerospace Workers (1300 Connecticut Ave., N.W., Washington, D.C. 20036) has undertaken an interesting initiative by formulating aspects of economic plans for "Rebuilding America in the 80s."

the theory and use of complex machines. The implication is that many people now trained into "engineering science" are badly needed to work in a hands-on capacity in many industries. To be sure, such a change requires a transformation of values. Young people must be taught in theory and by example that physical work is necessary, that it demands high skill for excellent performance, and that in turn it confers status on the person so equipped. This implies that the young people now entering schools of business and law must in large part be directed into training for high-tech occupations that include hands-on performance.*

National economic policy will surely be required for energy production and conservation. Shortly after the Three Mile Island nuclear accident, and at about the time when David Inglis was calling attention to the practicability of wind power, the New York State legislature received a report surveying developable hydropower sites within the state. "It found in excess of 1,700 that have economic potential. They range in output capability from 50,000 to 1.5 million watts. Their combined power could be equal to three nuclear power plants. Surprisingly, some 1,100 come complete with dams."[50] David Lilienthal, the third chairman of the Tennessee Valley Authority, and responsible for much of its early constructive quality, calls attention to the finding of the Federal Power Commission that "America's underdeveloped water power could supply the electric needs of 40 million people and replace 2 million barrels of oil a day. Even this large figure does not take into account the opportunities of small rivers and in existing dams and canals and locks not now equipped for electric production." Lilienthal points out that "restoring the economic vitality of scores of small once-prosperous communities may be the most important social reason for utilizing to the full the energy in our medium-sized and small streams and water courses. This is notably true of the Northeast, which historically owed its manufacturing preeminence to the power of falling water."[51]

From the standpoint of economic return on investment in the energy field, there is hardly a match for energy conservation. One serious estimate is that "the two-fifths of our electricity now used to heat and cool buildings can be replaced by good architecture more cheaply than the running costs alone for a nuclear plant. . . ."[52]

A national policy for productivity growth will be required to unify the impetus for rebuilding production competence. Such a policy must take into account a neglected aspect of industrial productivity: the large differences

---

*During the winter of 1982 I visited a number of New England machine tool factories and noted a preponderance of skilled machinists who were slated to retire within five to ten years, and the absence of any notion among the managers of these plants as to where or how they would get promising replacements.

among factories in the same industries. The last data available for gauging this are from 1967. At that time the average productivity of the top 25 percent of factories in many industries was, on the average, 2.4 times the average productivity of the bottom 25 percent.[53] In the automobile industry that productivity range was 2.5 times, in the steel industry 2.3, and in petroleum refining an astonishing 4.8. This means that very large opportunities for improvement of performance are available within particular industries simply by applying to the less productive factories the technologies already adopted by the "best performing" factories. This approach to productivity improvement would make possible large gains, even before major new technologies were brought to bear.*

Environmental protection is yet another indispensable requirement for the prudent operation of modern industry. There is no substitute for national policy to cope with the country's massive neglect of this matter in the recent past. For example, the Environmental Protection Agency has reported that from 1975 through 1978 fully 90 percent of industrial waste was disposed of improperly. Appropriate public policy can not only protect the population from grave environmental hazards but also induce firms to develop methods of waste utilization which have often been found to be economically beneficial.[54]

Local planning by communities can be vital to a workable, decentralized building program for a productive American economy. According to Derek Shearer, "Local democratic planning [could] begin with neighborhood-based programs that provide residents with technical help to come up with an assessment of the goods and services needed by their community. This might include public amenities like parks and street repairs, and private needs, like particular kinds of stores or, simply, jobs for the unemployed. . . . Cities [could] obtain capital to plan for new jobs and neighborhood improvements from municipally owned banks that would loan funds and provide equity for development projects." The idea of using local banks that are linked to community control and local decision processes is a major alternative to the pattern of centralism with its requirement for endless paper and impersonal dealings with poorly informed, distant bureaucrats.[55]

The goal of useful work for all is no pipe dream. Its realization, however, requires recognition of and response to the breakdown of the long-standing

---

*The R & D process for new technologies will have to take into account the limits that derive from the attempt to get "economies of scale"; that is, trying for higher productivity by enlarging mechanisms and factories. The limits of the "economies of scale" approach have been defined by John E. Ullmann in *The Improvement of Productivity: Myths and Realities* (Praeger, 1980).

tacit social contract between management and the rest of society. Management has been expected to organize work, and in exchange has been permitted to control production and to take a large share of the profits and power. But managerialism, oriented with primacy to profits/power, has developed a trained incapacity to organize work. The traditional basis for legitimacy of managerial power is being destroyed by the controlled deterioration of the U.S. production system and the parallel efforts of management to sustain its money-making in the presence of a growing workless population. Once the social contract breakdown is displayed for all to see, there will come a national demand for alternative ways to organize work and rebuild the American economy. The underlying requirements include initiatives by all the production occupations for progressively enlarged workplace democracy, moves toward production-oriented management, more decentralized decision-making and a substantially smaller military economy.

The analyses of this book can be used to evaluate the merits of economic/industrial policy proposals for the United States. Thus, conservative opinion favors laissez faire, with the removal of many constraints ("regulation") on management. Proposals from the liberal center stress "industrial policy" and "reindustrialization" plans with state support to managements in "sunrise" industries. The classic socialist orientation features state ownership of industry as a primary measure.

This array of policy options contains a common flaw: a reliance on private and/or state management, and so on the classic social contract—that is, on the ability and willingness of management to carry out the efficient organization of work that has historically been its major function. But, as it has been a basic aim of this book to demonstrate, that contract no longer holds. The achievement of economic renewal will therefore require new modes of governance in economic life—and, most fundamentally and critically, the extension of decision-making power to those within the producing occupations.

APPENDIXES, NOTES, INDEX

Foreign Assets of U.S. Multinational Manufacturing Firms, 1979

Company	Foreign assets ($ millions)	Foreign as % of total assets
CPC International	1,413	68.3
Gillette	926	60.6
Black and Decker	505	55.5
Ford Motor	12,814	54.5
Dow Chemical	5,389	52.6
Colgate-Palmolive	1,262	52.0
IBM	12,345	50.3
Sterling Drug	571	49.6
Pfizer	1,482	48.6
NCR	1,360	46.6
Xerox	3,023	46.1
Singer	672	45.3
Kimberly-Clark	951	45.2
Johnson & Johnson	1,253	43.6
Avon Products	607	43.2
Goodyear	2,295	42.7
Sperry	1,588	42.6
American Standard	597	42.0
Burroughs	1,418	41.9
Scott Paper	763	41.7
Foster Wheeler	369	41.3
Merck	1,044	39.9
Warner Lambert	1,111	38.7
United Brands	465	38.2
Firestone	1,311	37.9
Eli Lilly	818	37.5
HJ Heinz	609	37.5

Company	Foreign assets ($ millions)	Foreign as % of total assets
TRW	952	36.4
Ingersoll-Rand	754	35.4
Consolidated Foods	730	34.9
Bristol-Myers	665	34.6
American Brands	1,245	33.9
Eastman Kodak	2,536	33.6
Litton Industries	954	33.4
American Home Products	669	32.0
Uniroyal	521	31.2
Levi Strauss	400	31.0
Bendix	716	31.0
Chrysler	2,055	30.9
Fluor	389	30.7
Halliburton	1,196	30.5
Monsanto	1,680	30.3
Kraft	760	30.1
Texas Instruments	571	29.9
Union Carbide	2,517	28.6
Motorola	542	28.5
Honeywell	941	28.2
Hewlett-Packard	532	28.0
Borg-Warner	503	27.7
Eaton	653	27.7
International Harvester	1,432	27.3
Carnation	404	27.2
American Cyanamid	767	27.1
General Foods	675	26.3
Deere	1,101	26.3
General Motors	8,369	26.1
Allied Chemical	1,086	25.8
United Technologies	1,651	25.7
General Electric	4,049	24.3
Procter & Gamble	1,360	24.0
Owens-Illinois	690	23.7
Borden	575	23.3
Dresser Industries	584	23.3
Gulf & Western Inds	1,106	21.4
Caterpillar Tractor	1,055	19.5
Pullman	239	18.4
General Tel & Elec	3,292	17.9

Company	Foreign assets ($ millions)	Foreign as % of total assets
Ralston Purina	378	17.3
RCA	902	15.1
Rockwell International	606	14.7
International Paper	706	14.6
Armco	455	13.9
Esmark	290	12.1
Westinghouse Electric	633	9.3
Control Data	536	7.9

Source: *Forbes,* July 7, 1980.

APPENDIX II

Regular Reports Prepared
in the ABC Company on
Accounts Receivable in 1975

D1 Report   A daily summary report which contains information concerning previous day's opening balance, sales, cash transfers, discounts, costs, vouchers, write-offs, journal entries, and closing balance. This record is one page for each of the firm's three divisions, and is kept by the control coordinators in charge of these divisions in the credit and receivable department. . . .

D2 Report   A daily input report which lists the customers' transactions against the previously assigned credit and receivable department's employee. . . . The control coordinators receive and check the report to verify that no employee violated his limit in giving discounts the day before. This report is 150 pages per day on the average. . . .

D3 Report   A daily report which demonstrates sales per customer in the previous day. The information on this report can also be found on report No. 2 with the exception of the customer's address which appears in report No. 3. The report is, on the average, 85 pages long. No action is taken by any individual employee in the company on any of the items printed on this report.

D4 Report   A daily report which contains information on regional banks' up-to-date balance. It also lists individual deposits for each bank. The report is 200 pages long on the average. . . .

D5 Report (Unearned Discount Letters)   These reports are copies of the letters which are sent to those customers who deducted discounts to which they were not entitled. This report is about ten pages each day and is filed and retained in the department. No action results from inspecting these reports. . . .

D6 Report (Machine Created Note Report)   A daily report which lists the allowed discounts which were not taken by the customers in different transactions and adds them to a special account. The control coordinators add up all these discounts to check against the total unearned discounts appearing on report D1. This report, one page per customer, is about 100 pages long.

Source: Heskia Heskiaoff, "Computers and Productivity in Production Operations and Administrative Functions in Manufacturing Industries in the United States" (Ph.D. dissertation, Columbia University, 1977).

D7 Report (Customer Master File Cash Announcement)   A daily report which lists the account number, the bank number, the division, the check number which was deposited, the check date, and the amount deposited. The control coordinators give the report to other employees in the credit and receivable department who check to see whether the checks were applied toward the individual accounts by the computer or not. This report is about 200 pages long.

D8 Report (High Balance Report)   A daily report which lists each customer (account) whose outstanding balance exceeds his individual limit. The credit and receivable department then decides to approve or disapprove further shipment to the customer until the company receives additional payments. This report is about 50 pages long.

D9 Report (Referral Activity Report)   A daily report which lists the payments by those customers who were late in making payments. The credit and receivable department decides whether each payment was large enough not to warrant stoppage of further shipment to the customer. The report is 100 pages long.

D10 Report (Cash Exception Report)   The largest daily report, it lists the [50 percent of] customer payments and deposits whose accounts, due to some irregularities in the input data, cannot be properly updated by the computer. The payments are then manually entered in the system through video terminals in the credit and receivable department. The report is about 1,000 pages long. . . .

M1 Report (Trial Balance)   A monthly report reflecting all customer balances is sent to the credit and receivable department. These reports are prepared on microfiche and are kept in the credit and receivable department for reference.

M2 Report (Customer Statements)   A monthly statement which is mailed to each customer, listing the unpaid items and the total amount owed to the company. There are about 60,000 statements issued each month to the active customers. . . .

M3 Report (Red Tab Report)   A monthly report which lists the customers who are late in payments. The credit and receivable department studies the warnings and decides whether any warning should be removed. Meanwhile, if the customer orders additional merchandise prior to the removal of the warning, the credit and receivable department must approve the order. This report is about 150 pages each month.

M4 Report   A monthly managerial summary report, it indicates the terms of payments for all active accounts. The management in the credit and receivable department by using this report predicts the cash flow for the coming month. This report is two pages each month.

M5 Report (Retention Report)   One of the two largest monthly reports, it provides the credit and receivable department of the firm with a list of customer accounts which are fully paid. It is estimated that the computer center prints 15,000 pages of this report each month. . . .

M6 Report (Delinquency Report)   This report . . . lists the accounts which are late in payment. It is prepared to show the associated salesman and the territory. The credit and receivable department sends these reports to each salesman and his regional sales manager. This report is about 15,000 pages each month.

Q1 Report   A quarterly report, it is prepared on microfilm and sent to the credit and receivable department. The report contains the monthly retention reports of the three previous months and is kept in the departmental records.

PRODUCTIVITY IN THE CREDIT AND RECEIVABLE DEPARTMENT
BEFORE AND AFTER COMPUTERIZATION IN THE ABC COMPANY

	1961	1975	% Increase
Number of full-time employees performing credit and receivable functions	30	90[1]	200
Overtime (equivalent full-time employees)	5	0	—
Data processing budget allocated to the credit and receivable department	$55,000[2]	$607,000[3]	1003
Average number of customers (accounts) kept on file	75,000	95,000	26
Average number of active accounts kept on file	35,000	55,000	57
Equivalent number of full-time employees per 10,000 accounts kept on file	4.66	9.47	103
Equivalent number of full-time employees per 10,000 active accounts	10	16.36	63
Data processing budget per 10 customers kept on file	7.33	63.89	771
Data processing budget per 10 active accounts	15.71	110.36	602

1. The number of employees in the department in 1975 varied between 85 and 95.
2. The estimated rental of the unit-record machines used by the department in 1961.
3. The hardware rental and the cost of computer center personnel allocated to the credit and receivable department in 1975.

How the Military Economy Maximizes Cost

The military services of the Department of Defense characteristically develop ever more elaborate specifications and performance requirements for weaponry. Thus the electronic control systems (avionics) of several weapons have been identified as costing more than two times their weight in gold (Fox, 23). During the program evaluation process for new weapons systems, costs are characteristically given little consideration until a problem of adequacy of funding arises (Fox, 76). Military and civilian managers in the Department of Defense have opposed industrial engineering studies of contractor practices since recommendations for reducing cost or price might imply that the managers concerned had been doing a poor job (Fox, 80). On numerous occasions, progress reporting through Pentagon channels on weapons systems has been "adjusted" to delete bad performance reports at firms under Pentagon supervision, or at military installations involved in weapons testing (Fox, 80).

Committees of Congress have repeatedly approved military budget requests under incredible conditions, disclosed here for the first time to my knowledge. Fox describes proceedings at secret hearings of various Congressional committees: the small number of members present; the poor quality of questions asked; the fact that the Pentagon is frequently asked to prepare the questions which the Congressmen on the Armed Services Committees use for questioning Pentagon witnesses; the perfunctory style of the whole procedure; intervention by members of Congress to enlarge particular budget items so as to generate income and employment in their districts or states (Fox, Ch. 7).

The Department of Defense central office staffs for regulating military industry total about 55,000 people (Fox, 34–36, 215), including 10,000 persons in each of the armed services and 25,000 in the Defense Contract Administration Service which administers 80% of industrial contracts.

Ordinarily, the cost of weapons systems plays a minority part in the selection of

Sources: From S. Melman, Review Essay on "Operating Characteristics of Military Economy," *Journal of Political and Military Sociology* 5 (1977), pp. 295–300; J. R. Fox, *Arming America: How the U.S. Buys Weapons* (Harvard University Graduate School of Business Administration, 1974).

industrial firms to do the work. Thus in the weighting system for grading potential industrial contractors, cost is given a 15% weight among all other factors (Fox,
262).

By 1971 the Pentagon was attempting to reduce cost growth by the device of raising
initial estimates (Fox, 167). Pentagon program managers have characteristically been
rewarded professionally as their programs become larger; that is, involving larger
budgets (Fox, 180). Typically, military personnel assigned as program managers to
weapons systems are given efficiency ratings that are independent of the costs, or
scheduling, or technical performance factors of the weapons system they are supervis-
ing. Thus, in one period 85% of the colonels in one of the military services' procurement organizations were rated as being in the top 12% of officers in terms of efficiency
(Fox, 189).

J. R. Fox finds that, typically, the argument for more money starts at the top levels
of the White House and the Department of Defense (Fox, 289). At the same time
senior military officers have typically been critical of "should cost" engineering studies aimed at cost reduction (Fox, 343).

There has been steady intensification of administrative controls over the underlying military industry firms that are charged with doing weapons research, development and production. *The Armed Services Procurement Regulations* when first
formulated in 1947 comprised 100–125 pages. By 1973 this set of rules for the functioning of military industry firms and Pentagon supervisors totaled 3,000 pages in loose-
leaf format with thick batches of monthly replacements as a continuing pattern (Fox,
14). The Department of Defense spends, internally, not less than $225–$450 million
annually for data and allied management systems (Fox, 400).

The establishment of the Defense Contract Audit Agency was part of the
McNamara reorganization of the Pentagon (Fox, 2). As implied by the title and
the terms of reference of this agency, this was supposed to be the strong right arm
of the Department of Defense top management for control of costs and other aspects
of operation in the largest industrial organization in the world. However, in the words
of a senior military procurement official, "The Defense Contract Audit Agency has
the responsibility for controlling the reasonableness of costs. The reason that *we*
forecast the trend of dollar cost increases on a contract is to determine what additional
funds we will need" (Fox, 423). This purpose is obviously well removed from any
auditing function that is designed to serve a cost-minimizing objective. A Pentagon
official characterized his program management colleagues in the following terms:
"These men believe that their job is to get the most technically sophisticated hardware
in the shortest time-frame. Their point of view is supported by contractors' interests
in maximizing reimbursed cost to build and retain their technical base." The Chief
of Naval Operations, Admiral Zumwalt, admonished his subordinates to be sure to
spend the full sums allotted for a given year. The Admiral wrote: "Anticipate any
shortfall in fiscal year 1972 outlay target could be translated into program loss under
fiscal year 1973 ceiling" (Fox, 136). Junior military officers assigned to various military
purchasing offices (service academy graduates in these instances) have reported being
ordered to "misrepresent the facts on the program, to improve the likelihood of
obtaining the required additional funds from the Congress." Other junior officers and

civilian officials reported pressures not to identify or report cost growth (Fox, 434, 442).

A manager in a military industry firm reported that "the only thing worse than a serious cost over-run is a cost under-run of 15% or more. If such an under-run occurred, we would make the government contracting officer look bad. This, in turn, would endanger our relationship with him and motivate him to negotiate a lower target price with us on the next contract" (Fox, 440). Apparently, such endangerment has been effectively minimized throughout the system.

Within military industry firms there is a collateral pattern of practices with those operated by the Pentagon. Cost estimates for new weapons systems tend to follow the budgeted amounts of money for those systems (Fox, 101). Administrative and technical staffs tend to be from 5 to 10 times as large as the staffs of French or German military industry firms producing similar products. Program managers are graded in terms of Pentagon satisfaction with the weapons system delivered. Cost considerations play a definitely lesser role (Fox, 209). The management and engineering policies within military industry firms include incentives for ever more complex designs of weapons products. Since the salaries of military industry executives are mainly a function of sales volume (Fox, 298), cost increase is favored.

Military industry firms' overhead comprises 40% to 70% of total costs (Fox, 327). Management consultants with wide experience in military industry have estimated that these classes of overhead costs are readily reducible by 25% to 35% (Fox, 329). Major U.S. military industry firms have employed 10 to 100 times the number of engineers required to carry out particular tasks (Fox, 332).

Military contractors typically use historical cost trends for both cost and price estimating. This cost-escalating practice is not only permitted: it has been preferred by Pentagon top managers. The consequence of this practice is to incorporate all manner of causes of cost growth into the estimating base for the costs and prices of new products (Fox, 331).

A financial manager of one large firm reported that "the contractor's internal budgets were developed by allocating all unassigned personnel to the program, rather than by estimating the effort required for an individual task or set of tasks" (Fox, 413). Profit policy is consistent with the rest, for cost-reducing investment is not rewarded, indeed may even become a source of profit penalty. Therefore military industry firms have had a profit incentive to maintain and enlarge costs (Fox, 317).

Cost increase operates even where "incentive" contracting is utilized. For example, a very small penalty rate for exceeding planned costs can become an incentive to spend well beyond planned costs. Thus, "most incentive contracts are written so that contractors must pay no more than 20¢, and usually less, of each dollar increase in cost above the target cost. Since the contractors' share of cost over-runs is tax deductible, and since large defense contractors are in the 50% or higher tax bracket, the actual cost of each dollar over-run to a contractor is 10¢, and often less. To state this another way: if the contractor spends an additional dollar on direct or overhead costs (thus enhancing his commercial business or future defense business) and charges the cost to the incentive contract, the dollar investment will cost the contractor no more than 10¢. Thus, in many cases, it is to the contractor's advantage to spend as much on a contract as the market will bear (Fox, 242).

Engineers are expected to elaborate product designs and, typically, are not rewarded for cost reduction (Fox, 443–4). Production workers are under similar pressures (Fox, 443–4). As a group, the engineers working in military industry have not been trained to design for cost-minimization (Fox, 475).

Both Department of Defense and military industry firm managers cooperate to start the production of weapons systems before their development as products have been completed. This necessarily results in considerable rework owing to redesign of parts and the need to re-do tooling, equipment, materials, and final products (Fox, 107). The Defense Contract Administration Services' field agents usually avoid seeking out poor quality, or practices within their firms that would enlarge costs, so as not to endanger good working relations with the staff of the Pentagon-serving firm (Fox, 219).

Such practices became part of the Total Package Procurement Contract. This was developed under McNamara and applied with much public flourish to the C-5A contract. These contracts, designed to place responsibility from initial research and development to final production in the hands of one firm, permitted the firm to offset any initial losses by price increases on production beyond the initial quantities ordered (Fox, 245).

At the very start of a firm's relationship with the Pentagon on a prospective weapons system, a pattern is established for lavish administrative outlays. Thus the Pentagon has issued *Requests for Proposals* which range from 1,200 to 2,500 pages in length. The proposals submitted by contractors for prospective weapons systems have been in the colossal range of size. In the case of one weapons system cited by J. R. Fox, the proposal required 22,990 pages. For a set of contracts involving diverse weapons systems, the range of proposal length was 23,000 to 38,000 pages. "The five competitors on the C-5A programs submitted proposals that totalled 240,000 pages. With all the required copies, the proposals weighed 35 tons" (Fox, 265–6).

Obviously, the preparation of proposals of such length requires large staffs. Thus the Boeing, Lockheed, and Douglas companies employed, together, about 6,000 people to write the proposals on the C-5A aircraft (Fox, 295).

It may not be assumed that the contracts include meaningful guarantees of performance for products finally delivered to the military. Indeed, "guaranteed performance" clauses have been nullified by the absence of penalty for failure to meet standards (Fox, 356). The technical performance of major weapons systems (the C-5A is a prime case) has tended to diverge widely from the specifications that had been set at the outset (Fox, 3, 393–4).

The Reagan Budget's Contribution to Unemployment in Fiscal 1982

	Job Loss
Jobs and Training	
CETA	340,000
Young Adult Conservation Corps	18,000
Youth Conservation Corps	2,000
General Employment and Training/Youth Programs	160,000
Transportation	
Federal Highway Construction	44,000
Mass Transit Grants	33,000
Amtrak	10,000
Local Rail Service and Conrail	2,300
Northeast Rail Corridor Improvement	2,000
Airport Construction	6,000
Commerce, Credit, Housing, etc.	
Farmers Home Administration	41,000
HUD Rehabilitation Loan Fund	4,000
Economic Development Administration	116,000
Rural Electrification Administration	158,000
Subsidized Housing	51,000
Public Housing Modernization	13,000
Natural Resources and Environment	
Water Resource Development	2,000
EPA Water Treatment Plants	91,000
Energy	
Synthetic Fuel Subsidies	91,000
Solar Energy and Conservation Bank	2,700

Solar Energy	2,500
DOE Fossil Energy Programs	4,600
DOE Energy Conservation	17,000
Federal Employees	
Reductions in Federal Civilian Employment	43,100
Postal Subsidy	N.A.
State Employment Security Agencies	5,000
TOTAL JOB LOSS	1,259,200

Source: *AFL-CIO News,* March 28, 1981.

Estimates of Average Employment Impact of Military Spending (1977–78)

New York	− 288,200	Montana	− 2,300
Illinois	− 160,700	Delaware	− 1,200
Michigan	− 139,100	South Dakota	− 600
Ohio	− 131,900	Kansas	+ 600
Pennsylvania	− 112,900	New Hampshire	+ 600
New Jersey	− 71,900	Maine	+ 2,300
Wisconsin	− 71,700	Alabama	+ 3,500
Indiana	− 64,500	Connecticut	+ 3,900
Minnesota	− 54,600	North Dakota	+ 4,400
Tennessee	− 47,200	New Mexico	+ 7,400
Florida	− 40,100	Utah	+ 9,300
Massachusetts	− 39,800	Kentucky	+ 11,100
Iowa	− 38,500	Colorado	+ 11,200
Oregon	− 37,800	Texas	+ 15,400
Nevada	− 24,100	Alaska	+ 15,700
Louisiana	− 23,300	Oklahoma	+ 16,000
West Virginia	− 18,900	Maryland	+ 17,000
California	− 13,800	Washington	+ 20,200
Arkansas	− 12,300	Georgia	+ 20,900
Nebraska	− 6,200	Mississippi	+ 23,400
Missouri	− 4,500	N. Carolina	+ 23,800
Vermont	− 4,200	S. Carolina	+ 29,200
Rhode Island	− 3,600	Hawaii	+ 45,200
Wyoming	− 3,000	Virginia	+ 125,900
Idaho	− 2,800		
Arizona	− 2,800	NET JOBS LOST	1,015,000

Source: Based on data in Marion Anderson, *The Empty Pork Barrel: Unemployment and the Pentagon Budget,* 1982 ed. (Employment Research Associates, 400 S. Washington Ave., Lansing, Mich. 48933, 1982), p. 3. Note: The sum of the states data does not equal the overall U.S. total because of rounding.

NOTES

Introduction

1. The following are the best estimates of "hourly compensation costs" to employers, for production workers in manufacturing, in thirty countries, for 1980. These are unpublished data prepared by the U.S. Department of Labor, Bureau of Labor Statistics, Office of Productivity and Technology, April 1982. "Hourly compensation costs" to management include money payments as well as payments "in kind." All data are in U.S. dollars.

United States	10.00
Canada	9.04
Brazil	1.70
Mexico	2.97
Venezuela	3.85
Australia	7.25
Hong Kong	1.30
Israel	3.79
Japan	5.61
Korea	1.09
New Zealand	5.02
Singapore	1.24
Taiwan	1.27
Austria	7.88
Belgium	13.18
Denmark	10.44
Finland	8.22
France	9.23
Germany	12.26
Greece	3.12
Ireland	5.95
Italy	8.26
Luxembourg	11.81
Netherlands	12.17
Norway	11.29
Portugal	2.03
Spain	5.93
Sweden	12.51
Switzerland	11.15
United Kingdom	7.37

2. Seymour Melman, *Our Depleted Society* (Holt, Rinehart & Winston, 1965).

Prologue

1. Various publications of the U.S. Bureau of Labor Statistics, cited in Seymour Melman, *Dynamic Factors in Industrial Productivity* (John Wiley, 1956), p. 152.

2. William A. Hadley, "Why the United States Is Strong," *Mechanical Engineering,* September 1956.

3. *Business Week,* February 5, 1979.

4. A. E. Fitzgerald, *The High Priests of Waste* (Norton, 1972), ch. 5.

5. *Defense Week,* October 27, 1980, p. 1. For a description and analysis of how cost-maximizing operates in a military industry firm, see Seymour Melman, *The Permanent War Economy* (Simon & Schuster, 1974), ch. 2.

6. Special communication from the Department of Defense, Office of the Under Secretary of Defense, Defense Industrial Resources Support Office, February 20, 1981.

7. John R. Fox, *Arming America, How the U.S. Buys Weapons* (Division of Research, Graduate School of Business Administration, Harvard University, 1974), p. 262.

8. Another thing that happened to the U.S.

machine tool industry after 1960 is that the pace of machinery design improvements slowed down. There is no well-defined explanation for that development. It showed up in a rating system for machine productivity called the *Productivity Criterion Quotient,* formulated by Dr. Lawrence Hackamack of Northern Illinois University and published in *American Machinist;* see issues of November 11, 1963, June 7, 1965, and October 7, 1968. This may have been one effect of the concentration of R & D effort, within the major machine tool firms, on the new numerical control technology. A handful of leading firms have been the concentration points of research effort in that industry.

9. U.S. Bureau of Labor Statistics, *Wholesale Prices and Price Indexes,* January 1967; *Monthly Labor Review,* January–June 1978; Bureau of Labor Statistics, Bulletins 1705, 1865, 1966; *Monthly Labor Review,* August 1980.

10. The Bank of Japan Statistics Department, *Economic Statistics Annual,* 1963, 1969, 1978; *Price Indexes Annual,* 1975, 1979.

11. National Machine Tool Builders Association, *Economic Handbook of the Machine Tool Industry, 1980/81* (McLean, Va., 1980), p. 249.

12. U.S. Bureau of Labor Statistics: *Productivity and the Economy,* Bulletin 1710, 1971, p. 30; *Productivity and Costs,* USDL 81-209, April 27, 1981.

13. *American Machinist,* December 1980, p. 133.

14. *Business Week,* October 5, 1981.

15. National Machine Tool Builders Association, op. cit., p. 98; Japan Machine Tool Builders Association, *Machine Tool Industry,* p. 21.

16. Unpublished federal report on the machine tool industry, 1972.

17. National Machine Tool Builders Association, op. cit., p. 250.

18. U.S. Bureau of the Census, *Census of Manufacturers, 1977, General Summary* (Government Printing Office, 1980), pp. 1–40.

19. U.S. Air Force Wright Aeronautical Laboratories, Lawrence Livermore National Laboratory (University of California), *International Machine Tool Task Force Conference,* October 16–17, 1980.

20. Seymour Melman, *Report on the Productivity of Operations in the Machine Tool Industry of Western Europe,* European Productivity Agency, Organization for Euro-

pean Economic Cooperation (Paris, October 23, 1959).

21. U.K. Board of Trade, *The Machine Tool Industry: A Report by the Subcommittee of the Machine Tool Advisory Council Appointed to Consider Professor Melman's Report to the European Productivity Agency* (H.M.S.O., 1960). This subcommittee was chaired by Sir Stuart Mitchell.

22. *The New York Times,* October 26, 1959.

23. Seymour Melman, "Russia—a New Lathe Every Fifteen Minutes," *Mechanical Engineering,* October 1960, pp. 42–45; *Mechanical Engineering,* June 1961, pp. 102–103.

24. In 1977, an engineering group formulated a research proposal aimed at developing methods for improving productivity in the U.S. machine tool industry. Federal research administrators could not see why it should be necessary to examine proposals for improving productivity in the machine tool industry, since if such ideas were relevant at all, then the managements of the industry must surely have thought of them. Furthermore, several of the government men had long experience with NASA operations, where there had never been any difficulty in obtaining satisfactory machine tools for the work to be done. These staffers had never been trained to understand that managements might operate by other than cost-minimizing rules. Therefore, they were unable to "see" the cost-and-subsidy-maximizing character of their state-managed NASA environment and its consequences for the unique high-tech machine tools that were available to them.

1

1. *The Wall Street Journal,* September 23, 1980.

2. *U.S. News and World Report,* October 10, 1977.

3. *The New York Times,* February 19, 1981.

4. U.S. Steel Corporation, *Annual Reports* and 10K reports to the Securities and Exchange Commission (Pittsburgh, Pa., 1975–1979), cited in Barry Bluestone and Bennett Harrison, "Why Corporations Close Profitable Plants," *Working Papers,* May–June 1980.

5. Thomas Brom, "U.S. Investment Dollars Are Deserting America," Pacific News Service, July 1, 1980.

6. *The New York Times,* February 19, 1981.

7. *The New York Times,* April 2, 1981.

8. *The New York Times,* February 19, 1981.

9. *The New York Times,* November 29, 1976.

10. *The New York Times,* September 21, 1980.

11. Ibid.

12. U.S. Senate, Subcommittee on Antitrust and Monopoly, Committee on Judiciary, *Hearings on Economic Concentration,* 91st Cong., 1st sess., 1969, pt. 8A, appendix, Staff Report of the Federal Trade Commission on Corporate Mergers, p. 63. These data cited in Barry Bluestone and Bennett Harrison, *Capital and Communities: The Causes and Consequences of Private Disinvestment* (Washington, D.C.: The Progressive Alliance, 1980), p. 123.

13. Bluestone and Harrison, *Capital and Communities,* pp. 41, 20.

14. *The New York Times,* February 23, 1981.

15. *The New York Times,* November 10, 1980.

16. *The Wall Street Journal,* November 6, 1980.

17. Edward Kelley and Lee Webb, *Plant Closings,* Conference on Alternative State and Local Policies (Washington, D.C., 1979), pp. 16–17.

18. Bluestone and Harrison, *Capital and Communities,* pp. 200–202; Jonathan Kwitny, "Tube Plant, 600 Jobs Saved in Indianapolis— in the Nick of Time," *The Wall Street Journal,* March 22, 1978, p. 1.

19. Researches on deindustrialization within the United States note that a vice-president of Fantus, a principal consulting firm on plant location, has explained the movement of many Northeastern and Midwestern firms to the U.S. South, saying: "Labor costs are the big thing, far and away. Nine out of ten times you can hang it on labor costs and unionization." Akron *Beacon Journal,* February 20, 1977; cited in Edward Kelley, *Industrial Exodus,* Conference on Alternative State and Local Policies (Washington, D.C., 1977), p. 3.

20. Bluestone and Harrison, *Capital and Communities,* p. 53.

21. Richard Barnet and Ronald Müller, *Global Reach* (Simon & Schuster, 1974), p. 307.

22. Seymour Melman, *The Permanent War Economy* (Simon & Schuster, 1974), Appendix 3, pp. 333–353.

23. Bluestone and Harrison, *Capital and Communities,* pp. 52–55.

24. *The Wall Street Journal,* March 11, 1981.

25. *The New York Times,* November 9, 1980.

26. Ibid.

27. Ibid.

28. Ibid.

29. William Serrin, "Detroit Strikes Back," *The New York Times,* September 14, 1980.

30. U.S. Department of Transportation, *The U.S. Automobile Industry, 1980,* Report to the President from the Secretary of Transportation, January 1981.

31. Serrin, op. cit. The closings process continues. For example, G.M. announced four more plant closings, affecting 9,620 workers in Trenton, Cleveland and Detroit (2). *The New York Times,* February 26, 1982.

32. Harley Shaiken, "How Auto Workers Will Pay for Big Three Recovery," Pacific News Service, July 23, 1980.

33. *The New York Times,* November 7, 1980.

34. *The New York Times,* August 29, 1980.

35. *Viewpoint* 5, no. 4 (1975), pp. 7, 8, AFL-CIO, Industrial Union Dept., Washington, D.C.

36. Ibid.

37. Peggy Musgrave, *Direct Investment Abroad and the Multinationals: Effects on the United States' Economy,* prepared for the U.S. Senate, Committee on Foreign Relations, Subcommittee on Multinational Corporations (Government Printing Office, August 1975), pp. xi, 11, 12.

38. Musgrave, op. cit., p. 13.

39. *UE News,* December 8, 1980.

40. This estimate was derived by Robert Frank and Richard Freeman, *The Distributional Consequences of Direct Foreign Investment* (Academic Press, 1978). Frank and Freeman at Cornell University carried out a careful industry-by-industry analysis of the consequences of foreign investment for domestic employment. Their estimates include a comparative cost pattern of U.S. domestic compared with foreign production. The estimates of employment effects do not include derived job displacement as in services, trade, etc. The Frank and Freeman estimates are based upon 1970 data.

41. An array of methodological issues are involved in estimating the employment loss that is associated with direct foreign investment. A sophisticated analysis of the main studies in this field is found in the monograph by Musgrave, op. cit., especially chs. 8, 9, and 10.

42. Musgrave, op. cit., pp. 14, 15.

43. Machinery and Allied Products Institute, *The Role of U.S. Manufacturing and Machinery Investment Abroad—a Review and Current Appraisal* (Washington, D.C., November 1979).

44. Ibid.

45. *In These Times,* April 22–28, 1981, p. 4.

46. *The Wall Street Journal,* March 11, 1981.

47. *The New York Times,* January 4, 1981.

48. *Monthly Economic Letter,* Citibank, December 1978, p. 13.

49. Unpublished data from the U.S. Bureau of Labor Statistics.

50. U.S. Department of Labor data cited in *Viewpoint,* op. cit., p. 14.

51. Musgrave, op. cit., p. 107.

52. Robert Gilpin, quoted in *Viewpoint,* op. cit., p. 15.

The abandonment of England by British investors has been followed by the out-migration, especially of middle-class professionals and skilled workers, to the main Commonwealth countries. *The Nation,* November 21, 1981.

2

1. In the case of the important new product, titanium dioxide, Du Pont required ten years for product research and development. *Business Week,* July 3, 1978, p. 48.

2. *Business Week,* July 3, 1978, p. 46.

3. *Business Week,* February 16, 1976, p. 58.

4. U.S. Bureau of the Census, *Statistical Abstract of the United States: 1980* (Government Printing Office, 1980), p. 566.

5. *Business Week,* February 16, 1976, p. 60.

6. *Business Week,* July 3, 1978, p. 52.

7. *The New York Times,* editorial, March 9, 1981.

8. *Statistical Abstract of the United States: 1980,* p. 907.

9. Patrick Wright, *On a Clear Day You Can See General Motors* (Wright Enterprises, 1979), p. 230. Mr. DeLorean's well-publicized troubles in 1982 in no way vitiate the significance of his account.

10. Heskia Heskiaoff, "Computers and Productivity in Production Operations and Administrative Functions in Manufacturing Industries in the United States" (Ph.D. dissertation, Columbia University, 1977).

11. Wright, op. cit., p. 217.

12. *The New York Times,* November 7, 1980; September 14, 1980.

13. *The New York Times,* September 12, 1980. The report discovered that "the large car's share of the market fell from 47.1 percent to 29.2 percent during the period (January–June 1980), while imports rose from 24.7 percent to 34.5 percent."

14. Wright, op. cit., p. 211.

15. At the end of 1980, all manufacturing corporations in the United States were utilizing capital from stock issues worth $176.2 billion and from bank loans of $55 billion. U.S. Federal Trade Commission, *Quarterly Financial Report for Manufacturing, Mining and Trade Corporations, First Quarter, 1981,* June 22, 1981, Table A-2, p. 20.

16. *The New York Times,* January 4, 1981.

17. *Business Week,* April 6, 1981, p. 42.

18. National Machine Tool Builders Association, *Economic Handbook of the Machine Tool Industry, 1980/81* (McLean, Va., 1980), p. 249.

19. *Time,* July 6, 1981, pp. 46–48.

20. Wright, op. cit., p. 12. The reader will find an especially informative discussion of the impact of cost-cutting on product quality in the chapter titled "Turning Chevrolet Around."

21. *Business Week,* February 16, 1976, p. 58.

22. See, for example, the *Wall Street Journal* series on plant maintenance problems, January 7–9, 1981.

23. *Statistical Abstract of the United States: 1980,* p. 622.

24. William V. Rapp, vice-president of the Morgan Guaranty Trust Company, *The New York Times,* February 8, 1981.

25. *The New York Times,* July 25, 1982. Steve Lohr, "Japan Reaps Benefit of Early Smart Shopping."

26. *Statistical Abstract of the United States: 1980,* p. 559.

27. *The New York Times,* January 4, 1981.

28. *The New York Times,* March 29, 1981. An untutored observer might, of course, ask: "Couldn't they just reduce prices?" But that sort of strategy hasn't been part of mainline management thinking for some time.

29. Wright, op. cit., p. 178.

30. Wright, op. cit., pp. 6, 7.

31. Irwin Ross, "How Lawless Are Big Companies?" *Fortune,* December 1, 1980.

32. In *The Gentlemen Conspirators* (Grove Press, 1962), John G. Fuller summarized the federal cases involving criminal and civil misconduct in which the principal firms of the U.S. electrical-machinery-producing industry were found guilty of various criminal and civil violations. The violations were, all of them, fast money-making schemes.

33. *The New York Times,* October, 19, 1980. See letter, "A Thriving American Forced-Labor Industry," *The New York Times,* February 12, 1982.

34. *The New York Times,* May 27, 1982. Lydia Chavez, "Toxic Waste Entrepreneur."

35. *The New York Times,* January 4, 1981.

36. *In These Times,* January 14–20, 1981, p. 2.

37. *The New York Times,* April 13, 1981.

38. *Business Week,* May 12, 1980, p. 47.

3

1. *Time,* May 4, 1981; U.S. Bureau of the Census, *Statistical Abstract of the United States, 1980* (Government Printing Office, 1980), p. 174.

2. *Time,* op. cit.

3. *The New York Times,* May 23, 1980.

4. Abbott, Langer and Associates, *Compensation of MBAs, 1976* (Park Forest, Ill., 1976).

5. Patrick Wright, *On a Clear Day You Can See General Motors* (Wright Enterprises, 1979), pp. 191 ff. Wright gives important detail on how the dominance of financially oriented managers affected the policies and style of operation of the General Motors Corporation.

6. *Business Week,* June 30, 1980. A special issue, "The Reindustrialization of America."

7. An extensive text and periodical literature is produced by and serves the business schools. A useful entry to this literature is provided by William H. Newman and James P. Logan, *Strategy, Policy and Central Management,* 8th ed. (South-Western Publishing Co., 1981). Note the Selected Bibliography, pp. 765 ff.

8. *The New York Times,* July 16, 1980.

9. Ibid.

10. *The New York Times,* July 27, 1980.

11. See the advertisement by *Fortune* that appeared in *The New York Times* of January 28, 1981.

12. U.S. Congress, House, Report of the Committee on Small Business, *Conglomerate Mergers—Their Effects on Small Business and Local Communities,* 96th Cong., 2d sess., 1980, p. 46.

13. *The New York Times,* February 19, 1981.

14. *Time,* May 4, 1981.

15. Summary data on multi-unit firms in U.S. manufacturing are found in *Statistical Abstract of the United States, 1980,* p. 807; see also *1967 Enterprise Statistics, Pt. I, General Report on Industrial Organization,* Series ES67-1, 1972, p. 326, and in the same title for 1977, Table 1.

16. *Time,* July 6, 1981, pp. 46ff., "A Shortage of Vital Skills."

17. *The New York Times Magazine,* January 4, 1981, p. 42. This was a comment about American management by the president of the Sony Corporation.

18. *Business Week,* May 11, 1981, p. 87.

19. *The New York Times,* August 2, 1953.

20. David Riesman, "The Dream of Abundance Reconsidered," lecture at the American Psychiatric Association Meetings, New Orleans, May 12, 1981.

21. This essay was published in the collection entitled *Mass Leisure,* The Free Press, 1958.

22. A fairly comprehensive review of these developments is found in the volume by Daniel Bell, *The Coming of Post-Industrial Society* (Basic Books, 1973), pp. 36, 37, 461, 462.

23. *Statistical Abstract of the United States, 1980,* p. 166.

24. *Forbes,* September 15, 1971, p. 58.

25. See the articles by Robert H. Hayes and William J. Abernathy, "Managing Our Way to Economic Decline," *Harvard Business Review,* July–August, 1980; also the shorter article by the same authors in *The New York Times,* August 20, 1980; see also Robert H. Hayes and Modesto A. Maidique, *The New York Times,* June 2, 1981. A wide-ranging evaluation of operations research/management science, as practiced in the United States, was produced by one of the American "founding fathers" of O.R. See Russell L. Ackoff, "The Future of Operational Research Is Past," and "Resurrecting the Future of Operational Research," *Journal of the Operational Research Society,* 1979, pp. 93–104, 189–199.

26. Chile Nakane, *Japanese Society* (University of California Press, 1970), ch. 1. See dispatch by Steve Lohr, "Japanese Earned Labor Harmony," *The New York Times,* February 13, 1982.

27. Letter to the Editor, *The New York Times,* April 5, 1981.

4

1. Seymour Melman, *Dynamic Factors in Industrial Productivity* (John Wiley, 1956), ch. 17.

2. Ali Dogramaci, "Methodological Considerations for Research on the Size of Administrative Overhead and Productivity," *Administrative Science Quarterly,* March 1977.

———, "Administrative Overhead and Industrial Performance Under State Managerialism" (Ph.D. dissertation, Columbia University, 1975). Nelson M. Fraiman, "Growth of Administrative Employment and Output in U.S. Steel Industry," *Journal of Economic Issues* 12, no. 2 (June 1977). Thomas O. Boucher, "Productivity and Industry Structure" (Ph.D. dissertation, Columbia University, 1978). Heskia Heskiaoff, "Computers and Productivity in Production Operations and Administrative Functions in Manufacturing Industries in the United States" (Ph.D. dissertation, Columbia University, 1977). Seymour Melman, *Decision Making and Productivity* (John Wiley, 1958).

———, "Managerial Versus Cooperative Decision Making in Israel," *Studies in Comparative International Development* 6, no. 3 (Rutgers University, New Brunswick, N.J.: distributed by Sage Publications. 1970).

3. See Lester Thurow, "Why Productivity Falls," *Newsweek,* August 24, 1981.

4. Seymour Melman, "The Rise of Administrative Overhead in the Manufacturing Industries of the United States, 1899–1947," *Oxford Economic Papers* (New Series), January 1951.

5. U.S. Bureau of the Census, *Statistical Abstract of the United States, 1980* (Government Printing Office, 1980), p. 811.

6. The 45 percent figure has particular interest insofar as the 50 percent tax rate under federal tax law starts for married couples at $60,000 net income per year, and for single persons at $31,500 per year. In other words, these nonsalary "perks" can substantially offset tax payment by the employees involved. *The New York Times,* August 27, 1980. See the article by Thomas C. Hayes on "perks" rising with inflation.

7. This is the text of the news report in *U.E. News,* March 23, 1981:

A $100,000 raise over 1979 brought the salary of General Electric chairman Reginald H. Jones to $1 million last year.

On top of this, Jones took $51,908 for expenses.

Now 63 years old, the company official is retiring on April 1 on an annual pension of about $400,000. If that isn't enough to show how magnanimous the giant corporation can be, Jones will receive, in addition to his pension, 1,094 shares of the company's stock each of the next 17 years plus $8,276 in cash.

The value of the stock based on the latest stock market price would be $73,708 a year.

Last year, Jones benefitted from stock options to the tune of over $150,000. Other options and benefits he holds have a potential value of over $803,631. . . .

See also the "Annual Survey of Executive Compensation," *Business Week,* May 10, 1982.

8. *Business Week,* May 10, 1982, pp. 76–102.

9. Mark Green, "Richer Than All Their Tribe," *The New Republic,* January 6, 1982.

10. Seymour Melman, "The Rise of Administrative Overhead in Manufacturing Industries of the United States, 1899–1947"; *Dynamic Factors in Industrial Productivity.*

11. Heskiaoff, *op. cit.,* ch. 4.

12. *The New York Times,* June 20, 1980 (see article, "Experts Find Abuse of Employee Rights"); August 7, 1980 (see article, "Lie-Detector Use on Jobs Growing").

13. *The New York Times,* April 1, 1981.

14. *The New York Times,* December 2, 1981.

15. Patrick Wright, *On a Clear Day You Can See General Motors* (Wright Enterprises, 1979), p. 160.

16. *Business Week,* September 14, 1981; July 6, 1981.

5

1. Special communication, Office of the Secretary of Defense, Comptroller, Directorate for Information, Operations and Reports.

2. U.S. Department of Defense, *Real and Personal Property,* September 30, 1980, Office of the Secretary of Defense, Directorate for Information, Operations and Reports.

3. U.S. Bureau of the Census, *Statistical Ab-*

stract of the United States, 1980 (Government Printing Office 1980), p. 570.

4. *Economic Report of the President, Transmitted to the Congress, January 1980*, p. 203.

5. *Statistical Abstract of the United States, 1980*, p. 474.

6. Such estimates are, of course, strongly affected by the methods of assigning money value, as well as the changing value of the money unit itself. If one calculates in "constant" (1972) dollars, the 1950 to 1980 estimate of national defense outlays comes to $2,074 billion. That can be compared with the estimated value for all business-owned equipment and structures in the United States by 1979, again in 1972 dollars, of $1,102 billion. See *Statistical Abstract of the United States, 1980*, pp. 366, 474.

7. Special communication, U.S. Department of Defense; *Defense Week*, June 14, 1982.

8. The 1946 Eisenhower memorandum was published as Appendix A to Seymour Melman, *Pentagon Capitalism* (McGraw-Hill, 1970).

9. Seymour Melman, *Our Depleted Society* (Holt, Rinehart & Winston, 1965).

10. President Eisenhower's Farewell to the Nation, U.S. Department of State, *Bulletin* 44 (February 6, 1961). The address was delivered on January 17, 1961.

11. The available U.S. data, in all the relevant categories, are to be found in the United Nations *Yearbook of National Accounts Statistics, 1979*, vol. 1, for 1960, 1963, 1965, and each year 1970–1978. The average value of the military/producers' fixed capital formation ratio for the United States for all those years is $52.40.

12. *National Science Foundation Highlights* (Washington, D.C., September 26, 1980). See also U.S. Office of Management Budget, *Special Analysis of the Budget of the U.S., 1980/1981*, Special Analysis K. From the details given here, I estimate that 63 percent of the R & D outlay by the Department of Energy is on behalf of military and closely related functions. That percentage was applied to the federal R & D budget funding as reported by the National Science Foundation. Separately, in a statistical tabulation titled *Federal R & D Obligations by Agency: FY 1978 and 1982*, the National Science Foundation reports R & D estimates by federal agency. From these 1982 estimates, using the same mode of estimation as for 1981, the military-related component of federal R & D was 72 percent in 1982.

13. *The New York Times*, June 26, 1981.

14. National Science Foundation, *Reviews of Data on Science Resources* (Washington, D.C., May 1976), p. 14.

15. The military-serving industries are identified here as: ordnance and missiles, chemicals and related products, electrical machinery and equipment, transportation equipment, and instruments and related products. These data were compiled by Michael Boretsky, *U.S. Technology: Trends and Policy Issues*, U.S. Department of Commerce (Washington, D.C., October 1973). See especially Table 3 and related footnotes.

16. *The New York Times*, December 23, 1980.

17. I have defined the theory and mode of operation of the cost-maximizing military economy in previous books: *Pentagon Capitalism* (McGraw-Hill, 1970), and *The Permanent War Economy* (Simon & Schuster, 1974). The present analysis and data supplement and update these earlier materials.

18. See the article on the Op-Ed page of *The New York Times*, May 14, 1981, by James Cramer, a staff reporter for *The American Lawyer*. He notes that "the firms are often staffed with attorneys who commanded or served in the legal divisions of the armed forces and who are well versed in the government's strategies for defending claims. The firms create claims that can't be settled quickly, developing endless points of contention, obscuring the merits of the case. The settlement that comes out of such a process is more of a horse trade than an intelligent estimate of the project's actual cost. To be sure, the government does authorize design changes that can raise the price of a weapons system but nowhere near the settlements that some attorneys have achieved. . . . In 1978, for example, the government paid more than $1.1 billion in overruns for ships with three major contractors, even though Navy analysts agreed that less than half that cost was justified. The Navy paid the rest, fearing the cost of never-ending litigation over $2.7 billion in claims that eight law firms submitted for those contracts. The claims, some running 60 volumes in length, simply defied a realistic challenge on the merits."

19. *Defense Week*, October 27, 1980.

20. *The New York Times*, November 21, 1980.

21. Special communication, Office of the Under Secretary of Defense for Research and Engineering. See also U.S. Department of Commerce, *Defense Materials System and Defense Priorities System,* December 1976.

22. See the report by Gordon Adams, *The Iron Triangle: The Politics of Defense Contracting* (New York: Council on Economic Priorities, 1981).

23. *The New York Times,* July 1, 1981.

24. *The New York Times,* April 16, 1981.

25. See the discussions and detail on this point in Melman, *The Permanent War Economy,* pp. 32, 33, 180–182.

26. James M. Suarez, "Profits and Performance of Aerospace Defense Contractors," *Journal of Economic Issues,* June 1976.

27. *Statistical Abstract of the United States, 1980* (Government Printing Office, 1980), p. 265; *The New York Times,* January 18, 1981, Op-Ed article by Herbert Kriedman, "Off Whose Back?"

28. *The New York Times,* March 25, 1981, article by Ann Crittenden, "Growers' Power in Marketing Under Attack."

29. *The New York Times,* March 30, 1981.

30. June 7, 1981, news broadcast on the Public Broadcasting System.

31. Seymour Melman, "The Federal Connection," *The New York Times,* November 2, 1975; for first sources of these data, see James R. Anderson, "The Balance of Military Payments among States and Regions," in Seymour Melman, ed., *The War Economy of the U.S.* (St. Martin's Press, 1971).

32. Northeast-Midwest Institute, *The Federal Balance of Payments, Regional Implications of Government Spending* (3588 House Annex No. 2, Washington, D.C. 20515; August 1980).

33. Disregarding the role of the federal government's managerial control over its military economy and the effect of its investment decisions, a report on "a national agenda for the '80s" found that the decay of cities in the "old industrial heartland" was part of a historically inexorable process, "the emergence of post-industrial urban America." In this case, the use of post-industrial ideology to rationalize the policies of the state management is the more galling because the recommendations of that report on urban policy came from a subcommittee headed by Charles E. Bishop, "an economist who is president of the University of Houston, which is in the heart of the so-called Sunbelt." *The New York Times,* December 27, 1980.

34. U.S. General Accounting Office, *Federal Paperwork: Its Impact on American Businesses* (Washington, D.C., November 17, 1978).

35. *U. S. News and World Report,* December 29, 1980.

36. *The New York Times,* January 18, 1981.

37. *The New York Times,* April 10, 1981.

38. Boston *Globe,* June 26, 1981.

39. The following papers by Franklyn D. Holzman contain crucial data and analysis on this subject: "Are the Soviets Really Outspending the U.S. on Defense?" *International Security,* Spring 1980; "Soviet Military Spending: Assessing the Numbers Game," *International Security,* Spring 1982; "Is There a Soviet-U.S. Military Spending Gap?" *Challenge,* September–October 1980.

40. See the discussion "Limits of Military Power," in ch. 6 of Melman, *The Permanent War Economy.*

41. The following are some of the findings that trace the erosion of the idea that wars can be "won" by "superior" armed forces. In 1975, the U.S. National Academy of Science produced a report, "The Long-Term Worldwide Effects of Multiple Detonations of Nuclear Weapons," that held out the prospect of a worldwide holocaust from a general nuclear war owing to depletion of stratospheric ozone and the ensuing intense ultraviolet irradiation of the earth. See Philip Handler, "No Escape," *The New York Times,* November 26, 1975.

By May 1981, the U.S. scientific community had become aware that, by triggering the electromagnetic pulse (emp) phenomenon, a single nuclear blast high above the United States could shut down the national power grid and knock out communications, including military communications, from coast to coast. See *Science,* May 29, 1981, and articles in the following issues. Data are also accumulating on the characteristics and number of accidents involving nuclear weapons in the hands of U.S. Armed Forces. See *The New York Times,* May 26, 1981; also, Lloyd J. Dumas, "National Insecurity in the Nuclear Age," *Bulletin of Atomic Scientists,* May 1976.

As nuclear weapons continue to be made and positioned or stockpiled, the control of material suitable for making nuclear bombs becomes a more urgent problem. Reports have been published to the effect that "thousands of pounds" of such material, thought to be in U.S. processing plants, are in fact unaccounted for (*The New York Times,* December 29, 1974). One of the rarely discussed problems is that of disposing of military nuclear waste materials, which in 1981 amounted to 10,196,000 cu. ft., or 98.8 percent of the high-level radioactive wastes from U.S. nuclear facilities of all kinds (*The Defense Monitor* 10, no. 1, 1981).

Also growing is the assertion that in a nuclear war "victory is possible." That is the title of an article by Colin S. Gray and Keith Payne, in *Foreign Policy,* No. 39, Summer 1980. The authors, on the staff of the Hudson Institute, a think tank, write that:

Strategists cannot offer painless conflicts or guarantee that their preferred posture and doctrine promise a greatly superior deterrence posture to current American schemes. But they can claim that an intelligent U.S. offensive strategy, wedded to homeland defenses, should reduce U.S. casualties to approximately 20,000,000, which should render U.S. strategic threats more credible.

The production and dissemination of a literature of this quality implies that with a sufficient show of force it should be possible, psychologically, to compel the Soviets to back away from whatever threat they may be rash enough to propose. If such a threat were to be offered, U.S. military planners dream of replaying the Cuban missile crisis. For an unconventional but relevant diagnosis of that crisis and its later significance, see Melman, *Pentagon Capitalism,* pp. 133 ff. (The Soviet attempt in 1962 to emplace short- and intermediate-range missiles in Cuba can be accounted for as an emergency military effort to restore a nuclear deterrence capability that had been seriously eroded by a combination of U.S. weapons buildups, plus U.S. intelligence coups that gave the U.S. command exact knowledge of the location, technical characteristics and plans for use of Soviet ICBMs.)

New Pentagon technology that heightens the risk of major military accidents includes a return to production of nerve gas (*Defense Week,* January 26, 1981) and plans for wars in outer space. See a summary article by John Markoff in *In These Times,* May 7, 1980. A reading of U.S. Army Field Manual 100-5,

Operations, 1976, discloses that basic U.S. military doctrine no longer takes care to separate conventional from nuclear military operations. U.S. strategy and tactics are described as "conventional-nuclear," and the Field Manual indicates that the U.S. Army's weaponry and tactical preparations are all in that category.

42. *Statistical Abstract of the United States, 1980,* p. 370; *The New York Times,* editorial, May 8, 1982.

43. *The New York Times,* June 20, 1976, John W. Finney, "Selling Arms Is a Pentagon Mission."

44. *The New York Times,* March 11, 1981, Washington dispatch, "U.S. Plans Military Loans for 16 Nations." The following are countries scheduled to receive increases under this program: Oman, Yemen, Tunisia, Turkey, Kenya, Sudan, Egypt, Morocco and other Persian Gulf and Southwest Asian nations; also, El Salvador, Thailand, and Israel.

6

1. See report on machine tools and woodworking machinery in U.S. Bureau of the Census, *Report on Power and Machinery Employed in Manufactures* (Government Printing Office, 1888).

2. David Noble, *Forces of Production* (Alfred A. Knopf, in press).

3. Frederick W. Taylor, *Shop Management* (Harper & Bros., 1911), pp. 98, 99.

4. National Machine Tool Builders Association, *Economic Handbook of the Machine Tool Industry, 1980/81* (McLean, Va., 1980), p. 250.

5. Benjamin Coriot, "The Restructuring of the Assembly Line: A New Economy of Time and Control," *Capital and Class* 11 (Summer, 1980), London, translated from *Sociologie du Travail,* no. 1 (January–March 1979), Seuil Editions, Paris. The bibliography attached to this article introduces the reader to a wider literature.

6. From an unpublished study (1980) by David Noble (Massachusetts Institute of Technology), *Pilot Program,* a recent six-year "job enrichment" program initiated by the management of the General Electric Co. at Lynn, Mass.

7. *The New York Times,* March 8, 1981.

8. The National Research Council, *Energy Choices in a Democratic Society,* Supporting

Paper 7 (Washington, D.C.: National Academy of Sciences, 1980), p. 34.

9. U.S. Bureau of the Census, *Statistical Abstract of the United States, 1980* (Government Printing Office, 1980), pp. 916, 917.

10. Lee Schipper and Allan J. Lichtenberg, "Efficient Energy Use and Well-Being: The Swedish Example," *Science,* December 3, 1976; also *Science,* May 20, 1977, p. 856.

11. *Statistical Abstract of the United States, 1980,* p. 605.

12. *The New York Times,* December 28, 1980. See article by Michael D. Hinds, "Despite a Trend Toward Conservation, New Homes Are Called Energy Sieves," *The New York Times,* May 17, 1981.

13. *Science,* December 3, 1976, p. 1003. When diverse fuels are converted to kwh-equivalent units, then: for the U.S. (1972), average kwh/passenger-mile: auto—1.41; bus—0.4; air—3.0; rail—under 30 miles, 0.21, over 30 miles, 0.87. John E. Ullmann, "The Interstate and Defense Electric Railroad," *Trains,* April 1980, p. 66: "A ton-mile of truck freight uses about 0.88 kwh compared with 0.19 kwh for a ton-mile of rail freight. . . ."

14. Larry Sawers, "American Ground Transportation Reconsidered," *Review of Radical Political Economy,* Fall 1979.

15. Pat Choate and Susan Walter, *America in Ruins* (The Council of State Planning Agencies, Washington, D.C., 1981), p. 1.

16. See the description of the British Railways advanced passenger train (APT) in *Technology Review,* October 1980.

17. *The New York Times,* September 15, 1981.

18. Charles Gray, Jr. and Frank Von Hippel, "The Fuel Economy of Light Vehicles," *Scientific American,* May 1981. See also Bob Shamansky, "To Join the Car Race," *The New York Times,* February 1, 1982.

19. *Mechanical Engineering,* December 1980, p. 59. It is worth noting that small size has been associated with less safety and higher fatality rates. But this is also owing to less priority attention to safety features as part of automobile design.

20. *Mechanical Engineering,* August 1980, pp. 43, 44.

21. "The Electric Car: Will There Be One in Your Garage?" *Harper's,* May 1979.

22. See, for example, the following papers by Victor Wouk. "Electric Cars: The Battery Problem," *Bulletin of the Atomic Scientists,* April 1971; *An Experimental ICE/Battery-Electric Hybrid with Low Emissions and Low Fuel Consumption Capability,* Society of Automotive Engineers, Warrendale, Pa., February 23, 1976, Technical Paper 760123.

23. Victor Wouk, "Another Way of Powering Vehicles," *The New York Times,* July 12, 1979; see also Hans G. Mueller and Victor Wouk, *Biberronnage Makes an Electric Car Practical with Existing Batteries,* Society of Automotive Engineers, Warrendale, Pa., February 25, 1980, Technical Paper 800204.

24. Hans G. Mueller and Victor Wouk, *Efficiency of Coal Use, Electricity for EVs versus Syn Fuels ICEs,* Technical Paper 800109, Society of Automotive Engineers, Warrendale, Pa., February 25, 1980.

25. The National Research Council, *Energy Choices in a Democratic Society,* Supporting Paper 7 (Washington, D.C.: National Academy of Sciences, 1980), p. 52.

26. U.S. Department of State, *Bulletin* 44 (February 6, 1961).

27. See, for example, the table on energy conservation policies and their impact on pp. 86 and 87 of the report—the National Research Council, *Energy Choices in a Democratic Society.*

28. U.S. Congress, Joint Economic Committee, *Pursuing Energy Supply Options: Cost Effective R & D Strategies* (Washington, D.C., April 27, 1981).

29. Joint Economic Committee, op. cit., p. 180.

30. Joint Economic Committee, op. cit., p. 138. It is of interest that the Sanyo Company of Japan has reportedly announced that it expects to reach the U.S. 1986 cost goals by 1983 or, at latest, 1984. See the advertisement in *The New York Times,* July 28, 1981, Op-Ed page, entitled "Made in Japan—Again?" The advertiser was Rodale Press of Emmaus, Pa.

31. Joint Economic Committee, op. cit., pp. 148 ff.

32. Joint Economic Committee, op. cit., pp. 195 ff.

33. Joint Economic Committee, op. cit., pp. 200 ff.; U.S. General Accounting Office, *Potential of Ethanol as a Motor Vehicle Fuel* (Washington, D.C., 1980).

34. Joint Economic Committee, op. cit., pp. 294 ff.

35. Joint Economic Committee, op. cit., pp. 316, 320.

36. *The New York Times,* August 14, 1980.

37. *The New York Times,* August 24, 1980.

38. *The New York Times,* February 15, 1981.

39. *The Wall Street Journal,* April 7, 1981. A rounded, authoritative comparative analysis of wind power is found in David R. Inglis, *Windpower and Other Energy Options* (University of Michigan Press, 1978); Joel Fagenbaum, "Harnessing Wind Power," *Mechanical Engineering,* April 1982.

40. *The New York Times,* August 5, 1980.

41. *The New York Times,* April 13, 1979.

42. This analysis of auto industry technology is based upon Seymour Melman, "The Impact of Economics on Technology," *Journal of Economic Issues,* March 1975.

43. Emma Rothschild, *Paradise Lost: The Decline of the Auto-Industrial Age* (Random House, 1973); *Statistical Abstract of the United States, 1980,* pp. 486–487.

44. *Statistical Abstract of the United States, 1980,* pp. 648, 653, 654, 487, 641, 646.

45. *Business Week,* September 15, 1973.

46. *The New York Times,* July 3, 1974.

47. Seymour Melman, *Dynamic Factors in Industrial Productivity* (John Wiley, 1956).

48. Ibid.

49. Ibid.

50. Boston *Globe,* July 16, 1972.

51. Martin Douglas, "G.M. Versus Its Workers," *The New York Times,* February 15, 1982.

52. Letter to *The New York Times* from Ross Stagner, "former president of the American Psychological Association's Division of Industrial Psychology," March 11, 1982.

53. Rudy L. Ruggles, Jr. and Vijay Kumar, "The Dark Side of Ford's Contract," *The New York Times,* March 1, 1982.

54. *Work in America: Report of a Special Task Force to the Secretary of Health, Education, and Welfare* (MIT Press, 1973).

55. Seymour Melman, *Decision-Making and Productivity* (John Wiley, 1958).

56. Seymour Melman, "Managerial Versus Cooperative Decision-Making in Israel," *Studies in Comparative International Development* 6, 1970–1971, no. 3 (Rutgers University Press, 1971).

57. For numerous illustrations of the variability of design according to the criteria used, see Victor Papanek, *Design for the Real World* (Pantheon Books, 1971). See the following Ph.D. dissertations which illustrate the detailed role of economic factors as determinants of design: John E. Ullmann, "Criteria of Change in Machinery Design" (Columbia University, 1959); and George E. Watkins, "Cost Determinants of Process Plant Design—Central Station Boilers" (Columbia University, 1957).

7

1. The field of engineering economy probably had its genesis in the famous lecture of Henry R. Towne, "The Engineer as an Economist," *Proceedings of the American Society of Mechanical Engineers,* May 1886.

2. Harold B. Maynard, *Industrial Engineering Handbook,* 3d ed. (McGraw-Hill, 1971), parts 2–5. See also the critical literature: Adam Abruzzi, *Work Measurement* (Columbia University Press, 1952); William Gomberg, *A Trade Union Analysis of Time Study* (Science Research Associates, 1948).

3. Harold B. Maynard, op. cit., p. 7.

4. Robert A. Karasek, "Job Demands, Job Decision Latitude, and Mental Strain: Implications for Job Redesign," *Administrative Science Quarterly,* June 1979; "Job Socialization and Job Strain: The Implications of Two Related Psychosocial Mechanisms for Job Design," in Bertil Gardell and Gunn Johansson, eds., *Working Life* (John Wiley, 1981).

5. Robert A. Karasek, "Job Decision Latitude, Job Design, and Coronary Heart Disease," in Gavriel Salvendy and Michael Smith, eds., *Machine Pacing and Occupational Stress* (International Conference; Purdue University Press, 1981).

6. Seymour Melman, *Dynamic Factors in Industrial Productivity* (John Wiley, 1956), p. 152.

7. Seymour Melman, *The Permanent War Economy* (Simon & Schuster, 1974), Appendix A. This is a list of machinery products whose prices had been increasing as fast as or faster than the wages of industrial workers.

8. Byung Hong, *Inflation Under Cost Pass-Along Management* (Praeger, 1979). Independent, qualitative confirmation of the cost pass-along mechanism and its extent comes from diverse data: from managers in various firms; from accountants with wide industrial experience; from journalists who have inquired into the recent mode of operation of managers in various industries. See, for example, *The*

New York Times, June 6, 1978, dispatch titled "Some Businesses Are Hurt by Inflation, Others Benefit."

9. For a general analysis of this pattern, see Melman, *The Permanent War Economy,* ch. 2. For independent collections of data that illustrate the operation of the cost-maximizing system, see John R. Fox, *Arming America* (Graduate School of Business Administration, Harvard University, 1974); Jacques S. Gansler, *The Defense Economy* (MIT Press, 1980). These two books have special importance, as their authors are experienced administrators within military industry firms and in the Department of Defense. See also the review of John R. Fox, *Arming America,* in Appendix III.

10. Ibrahim Ihtiyaroglu, "Health Care Under Cost Maximization" (Ph.D. dissertation, Columbia University, 1979). Government subsidies for many American hospitals—or insurance payments whose cost standards are regulated by government agencies—have encouraged patterns of internal operations that closely resemble the cost-maximizing practices found in military-serving firms.

11. Kirsten Nygaard, *Data Processing, Planning and Control: Basic Reader for the Trade Unions,* Research Report No. 1 of the Iron and Metal Project, Norwegian National Union of Iron and Metalworkers, Oslo, 1972.

—— and Olav T. Bergo, "The Trade Unions, New Users of Research," *Personnel Review* 4, no. 2 (1975).

——, "Trade Union Participation," lecture at N. Staffordshire Polytechnic, July 1977.

——, "The Role of Information Systems, A Citizen's View," lecture at N. Staffordshire Polytechnic, July 1977.

——, "Participatory Democracy Development," lecture at Third AOPAA Symposium (Tunis), Norwegian Computing Center, January 1978.

—— and J. Fjalestad, "Group Interests and Participation in Information System Development," Special Seminar on Microelectronics, Productivity and Employment, OECD, Paris, Norwegian Computing Center, 1979.

12. For early formulations of these ideas, see: Sebastian Littauer, "Stability of Production Rates as a Determinant of Industrial Productivity Levels," American Statistical Association, *Proceedings of the Business and Economics Statistics Section,* Montreal, September 10–13, 1954; Seymour Melman, *Decision-Making and Productivity* (John Wiley, 1958), ch. 13.

13. Melman, *Decision-Making and Productivity.*

14. This formulation is mainly the work of Harley Shaiken, Research Fellow at MIT, and evolved at a meeting on new technology sponsored by the International Association of the Machinists in New York City on April 30 and May 1, 1981.

8

1. U.S. Bureau of the Census, *Statistical Abstract of the United States, 1980* (Government Printing Office, 1980), p. 907.

2. *Business Week,* July 24, 1978.

3. Ibid.

4. U.S. General Accounting Office, *Correct Balance of Defense's Foreign Military Sales Trust Fund Unknown* (Washington, D.C., June 30, 1980).

5. Ibid. Digest of the report.

6. *Defense Week,* August 3, 1981; *The New York Times,* November 2, 1981.

7. U.S. General Accounting Office, *FA-18 Naval Strike Fighter: Its Effectiveness Is Uncertain* (Washington, D.C., February 14, 1980). From this report, one learns that the plane weighed 22,100 pounds. From other data on the budget of the Department of Defense, appropriations per F-18 plane have been running at $42.8 million per plane, hence $1,936 per pound of airplane.

8. Remarks by Representative Les Aspin, *Congressional Record,* September 9, 1981.

9. Special communication, U.S. Department of Defense; *Defense Week,* June 14, 1982.

10. *Statistical Abstract of the United States, 1980,* p. 474.

11. These data are from Seymour Melman, "Looting the Means of Production," *The New York Times,* July 26, 1981.

12. *Statistical Abstract of the United States, 1980,* p. 281. In 1980, 3.1 million civilians were working for the government, of whom 666,000 were in the postal service. Of the remaining 2.4 million, the federal judiciary employed 14,700, and the Congress and its staffs 20,200.

13. *The Budget of the U.S. Government, Fiscal Year 1980* (Washington, D.C., 1979). Apart from the funds to the Department of Defense, the U.S. national military outlays include mili-

tary assistance, atomic energy (weapons), space research and technology, interest on the national debt in payment for past wars and military programs, veterans' benefits, and an assortment of lesser activities that are related to military operations.

14. *Statistical Abstract of the United States, 1980,* p. 375; the number in military-serving firms is: 1980—2,022,000; 1981—2,230,000; 1982 —2,515,000. U.S. Department of Defense, *National Defense Budget Estimates for FY 1983* (March 1982), p. 83.

15. *Statistical Abstract of the United States, 1980,* p. 908.

16. Data are from various tables in United Nations, *Yearbook of National Accounts Statistics, 1979,* 1980.

17. Richard J. Power, "Innovations in Capital Investment for Productivity Enhancement." Paper presented at Spring 1981 Meeting of American Institute of Industrial Engineers. Mr. Power is a "productivity principal" in the U.S. Department of Defense.

18. U.S. Army, *Partners in Preparedness,* Information Booklet, 1981.

19. Tom Riddell, "The $676 Billion Quagmire," *The Progressive,* October 1973.

20. Special communication, Office of the Under Secretary of Defense for Research and Engineering, May 21, 1981.

21. See the full text of the 1946 Eisenhower memorandum in Seymour Melman, *Pentagon Capitalism* (McGraw-Hill, 1970), Appendix A.

22. William Greider, in the Washington *Post,* February 4, 1979.

23. U.S. National Science Foundation, *National Patterns of Science and Technology Resources, 1980,* NSF-80-308 (Washington, D.C., 1980), p. 34.

24. Ibid.

25. Testimony by Dr. Arden L. Bement, Jr., Deputy Under Secretary of Defense for Research and Advanced Technology, before the Research and Development Subcommittee of the Committee on Armed Services of the U.S. Senate, 96th Cong., 2d Sess., 1980.

26. U.S. Bureau of the Census, *Census of Manufacturers, 1977,* vol. 1, 1980, ch. 2; U.S. Bureau of the Census, *Current Industrial Reports, Shipments of Defense-oriented Industries, 1977,* Census Publication MA-175 (77)-1 (1979).

27. Washington *Post,* February 4, 1979.

28. *Defense Week,* February 23, 1981, pp. 4, 8.

29. *Business Week,* January 10, 1977.

30. *The New York Times,* August 30, 1981.

31. U.S. Department of Defense, Security Assistance Agency, *Foreign Military Sales and Military Assistance Facts,* December, 1980, p. 2.

9

1. An important contribution to its wide use was the publication by *Business Week* of a special issue (June 30, 1980) on "reindustrialization" in the United States. One of its central themes was the comparative decline in the rate of increase of output per person in almost every aspect of the U.S. economy.

2. Seymour Melman, *Dynamic Factors in Industrial Productivity* (John Wiley, 1956), p. 208. It should be noted that these productivity estimates are based on output per *production worker* man-hour. Beginning in the 1970s, the U.S. Bureau of Labor Statistics shifted to presenting productivity data as output per *employee.* This latter method has the effect of including administrative, technical, and clerical employees in the index. This produces a necessarily different effect in the computation of productivity, since over long periods of time the administrative, technical, and clerical employees have grown much more rapidly in manufacturing than the number of production workers. For discussion of the implications of this point, see ch. 4, above.

3. László Rostas, *Comparative Productivity in British and American Industry* (Cambridge University Press, 1948). This monograph was a key document in the post–World War II discussion of industrial policy in Britain.

4. U.S. Bureau of Labor Statistics, *Productivity and the Economy,* Bulletin 1710, 1971, p. 30; 1970–1975 data by special communication from the Bureau of Labor Statistics; 1975–1980 data from *Monthly Labor Review* (September 1981), p. 91.

5. Tabulation prepared by Lester Thurow, in "The Productivity Problem," *Technology Review,* November–December 1980. U.S. Department of Commerce, "National Income and Product Accounts of the United States," *Survey of Current Business,* July issues of various years.

6. U.S. Bureau of Labor Statistics, *International Comparisons of Manufacturing Productivity and Labor Costs, Preliminary Measures for 1979,* USDL 80-322 (May 22, 1980), Table 2.

7. *The New York Times,* April 5, 1981.

8. U.S. Congress, House, Subcommittee on Trade of the Committee on Ways and Means, *United States–Japan Trade Report,* September 5, 1980, p. 5.

9. Hrothgar J. Habakkuk, *American and British Technology in the Nineteenth Century* (Cambridge University Press, 1962), p. 4.

10. Ibid., pp. 105–106.

11. Ibid., p. 168.

12. Melman, *Dynamic Factors in Industrial Productivity,* p. 152.

13. U.S. National Science Board, *Science Indicators, 1978* (Washington, D.C., 1979), Table 1-3.

14. U.S. National Science Board, op. cit., Table 1-1.

15. Igor Radovic, "Instability as a Restraint on Industrial Productivity, with Particular Reference to the Machine Tool Industry" (Ph.D. dissertation, Columbia University, 1964).

16. Thomas Boucher, *Capital Investment and Productivity in Manufacturing* (School of Operations Research and Industrial Engineering, Cornell University, 1980), pp. 16–21. See also relevant sources in Prologue, above.

17. U.S. Bureau of Labor Statistics, Bulletin 1865 (1966); *Monthly Labor Review,* January–June 1978.

18. *The Wall Street Journal,* April 8, 1981.

19. Lester Thurow, "The Productivity Problem," *Technology Review,* November–December, 1980.

20. Boucher, op. cit., p. 31.

21. The data of this development are analyzed by Boucher, op. cit.

22. Boucher, op. cit., p. 31.

23. Byung Hong, *Inflation Under Cost-Pass-Along Management* (Praeger, 1979).

24. *The New York Times,* January 4, 1981.

25. National Machine Tool Builders Association, *Economic Handbook of the Machine Tool Industry, 1980/81* (McLean, Va., 1980), p. 249.

26. See the report on the age of plant data gathered by the Economics Department of McGraw-Hill, which show that by 1980 37 percent of U.S. private industry's plant and equipment was more than ten years old—an increase from 31 percent in 1978 (*Business Week,* December 29, 1980). It also appears that such estimates of the age of U.S. industrial plant and equipment understate the condition, since the work week for plant and equipment has been lengthened during the last decades. The more intensive use of industrial equipment therefore implies intensified "using up" of the means of production.

27. U.S. Bureau of Labor Statistics (unpublished data), *Estimated Hourly Compensation of Production Workers in Manufacturing, Ten Countries, 1960, 1965, 1970–79* (Washington, D.C., February 1980).

28. Ibid.

29. UPI, the Boston *Globe,* July 12, 1976.

30. Machinery and Allied Products Institute, *Capital Goods Review,* no. 102 (Washington, D.C., February 1976). The average ratio of fixed investment to gross domestic product in manufacturing, 1960–1973, was 11.1 for the U.S., 17.1 for Belgium, the same for Sweden, 19.0 for the Netherlands, and 24.4 for Japan.

31. *American Machinist,* February 1981, p. 100. The percentage of new machinery spending for automation equipment was 40.6 in 1978 in U.S. manufacturing industry but 27.7 in 1980. To the editors of *American Machinist,* "the most surprising set of percentages are for the auto industry, showing a decline of more than 40 percent (from 26.6 percent in 1978 to 15.6 percent in 1980)." This may not be really surprising, in view of the emphasis given by the big three U.S. auto companies on new investments outside the United States, and plans for increased reliance for parts production on factories in Western Europe, Latin America and Asia.

32. "Fixed Investment, Productivity and Economic Performance—Inter-Industry Comparisons," *Capital Goods Review* (Washington, D.C.: Machinery & Allied Products Institute, April 1982); also, in the February 1976 issue, "Fixed Investment and Productivity Growth in Major Industrial Countries, 1960–1973."

33. The original data on scientists and engineers per 10,000 in the labor force, 1965–1977, come from National Science Board, *Science Indicators 1978* (Washington, D.C., 1979), Table 1-3. But these data for the United States include all scientists and engineers—those serving civilian as well as military industry. I have adjusted the original data for the U.S. by removing one-third of the original U.S. count, on the assumption that that is a reasonable estimate of the proportion of U.S. scientists and engineers serving the military establishment.

34. *Science Indicators 1978,* p. 144.

35. Ibid., p. 149.

36. Ibid., pp. 146–147.

37. *The New York Times,* January 4, 1981.

38. Lloyd J. Dumas, "Payment Functions and the Productive Efficiency of Military Industrial Firms," *Journal of Economic Issues,* June 1976; also, by the same author, "Parametric Costing and Institutionalized Inefficiency," *Proceedings, American Institute of Industrial Engineers,* Spring 1978.

39. Joe G. Baker, *An Examination of Employment in the Atomic Energy Field* (Oak Ridge: Manpower Research Programs, Oak Ridge Associated Universities, February 1978), p. 46.

40. *Business Week,* July 28, 1980.

41. William N. Leonard, "Research and Development in Industrial Growth," *The Journal of Political Economy,* March/April 1971.

42. U.S. Department of Commerce, Michael Boretsky, *U.S. Technology: Trends and Policy Issues* (October 1973), Table 3.

43. Michael Boretsky, "Trends in U.S. Technology: A Political Economist's View," *American Scientist,* January 1975.

44. Granville W. Hough, *Technology Diffusion* (Lomond Systems, Inc., Mt. Airy, Md., 1975), p. 47. Cited in Bernard Roth, "The Impact of the Arms Race on the Creation and Utilization of Knowledge," paper presented at the Symposium on the Optimum Utilization of Knowledge, Amherst, Mass., November 5–8, 1981.

45. Pat Choate and Susan Walter, *America in Ruins, Beyond the Public Works Pork Barrel* (Washington, D.C.: Council of State Planning Agencies, 1981), p. 1.

46. For an informative discussion on the contrast between the details of U.S. (Pentagon) and Japanese (Miti) styles of encouraging high technology, see: Robert B. Reich, "High-Tech Rivalry," *The New York Times,* November 20, 1981.

10

1. Unpublished data made available by U.S. Department of Labor, Bureau of Labor Statistics.

2. A study on the competitive status of the U.S. auto industry (the influence of technology in determining international industrial competitive advantage) by the U.S. Academy of Engineering has yet to be released at this writing; a report by Jim Harbour, "Comparison and Analysis of Productivity in the U.S. and Japanese Automotive Industry" (October 1980), was commissioned by the U.S. Department of Transportation; the International Metalworkers Federation (Geneva, Switzerland) has prepared estimates of U.S. and Japanese auto productivity and costs, and so has the research staff of the International Union, United Automobile, Aerospace and Agricultural Implement Workers of America, in Detroit. See also William J. Abernathy, Kim B. Clark, and Allan M. Kantrow, "The New Industrial Competition," *Harvard Business Review,* September–October 1981. These studies are not based upon direct examination of the internal costs of, e.g., Ford, Toyota. There are therefore no accounting data on labor, materials, etc. costs per vehicle, and the relation of unit costs to capacity utilization.

3. National Machine Tool Builders Association, *Economic Handbook of the Machine Tool Industry, 1980/81,* p. 250.

4. Michael Boretsky, *U.S. Technology: Trends and Policy Issues* U.S. Department of Commerce, October 1973, Table 21.

5. Sebastian B. Littauer, "Stability of Production Rates as a Determinant of Industrial Productivity Levels," *Proceedings of the Business and Economics Statistics Section,* American Statistical Association, September 10–13, 1954.

6. Seymour Melman, *Decision-Making and Productivity* (John Wiley, 1958).

7. *Decision-Making and Productivity,* p. 114.

8. Ibid., ch. 10. The management policies of Standard changed with mergers into Leyland and British Motors, and the sale of the tractor factory to Massey-Ferguson.

9. Y. Sugimori, K. Kusunoki, F. Cho, and S. Uchikawa, "Toyota Production System and Kanban System; Materialization of Just-in-Time and Respect-for-Human System," *International Journal of Production Research* 15, no. 6 (1977), pp. 553–564.

10. William J. Harahan, Director of Technical Planning for Manufacturing Staff, Ford Motor Company, quoted in *Business Week,* September 14, 1981, p. 97.

11. U.S. Congress, Office of Technology Assessment, *Technology and Steel Industry Competitiveness* (Washington, D.C., 1980), p. 81. In this discussion on the steel industry, I have drawn extensively on data published in this authoritative study.

12. Ibid., p. 82.

13. Ibid., p. 140.

14. Ibid.

15. Ibid., p. 130.

16. Ibid., p. 59.

17. U.S. Steel advertisement in the Washington *Post,* August 25, 1981.

18. Office of Technology Assessment, op. cit., p. 285.

19. Ibid., p. 86. "European Community" includes West Germany (38 percent), France (27 percent), Italy (41 percent), and United Kingdom (15 percent) (p. 289) and other countries.

20. *Business Week,* April 27, 1981, p. 124.

21. Ibid.

22. Office of Technology Assessment, op. cit., p. 95.

23. Ibid., p. 140.

24. Ibid.

25. Ibid.

26. Nelson Fraiman, "Growth of Administrative Employment and Output in the U.S. Steel Industry," *Journal of Economic Issues,* June 1977.

27. Office of Technology Assessment, op. cit., p. 364.

28. Ibid., p. 367.

29. Joseph C. Wyman, *The Steel Industry: Quarterly Commentary* (Shearson, Loeb Rhoades Inc., December 31, 1980). In this bulletin, Mr. Wyman observed: "We think steel industry management has not been specifically different from American managements generally; it just seems that way because the results of the industry have been so poor.... American management tilted toward instant profitability; in the process, it depleted its technical store of value, in effect living off and spending its technical inheritance."

30. Office of Technology Assessment, op. cit., p. 5.

31. Ibid., p. 125.

32. Ibid., p. 126.

33. Ibid., p. 127.

34. *The New York Times,* March 20, 1981.

35. Office of Technology Assessment, op. cit., p. 273. The character of the steel industry's R & D also reflects their approach to pollution abatement. The Office of Technology Assessment reports that "... From 1973 to 1977, the industry reported spending on the average only 5 per cent, or $25 million, of its pollution abatement funds on CIP (Change in Process) equip-ment. . . . CIP equipment leads to more cost-effective environmental control because more efficient use is made of raw materials and waste products, but often it calls for more technologically complex changes. Furthermore, CIP equipment is most efficiently installed at the time of plant construction. But the slow pace of steel industry modernization and expansion has been a major constraint on the pursuit of this more cost-effective abatement approach. . . ." (p. 342)

36. Ibid., p. 278.

37. Ibid., p. 77.

38. Ibid., p. 369.

39. Ibid., p. 138.

40. Frederick W. Taylor, *The Principles of Scientific Management* (Harper & Bros., 1911), p. 137.

41. *The New York Times,* April 26, 1981, "Big Steel on the Long Road Back."

42. *The Wall Street Journal,* April 7, 1981.

43. *The Wall Street Journal,* September 23, 1980.

44. *The New York Times,* August 17, 1981. For details on non-steel investments, see *United States Steel Corporation 1980 Annual Report;* also the *1981 Report.*

45. *The New York Times,* February 19, 1981.

46. Ibid.

47. *The New York Times,* December 2, 1979.

48. The Japanese steel industry has been meeting pollution control standards that are at least as rigorous as those in the United States. Reportedly, this was a major factor in the design and mode of operation of the Ohgishima Steel Works. That plant, built on an artificial island in Tokyo Bay, is widely regarded as the world's standard for steel production, utilizing oxygen furnaces, continuous casting and computerized process control. I am advised that when this plant was being considered, the Tokyo city government expressed misgivings about possible pollution, in response to which the plant's designers and prospective managers not only guaranteed air quality but offered to install a duplicate of the plant's emission and air-monitoring equipment in the offices of the Tokyo municipality.

49. Office of Technology Assessment, op. cit., p. 36.

50. From a summary of remarks by Richard W. Anderson, general manager, Hewlett-Packard Computer Systems Division, at H.P. press

reception, Cupertino, California, October 21, 1980. By special communication from the Hewlett-Packard Company.

51. Office of Technology Assessment, op. cit., pp. 276–281.

52. *The New York Times,* July 5, 1978.

53. *The New York Times,* November 18, 1977.

54. *Twenty-fourth Annual Report of the President of the U.S. on the Trade Agreement Programs* (Washington, D.C., 1979).

55. For a survey of growing U.S. production infirmities, see the *Wall Street Journal,* December 23, 1981, "Ever Rising Imports of Machinery and Parts Raise Fears in the U.S."

56. Steve Lohr, "Japanese Earned Labor Harmony," *The New York Times,* February 13, 1982.

57. These contrasting data on the Mazda and Chrysler firms, together with comments by Japanese and American observers, were broadcast by CBS Evening News on April 30, 1981.

58. Seymour Melman, *The Permanent War Economy* (Simon and Schuster, 1974), p. 145; *Statistical Abstract of the United States, 1973,* p. 776.

11

1. *The New York Times,* December 22, 1980.

2. James Fallows, *National Defense* (Random House, 1981), p. 52.

3. Department of Defense, Defense Science Board, *Industrial Responsiveness,* Office of the Under Secretary of Defense for Research and Engineering (1981); U.S. Congress, 96th Congress, 2d Session, House, Committee on Armed Services, *The Ailing Defense Industrial Base: Unready for Crisis,* Report of the Defense Industrial Base Panel, 1980.

4. For the full history of this internal struggle in the Department of Defense, see A. Ernest Fitzgerald, *The High Priests of Waste* (Norton, 1972); U.S. Department of Defense, *Defense Procurement Circular No. 12,* October 16, 1964, p. 3.

5. U.S. Department of Defense, *Department of Defense Instruction,* no. 5000.2, March 19, 1980, pp. 12, 13. See also U.S. Congress, 96th Congress, 2d Session, House Committee on Armed Services, *Hearings on Military Posture, Research and Development,* Title 2, February-

March 1980, H.A.S.C. No. 96–37 1980, pp. 461ff.

6. *The New York Times,* May 2, 1974.

7. *Business Week,* August 11, 1980; see article "The New Defense Posture—Missiles, Missiles, and Missiles," and Harold Brown's admonition: "Our Technology Is What Will Save Us."

8. Pierre Sprey, "The Impact of Avionics on the Effectiveness of Tactical Air." This was a study prepared for the Office of the Assistant Secretary of Defense for Systems Analysis, June 1968 (declassified 1974), cited in Fallows, *National Defense,* p. 55.

9. *Science,* June 20, 1980, p. 1354.

10. *Science,* March 14, 1980, p. 1184.

11. Ibid., p. 1187.

12. Rhonda Brown and Paul Matteucci, "The High Cost of Whistle-Blowing," *Inquiry,* September 1, 1981.

13. *The New York Times,* January 11, 1981; Edward L. King, *The Death of the Army* (Saturday Review Press, 1972).

14. *The Wall Street Journal,* June 1, 1981.

15. *Defense Week,* October 13, 1981.

16. U.S. General Accounting Office, *XM-1 Tank's Reliability Is Still Uncertain* (Washington, D.C., January 29, 1980).

17. *Defense Week,* August 24, 1981.

18. Gary Hart, "What's Wrong with the Military?" *The New York Times,* February 14, 1982. An interested reader will want to check the full file of *Defense Week,* a Washington, D.C., newsletter (e.g., "Clothing Chaos: Protective Gear Could Sweat Soldiers to Death," *Defense Week,* November 2, 1981). See the *Wall Street Journal* series starting February 17, 1982, "A New Troop Carrier Is Remarkable—So Are Its History and Cost."

19. Seymour Melman, *The Permanent War Economy* (Simon & Schuster, 1974), pp. 44ff.

20. Franklin C. Spinney, *Defense Facts of Life,* an unofficial staff paper by a civilian employee of the Office of the Secretary of Defense, Dec. 5, 1980, pp. 45–48.

21. *Defense Week,* December 3, 1980.

22. *Defense Week,* December 14, 1981.

23. *Defense Week,* December 7, 1981.

24. Alexander Cockburn, "Never mind, they don't work," *In These Times,* October 7–13, 1981.

25. James E. Muller, "On Accidental Nuclear War," *Newsweek,* March 1, 1982.

26. U.S. General Accounting Office, *Effectiveness of U.S. Forces Can Be Increased Through Improved Weapon System Design,* January 29, 1981, p. 6.

27. *Defense Week,* February 9, 1981.

28. U.S. General Accounting Office, *Issues Identified in Twenty-one Recently Published Major Weapon System Reports,* June 12, 1980, pp. 23, 24.

29. Gordon Adams, *The Iron Triangle: The Politics of Defense Contracting* (Council on Economic Priorities, 1981).

30. U.S. Congress, House Committee on Armed Services, *Hearings on Military Posture,* 1980, pp. 477–478. For a fine general discussion of the subject, see Mary Kaldor, *The Baroque Arsenal* (Hill & Wang, 1981).

12

1. Wholesale prices of manufactured goods: average annual percent changes: 1960 +.8, 1965–70 +2.6, 1970–75 + 7.5, 1975–80 +9.0. *Monthly Labor Review,* various issues.

2. U.S. Department of Defense, Comptroller, *Selected Acquisition Reports, Fourth Quarter 1980* (Washington, D.C., 1981).

3. U.S. Department of Defense, Office of the Under Secretary of Defense for Research and Engineering, *Report of the Defense Science Board, 1980 Study Panel on Industrial Responsiveness* (Washington, D.C., 1981), p. 25.

4. *The New York Times,* March 30, 1981.

5. See, for example, Leslie Wayne, "The Coming Flood of Treasury Debt," *The New York Times,* June 27, 1982.

6. John Kenneth Galbraith, *The Affluent Society* (Houghton Mifflin, 1958).

7. Seymour Melman, *Our Depleted Society* (Holt, Rinehart & Winston, 1965).

8. Pat Choate and Susan Walter, *America in Ruins* (Washington, D.C.: The Council of State Planning Agencies, 1981).

9. Ibid., p. 1.

10. Ibid., pp. 1–7.

11. *Business Week,* October 26, 1981, p. 139.

12. Ibid., pp. 146–151.

13. John Herbers in *The New York Times,* April 9, 1978; July 18, 1982.

14. *The New York Times,* July 30, 1981. See reports on "Drinking Water Purity Dropping" and "Health Fears Grow as Debate Continues on Toxic Wastes," March 7, 1982 and January 2, 1982.

15. *The New York Times,* June 21, 1980.

16. Seymour Melman, "The Federal Connection," *The New York Times,* November 2, 1975.

17. *The New York Times,* July 27, 1977, July 6, 1980.

18. James R. Anderson and Marion Anderson have pioneered in studies on the flow of federal funds in and out of states and congressional districts, with particular reference to their effect on employment and income levels. See, for example, James R. Anderson, "The Balance of Military Payments Among States and Regions," in Seymour Melman, ed., *The War Economy of the U.S.* (St. Martin's Press, 1971), pp. 137 ff. Also, James R. Anderson, *Bankrupting America, The Tax Burden and Expenditures of the Pentagon by Congressional District,* Employment Research Associates, 400 S. Washington Ave., Lansing, MI 48933 (1982). See also "Federal Spending: The North's Loss is the Sunbelt's Gain," *National Journal,* June 26, 1976. In relation to American cities, see James R. Anderson, *The Pentagon Tax: The Impact of the Military Budget on Major American Cities,* Employment Research Associates (March 1979).

19. *The New York Times,* July 20, 1981; April 4, 1982 ("New York Paying a Price for Delaying Repairs").

20. Mark Hipp, *Capital Needs of New York City,* a Report to the Disarmament Project of the Riverside Church, New York, NY 10027 (February 1979).

21. *The New York Times,* Op-Ed page, August 4, 1977.

22. *The New York Times,* August 31, 1981.

23. *The New York Times,* April 15, 1981.

24. *The New York Times,* July 14, 1980.

25. *The New York Times,* June 18, 1978.

26. *The New York Times,* August 7, 1980.

27. *The New York Times,* July 30, 1980.

28. *The New York Times,* August 17, 1980.

29. *The New York Times,* January 14, 1982, "Auto Workers' Jobs to Decline." The officials' estimate clearly included the several auto parts-supplying industries, while my estimate is limited to the final auto-producing factories and their employees.

30. Harley Shaiken, "A Robot Is After Your Job," *The New York Times,* Op-Ed page, September 3, 1980. See also in *The Nation,* October 11, 1980.

31. Bryan Miller, "Computers Add to Ar-

chitect's Reach," *The New York Times,* July 8, 1982.

32. Seymour Melman, *The Permanent War Economy,* ch. 9.

33. These are from a summary report in *The New York Times,* October 31, 1976.

34. Ibid.

35. *The New York Times,* March 17, 1981. See *The New York Times:* March 23, 1982, "Family Tries with Welfare to 'Make Do' "; March 13, 1982, editorial, "Some Safety Net."

36. *The New York Times,* January 3, 1982; March 12, 1982, "Required Reading."

13

1. AFL-CIO, Industrial Union Department, *Blueprint for a Working America, Rebuilding our Economy for the 1980s,* Washington, D.C. (1980).

2. *Business Week,* October 26, 1981.

3. *The New York Times,* October 1, 1975.

4. See, for example, *Capital Goods Review,* June 1975. This issue discusses capital formation and exports.

5. Lester C. Thurow, *The Zero-Sum Society* (Basic Books, 1980). Also by Thurow, a shorter discussion of his analyses: "There Are Solutions to Our Economic Problems," *The New York Times Magazine,* August 10, 1980.

6. Peter G. Peterson, "No More Free Lunch for the Middle Class," *The New York Times,* January 17, 1982.

7. "Statement of the Ad Hoc Committee on the Triple Revolution," April 1964.

8. See Seymour Melman, ed., *Strategy for American Security* (privately published, 1963); and *Our Depleted Society* (Holt, Rinehart, & Winston, 1965).

9. Lester Thurow, *The New York Times,* May 3, 1981.

10. Paul J. Burnsky, "Depletion of Skilled Crafts Threatened by Cutbacks," *AFL-CIO News,* April 25, 1981.

11. Robert B. Reich, former director of policy planning for the U.S. Federal Trade Commission, in *Business Week,* October 27, 1980, p. 28. Reich notes further that "too many of our products fall apart too soon, need inordinate repair, and are too expensive to use and maintain. We are losing the battle for competitive survival because, all too often, 'made in U.S.A.' has become a symbol for 'second-rate.' . . . The failure rates of Japanese products are now a fraction of the rates of their American competitors. . . ."

12. Ernest J. Breton, "Reinventing the Wheel: The Failure to Utilize Existing Technology," *Mechanical Engineering,* March 1981, p. 54.

13. For a summary of the conditions of cost-maximizing within military industry firms, see Appendix 3, *How the Military Economy Maximizes Cost.*

14. The following are two official reports within the state government of California on the operations of the BART system: *Investigation of the Operations of the Bay Area Rapid Transit with Particular Reference to Safety and Contract Administration,* Legislative Analyst, State of California, State Capitol, Sacramento, November 9, 1972; The State of California Senate, Public Utilities and Corporations Committee, *Report on Safety of the Bay Area Rapid Transit Automatic Train Control System,* January 31, 1973, State Capitol, Sacramento, California.

These news reports on BART appeared in *The New York Times:* "Computerized Transit on Coast Facing a New Delay," April 18, 1971; "A Rapid Transit System of the Future Will Serve California Now," August 13, 1972; "Transit Line on Coast Runs Well—Most of the Time," May 6, 1973; "Coast Mass Transit Hailed Despite Woes," August 23, 1975; "Rough Ride in Rapid Transit," September 5, 1971; "Mass Transit, Little Mass," October 19, 1975; "Tube Beneath Bay Closed After Blast," January 19, 1979; "Three-Week Snarl Is Feared on Coast Transit System," January 21, 1979.

The following articles appeared in *The Wall Street Journal:* "Rohr Is Asked by BART to Stop Shipping It Cars," January 28, 1974; "BART District Sues for Damages of $237.8 Million," November 20, 1974; "Rohr Underestimated Difficulty of Making Rail Cars, Report Says," August 30, 1971.

See also: "The Tough Route from Jets to Rail Cars," *Business Week,* May 1, 1971; "BART Withholds Westinghouse Money," *Electronic News,* November 20, 1972; "BART Votes to Sue Suppliers," *Aviation Week and Space Technology,* October 14, 1974; "BART Plans to Sue Its Builders," *American Machinist,* October 28, 1974; "Battling with Baffling BART," Washington *Post,* August 24, 1975; "Rohr to Quit Rail Car Jobs," Washington *Post,* June 2, 1976.

15. Boston *Globe,* December 6, 1978.

16. On the Morgantown, West Virginia, story, see *Railway Age,* September 8, 1975, and *Business Week,* March 16, 1974. The Morgantown, West Virginia, people mover saga reads as either more industrial tragedy or high comedy, depending on the reader's mood.

17. *Business Week,* July 6, 1981, p. 48.

18. Ray Connolly, "Competition and the Weapons Welfare State," *Electronics,* February 10, 1982, p. 64.

19. Karl F. Willenbrock, in a signed editorial in *Science,* September 18, 1981, on "United States and Technological Preeminence."

20. Seymour Melman, "The Carnegie Report: Puff Piece for a War Economy," *The Nation,* May 8, 1981.

21. William Nordhaus, in *The New York Times,* May 17, 1981.

14

1. Robert B. Reich, "Why the U.S. Needs an Industrial Policy," *Harvard Business Review,* January–February 1982.

2. John Walsh, "Japan-U.S. Competition: Semiconductors Are the Key," *Science,* February 12, 1982.

3. *The New York Times,* February 1, 1982; see the article titled "Chip Challenge from Japan."

4. Ray Connolly, "Competition and the Weapons Welfare State," *Electronics,* February 10, 1982. See also the exchange of letters in the *New York Review* of March 18, 1982, between Messrs. J. J. Nangle, a "research engineer in the integrated-circuit industry," and Robert B. Reich, the industrial economist.

5. "Will Japan Leapfrog America on Superfast Computers?," *The Economist,* March 5, 1982, p. 95.

6. Seymour Melman, *The Permanent War Economy* (Simon & Schuster, 1974), p. 145.

7. Peter G. Peterson, "No More Free Lunch for the Middle Class," *The New York Times,* January 17, 1982.

8. From NBC White Paper, "If Japan Can . . . Why Can't We?" Broadcast on National Broadcasting Company, June 24, 1980.

9. Ibid.

10. *The New York Times,* letter to the editor by Al Bilik, deputy to the executive director of District Council 37, American Federation of State, County and Municipal Employees, February 11, 1982.

11. "How the Japanese Manage in the U.S.," *Fortune,* June 15, 1981, p. 98.

12. Ibid., p. 102.

13. *Business Week,* October 12, 1981, p. 86.

14. Ibid.

15. Prof. Martin K. Starr, letter in *Business Week,* July 28, 1980.

16. See letter by Richard B. Robinson, professor of international management at MIT, in *The New York Times,* April 7, 1982.

17. *Business Week,* December 21, 1981.

18. "How the Japanese Manage in the U.S." *Fortune,* June 15, 1981, p. 103.

19. Steve Lohr, "Japan's Enviable Jobless Rate," *The New York Times,* December 21, 1981.

20. Ibid. During a visit to Lincoln, Nebraska, in April 1982, I learned that the Kawasaki Company, manufacturing motorcycles in that city, had decided upon a cutback of production, but did not discharge the production workers. Instead, they were loaned, for an extended period, to the city government to perform all sorts of community improvement work, while being retained on the Kawasaki payroll. See *The New York Times,* Oct. 24, 1981.

21. *The New York Times,* April 19, 1981. That proposal was soon dropped, as it generated editorial rebuffs.

22. Robert H. Hayes, "Why Japanese Factories Work," *Harvard Business Review,* July–August 1981.

23. "Texas Instruments Shows U.S. Business How to Survive in the 1980s," *Business Week,* September 18, 1978.

24. See Joseph C. Wyman, *Steel Mini-Mills —An Investment Opportunity* (New York: Shearson, Loeb Rhoades, Inc., November 20, 1980).

25. U.S. General Accounting Office, *Productivity-Sharing Programs: Can They Contribute to Productivity Improvement?* (Washington, D.C., March 3, 1981).

26. See the articles in *Fortune,* June 15, 1981.

27. *The New York Times,* October 16, 1981. See the dispatch on "The Japanese Way at Quasar: Plant in U.S. Called Model of Efficiency."

28. *The New York Times,* December 14, 1981. "Foreign Management Lessons: Sony Succeeds Where British Business Fails."

29. Rosabeth M. Kanter and Barry A. Stein, "The Egalitarian Revolution," *Bell Telephone Magazine,* Edition 4, 1980.

30. Ibid.

31. *The New York Times,* February 13, 1982. See dispatch on "Japanese Earned Labor Harmony."

32. *The New York Times,* February 26, 1982. See dispatch by Thomas C. Hayes, "Behind G.M.'s Labor Troubles." Compare with the important dispatch by Steve Lohr, "Japan Places Markets Above Profits," *The New York Times,* April 19, 1982.

33. Robert Vasquez, "Saving a Steel Town," *The New York Times,* August 20, 1980.

34. Victor Gotbaum and Edward Handman, "Labor's Business," *The New York Times,* April 22, 1982. The same union officials added that "the definition of successful management is not what it used to be: corporate managers are no longer measured solely by the ability to produce and sell goods or to create new products and new markets. Successful managers covet huge tax losses. Profits can be generated by merging two corporations to produce less together than they did apart."

35. Jeremy Rifkin and Randy Barber, *The North Will Rise Again* (Beacon Press, 1978), p. 100.

36. Ibid., p. 236.

37. *Business Week,* March 28, 1977, p. 78.

38. James O'Toole, *Making America Work: Productivity and Responsibility* (Continuum, 1981). This account is abstracted from an article by O'Toole in *Industry Week,* August 10, 1981.

39. *The New York Times,* July 5, 1981; see dispatch by Thomas C. Hayes, "At G.M.'s Buick Unit Workers and Bosses Get Ahead by Getting Along."

40. The following books and collections of articles will open up a wider literature to the reader:

Daniel Zwerdling, *Workplace Democracy* (Harper & Row, 1978). This book is a "guide to workplace ownership, participation, and self-management experiments in the United States and in Europe."

Ithaca Work Group, *Democracy in the Workplace: Readings on the Implementation of Self-Management in the United States,* Strongforce Series (Ithaca, N.Y., 1977).

Paul Bernstein, *Workplace Democratization: Its Internal Dynamics* (Kent State University Press, 1976).

Gerry Hunnius, ed., *Workers' Control, A Reader on Labor & Social Change* (Random House, 1973).

Ken Coates, *Can the Workers Run Industry?* (Sphere Books, 1968).

Louis Davis and Albert B. Charns, eds., *The Quality of Working Life* (The Free Press, 1975).

Industrial Relations (Berkeley) 9, no. 2 (February 1970). (This is a special issue on worker participation.)

Katrina Berman, *Worker-owned Plywood Companies: An Economic Analysis* (Washington State University Press, 1967).

Carl Bellas, *Industrial Democracy and the Worker-owned Firm: A Case Study of Twenty-one Plywood Companies in the Pacific Northwest* (Praeger, 1972).

Paul Blumberg, *Industrial Democracy: The Sociology of Participation* (Schocken Books, 1973).

David Jenkins, *Job Power: Blue and White Collar Democracy* (Doubleday, 1973).

William Ronco, *Jobs* (Beacon Press, 1977).

Workers' Self-Management Group, *Democratizing the Workplace: From Job Enrichment to Worker Control* (American Friends Service Committee, 48 Inman St., Cambridge, Mass. 02139 [$1]).

Work in America: Report of the Special Task Force of the Secretary of Health, Education and Welfare (MIT Press, 1973).

James O'Toole, ed., *Work and the Quality of Life* (MIT Press, 1974).

Jeremy Rifkin, *Own Your Own Job: Economic Democracy for Working Americans* (Bantam Books, 1977).

For continuing access to literature on workplace democracy, see: Association for Workplace Democracy, 1747 Connecticut Ave., N.W., Washington, D.C. 20009, and the journal *Workplace Democracy.*

41. *The New York Times,* April 27, 1982. See dispatch by William Serrin, "An Experiment in Jersey: Workers Buy a Factory."

42. *Business Week,* September 15, 1980.

43. *The New York Times,* August 19, 1980.

44. *The New York Times,* March 3, 1982.

45. *The New York Times,* October 11, 1981; see dispatch by Richard D. Lyons, "A Troubled Upstate City Solving Its Labor Unrest."

Professor William F. Whyte (Cornell) advises that a forthcoming book authored by J. Rothschild-Whitt, William F. Whyte, and others, will include a chapter on "The Jamestown Model of Cooperative Problem-Solving," describing the mode of operation of a community or area labor-management committee as a "distinctive [American] social invention."

46. Ernest J. McCormick and Mark S. Sanders, *Human Factors in Engineering and Design,* 5th ed. (McGraw-Hill, 1982); Harold B. Maynard, ed., *Industrial Engineering Handbook,* 3rd ed. (McGraw-Hill, 1971), see chapter on "Human Factors Engineering," pp. 7–46ff.; Victor Papanek, *Design for the Real World* (Pantheon Books, 1971); see the journal *Human Factors.*

47. Seymour Melman, *Our Depleted Society* (Holt, Rinehart & Winston, 1965); *Pentagon Capitalism* (McGraw-Hill, 1970); and *The Permanent War Economy* (Simon & Schuster, 1974).

48. Pat Choate and Susan Walter, *America in Ruins* (Washington, D.C., The Council of State Planning Agencies, 1981).

49. U.S. Bureau of the Census, *Statistical Abstract of the U.S., 1980* (Government Printing Office, 1980), p. 474.

50. *The New York Times,* April 25, 1979.

51. *The New York Times,* December 28, 1976.

52. *The New York Times,* August 5, 1980.

53. Michael Boretsky, *U.S. Technology: Trends and Policy Issues,* U.S. Department of Commerce, October 1973.

54. See the column on "Technology" in *The New York Times,* June 19, 1980.

55. Derek Shearer, "Popular Planning," *The New York Times,* March 16, 1982. See also Martin Carnoy and Derek Shearer, *Economic Democracy: Challenge of the 1980s* (M. E. Sharpe, 1980).

INDEX

ABC Company, 76
absenteeism, reduction of, 282 *n.,* 283
accidents, 195, 285
accounting procedures, 24, 44, 57, 74–6
administrative costs (in industry): in Great
Britain, 70; and output, 70–1; rising trends
of, 9–10, 76–7, 81, 172, 192, 270
administrative employees: pay compared to
production wages, 73; productivity, 74;
ratio to production workers, 9–10, 70–1, 71
n., 73, 76, 81, 158, 192, 270; training of,
249, 251
Aegis anti-air warfare system, 220, 221
aerospace industry: administrative versus
production employees, 159; civilian
contracts of, 135–7, 253–8; competitive
position of, 201; cost-maximizing in, 135–8;
excess of industrial capacity, 157–8;
expansion of, 66; high-tech orientation of,
254, 256, 258; investment in new capital,
208; and machine tool industry, 10, 105,
106, 135, 167; military preemption of
resources by, 177; as "sunrise" industry,
264; *see also* military aircraft; missiles
affluent society, concept of, 65
AFL-CIO: *Blueprint for a Working America,*
247; Reagan budget study, 238; report on
multinational wage policies, 34; *see also*
labor unions; *and individual unions*
Agency for International Development, 35
agricultural commodity prices, 93
Agriculture, U.S. Department of, 96, 229
aircraft, civilian: Japanese-made, 201;
production costs compared to those for
military craft, 135–7, 177
aircraft, military, *see* military aircraft
Air Force, U.S., 10, 104–5, 168, 236

Air Force Advanced Logistics System
(ALS), 215
Akron, Ohio, 19
alcohol abuse (by nuclear weapons
personnel), 219
Alfred Herbert, Ltd., 12
Allied Corporation (Allied Chemical), 60
America in Ruins (report), 228, 287
American Machinist reports, 6
American Management Association, 77
and *n.*
American Motor Corporation, 33
American Shoe Machine Company, 26
American Society of Mechanical Engineers,
13
American Telephone & Telegraph Company,
260
Amsden, Alice, 7 *n.*
Anaconda Copper Corporation, 50
Anderson, Marion, 238
Anderson, Richard W., 199
Arab-Israeli wars, 215, 217
architectural drafting, 237
Armco, 16, 198
Armed Services Committee (House), 208 and
n., 209–11
arms race and disarmament, 66, 265, 266 *n.,*
287
Army Corps of Engineers, 229, 234
Aspin, Rep. Les, 148
assembly line, 107, 108, 126
Atlantic Richfield, 50
Atomic Energy Commission, 175
Atomics International, 92
Australia, 29
auto industry: big-car bias of, 45, 45 *n.,* 49,
183; decline of U.S. dominance in, 183–4;

A NOTE ABOUT THE AUTHOR

Seymour Melman is professor of industrial engineering at
Columbia University. He holds a B.S.S. from the City
College of New York and a Ph.D. from Columbia, where
he has taught since 1948. He is the author of numerous
articles and books, including *Our Depleted Society* and
Pentagon Capitalism. Mr. Melman is also Co-chairman of
the National Committee for a Sane Nuclear Policy (SANE).
He has been Vice-President of the New York Academy of
Sciences and an honorary member of the faculty of the
Industrial College of the Armed Forces, and in 1981
he received the Great Teacher Award at Columbia.

A NOTE ON THE TYPE

The text of this book was set in a computer version
of Times Roman, designed by Stanley Morison for *The
Times* (London) and first introduced by the newspaper
in 1932. Among typographers and designers of the
twentieth century, Stanley Morison has been a strong
forming influence as typographical adviser to the English
Monotype Corporation, as a director of two distinguished
English publishing houses, and as a writer of sensibility,
erudition, and keen practical sense.

Composed by The Haddon Craftsmen, Inc.,
Scranton Pennsylvania.
Printed by Fairfield Graphics,
Fairfield, Pennsylvania.

Book design by Sara Reynolds